IN SEARCH OF THE COMMON GOOD

Center of Theological Inquiry

Theology for the Twenty-first Century is a series sponsored by the Center of Theological Inquiry (CTI), an institute, located in Princeton, New Jersey, dedicated to the advanced study of theology. This series is one of its many initiatives and projects.

The goal of the series is to publish inquiries of contemporary scholars into the nature of the Christian faith and its witness and practice in the church, society, and culture. The series will include investigations into the uniqueness of the Christian faith. But it will also offer studies that relate the Christian faith to the major cultural, social, and practical issues of our time.

Monographs and symposia will result from research by scholars in residence at the Center of Theological Inquiry or otherwise associated with it. In some cases, publications will come from group research projects sponsored by CTI. It is our intention that the books selected for this series will constitute a major contribution to renewing theology in its service to church and society.

WALLACE M. ALLSTON JR., ROBERT JENSON,
and DON S. BROWNING
Series Editors

What Dare We Hope?
by Gerhard Sauter

*The End of the World and
the Ends of God*
edited by John Polkinghorne and
Michael Welker

*God and Globalization, Volume 1:
Religion and the Powers of
the Common Life*
edited by Max L. Stackhouse with
Peter J. Paris

*God and Globalization, Volume 2:
The Spirit and the Modern Authorities*
edited by Max L. Stackhouse with
Don S. Browning

*God and Globalization, Volume 3:
Christ and the Dominions of
Civilization*
edited by Max L. Stackhouse
with Diane B. Obenchain

*Redemptive Change:
Atonement and the Christian
Cure of the Soul*
by R. R. Reno

*King, Priest, and Prophet:
A Trinitarian Theology of Atonement*
by Robert Sherman

In Search of the Common Good
edited by Dennis McCann and
Patrick D. Miller

IN SEARCH OF THE COMMON GOOD

Edited by
Dennis P. McCann and Patrick D. Miller

t &t clark

NEW YORK • LONDON

T & T Clark International, Madison Square Park, 15 East 26th Street, New York, NY 10010

T & T Clark International, The Tower Building, 11 York Road, London SE1 7NX

T & T Clark International is a Continuum imprint.

Cover art: PowerStock/Superstock

Cover design: Wesley Hoke

Library of Congress Cataloging-in-Publication Data

In search of the common good / edited by Dennis McCann and Patrick D. Miller.
        p. cm. — (Theology for the twenty-first century)
    Includes bibliographical references and index.
    ISBN 0-567-02770-8 (hardcover)
    1. Good and evil. I. McCann, Dennis. II. Miller, Patrick D. III. Series.
    BJ1401.I5 2005
    261.8—dc22

                                        2004019088

Printed in the United States of America

05 06 07 08 09 10   10 9 8 7 6 5 4 3 2 1

Contents

Acknowledgments

The collection of essays brought together in this volume is the result of a three-year project on "Theology and the Common Good" carried on by a group of scholars from various disciplines: Bible, theology, ethics, political science, and law. The group met under the auspices of the Center of Theological Inquiry in Princeton, New Jersey. We are greatly indebted to all the staff of the Center for their assistance in various ways. Our special thanks goes first to Wallace M. Alston Jr., the Director of the Center, and Robert W. Jenson, Senior Scholar for Research, who conceived the idea of the project, brought its members together, and funded our meetings. We also owe a debt of gratitude to Kathi Morley, who helped us on all the many arrangements involved in bringing the members of the project together twice a year over the three-year period, and to Marion Gibson, who handled all matters relative to getting papers in and out on time for our discussions. One important member of the group, Robert George of Princeton University, was not able to finish with the group because of other commitments, but we are grateful for his contribution during his time with us.

Introduction

Dennis P. McCann and Patrick D. Miller

The papers comprising this volume are the results of a three-year engagement of persons from theology, law, ethics, Bible, and politics—under the auspices of the Center of Theological Inquiry. The group explored the meaning of the common good and what resources Christian theology, biblical studies, and ethics might contribute to our understanding of it.

We began our deliberations at the beginning of the millennium and during the 2000 presidential campaign. The first meeting in the second year was shortly after the terrorist attacks of 9/11, and our final meeting took place during the war in Iraq. In the course of the three years we witnessed the deepening division in our nation's public discourse. One polarizing battle after another was fought over wars and the rumors of war, the financing of domestic social programs, taxes and budget cuts, corporate oversight, the role of the government in stimulating the economy, and what should be done—and left undone—about "homeland security." In an even larger context, we were conscious of the changing international situation reflected in the many manifestations of globalization, the end of a bipolar world order, the rise of a more united Europe, and the plight of the peoples of Africa beset by war, AIDS, and extreme poverty. All of this made us aware how mammoth our topic was. It is to the credit of CTI that those invited to this theological conversation about the common good were by no means in solid agreement on how to view these issues and respond to them. Had there been a greater degree of consensus among us, it probably would have indicated that the group itself was unrepresentative of the range of informed opinions to be dealt with, and that the outcome of our theological conversation had been preempted before it even got started. To the credit of the project members, coming together in the process of discussion, argument, and friendship produced a common good deeper and more important than consensus.

After three years of semiannual meetings, drafts and redrafts of papers, what then have we to show for our efforts? We have no new definition of the common good to propose and no ten-point program for implementing it. Such a formulation would have failed to represent the diversity of the group while hiding serious and important differences among us. So rather than seeking a definitive formulation, we decided to concentrate instead on bringing forward the intellectual resources that each of us knew best, while engaging in the deep listening to each other that can lead to mutual learning. The contemporary social, economic, and political context described above made us all the more aware of what a mammoth topic we had taken on. Comprehensiveness was beyond our grasp, as has been true for others who have taken up the common good. We nevertheless grabbed hold of some important pieces of the discussion, pieces that ended up touching on a lot of things that matter. The result, as manifest in these essays, is a rich and complex treatment of the common good. Questions are asked and claims are made for where and how the common good is achieved and manifest. Both the questions and the claims provide possibilities for further discussion but also for decision and action.

Our often tested commitment to the project paid off also in unexpected ways. The best insights sometimes came in the easier moments of getting to know each other before, during, and after dinner rather than in the formal sessions in which we criticized each other's ideas and applauded or challenged their political, social, and theological presuppositions. Participants often came to appreciate each other, not in ideological argument, but in sharing their personal and family stories, their hopes and fears about being good parents and about children being able to make it, or the challenge of being good to their own aging parents and loved ones. Of course, such moments led to the discovery and acknowledgement that, despite apparent diversity in the group, the category of conventionally "married with children" was a category overrepresented in the group as a whole, despite differences over, say, family policy and related issues. Perhaps we were closer to consensus on some aspects of the common good than we were prepared to admit in public. The experience of worshipping together, whenever we were able to make room for it, was another moment, perhaps less surprising, when at least an inarticulate sense of the common good seemed within our grasp.

Thus we rediscovered the most difficult lesson about the common good: conversation about it is almost impossible today apart from some shared experience of community. As we became more of a community—albeit one that existed only in six sixty-hour segments that marked autumn and spring for the three years in which we met together—it became easier to have a productive conversation about the common good.

When we first looked across the table at each other, however uncertainly and apprehensively, it was clear that if we actually pulled it off, this would be a conversation about the common good not like many others. Some of us already knew of each other professionally, as members of the Society of Christian Ethics, the Society of Biblical Literature, or the American Academy of Religion. Some had actually read each other's works, reviewed them for journals and other publications, or collaborated previously in other projects. Even so, as a gathering of Christian scholars—theologians, ethicists, and students of the Bible—our group was unusual in its ecumenical character. As a theological and moral issue, the common good is identified with the discourse of Catholic social teaching, and it is often assumed that only Catholics have any real stake in discussing it. Our group, however, had not only an appropriately diverse representation of Catholic perspectives, but also a range of Protestant scholars. The latter enriched the conversation with critical biblical insights and theological and ethical agendas well attuned to the significance of the biblical covenant in its public, communitarian, ecclesial, and personal dimensions. Each of us eventually sought to confront the impact of his or her own social location, the ways in which race, gender, and social class both empower and disempower each of us for participation as public intellectuals. Yet the group was challenged and encouraged by the example of our African-American colleagues to be particularly careful in struggling for an understanding of the common good that would be uncommonly good to the extent that it was uncommonly common. At times, the conversation was difficult. But we came to realize how much better off we were taking the risks of unscripted new learning rather than retreating to some more orderly, less open-ended discourse within the familiar confines of academic camaraderie.

Our collective effort to achieve a common good sufficient to sustain a serious theological conversation about it, we came to realize, was but a microcosm of the challenges facing any public discourse or politics to be advanced on the basis of this notion. Everywhere we looked, the common good was in serious trouble. Perhaps ordinary people still had a rough idea that the term meant to signify the good of all, or as one of us once put it, "the good to be pursued in common."[1] Nevertheless, we knew ourselves to be living in an era whose economics and politics often failed to serve the public interest in its pursuit of one form or another of collective self-interest. Despite the short-lived drawing together of most Americans in their shared alarm and grief over 9/11, the new sense of national unity quickly unraveled as our leaders on all sides found themselves unable to resist the temptation of using this event for their own short-term political advantage. We went back to politics as usual in great things and small.

Even the controversies over what to do with the site once occupied by the World Trade Center demonstrated how quickly any pretense to the common good had simply evaporated: "When it's so obvious that people are asking What's in it for my group? it's hard to ask with a straight face, 'What is the public interest

---

1. Dennis McCann, "The Good to Be Pursued in Common," *The Common Good and U.S. Capitalism* (ed. Oliver F. Williams and John W. Houck; Lanham, MD: University Press of America, 1987), 158–78. It should be noted that while McCann's definition is simple, his analysis is quite complex and operates out of a sophisticated theoretical basis.

or common good?'" So reported the *New York Times*, quoting a political scientist observing the return to politics as usual. Indeed, according to the *Times*, a professor of urban design observed rather cryptically in conjunction with the competition over the design of a possible memorial on the site that "the common good doesn't exist any more, and that's been very liberating."[2] Even in casual appeals to the common good, such as those represented in these quotations, one is faced with knotty conceptual issues (Kirk-Duggan).[3] The author of the *New York Times* essay just quoted understands the notion of the common good to be "what is best for the most people." This is a utilitarian way of defining it that covers over a multitude of problems, including the degree to which the individual's good is a dimension of the common good.[4] There are other, equally obvious questions that need to be explored: Is it a presently shared good that is in view? Or is it an anticipated and teleological good (Jenson, McCann, Stackhouse)? To what extent is the common good a material good? Or is it a matter of the spiritual, the aesthetic, or the moral? The good to be pursued in common may or may not be understood theologically. While this book arises out of conversations on the part of persons for whom it is ultimately a theological issue, we both acknowledge and listen to those for whom the notion of a shared good is not a theological matter but still very important.

In addition to this universal, more popular, and less formal usage of the expression "common good," the concept has a long history as a philosophical, political, and theological notion. It goes back at least as far as the Greeks and passes into our own time particularly through Roman Catholic social teaching (McCann). Here one encounters a more formal and theoretical effort to describe the ways that individuals live in community and realize their best interests at least in part by means of common pursuits and shared goods. For Aristotle, the common good was a higher good than that of the individual, and the common good was very distinctly to be associated with the polis, with a people or the state. Cicero, on whom Augustine drew in his effort to define the conditions for a people or a public to exist (Jenson), tied the concept of justice closely to the pursuit of the common good. This constraint is confirmed in Scripture, but not apart from its larger vision of God's mercy and compassion (Lapsley).

A proper understanding of the community in which the common good is to be pursued is one of the central issues in the contemporary discussion, and one also informed by important historical antecedents (Cavanaugh, Porter). A strong

---

2. Kirk Johnson, "A Plan Without a Master: Rebuilding by Committee? Robert Moses Would Cringe," *New York Times*, April 14, 2002. The comments were made, respectively, by Kenneth Kolson, author of *Big Plans: The Allure and Folly of Urban Design* (Baltimore: The Johns Hopkins University Press, 2001), and Margaret Crawford, a professor of urban design at Harvard University.

3. Throughout this essay the various names in parentheses refer to authors in this volume whose essays pertain in some fashion to the matter in question.

4. For discussion of some of the problems of utilitarianism as a substitute for common good theory or for equating it with the common good, see Robert E. Rodes Jr., *The Legal Enterprise* (Port Washington, NY: Kennikat, 1976), 38–41.

part of the Catholic tradition, memorably restated in the modern period in Leo XIII's *Rerum novarum* but reaching back to Thomas Aquinas and his predecessors (McCann, Porter), has closely associated society with the state and placed responsibility for the common good in the hands of the rulers. Nevertheless, that same tradition has also proposed the principle of subsidiarity as a way of identifying the relationship between the good of the larger society, the commonweal, and the good of the various elements that make it up—family, church, local communities, education, the arts, and the like. The larger political entity has a responsibility for helping, or "subsidizing"—whether by resources, regulation, or other modes—these smaller, more immediate forms of communal life. Still other theories of civil society have tried to take account of the pluralist character of the contemporary society (Stackhouse) and its role in sustaining an interrelated set of commons.

While the Bible has not been a primary focus of the more technical discussion of the common good, its influence can be traced from the beginning. It has come into play afresh in the current discussion, and is well represented in this volume (Furnish, Kirk-Duggan, Lapsley, Miller, Stackhouse, Skillen, and others).[5] It was Augustine who insisted that the highest good is the love of God and that the common good is found in the communion of all persons with one another and with God. This understanding, deeply rooted in the biblical tradition and its notions of covenant, has created a permanent tension between political society and the religious community as the ultimate locus of the common good. More precisely, it has raised the question of how one speaks of the common good in political terms and what is the relation between the body politic and the *ekklēsia* as harborers and bearers of the common good. Insisting that the good of the polis is not the highest good, Augustine substantially reshaped the understanding of the common good.

Augustine, however, did not ultimately reject the role of the state. Indeed, his way of thinking leads to a vision of the common good marked by a theological struggle between human society and the communion of saints, neither one of which is to be identified with the city of God. But a commonweal may exist, in Augustine's view, wherever "a people is an assemblage of reasonable beings bound together by a common agreement as to the objects of their love."[6] The common good, then, is intentional: it is not simply the inevitable outcome of one or another sort of natural affinity, but involves some sort of commitment to a deliberative process involving the sharing of insights and the achievement of moral consensus.

Since Augustine, at least, the question of the nature of the community that pursues a common good has occupied the attention of all who have thought about

5. One may cite the essay by John Collins, "The Biblical Vision of the Common Good," in *The Common Good and U.S. Capitalism*, 50–69, but the literature is not loaded with invocations of the biblical tradition in its discussion of the common good.

6. For the references to Augustine and *The City of God*, see the important discussion of David Hollenbach, "The Common Good Revisited," *Theological Studies* 50 (1989): 70–94, (an important resource for the discussion in this essay generally) as well as the essay by Jenson in this volume.

these matters. In various ways, the essays that follow take up that question once more. In some instances they seek to raise the issue of the community generally (Mount). In other cases they deal with the role of the political authority—for good or ill—in the pursuit of the common good (Cavanaugh, Porter, Skillen). Or they explore the necessity of defining the common good in relation to God's own intentions and the community that is formed in worshipful response to God (Jenson). Given this Augustinian way of posing the question, it is not surprising that the biblical covenant has become a central part of the discussion of the common good (Miller, Mount). One of the issues it raises is the extent to which covenantal discourse provides a sufficient basis for a communitarian understanding of the good that is effected in both political and ecclesial communities. Among others, the eminent Jewish philosopher Daniel Elazar has helped to connect the biblical covenantal tradition with Western political theory,[7] a connection appropriately explored in this volume in relation to the common good (Stackhouse).

Thinking about the common good has been complicated in the modern period by the focus upon the individual and individual rights. Americans have tended to conduct public affairs mostly in the discourse of rights: moral and legal rights, human rights, and civil rights. Such discourse has served to define a politics in which it has been possible to assert the claims of individual rights. In the course of our history, however, it has not kept us from the enslavement of large numbers of persons (Young) and the pacification of others confined to reservations (Ball), on the implicit assumption that the common good was better served in so doing. That being the case, then why focus attention on the common good? Will not we be served better by more vigorous pursuit of the right of each individual citizen?

The short answer is that upholding the discourse of rights may be a necessary but surely not a sufficient condition for the achievement of genuine community, national or otherwise. There are at least two large problems arising from an exclusive focus on individual rights. One is the distortion of the truth that our life and death really are with our neighbor. One may speak in theological terms of love of neighbor (Furnish), in philosophical understandings of the other (Young), or in the moral language of responsibility and obligation (Miller). In any case, individual goods are finally not capable of being sustained without the consciousness of the neighbor who is always there, though often silenced and marginalized to invisibility (Young). The other problem is that, when acted upon consistently,

7. Daniel Elazar, *Covenant and Polity in Biblical Israel: Biblical Foundations and Jewish Expressions* (New Brunswick, NJ: Transaction, 1995); idem, *Covenant and Commonwealth: From Christian Separation through the Protestant Reformation* (New Brunswick, NJ: Transaction, 1996); idem, *Covenant and Civil Society: The Constitutional Matrix of Modern Democracy* (New Brunswick, NJ: Transaction, 1998); idem, *Covenant and Constitutionalism: The Great Frontier and the Matrix of Federal Democracy* (New Brunswick, NJ: Transaction, 1998); and Daniel Elazar and John Kincaid, eds., *The Covenant Connection: From Federal Theology to Modern Federalism* (Lanham, MD: Lexington Books, 2000).

rights discourse inevitably focuses attention upon the institutions of law and politics, which in turn become the privileged arenas of social conflict. Political struggles normally yield both winners and losers. Rarely are they accompanied by
sincere gestures of reconciliation, or genuine efforts to heal the wounds that political polarization has inflicted on both sides.

Discourse on the common good, despite the obvious risks that history reveals
as all too often attendant upon it, may be a useful way of addressing the long-term
corrosive effects of a politics geared exclusively to mobilizing and then deciding
conflicts among various rights claims. Such discourse can focus our attention on
what we still hold in common, or must hold in common, if we are to continue as
a more or less coherent and effective political community (Lovin). Some will warn
about the dangers of subsuming real difference in abstract or forced forms of commonality (Kirk-Duggan, Young). Others may argue that discourse in search of the
common good is a waste of time. They may feel that as long as we agree to certain minimal standards of procedural justice, as long as our common faith in the
legal system holds, we need neither seek nor arrive at consensus about the common good tacitly presupposed in all our various institutional arrangements. But
we see the erosion of our common faith in the legal system and our system of
checks and balances, more or less confirmed by an unflinching look at our actual
history as a nation. Precisely this erosion demonstrates how timely it is for us to
participate in a serious conversation about the common good.[8]

A return to thinking about the common good should not replace continuing
attention to human rights, but it may be helpful in defining the terrain where certain larger questions of social and political legitimacy may usefully be explored. As
David Hollenbach has written: "Community and solidarity are to be highly valued, but so are freedom and the dignity of each person. Therefore recent Catholic
discussions of the common good stand opposed to the extremes of both individualism and collectivism."[9] Catholic social teaching, for example, is bringing the
question of solidarity and individuality into mutual relationship around an
acknowledgement of the interdependence of all human beings and the dignity of
each individual. Such teaching is reinventing discourse on the common good in
order to illuminate the larger social context in which the claims of human rights
can be honored and implemented.

The rationale for the discussion that follows, though manifold, is ultimately
theological. Whether under the formal rubric of "common good" discourse or not,

---

8. In this regard see the study of the effects of litigation on the common good
in Philip K. Howard, *The Collapse of the Common Good* (New York: Ballantine
Books, 2001), and the analysis of the actions of the Supreme Court in handling the
impasse in the 2000 election by Alan Dershowitz, *Supreme Injustice: How the High
Court Hijacked Election 2000* (New York: Oxford University Press, 2001). For a
counter position to that of Dershowitz, see Richard A. Posner, *Breaking the
Deadlock: The 2000 Election, the Constitution, and the Courts* (Princeton: Princeton
University Press, 2001).
9. David Hollenbach, "Common Good," *The New Dictionary of Catholic Social
Thought* (ed. Judith A. Dwyer; Collegeville: Liturgical Press, 1994), 193.

the meaning of a commitment to community and the duties and claims of the individual vis-à-vis that community have never been more pressing concerns. Yet as a group of Christian scholars responsive to the claims of theology, we must recognize that thinking about the common good is intrinsic to the very character of Christian faith and the ethos it evokes. In a most profound way the biblical vision is a vision of the common good. One may work with notions of justice and mercy (Lapsley), the care of the weak, covenantal living, or the new Jerusalem. In any such expression, the meaning of being human, of being a child of God, and living with the neighbor (Furnish, Miller) are so intrinsically bound together that there is, for us, no escaping involvement in the search for a common good in our time. The search must go on, even if our Christian faith also prompts us to admit that we shall see it only later, or that our sinfulness obstructs any real possibilities of truly achieving a good for all in one and for each in all.

Biblical Dimensions

Introduction

Jacqueline Lapsley

In selecting a focus for thinking about the common good in the light of Scripture, the members of the project who work primarily as biblical scholars acknowledged at the start that any attempt at comprehensiveness would be mere pretense or superficial at best. Wanting to convey something of the variety of the biblical witness concerning the common good, the writers of these first three essays have selected texts that engage diverse biblical genres and come at the subject from quite different perspectives. Patrick Miller takes up the question of the common good in relation to the Decalogue, exploring what concern for the common good looks like in covenantal and legal material. Jacqueline Lapsley explores the book of Jonah, to see how the common good emerges in the context of one of Israel's stories. In the New Testament, Victor Furnish finds that Paul articulates considerable interest in and concern for the common good, despite his overarching apocalyptic framework.

While the texts we have taken up here are quite different in many respects, a certain coherence is evident. Thus, while they represent only a narrow selection of the biblical corpus in one sense, the Ten Commandments, Jonah, and Paul's letters testify to the integrity as well as to the diversity of the biblical witness in affirming the common good—the norm and authority for which resides in God alone—as a core biblical value. Ultimately, we perceive the interests of the common good to be central to the witness of Scripture taken as a whole, and as such we understand the Bible to be making an authoritative claim upon Christian communities to participate in making what is good, good for all.

The centrality of the Ten Commandments to the life and faith of both Israel and the church is undisputed. For the community of faith, life with God and with the neighbor is fundamentally shaped by and oriented toward the Commandments, both now and eschatologically. Miller ponders the implications of the Commandments for the way in which the community of faith orients itself to the common good, which is simultaneously to be sought as a goal, received as a gift, and enacted in the life of the community. Deuteronomy is the primary context for exploring how the Commandments shape the community and the individual's orientation to the common good. Nevertheless, Miller also explores the intrinsic openness of the Commandments to engage other, nonbiblical traditions in pursuit of a more widely shared understanding of the common good. He is careful to distinguish the genuine potential of the Ten Words in such an endeavor from their draft status in the current "culture wars." Encompassing not only other human communities, but also the natural world , the Commandments ultimately "mark out a sphere of moral space and action in behalf of the common good."

In a time of waning commitment to the common good, the book of Jonah makes a bold claim: God is not parochial, but cares for the good of all, even our most reviled enemies. Lapsley's essay explores multiple ways in which Jonah relies on the merciful character of God to forgive him his flight from his prophetic call, even as he finds abhorrent the possibility that God will be merciful to Israel's most violent and hated enemy, the Ninevites. This paradox at the heart of the story confronts us with the ways in which we, like Jonah, rely on God's mercy but would retain that mercy for ourselves. Divine mercy is motivated by compassion and must be understood not as opposed to justice, but as constitutive of justice. Yet this holistic form of justice is not for God alone; God prods Jonah to train his own heart in the ways of compassionate justice. The story suggests not only that God's mercy and justice extend beyond our parochial borders to our enemies, to animals, and to all of creation, but also that we, *in imitatione Dei*, must enlarge the boundaries of whom and what we consider "common" in the common good.

In recent years a consensus has emerged among scholars concerning the apocalyptic nature of Paul's thought—one facet of which is that Paul sharply contrasted the present age with the age to come, and urged believers "not to be conformed to this age." This emphasis on apocalyptic thought has led many to understand Paul as advocating a sectarian view, which would seem to leave little room for the common good. In contrast to this trend, Victor Furnish returns to the Pauline corpus and, instead of exhortations to form Christian communities in absolute opposition to the wider culture, he finds there a commitment to the common good of all, a commitment that is to be nurtured and lived out within the community of believers. For Paul, promoting the common good is authorized and mandated by the "uncommon love of God," already poured out for all people in the person and work of Christ. Thus Furnish argues that Paul did not understand believers to be anything akin to "resident aliens," as is sometimes urged. While Paul asserts that believers are ultimately "citizens of a heavenly commonwealth" (Phil 3:20), they are also simultaneously, albeit temporarily, citizens of the wider society, with all the responsibilities pertaining thereto. In this context, Paul urges the believing community to adopt a posture of critical engagement with the world, assessing the values and claims of the world against the values and claims of the gospel, "affirming what it can and opposing what it must." The integrity of Christian moral witness depends on such discernment and on the extent to which we act upon it, advancing the good that resounds in the life of all.

The common good, as goal and as gift, comes from God. The biblical witness to its centrality for the life of faith is born out of those ancient communities' conviction that God's "uncommon" love is poured out for the whole world. We begin this volume with these traditions because they are the unique and authoritative witnesses to that love, and because all else rests upon them.

"That It May Go Well with You"

The Commandments and the Common Good

Patrick D. Miller

The centrality of the Decalogue for marking the contours of trust in God and life with our neighbor is an assumption that both guides the discussion that follows and is further undergirded within it. In this essay I intend to uncover the various ways in which the Commandments, particularly within the context of their presentation in the book of Deuteronomy, provide a way of thinking about the common good. This is with reference to the community of faith that receives the Commandments as the way to live for those redeemed and ruled by the living God, the Lord of Israel and the Lord of the church. Identity is given and community is formed by the word of God to ancient Israel in the Commandments, a word that continues to tell us who we are and how we are to live. Because Christians discover that what they receive as God's word for life resonates with the experiences and stories of others who may not identify with the story of God's way with Israel and the church, it is appropriate also to explore any possibilities for a wider conversation about the common good in light of the Commandments.

The Commandments in the Context of Deuteronomy

While the giving of the Commandments occurs in the Sinai pericope in Exod 19–24 and is thus set as a part of and response to the Lord's delivery of the Israelites from Egyptian slavery, it is the book of Deuteronomy that is framed from beginning to end as an elaboration of the Commandments as the covenant that orders Israel's life.[1] As the context for the Commandments, Deuteronomy

---

1. I am assuming here the various studies of the book of Deuteronomy that have pointed to signs that the Deuteronomic Code (chs. 12–26) is ordered or structured

presents itself as a combination of *teaching* and *constitution*, of *instruction* and *polity* for the people of God about how they are to live as the Lord's people and as a community of brothers/sisters/neighbors.[2]

1. The *instruction* is developed in relation to the way in which the community's good, defined often as life, is something to be taught and learned and in that process also rationalized and urged. This teaching is to be written down, read again and again, repeated and talked about (Deut 6:4–9). Specifically in the context of Moses' retelling the story of the Lord's giving of the Commandments, Deuteronomy sets to the fore the need to learn and teach these words:

> "Assemble the people for me, and I will let them hear my words, so that they may learn to fear me as long as they live on the earth, and may teach their children so." (4:10b)[3]
>
> And the LORD charged me at that time to teach you statutes and ordinances for you to observe in the land that you are about to cross into and occupy. (4:14)

---

along the lines of the Decalogue and so is to be understood as a development, specification, and illustration of the meaning and force of the Commandments. See, for example, Dennis Olson, *Deuteronomy and the Death of Moses: A Theological Reading* (Overtures to Biblical Theology; Minneapolis: Fortress, 1994). That this is not a modern construct is evident in Luther's lectures on Deuteronomy, where he begins his commentary on each chapter by relating its subject matter to one of the Commandments. Indeed, he comments at the beginning:

> If you want to give this book a name suitable for our use, you will correctly call it a most ample and excellent explanation of the Decalog. After you know it, you could want nothing more that is needful for understanding the Ten Commandments. For it teaches this people to live well [a theological definition of the common good?] according to the Ten Commandments in both spirit and body.

Lectures on Deuteronomy, in *Luther's Works* (ed. J. Pelikan and D. Poellot; American ed.; Saint Louis: Concordia, 1960), 9:14.

2. For a more extended development of this dual purpose for the Book of Deuteronomy, see Patrick D. Miller, "Constitution or Instruction? The Purpose of Deuteronomy," in *Constituting the Community: Studies on the Polity of Ancient Israel in Honor of S. Dean McBride Jr.* (ed. Steven Tuell and John Strong; Winona Lake, IN: Eisenbrauns, 2003). The case for Deuteronomy as a form of polity has been set forth in convincing fashion by S. Dean McBride, "Polity of the Covenant People," *Interpretation* 41 (1987): 229–44. The character of Deuteronomy as teaching and instruction has often been noted. For a recent defense of this way of perceiving the book, one that is in conversation with McBride, see Olson, *Deuteronomy and the Death of Moses*.

3. Scripture quotations are from the NRSV unless otherwise indicated. The abbreviation "lit." denotes the author's literal translation.

Behavior in conformity to this mode of existence, however, is something that needs exhortation and explanation, reasons for obedience, and motivations indicating the attractiveness of the way described therein.[4] That is a part of the learning and appropriation. Further, a strong emphasis is placed upon the need for *future generations* to be taught the Commandments and to learn them and their specific implications. So the teaching has to do with inculcating a way that is open to the future and can guide the future.

2. The *polity* and *constitutional* dimension is developed in relation to the character of the community as a sociopolitical entity that organizes its life in all its dimensions and understands its covenantal shape as having to do with all facets of its life. The constitution or polity has to do with the sacral/cultic, the political, and the social. The polity envisioned transcends the distinction between religious and political community and thus provides an opportunity for thinking about and conceiving the common good in a way that incorporates both.[5] The Deuteronomic vision, embodied constitutionally and foundationally in the Commandments, is a complex pluralistic system where the political, the theological/religious, the educational, and the moral can be identified. They coalesce, however, in such a way that it is not possible to identify the good of the whole in any one category or social system apart from the other spheres.

Interpersonal relationships are at the center of the moral space in which the Commandments provide an orienting perspective. Yet the body as a whole, the political entity of Israel, is the addressee or recipient of the Commandments, and the consensual response is a response of that entity. So while one may speak of "community," "people," and the like, one does so in cognizance of the fact that this is also a political order, traditionally described as a state.[6] The nature of the

---

4. Here, therefore, Deuteronomic understanding of the law and indeed the formulation of the moral good in the directives of the Commandments anticipate Aquinas's emphasis on the character of the law not only as orienting one toward the common good but also as a norm of reason. In every instance of the inclusion of an explanatory or hortatory clause, the rationality of the Commandments and the law is asserted. In this respect, see Jean Porter, "The Common Good in Thomas Aquinas" (in this volume). On the importance of a public discourse about the common good, see Robin W. Lovin, "Public Discourse and Common Good" (in this volume). While Lovin's concern is for a discourse that brings various elements into conversation about the common good, Deuteronomy points to another kind of rationality that centers in education and persuasion of a good already conceived.

5. This assertion carries with it the recognition that there are more complex manifestations of contemporary, social, political, and religious communities than envisioned by Deuteronomy, and that it is precisely when these communities are differentiated from one another in some fashion that the difficulties often arise. Nor does Deuteronomy have a sense of a global community, though it does address questions of relation to other political entities.

6. The self-presentation of the book of Deuteronomy is, of course, that of a community without official political structures, wandering in the wilderness, and about to enter the promised land. But the actual context of the book is fully in the

community whose common good is sought, protected, and enhanced via the Commandments is complex rather than simple. It ranges from cultic to socioethnic, from kin to polity.[7]

The book of Deuteronomy presents itself further as a constitutional document that is *appropriate for changing situations.* Its instruction guides the community, but its application to changing circumstances, including changes to the shape and character of the social and political order, invites the community to keep asking how the fundamental directions suggested here are to be worked out in new situations.[8] There is an assumption that the common good of the community is discernible and can be formulated. It is also assumed that the community will have to keep seeking to discern that common good, while continuing to be directed by the foundational instruction. The community has torah and no longer needs a Moses, but it will have to keep asking what the specifics of the instruction are in each new time.

3. The coming together of instruction and polity is in the conception of "this torah" as "covenantal law, the divinely authorized social order that Israel must implement to secure its collective political existence as the people of God."[9] A covenantal structure for the life of the people is presumed and implemented in both the Decalogue and the Deuteronomic instruction. Thus the good of the community's life is framed in a sociopolitical structure involving voluntary commitment and obligatory actions. While one may use such terms as guidelines,

---

monarchical and state period. All sorts of clues within the book point to such, not least being chapters 16:18 through 18:22, which provide for various courts and authority figures and how they are to operate in the community. Chapter 1 also specifies the system of officers set up by Moses, which is probably a reflection of a judicial reform in the ninth century or later (2 Chr 19:4–11). For a more precise history of the notion of "state," see William Cavanaugh, "Killing for the Telephone Company" (in this volume).

7. On issues of definition and character of the "community," the significance of identity and participation, see Eric Mount, "It Takes a Community—or at Least an Association" (in this volume) and his earlier work, *Covenant, Community, and the Common Good: An Interpretation of Christian Ethics* (Cleveland: Pilgrim, 1999).

8. The necessity of developing ways in which the constitutional and normative directives of the Commandments are played out in the life of individuals and the community is indicated by the differences between the Book of the Covenant in Exod 21–23 and the Deuteronomic law in Deut 19–26. Both are to be understood as specifying and illustrating the way in which the Commandments are to guide in particular cases. At least some of the differences seem to reflect a changing social and economic setting behind the two bodies of statutes and ordinances.

9. McBride, "Polity of the Covenant People," 233. Cf. the comment of Norbert Lohfink growing out of his study of the term "assembly" (קהל = *qāhāl*) in Deuteronomy and its place in the narrative setting of the giving of the Commandments in Deuteronomy: "Israel as such was perfectly constituted only through the Horeb [Sinai] covenant. Only by this event did it *become a* קהל *in the exact sense of the word*" ("Reading Deuteronomy 5 as Narrative," in *A God So Near* [ed. Brent A. Strawn and Nancy R. Bowen; Winona Lake, IN: Eisenbrauns, 2003], 274).

basic principles, foundations, and the like, the Decalogue is not presented as such. It is not set forth as an abstraction from the specific context that defines the Decalogue or is defined by the Decalogue, the covenant. What we therefore find in the Decalogue are covenantal stipulations (familiar from analogous forms in the ancient Near East). These stipulations serve to "constitute" a community of relationships—the relationship between God and the people and the inner-working relationship among the people. The covenantal ethos is a community ethos.[10] And the stipulations are not primarily to give general principles but to effect a community of harmonious relationship, a community of peace and blessing, doers of the good and the right and thus recipients of the good and blessing (see below).

Both the Commandments and the book of Deuteronomy assume and depend upon an intimate connection between the community as a whole and its individual members and thus an interaction between thinking about the *community* and the *individual*.

1. One of the ways this interaction is evident in the text is a feature usually relegated to stylistic or source-critical functions, that is, the constant interchange between second person singular and second person plural in Deuteronomy. Moses' address to the people, therefore, moves back and forth between plural and singular address in a way that defies easy explanation. One thing that happens is that the reader/listener hears a "you" and a "you all," fully interchangeable, and thus is constantly being addressed both as part of the larger whole and as individual recipient of the divine/Mosaic instruction. This interchange between personal and communal modes of address is intrinsic to the Commandments, which are singular in form and so address the community as individuals. But the Commandments in their narrative context are addressed to the *assembled community*. A further implication of this dual mode of address is that the singular mode, which clearly is a way of setting the covenantal stipulations upon each member of the community, may also be received as a singular address to the community as a whole. That is, Israel hears itself addressed as "you" and thus *as a community* faces the responsibility of continuing to decide about who is its neighbor.[11]

2. The Commandments offer a definition of the community that seeks a common good. The community is individuals existing in a complex of various relationships.

---

10. See Mount, "It Takes a Community."

11. It is not surprising, therefore, that ethnic issues arise in the question "Who is my neighbor?" as posed to Jesus. The Deuteronomic Code distinguishes between the way of treating the neighbor and the resident alien on one hand, and relations with the foreigner on the other. Yet the Commandments open the issue for the community as a whole vis-à-vis others outside the community and do not let the question of the neighbor remain a purely intracommunity definition.

The beginning and ending of that complex is the relationship to God and the relationship to the neighbor. Thus the first four commandments explicitly have to do with the fear and worship of "the LORD (= YHWH) your God" (but with significant social, legal, and political implications—see below),[12] and the last two (or three, depending on the numbering) make explicit reference to "neighbor" (4x). In between, there is a transition from the relationship to the Lord to the relationship with others, ultimately the neighbor, but not only the neighbor. Covenantal obedience and its outcome in the good of the community also involves familial relationships (honoring parents), responsibilities falling upon those who have oversight of others, and relationships to those who are in some sort of dependence or service that does not leave them free to act on their own (the Sabbath commandment). The complex of relationships also includes the world of nature and specifically the animal world. In the reflexes of the Sabbath commandment in the book of the covenant, the release and rest include the agricultural realm as well (Exod 23:10–12).[13]

3. The moral space effected by the Commandments and specified in the Deuteronomic Code (chs. 12–26) thus incorporates a variety of complex relationships and systems: power relationships (e.g., king and subject, master and bonded servant, husband and wife, employer and employee, priest and lay person, lender and borrower, judge and plaintiffs, landowner/property owner and landless, and so on), family relationships, communal relationships, property definition, systems of loans, systems of welfare, accessibility to economic goods, management of agricultural systems and animal needs, judicial structures, and the like.

4. It is not necessary to argue the issue of whether or not rights theories focus excessively upon the individual or to challenge the legitimacy of rights arguments in seeking the common good in its moral dimension. It is important in this context, however, to note that the way in which the Commandments provide a structure and space for the moral life is not in terms of *rights* but in terms of *responsibilities*. In this respect one may use other terms, such as, "duties" or "obligations," but the term "responsibility" better connotes what takes place in the Decalogue. The Commandments deal with several primary spheres of human

---

12. This specifying of the name of the deity is not to be skimmed over lightly. The one who claims the allegiance, obedience, and worship of the people *this way*, by the keeping the Commandments, is "the LORD [YHWH]," the one attested by the words and deeds recounted in the story. In the reception of the Commandments, one does not have to do with a general notion of deity but with the one who led the Hebrew slaves to freedom and showed them how to live in freedom *this way* (see below).

13. Note that the issue is not posed in terms of crop rotation in the modern sense but a provision of rest for the land as well as for its occupants. Also, once again, it is a rest for the land so that those without means of productivity may avail themselves of its volunteer crops. In Job 31:38, one of Job's claims of innocence and obedience to the law is that his land has not cried out against him and its furrows have not wept (see W. Janzen, *Exodus* [Scottdale: Herald Press, 2000], 312–13).

good—work and rest, family and household, marriage, reputation and truth, the administration of justice, goods and property (economics in a broad sense), life and freedom, and human desire. These are areas in which human flourishing, and so the good of the community as a whole, are protected by the assumption of responsibility for the good of the other, for the good of the neighbor. The orientation of the Commandments is always toward the other, whether the other is the God whose proper worship is the ground of all other acts or the neighbor/brother/sister.[14]

The rights of the individual are presumed, but the way into those rights is always by way of responsibility for the neighbor. "My" rights, "my" well-being, and the like are insured and protected not by any claims or actions of my own but by my being a neighbor to others who stand under the same responsibilities toward me that I have toward them.[15] Thus a reciprocal responsibility is operative.[16] The implicit reciprocality is what enables the Commandments to chart the moral space for a *common* good. One may indeed derive from the Decalogue an implicit set of rights that belong to being and staying human, but they are inferential and as such do not define the moral space of the Commandments at its primary level.[17] In this respect, Paul Lehmann's formulation is appropriate, not being and

---

14. The Commandments are where the category of "neighbor" is introduced into the biblical story. With the Commandments, the reality of "your neighbor" becomes controlling for the moral life of the community. Its continuing significance as a moral category is indicated by its reappearance as a major issue in the parable of the Good Samaritan in the New Testament (Luke 10:29–37).

15. A recent advertisement by Liberty Press for the publication of the writings of the Scottish philosopher Gershom Carmichael speaks of "the manner in which he justified the natural rights of individuals. Those rights included the natural right to defend oneself, the natural right to own the property on which one has labored, and the natural right to services contracted with others." From the perspective of the Commandments, those "rights" are "natural" and safeguarded only by being and having a neighbor. On the place of responsibility in and for community, see also Mount, "It Takes a Community."

16. On the notion of reciprocal responsibility, see P. Lehmann, *The Decalogue and a Human Future: The Meaning of the Commandments for Making and Keeping Human Life Human* (Grand Rapids: Eerdmans, 1995). Lehmann speaks of rights being transformed as responsibilities, which is intrinsic to the ethical perspective of the Commandments.

17. A recent formulation of this reciprocality is that of John Witte Jr.:

> Protestants have thus long translated the moral duties set out in the Decalogue into reciprocal rights. . . . Each person's duties towards a neighbor . . . can be cast as a neighbor's right to have that duty discharged. One person's duties not to kill, to commit adultery, to steal or to bear false witness thus give rise to another person's rights to life, property, fidelity and reputation.

"Between Sanctity and Depravity: Law and Human Nature in Martin Luther's Two Kingdoms," *Villanova Law Review* 48 (2003): 762.

staying human but making and keeping human. Precisely out of *orientation toward the other* , the Commandments open up *the natural world* as a full part of the realm of responsibility. This opening is readily apparent in the way in which the illustrative cases spell out the particularities and force of the Commandments in the legal codes (see above) but is already evident in the inclusion of the animal world in the Commandments themselves (Deut 5:14, 21).

Intrinsic to the Decalogue, therefore, is a way of thinking and acting that is toward the common good. It assumes a shared understanding and actions that shape human life in terms of responsibility for the well-being of others and not simply as a general good ("Love your neighbor") but articulated and worked out in the primary spheres of human existence and common life. The preference for responsibility over rights is intrinsic to the vision of the common good of the Commandments. That has large implications for the way in which the community develops law, juridical procedures, welfare systems, and modes of protection in all spheres.

The book of Deuteronomy sets "the good" as a primary topic of conversation and understands it as *way, gift,* and *goal* for the community's life.[18] In all these respects the good is something that comes from outside. As a conformity to the covenantal stipulations, the Commandments, by definition, assume a kind of moral realism, a claim that the goods belonging to or defining this living space are independent and outside of the ones who orient themselves thereby even if manifest only in the acting and doing of the community.[19] But the good comes from outside in another sense, as *blessing*[20] and *gift.*[21] At the same time, the good is also brought into reality and experienced by the actions of the people. Go the good way "so that . . . it may go well with you" (Deut 5:16). The common good, therefore, is not simply *achieved*; it is both *sought* and *received.* The characteristic modes of the community in its pursuit of and enjoyment of the common good are thanksgiving

---

18. In this respect see Victor Furnish's identification of the good that is found in an uncommon love as both a gift and a claim ("Uncommon Love and the Common Good: Christians as Citizens in the Letters of Paul"). Relative to Deuteronomy and the Commandments, it is important to see how the good is that path along which one walks and also the goal of all one's actions.

19. Such an understanding is presumably inherent in a theistic approach, but it is confirmed in this case by the way in which the Commandments are received by the community as a theophanic word. On the varying kinds of moral realism, see the helpful discussion of Ruth Abbey, *Charles Taylor* (Philosophy Now; Princeton: Princeton University Press, 2000), 26–31.

20. Note Deut 8:10 "When you have eaten and are satisfied, then be sure to thank the LORD for the good land that he has given you" (lit.). The text also includes a warning against thinking "My hand and my power have gotten me this" (8:17, lit.).

21. The "good land" is often spoken of as "given" by the LORD (1:25, 35; 4:21; 6:18; 8:10; 9:6; 11:17). See also the Mosaic instruction to "rejoice in all the good the LORD is giving to you" (26:11, lit.).

and obedience. The flourishing of the community is both gift and goal, but it is found by choosing to walk the way.

Along with the *good* as a gift and way, Deuteronomy sets *life* as the goal, reward, and outcome of proper conformity to the responsibilities defined by the covenantal relationship and indeed suggests an implicit correlation of the good and life. In this regard, attention should be drawn to the book's decisive and climactic moment in enacting the covenant at Moab. After Moses has reminded the community of the Decalogue and further instructed them about its implications in the specifics of the law, he sets the decision before the people:

> See I have set before you life and . . . [good (lit.)], death and . . . [disaster (lit.)]. . . . Choose life so that you and your descendants may live, loving the LORD your God, obeying him, and holding fast to him; for that means life to you and length of days, so that you may live in the land that the LORD swore to give to your ancestors, to Abraham, to Isaac, and to Jacob. (Deut 30:15–20)

In Deuteronomy, the good of others is not something that is enjoined as a separate act apart from the regular activities of life. It is something that is achieved within them. Two cardinal examples can be cited. One is the way in which the enjoyment and celebration of God's gift in and through the regular celebratory festivals is something that is inclusive of all the community so that all are provided for. *Rejoicing* in the good that God has given *includes within it* the *doing* of the good, including everyone in the celebration of the good gifts, providing for the whole of the community.[22] Within the context of this community, the centrality of an inclusive and celebratory meal "before the LORD" is unavoidably a eucharistic anticipation.

Second, the laws do not so much instruct one on how to add good to the life of the neighbor as they indicate how each member of the community is to carry on his or her life. The purpose is so that he or she does not inhibit the good for all that is inherent in the life of the community living by this instruction and constitution. The good of the neighbor is not "in addition to" but worked out in the everyday activities of human life. The laws do not set forth a lot of good things to do. The good is found in making sure—in one's enjoyment of the good gifts, God's good and "the work of your hands"—that others are not cut off from the good.[23]

Michael Welker has suggested that one begin to see the laws not simply as requirements to be done but as provisions for securing expectations. A culture of

---

22. See, for example, the festival laws of Deuteronomy in 14:22–29 and 16:1–17; cf. 12:17–19.

23. On the purpose of the Sabbath commandment to provide rest for male and female bond servants, see below.

expectations is secured through the community's attention to the covenantal stipulations and the particulars of living this way. That security of expectations, arising out of a structure of responsibility to the other identified as both "the LORD your God" and "your neighbor," is another way of speaking about the common good.[24]

Securing the Common Good through the Commandments

Relative to the *substantive* character of the common good, the Commandments help to mark out a sphere of moral space and action in behalf of the common good. Such delineation is evident as one examines the particular commandments.

The first four commandments explicitly have to do with the fear and worship of God. Several implications may be drawn from that fundamental fact:[25]

First, the good of the individual and of the community, the possibility of their flourishing, is directly related to their recognition of the Lord of Israel as determining their life and receiving their full obedience and worship. This means that there is no other possible ultimate concern, no other center of meaning or value on which those who live by this word can rely.

Second, in the Jewish tradition, the first of the Commandments, or more literally of the Ten Words, is what others call the Prologue, the self-presentation of the Deity as redeemer of an enslaved people and the one who comes to them as "your God." The Commandments are before the people not simply as a good way to go but as a claim on their lives. They do not stand outside the ground of the Lord's liberation of the people from oppression. They are received as directives for living, but living as those who have been freed from political and social servitude in order to be the servants of the Lord.

Third, all other facets of life in community, for the good and for the other, flow out of the worship of the Lord alone. The double-sidedness of this is implicit in the First Commandment and explicit in the Shema (Deut 6:4–5), the positive form of the First Commandment:

- The love and service of the Lord as God. There is a positive obligation to commit oneself fully (heart, soul, and everything) to the Lord.
- The exclusion of any other possible ultimate loyalties. The commandment's prohibitive form is critical for its resistance to the transformation of penultimate claims to ultimate ones.

---

24. M. Welker, "Security of Expectations: Reformulating the Theology of Law and Gospel," *The Journal of Religion* 66 (1986): 237–60.

25. The numbering of the Commandments in this essay is according to the Reformed tradition, which separates the prohibition of the worship of other gods (the first commandment) from the making and worship of images or idols (the second commandment).

The commandments of the first table of the Decalogue have significant social, legal, and political implications:

1. The First Commandment has to do with the one in whom we trust and the locus of our ultimate obedience. It is a *political* claim and often has played out quite specifically in the political realm. Both praise and prayer are basic manifestations of living by the First Commandment. They are political acts that signify where one's ultimate obedience lies and one's judgment about what power is finally operative in the world.[26] Obedience is a form of discipleship, and the language of discipleship begins with the first commandment. The *economic* dimension of the worship of other gods is widely evident in the biblical story. Violation of the first commandment centered heavily on systemic and communal devotion to the economic gods (for example, Baal in Hos 1–3; the Queen of Heaven in Jer 44; and Mammon in Matt 6:24 // Luke 16:13).[27]

2. The prohibition of the making and worshipping of images has political and economic implications as well, if some of the contemporary investigation is on target. Because of the close relation to the image of the god and the image of the king, the resistance to divine images may be an early manifestation of Israel's resistance to human kingship in light of its covenantal polity under the rule of the sovereign Lord of Israel. In addition, a number of texts indicate that the prohibition has some connection with the character of idols and images as being cast in silver and gold. Thus, the Israelites are warned against coveting the silver and gold of the idols, both because one may be drawn away from the worship of God and because the silver and gold are themselves tempting. There is an economic danger in the worship of the idols, whether they are images of the Lord or of other gods (see Exod 20:23; Deut 7:25; Josh 7; Judg 8:24–27; 17:1–13).[28]

3. The misuse of the name operates especially in the law court, in the judicial sphere. See the "swear falsely" in Deut 6:13, which is a positive formulation of this commandment, and the Jewish Publication Society Tanakh's translation of the Commandment: "You shall not swear falsely by the name of the LORD your God." In Deuteronomy, the term "in vain" is the same word used for "false" in the ninth commandment that forbids "false" witness. The social dimension of the commandment has to do with *truth in the courts* and the possibility of a *proper administration of justice*. That is seen to be a matter of the relationship with God (third commandment) as much as with the neighbor (ninth commandment). The political and

---

26. Note in this connection, Karl Barth's insistence that the resistance indicated in the Barmen Declaration was a manifestation of obedience to the first commandment, not simply a resistance to tyranny. The First Commandment also played a significant role in forming a basic ground for resistance to the Vietnam War in the 1960s.

27. On the connections between political and economic power in the nation state, see Cavanaugh, "Killing for the Telephone Company" (in this volume).

28. For further discussion and references to the secondary literature, see P. D. Miller, *The Religion of Ancient Israel* (Louisville: Westminster, 2000), 21–23.

religious dimensions of this commandment, however, are not to be overlooked. It sets a resistance to the light or empty invocation of the Deity's name or the appropriation of the name of God as a ground for one's own agenda in full awareness that such a move actually turns the ultimate into the penultimate and the holy into the profane. Even the invocation or promulgation of the Commandments to serve one's own political and cultural ends can be a violation of the name of God. The same is true for the easy and common tendency to trivialize the Commandments in jokes, cartoons, or simplistic and reductionistic dismissal of their pertinence for life. Discernment between appropriate and inappropriate invocation of the divine name is not always an easy task. But this does not release the community from engaging in just such discernment (see "The Endangerment of the Commandments" on page 37).

4. The Sabbath rest is rooted in both the creative work of God, as a rest after labor that imitates the divine order (so the Exod 20 grounding), and in the work of God to liberate the oppressed and give freedom to those in bondage (so the Deut 5 grounding). The work-rest cycle belongs both to an acknowledgement of the ground of life in the work of God and to what is needful to make and to keep human life human. In its nonutilitarian purposelessness, Sabbath rest, therefore, is clearly a part of devotion to the Lord. At the same time it is given a purpose that is both humanitarian and socioeconomic. It is the first specific instance of protection of the good of the neighbor, in this case, the economically dependent neighbor, "your male or female slave" (Deut 5:14). The Sabbath is set to protect or provide for regular rest for those who are in one's service or economic control and incapable of getting the rest unless it is structured into the system.

As the Deuteronomic Code interprets the Sabbath commandment of the Decalogue and applies it specifically to cases, it makes clear that this has to do with both *money* and *labor as commodities* or as means of becoming economically endangered. That is evident in Deut 15, the first part of which has to do with loans and the remission of loans and pledges every seventh year. The second part of Deut 15 has to do with bonded service because of debts. Such labor is not to continue past the seventh year and is to be rewarded by provision of the means for the formerly indebted or bonded person to begin life with sufficient economic resources not to be endangered again. The cases and specifics growing out of the commandment against *stealing* incorporate all sorts of ways in which economic endangerment is addressed and economic support is protected. To the extent that the Commandments chart the moral space in which the community may find a shared good, that enterprise is heavily oriented around the safeguarding of economic sufficiency against its undoing.[29] In the Commandments, the common good is effected largely by the protection and provision of economic goods.

---

29. For a more detailed exploration of this claim, see P. D. Miller, "The Economics of the Straying Ox: Property and Possessions in the Light of the Commandments,"

The preceding discussion indicates that the distinction between the right and left tables of the Commandments is a blurred one. Nevertheless, the "other" envisioned as the direction toward which life and thought are directed is more specifically the focus in the second table of the Commandments.

1. The orientation in moral space (see below) is provided by the Commandments and the sense of the common good that they encourage. In no small measure this orientation rests upon the way in which the Sabbath commandment and the commandment to honor parents serve as bridges between the love of God and the love of neighbor. That is especially the case with regard to their effecting a starting point for the relationship with the neighbor. There is a logical starting point and an illogical one. The *illogical* one is already indicated in the discussion of the Sabbath commandment above. The purpose of the Sabbath rest in the Deuteronomic form of the Decalogue is so that your male and female slave may have rest such as you have, that those whose work and labor are under your control may be released. This illogical starting point is rooted in the fundamental *theological* logic of Israel's story, evident not only in the grounding of the Commandments in the story of God's liberation of this people from slavery but articulated precisely as the meaning of the Commandments and the statutes and ordinances.

In future generations, the children will ask their parents, "What is the meaning of the decrees and the statutes and the ordinances that the LORD our God has commanded you?" The mothers and fathers are to answer: "We were Pharaoh's slaves in Egypt, but the LORD brought us out of Egypt with a mighty hand"(Deut 6:20–21). The redemption from slavery has set a different kind of logic at work: The initial and special concern is for the oppressed, dependent, vulnerable, and nonfree members of the community. It is only after that point is made and insured in the Sabbath commandment and the sabbatical principle growing out of it that one can then move on to the neighbor, who is met in the other relationships of communal life. Here, as elsewhere in the Commandments, the orientation is toward responsibility. One may indeed infer a *right* to rest from hard labor. But the Commandments do not make such a claim. They assume the human need and see the common good not in assertion of that right but in making sure that it is protected for those who cannot assume it for themselves.

The *logical* starting point for protecting the good of the neighbor, as already implicit in the Sabbath commandment, is the *family*.[30] That starting point is

---

in *Having: Property and Possession in Social and Religious Life* (ed. William Schweiker; Grand Rapids, MI: Eerdmans, 2004), 17–50.

30. The way in which this commandment serves as the starting point for thinking about life with the neighbor and responsibility of the other is demonstrated in Lev 19, the text most closely connected to the Decalogue. Samuel Balentine has pointed to a chiasm in the structure of the chapter that "reverses the order of the Commandments in the Decalogue, elevating Commandment number five, reverence for father and mother, to the position of first importance. . . . The lead commandment to revere father and mother (v. 3a), who represent the most intimate union in the family structure, is amplified with further commandments (vv. 9–35)

provided in the commandment to honor parents. As such, the family is opened up as an important part of the moral framework provided by the Commandments. The reciprocal responsibility inherent within the neighbor commandments would seem, at first glance, to be inoperative in this commandment. Thus it suggests a hierarchy of human relationship that insures the good of the ones at the top of the hierarchy. There is, however, an implicit reciprocality operative within this commandment. That reciprocality is made explicit in the development of the trajectory of this commandment in Ephesians, where the commandment is quoted as the ground for the "Pauline" injunction: "Children, obey your parents in the Lord" (Eph 6:1). That injunction, however, is followed directly by its corollary, thus achieving reciprocity even in this hierarchical situation: "Fathers, do not provoke your children to anger." The reciprocal enhancement of the good is further indicated in the setting of the Commandment in a *generational* pattern. There is an implicit awareness that while the young are to honor the old, the children their parents, it is inevitably the case that the young grow old. The children become parents so that their good is protected by the establishment of a pattern that begins with their insuring the good of their parents. But the pattern will carry through for their own well-being into the next generation.

There are two other things to be observed in the commandment that structures family relationships. Here the Decalogue explicitly identifies the "good" as the goal of living according to this pattern, the description of life under God embodied in the Commandments. The motivational clause "that it may go well with you" (Deut 5:16) is explicitly underscored in the Ephesians text (6:3). It reminds the community that this is the one commandment with a promise, a promise of the good as an outcome of the mode of behavior and life prescribed in the commandment(s).

The second significant dimension of the Commandment is its opening up a larger sphere of good, specifically, the way in which persons in the community relate to authorities and leaders. Paul Lehmann's comment on this is worth quoting in full:

> The crux of Luther's interpretation of the fourth commandment is its insistence that the relations between parents and children are paradigmatic of human wholeness.[31] This is the case because the relations

---

that extend the requirement for ethical relationships to the broader "community" of all God's creation. The land must be harvested with a compassion that does not ignore the needs of the poor (vv. 9–10; see also vv. 23–25), and plants and animals must be protected against mixed breeding that weakens the species God has created (v. 19). The welfare of the human community must not be jeopardized by dishonesty (vv. 11–12), oppression (vv. 13–14), economic injustice (vv. 15–16, 35–36), hate and vengeance (vv. 17–18), abusive sexual practices (vv. 20–22, 29), or disrespect for elders or aliens (vv. 32–33)" (*Leviticus* [Interpretation; Louisville: Westminster John Knox, 2002], 161–62).

31. This reading of the trajectory of the commandment to honor parents is not, of course, peculiar to Luther. It is widespread in the history of interpretation of the

between parents and children are pivotal to the nurture of a humanizing apperception that converts the otherwise dehumanizing polarization between inequality and equality, and between authority and freedom, into a creative and fulfilling congruence. The secret of this conversion is the reciprocal responsibility in, with, and under which inequality and equality, authority and freedom are joined.[32]

The filial responsibility to honor and treat well one's parents and the reciprocality inherent in that responsibility make an appropriate starting point for thinking about necessary asymmetrical and hierarchical relationships of all sorts: employer-employee, teacher-student, judge-petitioner, ruler-subject, and the like.

2. We have recognized the family as a social unit of reciprocal responsibility for the good across generations and the parent-child relationship as the starting point for discerning the good in relation to the other. These are then given further direction and support as a sphere of the common good by the prohibition against *adultery*. The orientation of the commandment is toward the neighbor, not towards one's own marital relation. What is being protected in the commandment is the marital relation, the husband-wife relation, of one's neighbor. So both aspects of the family relationship—the husband-wife relation and the parent-child relation—are nurtured and undergirded, in one case by encouraging an esteem and respect across the generations, and in the other by securing the basic relationship from encroachment by any other that would effect a breach in the marriage.

Once again, the character of the Commandments as effecting responsibility toward the neighbor's good has the concomitant outcome of securing one's own marital relation from violation and harm. This happens both by my not having violated my own marriage in committing adultery with the wife of another, but also by my neighbor's care in protecting my marital relationship by not committing adultery with my wife. Thus, a major feature of the common good secured by a community that lives under this direction and instruction is that each member is concerned for protecting the good of his neighbor(s) rather than being focused on securing her own good.

3. At this point it is appropriate to recognize an important feature of the long history of interpretation of the Commandments that is central to the prohibitions of the second table of the Decalogue but is not confined to it. The meaning of the

---

Commandment and has clear rootage in the Deuteronomic polity. Deuteronomy orders the Deuteronomic Code in chapters 12–26 roughly according to the outline or order of the Decalogue and thus underscores the character of the code as specifying and illustrating the force of the Commandments in various specific instances and cases. Immediately after Deut 15, which deals with the sabbatical principle releasing debts and slaves in the seventh year, comes a section in chapters 16–18 dealing with the leaders or "authorities" in the community, explicitly judges and elders, prophet and priest. This spells out the force of the family commandment.

32. Lehmann, *The Decalogue and a Human Future*, 152.

Commandments and the way in which they provide direction for faith and life is to be found in recognizing that every prohibition contains within itself a positive responsibility. Likewise, every positive command contains within itself a negative warning (keep the Sabbath—do not do any work on the seventh day; honor your father and mother—fathers, do not provoke your children to anger).

While not confined to a single strand of tradition, such an understanding of the Commandments has been central to their interpretation in the Reformed tradition. For John Calvin, there was always a three-part approach to the interpretation of each commandment. One sought after the subject of the commandment, the end of the commandment, and its *opposite*, that is the injunction to good in the prohibition and the warning against the bad in the command. His classic example was the commandment against killing, which, in light of its subject and its end, clearly meant not simply a prohibition of killing or murdering somebody else but a warning against harming one's neighbor in any way. Further, the opposite was inherent in the commandment in its full sense. One is enjoined to do all one can for the neighbor's good, or as Calvin put it, "We give our neighbor's life all the help we can."[33]

4. A further aspect of securing the common good through the appropriation of modes of conduct identified in the Commandments is the recognition of the strong connection between *thought* and *deed*, between *intention* and *act*. This is the critical point of the final commandment(s) that prohibits coveting anything that belongs to one's neighbor. In various ways it intensifies the nature of responsibility opened up in the second table by recognizing that what is guarded there is vulnerable first of all through the inner workings of envy, greed, and desire that can lead to acts prohibited by the other commandments.[34] That *acting* is the mode of endangerment of

---

33. John Calvin, *Institutes of the Christian Religion* (ed. and trans. John T. McNeill and Ford Lewis Battles; 2 vols.; The Library of Christian Classics; Philadelphia: Westminster, 1960), 2.8.9. Consistent with this understanding of the Commandments, the former Presbyterian Church in the United States, before its reunion with the United Presbyterian Church, prepared an extensive statement on "The Nature and Value of Human Life." It dealt with such issues as war, suicide, euthanasia, abortion, and capital punishment on the basis of an understanding of the commandment against killing in both its negative and positive dimensions.

34. "If the Decalogue devotes its final commandment to prohibiting desire for whatever belongs to the neighbor, it is because it lucidly recognizes in that desire the key to the violence prohibited in the four commandments that precede it. If we ceased to desire the goods of our neighbor, we would never commit murder or adultery or theft or false witness. If we respected the tenth commandment, the four commandments that precede it would be superfluous." (René Girard, *I See Satan Fall Like Lightning* [trans. James G. Williams; Maryknoll: Orbis, 2002], 11–12). In the tenth commandment Girard sees a perception of the centrality of mimetic desire in human nature, which, while good in itself, turns constantly to violence. The commandment signals a "revolution" in the handling of mimetic desire that is carried through in Jesus' call for an imitation or mimesis of himself, thus setting human desire away from self-love and the violence of rivalry against the neighbor and toward the imitation of God.

the neighbor's good is clear because the language for coveting most often occurs in biblical stories and prophetic sayings that go on to describe the act that erupts out of the envy and greed. Indeed, it is the connection between envy and greed that is at stake here, greed being the acquisitive move against the neighbor to enhance one's own well-being at the expense of another member of the community.[35]

It is this dimension of the working of the Commandments that is accentuated in Jesus' teaching of them. His antitheses in the Sermon on the Mount do not represent a critique of the Commandments or another and different or better teaching. Rather, Jesus here uncovers and unpacks the force of the commandment against coveting and focuses much of his teaching on the close relationship between what goes on in the heart and how one acts. Instead of going beyond the Commandments, Jesus takes them further and gets to the "heart" of the matter (pun intended). He also continues the tradition that began in the Old Testament and continues on in Paul, the tradition of seeing in the whole and the particularity of the Commandments a fundamental principle: "Love your neighbor." So the Commandments provide both complex and simple ways of seeking the good of the whole.

The complexity is in the particular working out of what the Commandments are after, a development that begins in Scripture with the stories, the prophetic sayings, the wisdom literature, and all the many pieces of case law in the Torah. That working out continues in the teaching of the church, beginning with Jesus and Paul and continuing through the history of the church to the present, exemplified in but not confined to the centrality of the Commandments in the church's catechesis.[36] The simplicity is in the accurate reduction of the pursuit of the good of all to the continuing enactment of the love of God and neighbor-love.

The Commandments as Moral Framework

The present discussion is about the common good, and that "common" is open and not finally determined. Therefore, it is appropriate now to ask about the possibility

---

35. As Girard recognizes, the term that is used in the tenth commandment is simply the word for "desire," which can often be an appropriate or acceptable feeling. The problem is the mimetic desire that becomes rivalry, the desire for what belongs to one's neighbor. The deep problematic and danger of desire is, of course, signaled early in the biblical story in the decision of the first woman to eat of the fruit of the forbidden tree because it was "desirable" (Gen 3). The term that is used there is the same as the term in the commandment (*ḥāmad*). Without the control of desire, there is no chance for a *common* good.

36. Note how the catechisms not only include the Commandments but go on to offer extensive development of the trajectory of meaning that arises out of each commandment. Obvious examples may be seen in Luther's Shorter and Larger Catechisms and the Westminster Larger Catechism, but there are many more. For the central role that Augustine played in setting the Commandments within the catechesis of the church as well as developments before and after Augustine, see Paul Rentschka, *Die Dekalogkatechese des hl. Augustinus: Ein Beitrag zur Geschichte des Dekalogs* (Kempten: Jos. Kösel'schen Buchhandlung, 1905). Cf. Bo Reicke, *Die zehn Worte in Geschichte und Gegenwart* (Beiträge zur Geschichte der biblischen Exegese 13; Tübingen: Mohr [Siebeck]), 8–50.

that the community whose identity is worked out and whose life is defined by these words from the Lord, by the Commandments, may find some companionship. Can it find some commonality with others who may not share the same identity or story? On the way to that question, and as a bridge between the community whose identity and direction are given at Sinai and other communities, I propose two metaphors for thinking about how life is lived, two metaphors for the moral that are appropriate for thinking about the function of the Commandments but may and do have wider applicability.

Both for the self and for the community, however limited or widely the "community" is defined, the need for some moral *framework* or *structure* belongs to the character of being human and to the possibility of being human or of making and keeping human life human (Lehmann's powerful cliché). Such a moral framework may be understood by some to be autonomous, by others as heteronomous, and by still others as theonomous. Some such frames of reference may be more grounded in story and shared communal experience (family, political, sacral communities, and the like). Others are rooted more in some rationality or inferred system of virtue. However such structures are erected, it is difficult to avoid some moral framework, at least within a communal life of even the most minimal sort.

At the same time, it is clear that in the modern world moral frameworks are problematic precisely at the point of assuming there is a *single* moral framework. No moral framework can be taken for granted as *the* moral framework, universally applicable to all.[37] The result may be reduction to a moral pluralism, at least in principle. Different structures, providing varying senses of identity and orientation or of identity and the good, coexist alongside each other within single communities or among and across different communities.[38] Or persons identify with a particular moral framework to a high degree while others approach the same framework more tentatively, appropriating some aspects and reticent about others. Still others may stand within a framework while understanding it as only one among other possibilities. And even in this case, one may be more or less positive about other possibilities.

Such a moral framework seems to be a presupposition of a common good. At a minimum, the very terminology of "common good" builds in assumptions about some moral framework undergirding or supporting it or providing a moral space in which one may live out, search for, discover, and experience the common good. And here I put forth the second metaphor for the moral. To the extent that the common good presupposes a commons, then it is appropriate also to speak of a moral *space* in which the self and others determine and share a common good. This is a space in which the self and others find a shared identity and a common orientation about how to live. The structural and spatial concepts of moral *framework* and moral *space* provide metaphors for development of a multidimensional

37. Charles Taylor, *Sources of the Self: The Making of the Modern Identity* (Cambridge: Harvard University Press, 1989), 17. For discussion of some common examples of moral frameworks, such as the honor ethic, the rule of reason, transformation of the will, and the like, see pages 20–24.
38. Ibid., 25–40.

and complex depiction of the moral life as a central dimension of the common good. The danger of such concepts also becoming static and fixed[39] is offset if both *structure* and *space* are set in a temporal and spatial *arc of understanding*. This is a trajectory of meanings, acts, and effects that receive their grounding in the moral framework and their orientation in the moral space but attend to ever changing contexts of varying sorts (personal, communal, historical, geographical, economic, and so on).

The Commandments create, in effect, a defining community. By its structure the questions of value and norms, the patterns of interaction among members and in relation to others, and the fundamental definition of one's self are determined as provided by the Ten Words of God. The very definition of the community and the identity of its individual members are all wrapped in and shaped by the moral space provided by the Commandments.[40]

The Openness of the Commandments

The question that remains, however, is whether there is any possibility that the shape and space for life as defined and laid out, constructed and landscaped by the Commandments, have any connection with the moral framework and moral space that others perceive and by which they live. It is not essential that that be the case. Dialogue may go on from utterly different vantage points and out of quite different stories. At the same time, there may be fruitful interchange precisely when one discovers some common ground.[41] In what follows, various reasons are given *from within the tradition itself* that suggest the possibility of the Commandments contributing to a more broadly shared understanding of the common good.

1. Within the literary and theological context in which the Commandments are given as divine word, they are seen to be *foundational* and *perduring*, not restricted to times and places. They are foundational in that they open up a way of living in freedom and in covenant with the redeeming God that is worked out in various ways in different contexts and new situations. The Commandments are related to the other legal collections in the Torah. While the collections are

---

39. The terms "static" and "fixed" are not inherently pejorative. Stasis may be life-saving; foundations keep things from falling down. But stasis that is not attentive to changing conditions may create obsolescence; and some structures need to be mobile or capable of moving if there is an earthquake.

40. For a more extensive elaboration of this point than is possible within the confines of this essay or as a supplement to the points being made here, see Patrick D. Miller, "The Good Neighborhood: Identity and Community through the Commandments," in *Character and Scripture: Moral Formation, Community, and Biblical Interpretation* (ed. William P. Brown; Grand Rapids: Eerdmans, 2002), 55–72.

41. See, for example, the essay in this volume by Milner Ball on Black Elk: "Common Good in Performance."

specific cases and illustrations of the force and bearing of the Commandments in the land and through time, the Commandments continue as the unchanging constitutional directives. The collections of case law (Exod 20:22–23:33; Deut 12–26) follow each account of the revelation of the Commandments (Exod 20; Deut 5) as the direct word of God. Narrative device explicitly separates them (Deut 5:22–33; cf. Exod 20:18–20), and they vary significantly from one another even as they deal with much common subject matter, thus signaling the difference between the legal collections and the Commandments. The Commandments are perduring both by the narrative and their continuing force. The narrative does not set them as belonging to a particular time and place;[42] they are for "the land you are about to occupy" (Deut 5:33, lit.). Their continuing force and character are a starting point in the divine instruction about the good and the right, about life in community with God and neighbor, exemplified in both the prophets and the Sermon on the Mount. In itself, this dimension of the Commandments does not take one outside the community that receives them in covenantal obedience, but it indicates their openness in time and space.

2. The Book of Deuteronomy explicitly identifies the "statutes and ordinances" as kept by Israel as evidence to the other peoples of what a wise and discerning nation Israel is:

> You must observe them [the statutes and ordinances] diligently, for this will show your wisdom and discernment to the peoples, who, when they hear all these statutes, will say, "Surely this great nation is a wise and discerning people!" . . . And what other great nation has statutes and ordinances as just as this entire law that I am setting before you today? (Deut 4:6, 8).

Other peoples can recognize the wisdom and justice of the statutes and ordinances Moses teaches as trajectories of meaning and action flowing out of the Commandments. There is an implicit suggestion that others desire these statutes and ordinances, that other nations envy Israel because of its wise and discerning laws. Jon Levenson comments with regard to this text:

---

42. Sinai, while a specific locus at a moment in the story of Israel, moves beyond that to become a kind of metaphor for the moral space of the community. New teaching goes on about the meaning and force, the particularity and ramifications of the Commandments, starting with Sinai. But though Moses teaches the meaning of the Commandments afresh on the plains of Moab (Deuteronomy), there is no second or new revelation of the Commandments or an equivalent covenantal structure. Moses refers *back* to Sinai (Horeb) in remembering the revelation of the Ten Words. But he teaches the community afresh at the border of the promised land what these words are all about, what is the meaning of covenantal existence in the new territory, now far from the wilderness of Sinai.

The commandments in question are the unique heritage of Israel granted her at a particular moment in her sacred history. But the desirability of these laws is presented as something universally recognized. . . . They are the universal, undeniable proof of the intellectual acuity of Israel. . . . Deut 4:5–8 views observance of the commandments as the fruit of both faith and reason, of Israel's unparalleled *Heilsgeschichte* and universal human perceptivity. Torah is the intersection and consummation of the particular and the universal.[43]

To these considerations one may add the recognition, precisely within Deuteronomy—though not alone there—that the Lord has other stories with the other nations.[44] The gods whom Israel is not to worship have been "allotted to all the peoples everywhere under heaven" (Deut 4:19; cf. 29:26; 32:8–9). There is an implicit assumption that the worship of the other nations, identified in relation to other deities and other religious systems, is, in fact, a provision and work of the Lord of Israel. One may set alongside this Deuteronomic hint the indication of exodus stories among other nations in Amos's oracle:

> Are you not like the Ethiopians to me,
>   O people of Israel? says the LORD.
> Did I not bring up Israel from the land of Egypt,
>   And the Philistines from Caphtor and the Arameans from Kir?
>   (Amos 9:7)

The notion of shared moral structures is not explicit in these texts but it may be inferred.

3. In their original sociohistorical setting, the world of the ancient Near East, certain of the concerns of the Commandments were shared by other religious and political communities. In his articulation of the foundations of a moral code operative in Israel and Mesopotamia, Karel van der Toorn finds them in the second table of the Decalogue and documents this with extensive reference to all sorts of Mesopotamian texts. He shows that respect for the gods and particularly

---

43. J. Levenson, "The Theologies of Commandment in Biblical Times," *Harvard Theological Review* 73 (1980): 26.

44. Patrick D. Miller, "God's Other Stories: On the Margins of Deuteronomic Theology," in *Realia Dei: Essays in Archaeology and Biblical Interpretation in Honor of Edward F. Campbell, Jr. at His Retirement* (ed. Prescott Williams Jr. and Theodore Hiebert; Atlanta: Scholars Press, 1999), 185–94; reprinted in P. D. Miller, *Israelite Religion and Biblical Theology: Collected Essays* (Journal for the Study of the Old Testament Supplement Series 267; Sheffield: Sheffield Academic Press, 2000), 593–602.

avoidance of lighthearted use of the divine name in frivolous oaths and blasphemy was characteristic of both Akkadian texts and the Bible.[45]

Further, one may observe, the Sabbath per se is not a shared religious practice in the world of the Bible. Nevertheless, there is a parallel in the provision for release of slaves and debts. Such action is at the heart of the Deuteronomic understanding of the purpose of the Sabbath commandment. It also significantly appears as a part of Mesopotamian practice in the royal proclamations of release of debts and taxes as well as in other procedures that released slaves from their labor.[46]

4. There is a long association of the Decalogue with the natural law.[47] From the patristic period onward, both the Golden Rule and the Decalogue are seen as providing the substance of the natural law, which is to be understood as of universal validity, to be recognized by persons. Jean Porter comments: "It makes sense to take these precepts [of the Decalogue] as statements of fundamental moral norms that are both generally known and foundational in the sense that other norms can be derived from them."[48] On inner-scriptural grounds the same thing can be argued, as I have mentioned above.[49] The theological grounding of the natural law is that it is contained in the divine law, as Porter argues for the scholastic

---

45. K. van der Toorn, *Sin and Sanction in Israel and Mesopotamia: A Comparative Study* (Studia Semitica Neerlandica 22; Assen/Maastricht: Van Gorcum, 1985), ch. 2. The same point is made by J. J. M. Roberts: "Even the Ten Commandments, delivered to the Israelites at Mount Sinai/Horeb by the voice of Yahweh, contain little that would not have been acknowledged everywhere else in the Near East." Then, however, he adds an important caveat that continues to have significant relevance for the appropriation of the Commandments: "Apart from the limitation of worship to the one God, the prohibition of images, and perhaps the observance of the Sabbath, these commands simply embody in a very pithy formulation the ethical standards common in the region" ("The Bible and the Literature of the Ancient Near East," in Roberts, *The Bible and the Ancient Near East: Collected Essays* [Winona Lake, IN: Eisenbrauns, 2002], 45). A significant tension is inherent in this mix of commonality and differentiation that continues to be an issue in the openness of the Commandments to their wider appropriation. As van der Toorn notes, however, even in the first table there are correspondences within the wider world of the Commandments that may be of significance for the conversation.

46. For the evidence and discussion of relation to biblical practices, see J. M. Hamilton, *Social Justice and Deuteronomy: The Case of Deuteronomy 15* (SBL Dissertation Series 136; Atlanta: Scholars Press, 1992), 45–72; and M. Weinfeld, *Social Justice in Ancient Israel and in the Ancient Near East* (Minneapolis: Fortress, 1995), 75–96.

47. See especially J. Porter, *Natural and Divine Law: Reclaiming the Tradition for Christian Ethics* (Saint Paul University Series in Ethics; Grand Rapids: Eerdmans, 1999), especially ch. 3.

48. Ibid., 168.

49. See, for example, P. D. Miller, "The Place of the Decalogue in the Old Testament and Its Law," *Interpretation* 43 (1989): 229–42.

tradition. Scripture provides a normative formulation of the natural law (Golden Rule) and "offers the paradigmatic statement of the immediate moral implications of the natural law, in the form of the Decalogue."[50]

While Porter's argument is an analysis of the tradition, it is in behalf of reclaiming such an understanding for contemporary Christian ethics, as her subtitle indicates. Others have sought to do the same in different ways. Reinhard Hütter has argued for a close association of the Decalogue with the natural law in contemporary ethical discussion. His suggestion is that the Decalogue helps us "remember" the natural law more fully in various contexts that all human beings share:

> Christians individually and the church corporately do not have any privileged knowledge in detailed practical moral matters. They, however, find themselves bound by the perspectives and insights of a path that God has willed for all humanity. The commandments as the way of human freedom in communion with God are the basis for re(dis)covering the "natural law." . . . Natural law is not "something out there" that we eventually "bump" into if we search long enough. Neither is it to be found "written" in our genes or in the stars. . . . While some principles of practical reason are accessible to all of us, the natural law in its fullness is not simply inscribed in our minds. Instead, diverse practices and traditions that structure human society display a matrix of contingent and unpredictable resonances with God's purpose for humankind as articulated in the narratives of Israel and Jesus. In particular structures of responsibility (their vocations), Christians have to discern and judge the resonances and dissonances in light of God's commandments.[51]

Robert Jenson has seen in the negative formulations of the Commandments (as well as in their substance) something of a kind of natural law:

> In their bare negative formulation . . . the commandments of the second table apply to all polities, including those that do not belong to the narrative in which the commandments appear and that must therefore substitute joint pursuit of self-interest [a secular definition of the common good?] for love of God. In this role the commandments state minimum conditions: no society can subsist in which the generations turn against each other; in which vendetta has not been replaced by public organs of judgment and punishment.
>
> Whether or not we wish to call the commandments in this negative abstraction natural law is perhaps mostly a matter of conceptual taste. The commandments are explicitly given by God to Israel and the church,

---

50. Porter, *Natural and Divine Law*, 132.
51. Reinhard Hütter, "The Twofold Center of Lutheran Ethics: Christian Freedom and God's Commandments," in *The Promise of Lutheran Ethics* (ed. Karen L. Bloomquist and John R. Stumme; Minneapolis: Fortress, 1998), 50–51.

but any people must know them in their negative mode if it is indeed to be a people even by less stringent definition. And existing peoples show that they do know them.[52]

It is possible also to see the incipient application of the norms of the Commandments already in the biblical narrative before their utterance by the Lord at Sinai. So James Skillen maintains in his essay in this volume, where he argues for "the creational origin and foundation of these responsibilities.[53] The presence of unacceptable desire in Gen 3 has already been mentioned (see n. 35). To that one may add the judgment of Cain because he murdered his brother (4:1–16; cf. 9:5–6); the emphasis on the Sabbath in the Priestly creation account, which is then drawn into the Sabbath Commandment (Exod 20:11); and Ham's dishonoring of his father, Noah (Gen 9:18–27).

The Endangerment of the Commandments

It thus should not be a matter of surprise that the Commandments belong to a larger realm of moral space than is represented by Sinai. The tradition itself so indicates and, in fact, we find evidence of them in other polities. Furthermore, Christian ethics has always overlapped in various ways with more general ethical modes.[54] In the case of the Commandments, one indication of this is the way in which they have become a kind of cultural code for the common good. There is a sense that the culture needs these commands to order its life, whether or not they are firmly rooted in a religious tradition. Or it may be that the religious tradition is acknowledged but is not perceived as critical for the cultural appropriation. It is

---

52. R. Jenson, *Systematic Theology*, vol. 2, *The Works of God* (New York: Oxford University Press, 1999), 86. Cf. the concluding sentence of his essay in this volume, "The Triunity of Common Good": "As for the ground of such judgments [that is, of earthly polities], the church need look no further than the Ten Commandments; if there is natural law, they republish it; if not, they are all we have or need."

53. "'The Common Good' as Political Norm."

54. See, e.g., the comment of Gilbert Meilander: "Even if Christian moral knowledge is built upon no foundation other than the biblical narrative of God's dealings with his world, that story itself authorizes us to seek and expect some common moral ground with those whose vision is not shaped by Christian belief. Thus, although the Christian way of life is itself a particular one sustained within particular communities, it has within it more universal elements. And the understanding of life which faith seeks, if it is truly understanding, will to some extent admit of 'translation' into the language of public life—which life it both affirms and seeks to transform. Moreover, biblical faith calls for trust in the free God, whose grace alone can ultimately sustain the life of discipleship in the world. For all these reasons it seems best to describe Christian ethics as a two-tier ethic—in part general and able to be defended on grounds not peculiarly Christian: in part singular, making sense only within the shared life of the faithful community" (*Faith and Faithfulness* [Notre Dame: University of Notre Dame Press, 1991], 19–20). In this regard Meilander's more extended discussion of this issue in his chapter on "The Singularity of Christian Ethics" is helpful.

perceived that the common good is enhanced as all live by these directives, whether or not they associate themselves with the communities of faith out of which the Commandments and their keeping originate or in any way with the religious grounds that may be inherent in them.

Precisely at the point of the broader cultural use of the Commandments, however, one can perceive special dangers to their proper appropriation, dangers found precisely in their capacity for openness. Like any icon they can be genuine windows to the Holy One or superficial and idolatrous covers for the proper worship of the Lord. Indeed, they may be both at the same time. There are probably several ways in which the openness of the Commandments also endangers them, but I shall mention only three:

1. Perhaps the largest endangerment of the Commandments is the one already mentioned: the use of the Commandments against the Commandments. This specifically is the way in which cultural uses of the Commandments may become incipient violations of the second and third commandments. Perhaps that is nowhere more vividly exemplified than in the actual turning of the Commandments again into tablets of stone, bronze, and so on, as they are set up in front of governmental buildings, hung on the walls of courthouses, and the like. There may be good motives behind such moves, but the outcome is often a civil or cultural manipulation of the Commandments that ignores their context and gives only lip service— if even that—to the first table of the Decalogue. The divine authority is assumed as a ground for enforcing the second table, but the fear and love of God that is embodied in the first table is not really at stake. The Commandments have become an end in themselves.

As the icon becomes an object of devotion and the God who speaks through it disappears, not only have the tablets become an idol, but the name of God has also been co-opted for secular and political ends, valid as those ends may be. So the community that engages in such practices is in danger of violating the commandment that safeguards the use of the divine name. Paul Lehmann's translation of Luther accurately catches up what is at stake and what is violated in the casual appropriation of the Commandments: "You shall not go about with the name of God as though it makes no difference."[55]

2. Overlapping with the danger of idolatry and empty use of the divine name is the tendency to trivialize the Commandments. That happens immediately, of course, when the first table is ignored. It is dismissed as of little account other than to provide a stamp of approval on the prohibitions that really matter. The

---

55. *The Decalogue and a Human Future*, 101. I recently heard of a hotel that has in its elevators posters of the American flag with the Beatitudes inscribed across it and on the breakfast serving table a stone replica of the Commandments with a cross on them. Thus the sacred is treated casually, the Christian tradition is appropriated for political ends, and the Ten Words of God are placed on a par with sausage and eggs, though the food surely gets more serious attention.

trivialization is most apparent, however, in the way that the Commandments have become a kind of slogan, one that is tossed about in an unsubstantial way. The Commandments become either a joke, the subject of cartoons and actual jokes, or they become a catchall category for all sorts of things that have nothing to do with the Commandments. Thus we have web sites on "The Ten Commandments of Golf" and books on *Thou Shall [sic] Prosper: Ten Commandments for Making Money* (by a rabbi, no less!). The word of the Lord has become a cultural cliché.

3. Finally, one cannot ignore the reductionistic and simplistic handling of the Commandments that arises out of their familiarity. They are seen as simple and obvious rules whose sphere of significance is self-evident and quite narrow. The ubiquity of the Commandments leads many to dismiss them as a negative and simplistic approach to morality. They are as helpful and useful as the next self-help book. Indeed, the next self-help book will probably confirm that as it uses the rubric trivially: "The Ten Commandments of. . . ."

I have cautioned against the endangerment of the Commandments that is incipient in their openness and familiarity. One must go on to warn also against an understanding of the Commandments in context that implicitly seems to forbid their appropriation by those who do not share that context, the story and experience in which the Commandments come to us, or do not take that context seriously. Fighting against the endangerment and misuse of the Commandments needs to take place in a way that does not close off their serious appropriation by others who see in them—or even in some of them—a way to a larger good.

All of this suggests that in the Commandments, which Christians receive out of the story of God's redemptive purposes for Israel and the whole human race, there is at least some significant theoretical and actual common ground for thinking with others who do not share that story about what constitutes community, the moral, and the good of each and all. This potential and actual common ground may be muddy at times. The Commandments may become more cultural icon than actualized modes of living by trust in the living God and in responsibility for the good of the neighbor. Yet all this does not mean that one should give up the effort to identify in these modes directions that many in various communities find conducive for the common good. Christians and Jews bring these "Ten Words" to the table for conversation about how we find, enjoy, and live the good. We may find that our partners in the conversation will already understand.

The Eschatological Trajectory of the Commandments

Finally, it is important to recognize that to the extent the Commandments point us to God's intended good, they reflect another kind of openness. Insofar as the Commandments are descriptive as well as prescriptive, they give us some picture of the kingdom of God, and so they speak not only about the life we live but also about the life to come. Surely that is intended when Jesus draws the Commandments prominently into his Sermon on the Mount, the intention of which is to instruct his disciples in the kingdom of heaven or the kingdom of God. The mix of the ethical and the eschatological in the Sermon is true of the Commandments, which are a part of the Sermon. One Christian theologian has put it this way:

> We are promised the day when God's intentions for us will be done. The ultimate purpose of the Decalogue is to tell us how things then will be. When we teach them to ourselves and our children, this is the last and best thing we are to say: "God is making a world of love to God and one another. See how fine that world will be. We will be faithful to God. We will be passionate for one another. We will be truthful for one another. We will . . ."[56]

The rabbis made the same point in one of their own stories:

> At the same time when God was giving the Torah to Israel, he said to them, "My children, if you accept the Torah, and observe my command-ments, I will give you for all eternity a thing most precious that I have in my possession." "And what," asked Israel, "is that precious thing which thou wilt give us if we obey the Torah?" "The world to come— the world to come," said the Lord. "Show us in this world an example of the world to come," says Israel. "The Sabbath—the Sabbath is an exam-ple of the world to come."[57]

As Christians keep the Sabbath on Sunday, the day of Jesus' resurrection, and— synecdochically—in their keeping of all the Commandments, they anticipate the coming of the kingdom and receive a glimpse into the world to come.[58]

---

56. Robert W. Jenson, *A Large Catechism* (2d ed.; Delhi, NY: American Lutheran Publicity Bureau, 1999), 12.

57. Abraham J. Heschel, *The Sabbath* (New York: Farrar, Straus & Young, 1951), 74.

58. On the importance of synecdoche (the whole found in a part) for interpreta-tion of the Commandments, see John Calvin, *Institutes*, 2.8.8. Note his own com-ment on the Sabbath commandment: "It would seem, therefore, that the Lord through the seventh day has sketched for his people the coming perfection of his Sabbath in the Last Day, to make them aspire to this perfection by unceasing med-itation upon the Sabbath throughout life" (2.8.30).

"When Mercy Seasons Justice"
Jonah and the Common Good

Jacqueline Lapsley

The quality of mercy is not strain'd,
It droppeth as the gentle rain from heaven
Upon the place beneath: it is twice blest;
It blesseth him that gives and him that takes:
'Tis mightiest in the mightiest: it becomes
The throned monarch better than his crown;
His sceptre shows the force of temporal power,
The attribute to awe and majesty,
Wherein doth sit the dread and fear of kings;
But mercy is above this sceptred sway;
It is enthroned in the hearts of kings,
It is an attribute to God himself;
And earthly power doth then show likest God's
When mercy seasons justice.
(Shakespeare, *Merchant of Venice*, act 6, scene 1, lines 184–98)

Jonah's Failure and the Common Good

Compared to the clamor of sectarian voices, the language of the common good is whispered only faintly. A student says in class that we should attend to oppressive conditions in China because "there are many Christians there." Christian parents abandon public schools (or the very concept of school) because the atmosphere might "contaminate" their children. War in Iraq is justifiable because "'they' started it on 9/11." We are under no obligation to offer debt relief to foreign nations, though the weight of the debt severely hinders their economic life. Where in all of this is there any concern for the good of the whole world, or more modestly, the whole community? Does God care about people outside the Christian community? Does God care about those outside the United States? Anecdotal evidence suggests that God's care for those within these borders is clear and strong, but whether God cares much about the rest of the world is much fuzzier, and even doubtful. As is often the case, Scripture, in this case in the book of Jonah, serves to clarify matters and to remind us again of the depth of God's love for the whole world.

People get what they deserve—or at least they should if justice is to prevail. To this end, God lifts the trampled out of the dust and judges the ones doing the trampling with severity. While imperfectly observed, the underlying principle of justice in the Old Testament is equity. The Scriptures testify that God is both the ultimate judge and guardian of justice. This has two significant implications. First, God is especially concerned about those who are denied justice, fair treatment in the social, economic, and political realms.[1] This justice may include the poor, widows, orphans, and the oppressed. This is most obvious in the prophets (Isa 11:4; 32:7; Mic 6:6–8; Amos 4:1; 5:11; etc.), although such concerns are widely evident throughout Scripture.[2] The second implication follows logically from the first. Those who impede others from attaining justice, who treat others unfairly (the wicked), will also "get what they deserve." "I will punish the world for its evil, and the wicked for their iniquity; I will put an end to the pride of the arrogant, and lay low the insolence of tyrants" (Isa 13:11).[3] While God judges the nations according to the principle of retributive justice sketched here, the prophets were acutely, painfully, aware that God offers no exemption to Israel, despite its election.[4] On the contrary, Israel is held to even more exacting standards for being the chosen people of God, and so repeatedly comes under God's judgment (Amos 3:2).

With this background in mind, the prophet Jonah comes across as perfectly suited to the job he is assigned: he is steeped in the long and rich Israelite

---

1. The economic and legal systems reflected in these texts possess, from our point of view, unjust features (debt slavery, the status of women, etc.). But within the ancient Israelite context these systems were designed to protect the vulnerable. It is against abuses of these systems that the prophets, especially, rail.

2. For further discussion see Moshe Weinfeld, *Social Justice in Ancient Israel and in the Ancient Near East* (Minneapolis: Fortress, 1995); and J. David Pleins, *The Social Visions of the Hebrew Bible: A Theological Introduction* (Louisville: Westminster John Knox, 2001).

3. Scripture is from NRSV unless marked as the author's literal (lit.) translation.

4. The phrase "retributive justice" is often applied to divine justice in the Old Testament, but it is in fact a bit confusing. "Retributive justice" applies more accurately to this second implication of God's justice, since the wicked have done something to deserve God's judgment/punishment (so they "get what they deserve"). The oppressed have not done anything "good" to merit God's judgment/uplifting. Simply because they are human beings, they deserve better than they have received at the hands of their fellow creatures.

prophetic tradition concerning God's justice, and he also understands the
Ninevites' particular sins (their history of violence). Jonah has a profound grasp of
theology and of the context for doing theology—what more could be wished for
any seminarian entering the ministry? Yet somehow it is not enough, and he
botches the job. Certainly he finally does what he is told, delivering his message
to the Ninevites. In that sense, he fulfills his prophetic task. Yet Jonah does fail,
and his failure is twofold.

First, Jonah suffers a failure of imagination. In the end, he is unable to step out
of his own identity and context to inhabit sympathetically, if only momentarily,
the identity and context of those radically different from him—the Ninevites.
Second, he fails to take full account of something in the character of God: compassion for those who deserve punishment, and care for those who seem beyond
caring for. Jonah knows that God is merciful, compassionate, but he rejects these
characteristics as at odds with God's role as guardian of justice. For Jonah, these
cannot be reconciled. This colossal refusal of imagination and of acknowledging
the fullness of God's character is worth exploring. In Jonah's failure lie clues to
reimagining the boundaries of "common" in the common good. For it is in the
interplay within God (and so, *in imitatione Dei*, within us) of these two seemingly
opposing qualities, justice and mercy, that we find our own imaginations stretched
to include even the most detested outsiders within the purview of God's care, and
thus within the common good.

The Enraging Mercy of God and Jonah's Utter Dependence on It

Jonah is called to go to Nineveh as God's representative.[5] Yet the narrator does
not disclose the exact nature of Jonah's commission, nor what aspect of it is so
repugnant or frightening that Jonah flees.[6] We must follow the story all the way
to the last chapter before Jonah discloses what he was thinking at the time of his

---

5. For a fascinating, idiosyncratic romp through the history of interpretation of
Jonah, see Yvonne Sherwood, *A Biblical Text and Its Afterlives: The Survival of
Jonah in Western Culture* (Cambridge: Cambridge University Press, 2000). The
interpretation of Jonah offered in this essay runs counter to the current trend (much
applauded by Sherwood) of deconstructing God in the book and of painting Jonah
as much maligned both by God and by the history of interpretation.

6. According to the Talmud, Jonah is not informed whether Nineveh will be
turned for good or for evil (*b. Sanh.* 89b). Rashi, among others, has suggested that
Jonah's prophecy could be read either positively (Nineveh will be transformed for the
good) or negatively (Nineveh will be destroyed), depending on how one reads the
verb. More recently, see Jack M. Sasson, *Jonah: A New Translation with Introduction,
Commentary, and Interpretation* (AB; New York: Doubleday, 1990), 295; and Alan
Cooper, "In Praise of Divine Caprice: The Significance of the Book of Jonah," in
Among the Prophets: Language, Image and Structure in the Prophetic Writings (ed.
Philip R. Davies and David J. A. Clines; JSOTSup 144; Sheffield: Sheffield Academic
Press, 1993), 145, n. 4. For another overview of the history of interpretation of
Jonah, see Thomas M. Bolin, *Freedom beyond Forgiveness: The Book of Jonah Re-
Examined* (JSOTSup 236; Sheffield: Sheffield Academic Press, 1997), 13–67.

initial flight: "O YHWH! [ET: LORD!] Isn't this just what I said when I was still in my own country? That is why I fled beforehand to Tarshish. For I know that you are a compassionate and gracious God, slow to anger, abounding in kindness, renouncing punishment" (4:2, lit.).[7] This is a shortened form of God's self-description from Exod 34:6–7: "YHWH! A God compassionate and gracious, slow to anger, abounding in kindness and faithfulness, extending kindness to the thousandth generation, forgiving iniquity, transgression, and sin" (lit.). Significantly, in Exodus this insight into God's character appears immediately following the episode of the golden calf, in which the Israelites experienced a depth of sin that becomes both unrepeatable and yet somehow prototypical for the rest of their history. The profundity of this salvific word is immeasurably enhanced by coming in the context of the absolute nadir of Israel's corporate life. It is at the moment when God is on the verge of rejecting Israel that the fundamental divine compassion and mercy are revealed.[8] Thus it does not surprise Jonah, nor should it surprise us, that this part of God's identity should come to the fore when dealing with the Ninevites, whose violence suggests that they, too, are at the nadir of their corporate life. The mercy of God is revealed when both Israel and Nineveh are at their most undeserving.

For Jonah, this declaration of the divine nature is not cause for rejoicing, but for complaint, a complaint that the prophet secretly nurtures throughout the story until, in a fit of pique, he finally blurts it out at the end. Only now are we privy to this aspect of Jonah's inner life, which in a sense is the fulcrum upon which the whole story turns. He is very angry that God has spared the Ninevites, not doling out to them the punishment they deserve.[9] Since the Ninevites are known for their violence and ruthlessness above all else, it appears that Jonah's refusal to prophesy to them derives from his firm belief that God should punish them. It also comes from his equally firm belief that in the end God will not. Jonah would rather die than live in a world that is not characterized by a consistently fair system of justice (4:3). After all, God exiled Israel for its sins; how much more deserving is Nineveh of punishment? Jonah's desire for a consistent ethic whereby everyone receives what she or he deserves is undermined by YHWH's concern not for an absolute principle of justice, but for the larger goal of the good of people outside the covenant community.[10]

---

7. Some question the veracity of Jonah's claim that this was his earlier opinion. See Sasson, *Jonah*, 296.

8. Variations on this description appear elsewhere, suggesting the significance of this understanding of God within Israel more generally (e.g., Num 14:18; Neh 9:17; Ps 86:15). See Brevard Childs, *The Book of Exodus: A Critical, Theological Commentary* (OTL; Philadelphia: Westminster, 1974), 612.

9. Here is a play on *rāʿāh* ("evil, wickedness, disaster"). When the Ninevites turn from their evil [*rāʿah*] way, God does not bring *rāʿāh* on the Ninevites (i.e., punish them). In turn, this refusal of God to punish them was a great evil to Jonah [*wayēraʿ ʾel-yōnāh rāʿāh gedōlāh*, 3:10–4:1].

10. Alan Cooper argues vigorously against this widely shared understanding, but he ignores important features of the text, and his overall view is not convincing ("In Praise of Divine Caprice," 144–63).

What is especially curious, indeed ironic, about Jonah's view is that he himself relies on the merciful nature of God. Jonah's knowledge of God's merciful nature is what makes him flee in disgust. Yet it also sustains him throughout his trials, while enduring the storm, his time in the belly of the fish, and finally outside Nineveh. He trusts that God will not allow him to perish, but instead will forgive him and deliver him. Jonah relies on God to forgive him this act of rebellion. This faith in God's mercy explains Jonah's strikingly nonchalant attitude in the midst of a succession of crises.[11] He is unconcerned enough to sleep in the belly of the fish while the storm rages, threatening to splinter the ship into pieces (1:4–5).[12] The sailors wonder at his serenity (1:6): "What are you doing sleeping?!? Get up, call upon your god!" (lit.). Jonah's casual attitude about the threat the storm poses to his life is connected to his reason for fleeing YHWH in the first place: he knows that God will be merciful to him. As readers we are acutely aware of the sailors' terror in face of the storm.[13] The transparency of their emotional state is only matched by the opacity of Jonah's. In fact, the intensity of the sailors' terror highlights Jonah's lack of fear; in contrast, he appears quite relaxed. Thus the desperation of the sailors' question emphasizes the tranquility of Jonah's blithe response: "Pick me up and fling me into the sea" (1:12, lit.). Jonah's insouciance suggests his confidence that even if he is hurled into the sea, God will deliver him because, as he later asserts, he knows that God is compassionate.

Jonah's faith in God's deliverance is not misplaced; immediately YHWH appoints a fish to rescue Jonah from the sea (2:1). As he did in the ship, Jonah in the belly of the fish relies on his conviction that God will deliver him. Even though there has been a lot of prayer and worship in the book thus far, Jonah has not been a party to it. The sailors were praying first to their own gods, and then worshipping and sacrificing and making vows to YHWH. But only now, in the belly of the fish, does Jonah pray to YHWH. The prayer in chapter 2 has long posed difficulties for interpreters because the situation of the prayer's speaker seems at odds with Jonah's situation. The prayer offers thanks to God for a *prior* act of deliverance from distress—this is no prayer for help in the present predicament! Jonah shrewdly affirms his faith in God's mercy by casting the prayer in the

---

11. This is often interpreted as an expression of the intensity of Jonah's disgust. According to this view, Jonah would rather die than be made into a false prophet. See Serge Frolov, "Returning the Ticket: God and His Prophet in the Book of Jonah," *JSOT* 86 (1999): 85–105. Frolov's overall interpretation of Jonah is quite opposed to the one I suggest here.

12. Psychologically, some have seen a drive toward death: sleep is often connected to death (giving the appearance of death). Jonah's willingness to be thrown overboard to save the sailors, when considered with the times he expresses an explicit desire to die (4:3, 8–9), could be viewed as considerable evidence that he does not care much whether he lives or dies. See Uriel Simon, *Jonah: The Traditional Hebrew Text with the New JPS Translation* (Philadelphia: Jewish Publication Society, 1999), 34; and Bolin, *Freedom beyond Forgiveness*, 172–75.

13. The text repeatedly describes the sailors as frightened, crying out about the misfortune that has come upon them [rā'āh], and finally crying out to YHWH and "fearing" YHWH. See esp. 1:5, 7, 8, 10, 14, 16.

past tense instead of as a petition. This unusual prophet offers no confession of sin and no repentance.[14] The prayer becomes intelligible, however, if we keep in mind that Jonah all along has been confident that God would deliver him from this series of disasters. The tone of Jonah's prayer is in keeping with his previous confidence in God's propensity to deliver and not to destroy. "In my trouble I called to YHWH, and he answered me. From the belly of Sheol I cried out, and you heard my voice" (2:3, lit.; ET, 2:3). This thanksgiving is rendered proleptically for a deliverance that is yet to be, but one that Jonah is confident will come.

Jonah's self-assurance is in keeping with his conviction that it is in the nature of God to rescue him from his present predicament. Jonah's view of the Ninevites' situation (they appear doomed, but Jonah knows God will deliver them) parallels Jonah's situation in the belly of the fish (he appears doomed, but Jonah knows God will deliver him). In one sense Jonah represents Israel in this story. Yet in his conviction that God will deliver him after he offers only a half-hearted prayer composed from the cribbed words of others, Jonah is unique among Israelite prophets.[15]

But before Jonah even thinks to offer this strange prayer, three days and nights go by in the belly of the whale, and *nothing happens*. Jonah would naturally assume, based on past experience, that he does not need to *do* anything for YHWH to deliver him.[16] By the start of the fourth day in the fish, however, Jonah decides to take some action and offers up a prayer, albeit a grudging one. The *Midrash Jonah* offers a similar interpretation:

> Jonah had been three days in the belly of the fish and had not prayed. Then the Holy One, blessed be He, spoke: "I have made a roomy place

---

14. Interpreters have offered a number of solutions for this apparent incoherence. For a sampling, see Hans Walter Wolff, *Obadiah and Jonah: A Commentary* (trans. Margaret Kohl; Minneapolis: Augsburg, 1986), 125–42. Several interpreters argue for the parodic or satirical nature of the poem. See John A. Miles, "Laughing at the Bible: Jonah as Parody," in *On Humour and the Comic in the Hebrew Bible* (ed. Y. T. Radday and A. Brenner; Bible and Literature 23; Sheffield: Almond), 203–15; R. P. Carroll, "Is Humour Also among the Prophets?" in ibid., 169–89; Athalya Brenner, "Jonah's Poem out of and within Its Context," in *Among the Prophets* (ed. Davies and Clines), 189–92; J. William Whedbee, *The Bible and the Comic Vision* (Cambridge: Cambridge University Press, 1998), 191–220.

15. Jonah's prayer is a kind of pastiche of psalmic material (Sasson, *Jonah*, 168–201). Most scholars see the prayer as an insertion, either by the author of the story (who got it from another source) or by a later editor. A few argue for the "integrity" of the poem (see, e.g., Brenner, "Jonah's Poem," 183–92). These genetic issues are not especially germane to the line I am pursuing here: how the prayer functions within the story. For further bibliography, consult Phyllis Trible, *Rhetorical Criticism: Context, Method, and the Book of Jonah* (Minneapolis: Fortress, 1994), 161, n. 10.

16. In this Jonah is not a typical Israelite. The lament psalms testify to the Israelite confidence that God will deliver, but it is quite unusual to think that communicating this need with God is unnecessary!

for him in the belly of the fish, so that he does not become anxious, and he is not praying to me. Now I will appoint a pregnant fish that has 365,000 small fish in it, so that he will become afraid and pray to me, because I desire the prayers of the righteous."

This midrash describes how Jonah, once inside the pregnant fish, becomes terrified of all the dirt and refuse from the small fish, and he immediately lifts his heart in prayer.[17] The type of prayer offered, of thanksgiving for past deliverance, offers a window onto Jonah's view of God's character, and of the Ninevites' situation in light of that character.[18] The Ninevites appear doomed, but Jonah knows God will deliver them, just as Jonah himself appears doomed in the fish, but knows God will deliver him.

The Sovereignty of God and the Good of All Creation

Throughout the book of Jonah, the sovereignty of God over creation is repeatedly emphasized. In the first two chapters God sends the storm to forestall the ship on which Jonah travels, and commands the fish to swallow Jonah and then to vomit him up. In the last chapter God provides, in rapid succession, a plant to shade Jonah, a worm to eat the plant, and a heat so oppressive to Jonah that he twice begs for death (first of God, then of his own soul). This portrait of God's power over creation—both natural forces like the sea and wind, and the smallest (worms) and largest (giant fish) of living creatures—casts into high relief Jonah's pathetic attempt to escape the deity. A man running away by hitching a ride on a ship appears quite ludicrous when faced with the awesome power of this God. Even Jonah knows how absurd this plan is. Queried about his identity when the storm is raging against the ship, he tells the sailors, "I am a Hebrew. . . . I worship YHWH, the God of Heaven, *who made both sea and land*" (1:9, lit.). Implied is Jonah's awareness that YHWH is thoroughly in charge of the storm threatening them all to doom; he knows that his own resistance to the divine call is doomed to failure.

Creation theology is such a prominent theme in the book that it is worth attending to the places in the text where the established orders of creation are askew. The central event of the first two chapters, for example, portrays a bizarre inversion of the natural order set out in Gen 1.[19] According to that vision of creation, human beings are to "exercise dominion over the fish of the sea" (Gen 1:28, lit.), yet it is the fish who exercises dominion over Jonah. True, the text is clear that

---

17. Cited in James Limburg, *Jonah: A Commentary* (OTL; Louisville: Westminster John Knox, 1993), 110.

18. Brenner reads the satire of the poem as directed at Jonah ("It is plain that the man is satirized"), but I understand the irony of the poem as emanating from Jonah ("Jonah's Poem," 190; cf. Trible, *Rhetorical Criticism*, 171–72). For another discussion of the satirical function of the prayer, see John Miles, "Laughing at the Bible: Jonah as Parody," 209.

19. My thanks to Jim Skillen for suggesting this contrast.

God is behind the actions of the fish (2:1). But why does God permit such a radical reversal of the created order as to allow a human being to be completely dominated by a fish?

This inversion mirrors another inversion, this time in Jonah's view of divine justice and mercy. Jonah flees the divine call to prophesy because he strongly suspects that God's mercy will overrule what he perceives to be justice. From Jonah's perspective, a strict retributive justice should be the operating principle when it comes to Nineveh, the prominent city of a most detested and feared people, the Assyrians. The king's description of a people guilty of "evil" and with "violence on their palms," accurately sums up the reputation of the Assyrians throughout the ancient Near East (3:8, lit.).[20] These people are so despicable that they deserve to experience the full brunt of the wrath of God.

Jonah's vision of how the Deity should deal with Nineveh is an inversion of God's, just as his presence in the belly of the fish is an inversion of the divinely created order. The narrow view of retributive justice that Jonah espouses is like a man inside a fish: it is inappropriate to the sovereignty of God over creation. The inappropriateness of both his presence in the fish and his view of divine workings is portrayed vividly when the fish vomits Jonah onto dry land (2:11; ET, 2:10). Vomiting is an organism's response to disorder within, and Jonah's skewed view of the ways of divine justice mirrors the disorder in the fish's belly.

Thus far I have pointed to the ways in which the imagery of the book asserts the power of God over creation. But beyond raw divine power, there is another point to the creation imagery in Jonah: YHWH does not simply wield total power over creation; he also desires the good of all creation. This is apparent in a number of ways. The portrayal of the sailors and the Ninevites as quintessential outsiders to Yahwism, for example, is overall quite positive. Certainly the fervor of their piety stands in marked contrast to Jonah's casual attitude in his dealings with YHWH. The favorable portrait of these outsiders, accompanied as it is by God's deliberate deliverance of both groups from destruction, attests to an ethic of divine care for those outside Israel.[21]

God is concerned that the whole city of Nineveh be transformed so that everyone, including the very young and other nonrational creatures, can flourish (the large and the small don sackcloth in 3:5). God takes pains to demonstrate to

---

20. "The cruelty of the Assyrian conquerors was proverbial. Large numbers were impaled or decapitated, the dissevered heads being thrown together in large heaps. Principals were often drawn and quartered. Shalmaneser III boasted of having burned boys and girls alive in the city of Aridi (Monolith Inscription, line 17)" (J. W. Wevers, "War, Methods of," *IDB* 4:804.

21. If one considers the outsiders specifically with respect to the common good, one is immediately struck by the devotion of the sailors as well as the Ninevites to the common good. The sailors work for the common good of the ship while Jonah, asleep in the ship's bowels, deliberately avoids his task of seeking Nineveh's good, which is tied to the good of all. The sailors reluctantly, but necessarily, cast out the disruptive influence, the one whose actions deny that the good is one held in common. The Ninevites also devote themselves to the common good of the city, praying and fasting as one (though obviously there is an element of self-interest here).

Jonah the difference between Jonah's attitude toward the plant that shields him from the sun, and God's attitude toward Nineveh: "You cared about the plant, which you did not work for and which you did not grow. May I not care about Nineveh, that great city?" (4:10, lit.).[22] The clear implication here is that God did work for Nineveh and did cause it to grow,[23] meaning that God's concern for Nineveh will have an intensity far beyond that which Jonah feels for the plant (and he is ready to die over the loss of the plant [4:9]).[24]

God's concern extends beyond human beings, however. The image of the beasts in sackcloth, crying out to God, has long provoked laughter among readers, as has the last line of the book. There God notes that in addition to the more than hundred thousand people in Nineveh who, on account of their ignorance and vulnerability, require care, also "many beasts" require attention (4:11). Beyond the humor is a more serious point, however. Throughout the book YHWH has consistently exhibited care toward all those outside of Israel, including not only the sailors and Ninevites, but also all the animals. The animals' "repentance," and the related reference to them in the last line of the book, foregrounds their solidarity with human beings and their significance in the divine economy of creation.[25] It would be a bizarre misconstrual to read in this an ethic of animal "rights." Yet it is not off the mark to perceive an ethic that attends to the flourishing of all animals (what it means to "flourish" being somewhat differently defined for each species) within the hierarchy of creation derived from the Old Testament creation traditions. At the top of the hierarchy, God cares for the "many beasts," and so should we.[26]

Particularity, Compassion, and Mercy

Pace Jonah, God does not abandon justice in favor of mercy. Rather, God incorporates mercy into the divine conception of justice by taking into account the mitigating circumstances surrounding the Ninevites' situation. Two reasons are given for God's renouncing the punishment against the Ninevites. First, they repent of

---

22. Cooper's argument that this is declarative ("I do not care about Nineveh") and that YHWH certainly did not create Nineveh is a stretch ("In Praise of Divine Caprice," 157–58). Bolin argues similarly in *Freedom beyond Forgiveness*, 159–64. Terence E. Fretheim, on the other hand, persuasively translates "May I not . . ." because it focuses on God's sovereign right to spare Nineveh, but does not assume that God must do so ("Jonah and Theodicy," *ZAW* 90 [1978]: 237).

23. This may indicate that Jonah's dispute with God goes beyond issues of justice to theodicy. See Fretheim, "Jonah and Theodicy," 227–37.

24. Although ambiguous in its meaning, the city is described as "a great city of/to God" in 3:3 (lit.). On the issue of responsibility in community and its relative depth or shallowness, see Eric Mount, "It Takes a Community," in this volume.

25. See Limburg, *Jonah*, 97; and also Patrick Miller's observation ("'That It May Go Well with You,'" in this volume) that the Commandments include animals in their openness toward the natural world.

26. See Michael Welker, *Creation and Reality* (trans. John F. Hoffmeyer; Minneapolis: Fortress, 1999), 70–73. The practices of agribusiness fall grimly and abysmally short of this.

their evil ways (3:10).²⁷ The Ninevites have made the renunciation of punishment possible through their repentance. The significance of this should not be underestimated because it speaks to the difference between divine mercy and divine indulgence. But what is the intrinsic motivation within the divine will that would make such a renunciation desirable? Here the clue lies in the last verse of the book: "And may I not care about Nineveh, that great city, in which there are more than a hundred and twenty thousand persons *who do not know their right hand from their left*, and many beasts as well?" (lit.).²⁸ The reason to care about the inhabitants of Nineveh is that they are morally confused, and that confusion makes them exceptionally vulnerable to vice ("evil" and "violence," 3:8). The beasts are not implicated in the moral confusion, but they are mentioned because they suffer the effects of the viciousness of their human fellow inhabitants. Human moral ignorance and confusion are mitigating factors in the way God treats creation. The care that God expresses here (*ḥûs* means "having tears in one's eyes"²⁹) is the divine compassion for even the most notorious perpetrators of violence, along with those who suffer on account of them.³⁰

Why is God merciful and Jonah not? In other words, what does God see in the Ninevites that Jonah does not see? God sees Nineveh within the web of circumstances that has brought them to this point; God knows the story of Nineveh, their particular narrative that has shaped them. Jonah does not know Nineveh in its particularity; he only knows that *in a case such as theirs*, where a party is guilty of so much violence, they should be the object of retributive justice. Observing that mercy is intimately connected to particularity, Martha Nussbaum argues that attention to particularity should be understood as a key component not simply of merciful action, but of justice itself. "But no such rules [within the rule of law] can be precise or sensitive enough, and when they have manifestly erred, it is justice itself, not a departure from justice, to use equity's flexible standard."³¹ In order to perceive the particular, one must "judge with" the agents of a crime, viewing

---

27. Cooper does not see a causal connection in this verse ("In Praise of Divine Caprice," 156–57).

28. The JPS translation adds, "who do not yet know. . . ."

29. See Limburg, *Jonah*, 97. Fretheim rightly observes that this compassion should not be understood as a fixed attribute of God, but appears in concrete situations ("Jonah and Theodicy," 232). Bolin rejects "to pity" in favor of "to have concern for, be sorry to lose," insofar as it expresses "concern for the loss of goods or property, even things of little value" (*Freedom beyond Forgiveness*, 160). This relies heavily on the rabbinic meaning of the term. In any case, an emotional response is involved in all of these translations.

30. The beasts of Nineveh (and children) would suffer the punishment inflicted upon Nineveh along with the morally culpable human beings.

31. Martha Nussbaum, "Equity and Mercy," *Philosophy and Public Affairs* 22 (Spring 1993): 96. Nussbaum traces the "close connection between equitable judgment—judgment that attends to the particulars—and mercy, defined by Seneca as "the inclination of the mind toward leniency in exacting punishment" (85). See also Aristotle, *Nichomachean Ethics* 5.10; and the discussion by Victor Furnish, "Uncommon Love and the Common Good," in this volume.

events from their perspective.[32] In considering the ignorance and moral confusion
of the Ninevites, God sees the particularity of their story, what brought them to
do the evil that stains their "palms" with violence. The pattern for the common
good is to be found in the character of God, who is the source and norm for the
common good in this story.

Equally relevant is Nussbaum's criticism of the tendency in judicial circles to
exclude emotional responses in making rational judgments. Typical of this thinking, for example, is the Massachusetts Trial Juror's Handbook, which offers this
"creed": "I am a JUROR. I am a seeker of truth. . . . I must lay aside all bias and
prejudice. I must be led by my intelligence and not by my emotions."[33] According
to Nussbaum, the perceived contrast between morality and sympathy is a "nest of
confusion." This is true insofar as "sentiment, passion, and sympathy would be a
prominent part of the appropriate (and rational) deliberative process, where those
sentiments are based in the juror's 'reading' of the defendant's history, as presented
in the evidence."[34] Milner Ball argues eloquently along similar lines: "In American
courts, on a rudimentary level, the expression of emotions like those contained in
tears that touch the heart simply cannot be excluded and should not be."[35] It is
therefore misleading to see mercy as somehow at odds with the requirements of
justice, which is the way Jonah views the situation. God's response of compassion
(eyes flowing with tears) is not an act outside of justice, but an act that constitutes
justice, in this case because God knows the Ninevites' situation.[36] The emotional
quality of the divine response to Nineveh is not merely a mitigating factor that
prevents true justice from being executed. Rather, the emotion is a crucial component of the act of judging since the emotional reaction is based on the "facts" of
Nineveh's case. It emerges out of a holistic understanding of both their evil deeds
and their moral confusion that led them to such acts. This has implications for our
understanding of God's dealings with humanity. Abraham Heschel saw God's
compassion for the Ninevites as upsetting "the possibility of looking for a rational
coherence of God's ways with the world."[37] Divine inscrutability may still be a

---

32. Nussbaum, "Equity and Mercy," 94.

33. Ibid., 120, n. 86.

34. Ibid., 120. The point is not to lump these reactions in with the ones that do
require exclusion (conjecture, prejudice, public opinion, and public feeling). Martha
Nussbaum distinguishes between compassion and mercy (both of which require an
exercise of imagination): "The only difference . . . [is] that mercy still judges that the
offender meets some very basic conditions of responsibility and blame" (*Upheavals
of Thought: The Intelligence of Emotions* [Cambridge: Cambridge University Press,
2001], 398). This is clearly the case with the Ninevites.

35. Milner S. Ball, *Called by Stories: Biblical Sagas and Their Challenge for Law*
(Durham: Duke University Press, 2000), 83. Ball offers an extended reflection on
the relationship between law and compassion, together with a discussion of some
theological implications.

36. Fretheim ("Jonah and Theodicy," 236) notes that the verb *ḥûs* often appears
in contexts where the administration of justice is taking place (often with the negative: "Do not have pity . . ."). See Deut 13:9 [ET, 13:8]; 19:13, 21; 25:12.

37. Abraham Heschel, *The Prophets* (New York: Harper & Row, 1962), 287.

daunting theological issue, but not because compassion is antithetical to rationality. "Rational coherence" and compassion are not necessarily mutually exclusive: appropriate emotional response is a constituent of appropriate moral judgment.

The story indexes the qualitative distinction between Jonah's response to the Ninevites and God's by spatially distancing Jonah from the city. Jonah refuses to say more than five (Hebrew) words before leaving the city. He shows his utter detachment in gazing upon its fate from afar. Such actions mark his lack of interest in and understanding of Nineveh as anything other than an archetype of evil (even when he was present in the city, he only made it a third of the way across before getting out of town [3:3–4]). His physical distance from the city is thus closely related to his inability to feel any concern for the inhabitants of Nineveh. YHWH provides a plant to show Jonah the kind of relationship that is envisioned between the prophet and the outsiders: "You cared about the plant, for which you did not work and which you did not grow, which appeared overnight and perished overnight" (4:10, lit.). As observed above, the kind of care Jonah feels for the plant is the type of care YHWH expresses for Nineveh. Yet the analogy is discordant in many ways. Jonah did not grow or nurture the plant; he only cares for it because it provides him with personal comfort.[38] The disjunctions in the analogy reveal God's care for Nineveh as being marked by a wholly different quality than Jonah's self-serving ethic. Because God "worked for" and "grew" Nineveh, God knows the "story" of Nineveh. Where Jonah's care for the plant is self-serving, God's care for Nineveh is based on knowledge of its inhabitants in their particularity and is therefore directed entirely toward the flourishing of the city.

Benevolence and Complacence in Jonathan Edwards and Jonah

The following may appear to be a contradiction of the discussion above, with its assertion of the significance of particularity for the moral life and the common good. I hope, however, that the contrast will emerge not as contradiction but as paradox: if Jonah is not focused enough on the particularity of the Ninevites, he is overly focused on the particularity of Israel. In an essay entitled "The Nature of True Virtue" (1755), Jonathan Edwards offers a useful discussion of the relation between particularity and the common good that illumines Jonah's situation.[39] For Edwards, "true virtue consists in a disposition to benevolence towards Being in general. . . . Love of *benevolence* is that affection or propensity of the heart to any Being, which causes it to incline to its well-being." Benevolence is contrasted to complacence, which presupposes the beauty of the object; benevolence encompasses every Being, ugly or not.[40] The "ugliness" of the Ninevites is certainly an

---

38. Fretheim argues that one can only feel this care if one has sovereignty over the object in question. On this view, Jonah has no right to feel pity for the plant, nor can he be expected to feel pity for Nineveh ("Jonah and Theodicy," 236).

39. Robert Jenson and Robin Lovin, in separate communications, suggested the relevance of Edwards here.

40. Jonathan Edwards, *The Works of President Edwards* (4 vols.; New York: Leavitt & Allen, 1852), 2:262–63.

issue for Jonah. As enemies and prone to violence, they are deeply repugnant, and Jonah cannot get beyond it. But Edwards goes on to make an even more crucial distinction between love of benevolence and what he terms "private system," in which love is directed toward a particular person without being grounded in the benevolence to "Being in general."[41] One might suppose that indifference to Being in general would be the result—an individual loves only within a private system, and feels indifferently toward the rest of Being. But Edwards pushes this further: commitment to private affection issues in "enmity to Being in general," the logical end of which is "a stated opposition to the Supreme Being."[42] The book of Jonah supports this logic: it is Jonah's love of Israel, and his own self-love, that fuels his anger against God. To hold dear the good of only particular persons or groups, ungrounded in the good of all, ultimately makes God your enemy. Inversely, love for God and love for "Being in general" amount to the same thing.[43]

Imitatio Dei

The book of Jonah offers a critique of Israel's understanding of justice, and it is clear enough that the appraisal is generated from within the tradition—this is self-critique.[44] While part of that self-critique targets overly narrow constructions of God's justice, another crucial aim of the story is to change the way the listeners and readers of the story understand *human* justice. From the beginning the story is told in such a way as to lead the listener to adopt the role of Jonah.[45] God's final speech and question to Jonah in 4:10–11 hang in the air ("May I not care for Nineveh?"), forever unanswered by Jonah and yet forever provoking answers from readers. The question is widely understood as addressed to us, the readers, as much as to Jonah, and as driving home the need for the reader to expand his or her understanding of the extent of God's care (beyond Israel, even to its enemies).[46]

41. Ibid., 2:268. James Sellers argues that Edwards "forges an alliance between the spiritual and the secular . . . to set them over against an unacceptable kind of morality, that of what he calls 'private systems'" ("Ways of Going Public in American Theology," *Word and World* 4, no. 3 (1984): 245.

42. Edwards, *Works*, 2:269.

43. "A benevolent propensity of heart to Being in general, and a temper or disposition to love God supremely, are in effect the same thing" (ibid., 2:270).

44. Michael Walzer sees Jonah's critique of Nineveh as an appeal to a thin "minimal code, a kind of international law" that proscribes acts of violence and brutality, and not to the thicker social values internal to a society. This is an outsider's critique. See Walzer, *Interpretation and Social Criticism* (Cambridge: Harvard University Press, 1987), 89. But the way the book functions as criticism is different. It is not directed to Nineveh; instead, it constitutes a thick internal critique of Israel's understanding of justice and mercy and God's dealings with the world.

45. Limburg notes the way that the eleven questions in the book are addressed to Jonah and the reader (*Jonah*, 25–26; see also Hans W. Wolff, *Studien zum Jonahbuch* [Biblische Studien 47; Neukirchen-Vluyn: Neukirchener Verlag, 1965], 52–53, 72).

46. Limburg, *Jonah*, 98.

Yet few have argued that the book asks readers to care for the Ninevehs of this world as God cares for Nineveh in the story. This, it is presumed, is for God to do; we are simply encouraged by the book not to resent it when divine compassion is directed toward objects we find objectionable. Sasson is a partial exception to this trend. He draws a parallel between the characteristics of Jonah's plant (divine rather than human involvement in its growth; the brevity of its existence) and those assigned to human beings in Pss 144:3–4 and 90:5–6. On this basis he argues:

> What is said about the fate of the *qîqāyôn* plant, therefore, is also about the fate of human beings; Jonah's indifference to its existence is also about the neglect with which human beings can treat each other; its death due to a "worm" is also about the destiny that awaits us all. It is in failing to grasp this analogy, then, that Jonah also deserves God's censure.[47]

On this reading what is subject to criticism is not simply Jonah's failure to allow God to care for human beings gone astray, but Jonah's failure to think of the Ninevites as human beings at all. Through the analogy of the plant, God admonishes Jonah (and therefore us as readers): "You feel the death of the plant keenly because you had a use for it, but you would rejoice over the death of a vast number of human beings, who resemble the plant in fundamental respects!" Jonah's moral barometer can only measure what is directly useful to him, not what might be in the interests of the common good.

In the last scene of the book the dialogue between Jonah and God employs markedly emotional language.[48] Twice God asks Jonah about the appropriateness of his anger, and twice God speaks of caring. Jonah is angry that God will not destroy the Ninevites (4:4) because it thwarts his desire for retributive justice, or more strongly, for revenge. Jonah is angry about the death of the plant because it symbolizes the withdrawal of God's mercy toward him and thus contrasts painfully with God's recent mercy toward the Ninevites.[49] God notes that Jonah is capable of an emotional response other than anger, however, since he "cared for" the plant in some sense (4:10). God discloses the shallowness of Jonah's care for the plant (he cares for it because it serves his need), and simultaneously God indicates that Jonah is on the right track. The "flowing of the eyes" is what is needed, but of a deeper nature than characterizes Jonah's care for the plant, and with a more appropriate object.

Two implications emerge: appropriate and inappropriate emotional responses, and the way these participate in making evaluative ethical judgments, are much to the fore in this scene. The book is not simply about the need for Jonah to allow

47. Sasson, *Jonah*, 318.
48. On the representation of the "inner life" in Jonah, see Kenneth M. Craig, *A Poetics of Jonah: Art in the Service of Ideology* (Columbia: The University of South Carolina Press, 1993), 124–43.
49. Sasson plausibly suggests that the plant symbolizes God's care for Jonah, and it is the loss of this sense of being cared for that makes Jonah angry enough to die (*Jonah*, 317).

God emotional freedom; it is deeply concerned with Jonah's emotional response to the world around him (the plant and the Ninevites).[50] In the divine dialogue with Jonah, then, God is teaching Jonah, and us as readers, how appropriate emotional response, and attention to particularity, can participate in our moral evaluations.[51] What is finally "overturned," then, is our own understanding of justice.[52]

A caution is in order here: I do not think that the book of Jonah advocates a thin, weak view of justice in which persons are not held accountable for their actions, and in which attention to particularity slides into moral relativism. Mercy is not the same as indulgence. The story implicitly invokes the Torah as the moral standard toward which all must strive (broadly here: violence as a way of life is unacceptable). This standard is not compromised by the mercy shown the Ninevites. Consideration of the Ninevites' history, of their ignorance and moral confusion, does not exonerate them of guilt for their atrocities. True, the book never tells us what happens to the Ninevites, whether their repentance endures or whether they backslide, as Jonah suspects they will, or to what extent they must bear the consequences of their actions. Nonetheless, their repentance, combined with the story of how they came to be this way, dictates a different kind of response to their situation than retributive justice would allow.[53] The book of Jonah challenges God's people (synagogue, church) to reimagine the boundaries of "common" in the common good, by affirming that an emotional response of compassion to even detested outsiders is part of a commitment to justice and the common good.

Reimagining the Boundaries of the Common Good

At the beginning of this essay, I observed that Jonah's failure is in part a failure of imagination. He cannot imagine what it is like to be a Ninevite, to be one who is

---

50. Walzer writes: "The regard for the people that God teaches [Jonah] at the end is only a rather abstract 'pity'" (*Interpretation and Social Criticism*, 78). I disagree about the quality of the pity, but Walzer's assumption that God is trying to teach Jonah something is worth noting. My thanks to Eric Mount for bringing Walzer's reading to my attention.

51. What kind of justice is appropriate for Native Americans and in the interests of the common good? See Milner Ball, "Common Good in Performance," in this volume. But perhaps in this case it is we (the U.S. government) who are the Ninevites.

52. As I see it, Josiah Young is exploring this same question from another angle in "Good Is Knowing When to Stop," in this volume. The attention Emmanuel Lévinas proposes ought to be paid the "sorrows of an entire world" in a just polity is akin to God's care for the Ninevites (Emmanuel Lévinas, "Peace and Proximity," in *Basic Philosophical Writings*, 163). Even if one holds that the book of Jonah hopes only to convince its readers to think of God's justice differently, and has no investment in a transformation of human justice, the theological question persists: How exactly is God's care for the Ninevehs of this world to manifest itself, unless God's people are agents of that care?

53. Jonah is read on Yom Kippur because of its emphasis on repentance. The book "rejects the ancient view . . . that only punishment can cleanse sin" (Simon, *Jonah*, vii).

outside of the covenant community, to be one who knows only violence. He cannot imagine caring for anything or anyone that is not directly useful to him. Furthermore, despite his certainty that God will show mercy to Nineveh, Jonah cannot bring himself to accept that God could be serious about including these ruthless outsiders within the boundaries of divine care, and by extension, within the common good. Certainly it is good for the Israelites, the animals, and the whole of creation that the Ninevites should turn from their violence. But the divine motivation for redrawing the boundaries of the common good to include the Ninevites goes beyond even this more or less self-serving reasoning. In the divine moral imagination, the deliverance of the Ninevites is good *for them*, and more importantly, it is simply good. This distinction is subtle, yet crucial. God is both the source and the standard for the common good. Therefore, the common good can never be reduced simply to self-serving reasoning. Instead, it resides in the life of God. Following Edwards, concern for the common good is a form of loving God—this cannot be reduced to self-serving logic either.

Biblical narratives are not usually perceived as possessing imperatival force in the same way that biblical law does,[54] yet it is not enough to say that the book of Jonah "invites" us to reimagine the boundaries of the common good. We are in the position of Jonah, and for Jonah such reimagining comes as divine imperative. Because God includes the most violent of enemies within the boundaries of the common good, we must do likewise. This necessarily alters the way we think about our involvement in, among other things, warfare. Care must be taken to consider the genuine welfare of people who will be directly affected by war, and special care must be taken to distinguish care for the welfare of the Other from forms of self-justification. A tension arises here: the behavior of the Ninevites was immoral with reference to *Israelite standards*, and so repentance and new life are envisioned for them. If this is a form of cultural imperialism, then so be it. This charge is, at any rate, a red herring. The real issue is the means by which God confronts the Ninevites: not by force, but by the prophetic word, borne by a "dove."[55] This is akin to the "critical engagement" with the world that Victor Furnish sees operative in Paul's letters ("Uncommon Love and the Common Good," in this volume). In this way, the Ninevites are made to see their own sin for what it is—the use of force generally forestalls any such self-understanding.

So Jonah is overly particular in drawing the boundaries around what he cares about, but not particular enough in relating mercy to justice. In this story the centrality of the role of compassion and particularity directs us to rethink how we should relate not only to the Ninevehs of this world, but also to those whose

---

54. Yet it is crucial to note how the story of Jonah depends entirely on the law. The five (Hebrew) words Jonah speaks to the Ninevites are only meaningful in the context of the divine law—and these violent foreigners, paradoxically, understand this.

55. The symbolic meaning of Jonah's name is disputed. The dove is often thought to connote a weak creature that whines in distress, though Frolov suggests that the sacrificial overtones of the word should be considered (Frolov, "Returning the Ticket," 97).

crimes are far less egregious.[56] Nearly everything in our common life, both local and global, requires reassessment, from declining commitment to common public education, to the ethics of global business practices, to the welfare of Christian and non-Christian people worldwide. The vexing problem of debt relief and foreign aid for developing countries, for example, might profitably be put into conversation with the book of Jonah. If particularity were viewed as a significant factor in the nature of justice, then the histories of the borrowing and lending countries, often entangled in complex and disturbing ways, might be part of the story. Similarly, compassion might be viewed not as somehow weak or beside the point in the hardball world of realpolitik, but as constitutive of good moral judgment, and in the interests of the common good.[57] Attention to both particularity and compassion not only thickens our sense of justice; it ultimately may also serve the common good better than previous incarnations of the concept. For "earthly power doth then show likest God's / When mercy seasons justice."

---

56. Some readers have seen the Nazis as the modern equivalent of Ninevites (e.g., Walter B. Crouch, "To Question an End, To End a Question: Opening the Closure of the Book of Jonah," *JSOT* 62 (1994): 112). Especially in Jewish discussions, the question of whether it is appropriate, or even possible, to forgive Nazis has been hotly debated.

57. See John Cassidy, "Helping Hands: How Foreign Aid Could Benefit Everybody," *New Yorker*, March 18, 2002, 60–66. Cassidy argues that despite its past failures, foreign aid can be successful if it is properly administered and is in the interests of the common good. Yet, "advanced countries" currently spend an average of 0.22 percent of gross national product on overseas aid; the United States spent 0.2 percent in 1990, and the current figure was half of that until quite recently (61–62). President Bush proposed a 50 percent increase in "core development assistance" to poor countries in March 2002.

Uncommon Love and the Common Good
Christians as Citizens in the Letters of Paul

Victor Paul Furnish

In their respective essays in this volume, Jacqueline Lapsley and Patrick Miller show how traditions as diverse as the story of Jonah and the Deuteronomic Decalogue nourish a vision of the good that looks not only to the interests of the believing community itself, but also to the interests of "outsiders." The present essay aims to show that the same may be said about the letters of Paul.[1] A careful reading of these letters strongly suggests that he did not hold a sectarian view of the church's status in the world, as sometimes claimed. Instead, he encouraged believers to be responsible members of society, concerned both for the well-being of their own community and for what was in the wider public interest.

Whether the apostle's view of life in the world was to some extent shaped by his knowledge of the Jesus traditions is a question that lies beyond the scope of this study. There is general agreement, however, about the eschatological orientation and apocalyptic character of both the preaching of Jesus and the gospel of Paul. For this reason, we begin with a few comments about the Jesus traditions as they relate to our topic, and about the allegation that the apocalyptic theology not only of those traditions but also of the Pauline gospel led necessarily to a world-denying ethic. Subsequently we turn to the Pauline texts themselves, giving special attention to some key passages in Philippians, Galatians, and Romans.

---

1. I wish to thank the president and faculty of Princeton Theological Seminary for inviting me to deliver the Alexander Thompson Lecture for 2002, from which this essay evolved. In its present form, it owes much to the discussion that followed the lecture, to critiques and suggestions offered by fellow members of the Common Good consultation convened by the Center of Theological Inquiry, and to an exchange of correspondence with J. Louis Martyn concerning several key points.

The Jesus Traditions: Eschatology and Ethics

The Gospels report Jesus as declaring that "no one is good but God alone" (Mark 10:18; Luke 18:19).[2] Hence, it is reasonable to suppose that whatever notions of a "common good" the Jesus traditions may yield are rooted in the understanding of God and of God's will, to which they bear witness. Indeed, integral to Jesus' preaching of the imminence of God's reign is an affirmation of the absolute justice and mercy of God. The corollary of this is the conviction that God is absolutely impartial in showing mercy and administering justice (Matt 5:45b–47; cf. Acts 10:34; Rom 2:11; Gal 2:6; Eph 6:9; Col 3:25).

Accordingly, the Gospels represent Jesus' ministry, and also the ministry to which he summons his followers, as devoted to the enactment of God's justice and mercy for all, expressly including the destitute, the exploited, and the reviled (e.g., Matt 25:31–46; Mark 1:40–41; 2:15–17; Luke 4:17–21; 14:16–21). Likewise, the Deuteronomic call to love the one God (Deut 6:5)—in the Jesus traditions joined with the Levitical commandment to love the neighbor (Lev 19:18)—resonates throughout much of the New Testament, sometimes radicalized as a call to love even one's enemies (Matt 5:44; Luke 6:27, 35a; Rom 12:14–21). Moreover, the so-called Golden Rule, a bit of moral wisdom at home in many ancient cultures and religions, has found its way into the teachings attributed to Jesus (Matt 7:12; Luke 6:31), thereby endowing those with a perhaps surprisingly universal aspect.[3]

In this connection, the parable about a "good Samaritan" (Luke 10:25–39) merits special attention. Luke represents it as Jesus' response to a certain lawyer's request for a definition of the "neighbor," whom the law commands one to love. Jesus, however, uses the story to shift the focus from the *object* of love—To whom should love be extended?—to its *subject*: what does it mean to *be* a neighbor to others? To this revised question, the story provides a surprising and thought-provoking answer. The good neighbor was neither the priest nor the Levite, even though both of them were, presumably, devoutly religious and committed to keeping the commandments of the law. Rather, it was the Samaritan—a member of a group the Jews regarded as unfaithful to the law and as even more of a threat to their way of life than the Gentiles.

This parable challenges Jesus' questioner—and Luke's readers—to redirect their attention from the question of the neighbor's identity to the question of their

---

2. Except as noted, all biblical quotations follow the NRSV ("alt." = NRSV has been altered by my translation; "vpf" = my own translation).

3. In addition to Patrick Miller's comments on the Golden Rule in relation to the Decalogue (chapter in this volume), especially see J. I. H. McDonald, "The Great Commandment and the Golden Rule," *Understanding Poets and Prophets* (JSOTSup 152; Sheffield: Sheffield Academic Press, 1993), 213–26; C. K. Barrett, "The First Christian Moral Legislation," *The Bible in Human Society* (JSOTSup 200; Sheffield: Sheffield Academic Press, 1995), 58–66; cf. John Hick, "The Universality of the Golden Rule," *Ethics, Religion, and the Good Society* (Louisville: Westminster John Knox, 1992), 155–66.

own. The issue is not how to define the other who is to be loved, but to allow one-self to be formed and motivated by the love that is commanded. Just so, the Samaritan was moved to interrupt his journey in order to give aid to a total stranger. Because the man in the ditch had been robbed, stripped, and left for dead, nothing was evident about his ethnicity, his religion, or his social status.[4] That Samaritan could recognize him only as a fellow human being who desperately needed help. Therefore, as Bernard Brandon Scott observes, this story disallows the imposition of any boundaries on the "map" of God's kingdom: "The world with its sure arrangement of insiders and outsiders is no longer an adequate model for predicting the kingdom."[5] By challenging such an arrangement, and the stereotypes that go with it, the parable engenders a vision of the common good that is no less inclusive than God's own justice and mercy.

Certain of these passages and themes have been employed in discussions of a Christian social ethic.[6] Yet some interpreters have argued that the eschatological expectations of the Jesus traditions and first-century Christianity gave them a "sectarian" character that was incompatible with such an ethic, and also with any notion of a universal "common good." Albert Schweitzer, for example, described the ethical teaching of Jesus as appropriate only for the brief interim before the expected coming of God's kingdom, and only for the end-time community itself.[7] Building on Schweitzer's view, Jack T. Sanders has claimed much the same for most of the New Testament, including the Pauline letters and Synoptic Gospels.[8] There is no disputing the apocalyptic-eschatological outlook of the Jesus tradi-

4. Cf. John R. Donahue, *The Gospel in Parable: Metaphor, Narrative, and Theology in the Synoptic Gospels* (Philadelphia: Fortress, 1988), 131; R. Alan Culpepper, "The Gospel of Luke: Introduction, Commentary, and Reflections," *The New Interpreter's Bible*, vol. 9 (ed. L. E. Keck et al.; Nashville: Abingdon, 1995), 229.

5. Bernard Brandon Scott, *Hear Then the Parable: A Commentary on the Parables of Jesus* (Minneapolis: Fortress, 1989), 201–2.

6. E.g., in the present volume: Patrick Miller notes how the concept of "neighbor" was taken up by Jesus and Paul, the "kingdom of God" motif figures prominently in the essay by Max Stackhouse, and various essays refer to Jesus' concern for the weak and disenfranchised. Also, the documents of the Catholic social tradition (discussed by Dennis McCann) frequently cite, inter alia, Jesus' concern for the poor, New Testament versions of the love commandment, and the parable of the Last Judgment (Matt 25:31–46). Elsewhere, Allen Verhey makes effective use of the parable of the Good Samaritan in his discussion of public policy toward health care; see "The Good Samaritan and Scarce Medical Resources," *Christian Scholar's Review* 23 (1994): 360–73; and idem, *Remembering Jesus: Christian Community, Scripture, and the Moral Life* (Grand Rapids: Eerdmans, 2002), 480–86.

7. E.g., Albert Schweitzer, *The Quest of the Historical Jesus* (ed. John Bowden; 1st complete ed.; Minneapolis: Fortress, 2001), esp. 200, 323, 332–33, 485; cf. idem, *The Mystery of the Kingdom of God: The Secret of Jesus' Messiahship and Passion* (New York: Schocken Books, 1964), 99–105.

8. Jack T. Sanders, *Ethics in the New Testament: Change and Development* (Philadelphia: Fortress, 1975).

tions and, in varying degrees, much of the New Testament, but it is another matter to claim that such an outlook undercuts any serious ethic.[9]

Paul: The Good News in an Evil Age

In the case of Paul, some interpreters argue that the apocalyptic outlook led him to establish his congregations as not just religious but also political assemblies. Paul must have thought these "local communities of an alternative society to the Roman imperial order" would have some kind of continuing existence in the coming kingdom of God.[10] Suppose, as claimed, the apostle urged these eschatologically oriented assemblies to be "exclusive communities, open to recruiting from, but otherwise not participating in, wider imperial society."[11] Then there would, indeed, seem to be little prospect of finding in his letters any social ethic, or any notion of a good held in common with society as a whole.

But what do the apostle's letters disclose? Does his "good news" of the uncommon love of God enacted in Christ for the ultimate redemption of the world preclude any notion of a "common good" *for* the world, which can be embraced by believers and unbelievers alike even in this present age?

The love that Paul regarded as definitive of God's self-disclosure in Christ is "uncommon" in the sense that it is uniquely an expression of God's own being and saving power, and is therefore present for humankind always and only as a *gift*. In the apostle's thought, considered as a whole, this love in fact constitutes "the good"—as God performs good, as God wills its performance by humankind, and as God promises its fulfillment in the coming age. The appeal in 1 Thessalonians to "pursue the good" (5:15, lit.) is therefore but an alternative formulation of the appeal in 1 Corinthians to "pursue love" (14:1). Put briefly, Paul's gospel concerns the *uncommon love* of God, through which the whole of creation is set free from its bondage to sin and death, and which faith receives as a gift, a claim, and a hope.

---

9. E.g., in ibid., Sanders argues that because of the imminent eschatology, "Jesus does not provide a valid ethics for today" (29); that while Paul's accent on love opens up the *possibility* of an ethics "not grounded in an imminent eschatology," the apostle himself does not present such an ethic, but in particular cases "tends to rely on tenets of holy law or sayings of the Lord," which are generally arbitrary and "often inconsistent" (65–66); that Mark "has only very little interest in the welfare of the world or its inhabitants other than to persuade as many of them as possible to repent and follow" (33); that Luke's emphasis on endurance while awaiting Jesus' delayed return renders him "unable seriously to deal with the problem of responsible ethical behavior" (39–40); and that what Matthew proposes about conduct "is so bound up with the expectation of [the] Parousia that it would be preposterous in the time of the non-occurrence of the Parousia" (45).

10. Richard A. Horsley, characterizing the view he shares with several other contributors to the volume *Paul and Empire: Religion and Power in Roman Imperial Society* (ed. R. A. Horsley; Harrisburg: Trinity Press International, 1997), 8, 209; see especially his own essay, "1 Corinthians: A Case Study of Paul's Assembly as an Alternative Society," 242–52.

11. Horsley, in ibid., 8.

The eschatological character of this Pauline gospel is evident and on the face of it would seem to render irrelevant any notion of a *"common* good" in the mundane, political sense, as it had been discussed for centuries.[12] References to what is in the general public interest regularly appear in the works of classical and Hellenistic writers, including Xenophon,[13] Plato,[14] Aristotle,[15] Cicero,[16] and the moral philosophers of Paul's day.[17] From at least the time of Augustine (354–430 C.E.), Christian writers also addressed the theme.[18] But Paul's thought might seem to leave little room for such an idea.

First, the apostle's apocalyptic theology led him to draw a sharp distinction between *"this* age" (e.g., 1 Cor 1:20) and a wholly "new creation," inaugurated in

---

12. The specific Greek phrase (*to koinon agathon*) is attested as early as Thucydides (fifth century B.C.E.), *History of the Peloponnesian War* 5.90.

13. Xenophon, *Cyropaedia* 1.2.2; 3.3.10; *Hiero* 11.1; *Agesilaus* 7.7.

14. Plato, *Republic* 7.519E–520A; *Laws* 4.875AB.

15. Aristotle, *Politics* 3.4.3–4 (1278b); 3.7.13 (1283b); 3.8.5 (1284b); *Eudemian Ethics* 1.8.11, 16 (1218a); *Magna moralia* 1.1.12, 15, 17, 19, 20 (1182b–1183a).

16. Cicero, *De republica* 1.25.39 ("A people is not a collection of human beings brought together in any sort of way, but an assemblage of people in large numbers associated in an agreement with respect to justice and a partnership for the common good [*iuris consensu et utilitatis communione sociatus*]"; trans. C. W. Keyes, LCL); *De finibus* 3.29.64; *De officiis* 1.7.20 ("The prime requirements of justice are that no man should harm another unless provoked by injustice, and that he should use common possessions for the common good [*communibus pro communibus utatur*] and only his own possessions for his own good"; trans. John Higginbotham, *Cicero on Moral Obligation: A New Translation of Cicero's 'De Officiis' with Introduction and Notes* [Berkeley: University of California Press, 1967]); 16.52 ("We should always be prepared to contribute to the common weal [*ad communem utilitatem*]"; trans. Higginbotham); 3.6.30 ("Neglect of the common good [*communis utilitatis*] is contrary to nature, for it brings injustice"; trans. Higginbotham); 6.31.

17. E.g., Seneca (d. 65 C.E.), *De clementia* 1.2.3 ("Man is a social creature, begotten for the common good [*communi bono*]"; trans. John W. Basore, LCL); *De otio* 1.4; *Epistulae morales* 48.2 ("You must live for your neighbour, if you would live for yourself"; trans. R. M. Gummere, LCL), 3; 85.36 ("The wise man's good is a common good [*commune bonum*]—it belongs both to those in whose company he lives, and to himself also"; trans. Gummere); Musonius Rufus (b. before 30 C.E.; cited and quoted from C. E. Lutz, *Musonius Rufus* [Yale Classical Studies 10; New Haven: Yale University Press, 1947]), 92–93, ch. 14, lines 17–33 ("Tell me, then, is it fitting for each man to act for himself alone or to act in the interest of his neighbor also, not only that there may be homes in the city but also that the city may not be deserted and that the common good [*to koinon*] may best be served?"); 96–97, ch. 15, lines 12–14 (The function of lawgivers is "to discern what is good [*agathon*] for the state and what is bad [*kakon*], what promotes and what is detrimental to the common good [*to koinon*]"); Epictetus, *Discourses* 1.19.7–15.

18. For Augustine see, e.g., Raymond Canning, "St Augustine's Vocabulary of the Common Good and the Place of Love for Neighbour," in *Augustine and His Opponents, Jerome, Other Latin Fathers after Nicaea, Orientalia* (ed. Elizabeth A. Livingstone; Studia patristica 33; Louvain: Peeters, 1997), 48–54.

Christ (2 Cor 5:17; Gal 6:15) and to be consummated at the Lord's return (e.g., 1 Cor 15:24–28; Phil 3:20–21).

Specifically, Paul viewed the present as an "evil age" (Gal 1:4) ruled by the "god of this age" (2 Cor 4:4 NIV), and creation itself as longing for liberation from its bondage to decay (Rom 8:19–22). He regarded everything that belongs to this age as "foolish" (1 Cor 1:20; 3:19), condemned (11:32), and doomed to pass away (2:16; 7:31b). It was precisely "to set us free from the present evil age," Paul said, that "the Lord Jesus Christ . . . gave himself for our sins" (Gal 1:3–4), with the result that in Christ "the world has been crucified to me, and I to the world" (6:14). Thus, unlike the "enemies of the cross of Christ" whose "minds are set on earthly things," believers belong to a "commonwealth in heaven" (Phil 3:18–20 NRSV alt.).

Second, and in keeping with this apocalyptic outlook, the apostle issued appeals like the one most memorably expressed in Romans: "Do not allow yourselves to be conformed to this age" (12:2a, vpf).

In support of such appeals and in accord with his overall apocalyptic outlook, Paul drew sharp moral as well as spiritual distinctions between the Christian community and society in general. He was not content to distinguish merely between "believers" and "unbelievers" (1 Cor 7:12–16; 14:22). More pointedly, we find him distinguishing the children of light from the children of darkness (1 Thess 5:5); the blameless and innocent from the crooked and perverse (Phil 2:15); those who know God from those who do not (Gal 4:8–9; 1 Thess 4:5); those who trust and serve God from those who worship idols (1 Thess 1:9–10); those who live by the Spirit of God from those who live by the spirit of the world (1 Cor 2:12); those who have been sanctified from those who remain unrighteous (6:1, 9–11); those who live honorably from those who have succumbed to debauchery and licentiousness (Rom 13:11–12); those who are being saved from those who are perishing (1 Cor 1:18; 2 Cor 2:15; cf. 4:3; Phil 1:28).

On this evidence, the rhetorical questions in 2 Cor 6:14–15 seem to be true to the apostle's outlook, even if they are not of his own composition:[19] "What partnership is there between righteousness and lawlessness? Or what fellowship is there between light and darkness? What agreement does Christ have with Beliar? Or what does a believer share with an unbeliever?" Terms like the ones used here— "partnership" (*metochē*), "fellowship" (*koinōnia*), "agreement" (*symphōnēsis*)—show up regularly in ancient discussions of what is good for society.[20] However, in Paul's letters such terms are applied not to the life of the civic community but to the life of the believing community. When he tells the Corinthians that the spiritual gifts have been given "for the benefit of all" (1 Cor 12:7, vpf [NRSV: "for the common

---

19. Some interpreters have argued that 2 Cor 6:14–7:1 is a later, non-Pauline interpolation; others, that it is non-Pauline material that the apostle himself drew into his discussion. For a discussion of the issues involved, see V. P. Furnish, *II Corinthians* (AB 32a; Garden City, NY: Doubleday, 1984), 371–83.

20. Examples from Aristotle's *Politics: metochē,* 2.2.6 (1261b); *koinōnia,* 3.3.7–4.3 (1276b); *symphōnēsis,* 2.5.14–15 (1263b).

good"]), he means, in fact, for the benefit of all believers.[21] Similarly, while other ancient writers had employed the image of the one body with its many members as a metaphor for the body politic,[22] Paul employs it as a metaphor for the body of Christ (1 Cor 12:14–26; Rom 12:3–5a).

If for these reasons our topic may seem less than promising, there are other, weightier reasons why it is nonetheless worth pursuing.

First, and most fundamentally, Paul understands the saving purpose of God to be cosmic in scope, inclusive of the whole of humankind, and indeed, of the whole of creation. He declares: "In Christ God was reconciling the world to himself" (2 Cor 5:19). "For as all die in Adam, so all will be made alive in Christ" (1 Cor 15:22). "Just as one man's trespass led to condemnation for all, so one man's act of righteousness leads to justification and life for all" (Rom 5:18). "Creation itself will be set free from its bondage to decay and will obtain the freedom of the glory of the children of God" (8:21).

Second, Paul does not summon his converts to withdraw from society but to live out their faith within it. For example, he assures the Corinthian Christians that he has never meant for them to turn their backs on the world. Paul calls on them, whatever their particular situation, to remain there with God (1 Cor 5:10; 7:24).

Third, there is good evidence that Paul presumes his own stated missionary strategy of accommodation—"I have become all things to all people, that I might by all means save some" (9:22)—is also an appropriate strategy for believers to adopt in their everyday dealings with outsiders. For example, he recognizes that some believers enjoy cordial relations with at least certain unbelievers (in Corinth, members of the congregation are sometimes guests in the homes of unbelievers, and unbelievers are sometimes present for the congregation's worship; 10:27; 14:20–25). He also urges believers to continue in their marriages to unbelieving spouses as long as there is harmony (7:12–16).

Finally, in some places Paul specifically encourages believers to include all people within their circle of concern. In other places he directs them to conduct themselves in ways that outsiders will consider respectable. There are clear instances of both in 1 Thessalonians. He prays that God will enable the members of the congregation to "increase and abound in love for one another and for all" (3:12). He admonishes, "See to it that no one repays anyone evil for evil; instead, seek always to pursue the good for one another and for all" (5:15, vpf). And he indicates that if they continue rather than abandon the work that brings them their

---

21. For the same phrase applied to what is in the interest of the *politeia*, see Aristotle, *Politics* 2.12.13 (1274b). In *Mechanical Problems* 847A (1284b), from the Aristotelian school, it is used more broadly, with reference to what benefits humankind (cf. Plato, *Laws* 9.875A). Quite often, however, Greek writers use this same expression somewhat negatively, to designate the pursuit of one's own interests without concern for what is in the public interest; especially see Aristotle, *Politics* 3.7.5 (1279b; over against pursuing the common good); *Rhetoric* 2.13.9 (1389b–1390a, living for one's own good [*agathon*] rather than for what is noble [*to kalon*]); Plutarch, *Pyrrhus* 12.3 (over against concern for what is just).

22. E.g., Aristotle, *Politics* 5.3.6 (1302b–1303a).

livelihoods, they will be conducting themselves "honorably in relation to outsiders" (4:12, vpf). Similarly, when Paul charges the Corinthians, "Give no offense to Jews or to Greeks or to the church of God," he is leaving no one out. He supports the injunction by referring to his principle of accommodation: "just as I try to please everyone in everything I do, not seeking my own advantage, but that of many so that they may be saved" (1 Cor 10:32–33). This distinction between one's own advantage and that of the many, as well as the terminology that Paul has used to express it, are typical of ancient discussions of the common good.

These four preliminary observations have been drawn mainly from 1 Thessalonians, the earliest of Paul's surviving letters, and 1 Corinthians, arguably the next earliest. This allows the present essay to be devoted, principally, to several especially instructive passages in Philippians, Galatians, and Romans.[23] These will be examined individually, in their likely chronological order.[24] Attention needs to be focused especially on what the apostle says about the relationship of the believing community to the wider civic community, and the relationship of the "good" that believers are called to pursue to the "good" that was valued by the unbelieving public. Does Paul's understanding of the uncommon love through which believers are redeemed by God and bound to one another in Christ leave any room or reason for believers to be concerned about what will serve the good of society in general?[25]

Being Citizens: Philippians

Philippians is the only Pauline letter in which citizenship language appears. The apostle may have thought it especially appropriate to employ such terminology in a letter being dispatched to this particular city. As a Roman colony, Philippi

---

23. The relevant passages in 1 Thessalonians and 1 Corinthians are discussed in my essay "Inside Looking Out: Some Pauline Views of the Unbelieving Public," in *Pauline Conversations: Essays in Honor of Calvin J. Roetzel* (ed. Janice Capel Anderson, Phillip Sellew, and Claudia Setzer; JSNTSup 221; Sheffield: Sheffield Academic Press, 2002), 104–24.

24. I assume the integrity of Philippians and regard it as written during an Ephesian imprisonment of Paul, which most likely took place between his dispatch of 1 Corinthians and 2 Cor 1–9. Galatians is notoriously difficult to date but was certainly written before Romans, perhaps about the time of 2 Cor 10–13.

25. Contrary to what the title might lead one to believe, these matters are not addressed in Bruno Blumenfeld's study, *The Political Paul: Justice, Democracy and Kingship in a Hellenistic Framework* (JSNTSup 210; Sheffield: Sheffield Academic Press, 2001). In part, this is because Blumenfeld's aim is broader, to demonstrate that "Paul's views in general" are coherent with classical and Hellenistic political thought (12). But more importantly, there are two further reasons: Blumenfeld seems to presuppose that the apostle's political thought can be understood in isolation from his theology (e.g., "My topic . . . is Paul's political thought and its context, not his theology and its background," 447–48). And he dismisses the apocalyptic and eschatological aspects of Paul's letters as superficial (e.g., "His missionary activity devalues the eschatological perspective," 449).

enjoyed a number of civic and legal privileges, including exemption from land and poll taxes. In Paul's day Philippi was a town of perhaps ten thousand residents, most of them Roman citizens. Although the religious life of the community was fairly diverse, the available evidence suggests that the imperial cult was especially popular and important. There appears to have been no significant Jewish presence, either in the town or in the congregation that Paul established there.[26]

Judging from the contents of this letter, the Philippian believers were coming under substantial pressure from the unbelieving citizenry, likely because of their exclusive allegiance to Jesus as "Lord." By thus rejecting, even if implicitly, the emperor's lordship as celebrated in the imperial cult, believers were opening themselves to the charge of impiety and therefore of being a threat to the political order.[27]

The tensions that Paul feared were developing *within* the Philippian church perhaps reflected two different ways of coping with the hostility of outsiders. Some believers may have responded by compromising their allegiance to Christ and returning to at least limited participation in the imperial or some other religious cult. This could explain Paul's warning about those who "live as enemies of the cross of Christ, . . . [whose] god is the belly . . . and [whose] glory is in their shame," with "their minds . . . set on earthly things" (3:18–19). Similarly, his sharp criticism of those who practice circumcision (3:2–11) would be understandable if other believers wished to be viewed less as Christians than as adherents of the Jewish law, and thus members of an ancient and honorable religious community.[28]

Whatever the precise situation within the congregation, there is no doubt that Paul understood its members to be at risk in society. Indeed, early in the letter he suggests that the congregation's difficulties are part and parcel of his own struggle (1:30). Toward the close of the letter, he declares that believers are responsible to a heavenly commonwealth (*politeuma*),[29] from which they expect the coming of their "Savior" and "Lord," Jesus Christ (3:20). This statement about being under the jurisdiction of a *heavenly* state, combined with the attribution to Christ of two titles used in the imperial cult as appellations of Caesar ("Savior," "Lord"), would seem to leave little room for thinking of believers as citizens also of the civic community. But in fact, such an idea does surface at several points in this letter.

---

26. Cf. Craig Steven de Vos, *Church and Community Conflicts: The Relationships of the Thessalonian, Corinthian, and Philippian Churches with Their Wider Civic Communities* (SBLDS 168; Atlanta: Scholars Press, 1999), 233–50; Mikael Tellbe, *Paul between Synagogue and State: Christians, Jews, and Civic Authorities in 1 Thessalonians, Romans, and Philippians* (ConBNT 34; Stockholm: Almqvist & Wiksell, 2001), 210–31.

27. Cf. de Vos, *Church and Community Conflicts*, 250–75; Tellbe, *Paul between Synagogue and State*, 231–78.

28. See, especially, de Vos, *Church and Community Conflicts*, 266–75.

29. For the meaning of *politeuma*, see, e.g., Andrew T. Lincoln, *Paradise Now and Not Yet: Studies in the Role of the Heavenly Dimension in Paul's Thought with Special Reference to His Eschatology* (SNTSMS 43; Cambridge: Cambridge University Press, 1981), 97–101; cf. Blumenfeld, *The Political Paul*, 119 n. 100.

Philippians 1:27–2:18

The appeals in this section have the congregation's own situation in view and are undergirded by the famous Christ-hymn of 2:6–11. Some of the appeals call for harmony within the congregation (2:2–5, members are to "be of the same mind, having the same love," and so on). But those with which the section opens and closes concern the everyday life of believers, their "public conduct," as it were.

The very first appeal in the letter (1:27–28) is concerned with the lives that believers must lead in the public sphere:

> 1 27Only, conduct yourselves as citizens in a manner worthy of the gospel of Christ, so that, whether I come and see you or am absent and hear about you, I will know that you are standing firm in one spirit, striving side by side with one mind for the faith of the gospel, 28and are in no way intim- idated by your opponents. For them this is evidence of their destruction, but of your salvation. And this is God's doing. (NRSV alt.)

The key verb here is *politeuesthai*, which means to *be* or *live as a citizen*. Many translations, disregarding the basic political reference, interpret it simply as the equivalent of *peripatein* (lit., "to walk"), which is the verb Paul commonly employs in his counsels about Christian conduct.[30] But his choice of *politeuesthai* here seems quite deliberate: It occurs nowhere else in his letters. It is peculiarly appro- priate in a letter to believers who resided in a Roman colony and were under pres- sure to be upstanding citizens. And it coheres with the metaphor of a heavenly "commonwealth," which Paul also employs only in this letter (3:20). The present appeal is not just a general one, urging the Philippians to "*live their lives* in a man- ner worthy of the gospel" (as in NRSV). By using a recognizably political term, the apostle is pointing specifically to the *civic, public context* in which believers are called to live in a way that is appropriate to the gospel they have embraced.[31]

It is important to observe that Paul has *not* chosen to describe believers as either "resident aliens" (*paroikoi*) or "transients [sojourners]" (*parepidēmoi*) in Philippi, although these very metaphors are used of Israel in the Septuagint (LXX), as in Gen 23:4, and also by the Jewish philosopher Philo.[32] After Paul, the authors of

---

30. Elsewhere, for example, he calls on believers to "walk" (i.e., lead their lives) according to the Spirit (Gal 5:16; Rom 8:4), to "walk" in love (Rom 14:15), and to "walk" in a manner worthy of God's call (1 Thess 2:12). See also Phil 3:17–18.

31. Cf. Raymond R. Brewer, "The Meaning of *POLITEUESTHE* in Philippians 1.27," *JBL* 73 (1954): 76–83; Edgar M. Krentz, "Military Language and Metaphors in Philippians," in *Origins and Method: Towards a New Understanding of Judaism and Christianity: Essays in Honour of John C. Hurd* (ed. B. H. McLean; JSNTSup 86; Sheffield: Sheffield Academic Press, 1993), 105–27; here, 115; Bruce W. Winter, *Seek the Welfare of the City: Christians as Benefactors and Citizens* (First-Century Christians in the Graeco-Roman World 1; Grand Rapids: Eerdmans, 1994), 98–100.

32. Philo, *Confusion of Tongues* 77–78 (trans. F. H. Colson and G. H. Whitaker, LCL): "This is why all whom Moses calls wise are represented as sojourners [*paroikountes*].

1 Peter and Hebrews do employ these terms to characterize the status of the Christian community in relation to the world (1 Pet 2:11; cf. 1:17; Heb 11:13; cf. 13:14). They could perhaps be appealed to as providing scriptural warrant for regarding the church, with Stanley Hauerwas and William Willimon, as "a colony . . . a beachhead, an outpost, an island of one culture in the middle of another," and its members as "resident aliens" in the world.[33] Remarkably, however, the only text that Hauerwas and Willimon cite to support their idea of the church as an "outpost" of heaven in an alien culture is Phil 3:20, which they quote according to the translation of James Moffatt: "We are a colony of heaven."[34] They describe Moffatt's translation simply as more "vivid" than others, overlooking the fact that it misrepresents what the text actually says. Paul's statement is not that the believing community as it exists on earth is a *colony of* heaven (in that case, he probably would have written something like *kolōnia tōn ouranōn*). He says, rather, that the believing community, already in its present, earthly circumstances, is under the jurisdiction of a "commonwealth" or "state" (*politeuma*) that exists "*in* heaven" (*en ouranois*).[35] Indeed, the terms "colony," "resident aliens," and "sojourners" do not appear anywhere in the apostle's surviving letters.

Paul's bypassing of such terms in favor of the expression "*to live as citizens*" shows that he endorses some level of continuing participation of believers in civic affairs. He does so notwithstanding the "necessary compromises of public life"[36] that such involvement will entail for them. Judging from Rom 13:1–7, two specific examples of civic participation would be paying taxes and, for anyone with the means, becoming a public benefactor.[37] Moreover, from Rom 16:23, where Paul identifies a believer named Erastus as "the city treasurer," one may infer that he regarded holding public office as another legitimate means by which Christians could contribute to the public good. In the passage at hand, of course, the apostle emphasizes one special point about Christians as citizens. In fulfilling their civic responsibilities, they must always conduct themselves "in a manner worthy of the gospel of Christ," as befits persons whose true citizenship is in a heavenly commonwealth.

The entreaties in 1:27–30 are carried forward in 2:14–16, where the relation of the believing community to the civic community is again in view.

Their souls are never colonists leaving heaven for a new home. Their way is to visit earthly nature as men who travel abroad to see and learn. So when they have stayed awhile in their bodies, and beheld through them all that sense and mortality has to show, they make their way back to the place from which they set out at the first. To them the heavenly region, where their citizenship lies [*en hō politeuontai*], is their native land [*patrida*]; the earthly region in which they became sojourners [*en hō parōkēsan*] is a foreign country."

33. Stanley Hauerwas and William H. Willimon, *Resident Aliens: Life in the Christian Colony* (Nashville: Abingdon, 1989), 12—but without a reference to these texts.

34. Ibid., 11; cf. 171.

35. See Lincoln, *Paradise Now and Not Yet*, 98–99, 220, nn. 57–58.

36. Allan M. Parrent, "Dual Citizens, Not Resident Aliens," *Sewanee Theological Review* 44 (2000): 44–49; here, 46.

37. See text on pages 78–81.

2 ¹⁴Do all things without murmuring and arguing, ¹⁵so that you may be blameless and innocent, children of God without blemish in the midst of a crooked and perverse generation, in which you shine like stars in the world. ¹⁶It is by your holding fast to the word of life that I can boast on the day of Christ that I did not run in vain or labor in vain.

The appeal to "do all things without murmuring and arguing" (v. 14) picks up a LXX term used of Israel's complaining to God during its time in the wilderness (e.g., Exod 16:7–12). But, given Paul's manifest concern for unity and harmony within the Philippian congregation (1:27; 2:2), he must be thinking, in the first instance, of complaints and arguments that believers have with one another, which are disruptive of Christian community.

However, when the apostle proceeds to state the aim of his appeal, the civic community also comes into view: "Do all things without murmuring and arguing, *so that you may be blameless and innocent, children of God without blemish in the midst of a crooked and perverse generation, in which you shine like stars in the world*" (2:14–15, emphasis added). The reference to "a crooked and perverse generation" echoes a passage in Deuteronomy (32:5) where the phrase describes disobedient Israel. Paul, however, now applies the phrase to pagan society. This is the setting in which believers have been called to be "blameless," "innocent," and "unblemished," truly "children of God."

Even here, where Paul accentuates the difference between the believing community and society at large, he does not portray believers as "resident aliens" or "transients" in the world. He employs a cosmological rather than a political image. By conducting themselves as God's children (= under the jurisdiction of a heavenly commonwealth) and "holding fast to the word of life" (2:16), they will be like the stars that shine in the cosmos. Because outsiders in this context are viewed more as opponents than as potential converts, it is unlikely that Paul's statement reflects a missionary concern.[38] Therefore, Matt 5:16 is not a true parallel ("Let your light shine before others, so that they may see your good works and give glory to your Father in heaven"). In the present case, the apostle summons believers to be blameless and innocent in *God's* sight, holding fast to the gospel (the "word of life") in spite of the pressures, threats, and hostile actions they may experience from an unbelieving society. He is not urging believers to try to disengage themselves from society. He is encouraging them to stand firm in their faith (cf. 1:27) despite the moral darkness of the world in which they presently live.

Philippians 4:5a

After appealing to Euodia and Syntyche to "be of the same mind in the Lord" (4:2–3), Paul offers three general and only loosely related counsels for the congregation as

---

38. Although *epechontes* could be understood as "holding *forth*," the usual interpretation of it as "holding fast" is the one that accords with the context.

a whole (4:4–6).[39] The second of these stands out from the other two. The first presupposes the congregation's relationship to "the Lord" (Jesus)—"Rejoice in the Lord always"—and the third calls on its members to "let . . . [their] requests be . . . known to God" in prayer (NRSV alt.). But the middle one is a counsel about how believers should conduct themselves in dealing with others: "Let your gentleness be known to all people" (v. 5a, NRSV alt.). The phrase translated "to all people" is an expression that, in Paul's letters as throughout the New Testament, almost always refers either to the whole of humankind or to all people with whom one comes into contact.[40] The latter meaning is unquestionably the one it has in the present case. Paul intends this counsel to apply not only within the believing community itself, but also as believers have dealings with unbelievers.

What exactly is the apostle commending? The expression he uses (*to epieikes*) has been variously translated as "gentleness" (NRSV), "consideration for others" (REB), and "good sense" (NJB). In the LXX, where the word group is used to describe a disposition of God as well as of people, it variously connotes kindness, forbearance, mercy, and even forgiveness. Paul himself uses it only one other time, when he entreats the Corinthians "by the meekness [*praütēs*] and gentleness [*epieikeia*] of Christ" (2 Cor 10:1).

Aristotle regarded *epieikeia* as the kind of moderation and generosity that should be exercised when the law, because of its generality, cannot take account of particular circumstances.[41] In line with this, and with wording similar to Paul's, 3 Maccabees (first century B.C.E.) represents the Egyptian king as writing that he has spared the lives of the Jews "in accordance with the clemency [*epieikeia*] that we have toward all people" (7:6). The term could also be applied to those who suffer unjustly, as in the Wisdom of Solomon (early first century C.E.). There the ungodly are represented as planning to torture the righteous man of God in order to "find out how gentle he is [*tēn epieikeian autou*], and make trial of his forbearance

---

39. Interpreters who regard Philippians as a combination of letters commonly assign 4:2–7 to the same letter as 1:27–2:18, situating these verses (4:2–7) just prior to that letter's formal close in 4:21–23 (e.g., J.-F. Collange, *The Epistle of Saint Paul to the Philippians* [London: Epworth, 1979], 8–12; cf. Helmut Koester, *Introduction to the New Testament*, vol. 2, *History and Literature of Early Christianity* [2d ed.; New York: de Gruyter, 2000], 136).

40. One example is Paul's declaration, "If for this life only we have hoped in Christ, we are of all people most to be pitied" (1 Cor 15:19). Another is his assurance, "By the open statement of the truth we commend ourselves to the conscience of all people in the sight of God" (2 Cor 4:2, NRSV alt.). Other examples (in all cases, NRSV alt.): "[The Jews] displease God and oppose the whole of humankind" (1 Thess 2:15). "You yourselves are our letter, written on our hearts, to be known and read by all people" (2 Cor 3:2). "Death spread to the whole of humankind because all have sinned" (Rom 5:12). "Therefore just as one man's trespass led to condemnation for the whole of humankind, so one man's act of righteousness leads to justification and life for the whole of humankind" (5:18). See also Rom 12:17–18, discussed on pages 77–78. In Paul's letters, the one possible exception is 1 Cor 7:7, where the phrase may mean "all believers."

41. Aristotle, *Nichomachean Ethics* 5.10.

[*tēn anexikakian autou*]" (2:18–19). In two further LXX passages, the same word is associated closely with *philanthrōpia*, benevolence toward other human beings.[42] The Vulgate renders both Pauline instances of the term (2 Cor 10:1; Phil 4:5) as *modestia*, a quality that Latin writers like Cicero regularly associated with the virtues of moderation and temperance.

Because Paul offers no specific example, his counsel to show gentleness toward all people might seem, on the face of it, to be a mere commonplace. It would not have seemed so to his Philippian congregation, however, if we consider the contents of the letter as a whole and their situation in Philippi, as well as the pointed reference to "all people." They would have heard it as a counsel to exhibit moderation and forbearance (perhaps also forgiveness?) even when dealing with unbelievers, including those who exhibited hostility toward them. In effect, albeit less explicitly, Paul is asking of this congregation what he had previously asked of his congregation in Thessalonica, which was also experiencing the hostility of unbelievers. "See to it that no one repays anyone evil for evil; instead, seek always to do good to one another and to all" (1 Thess 5:15, vpf).

Philippians 4:8–9

Like "gentleness," the qualities and dispositions that Paul mentions in Phil 4:8 were recognized throughout the Hellenistic world as benefiting the whole of society, and thus contributing to the common good.[43]

> 4 [8]Finally, beloved, whatever is true, whatever is honorable, whatever is just, whatever is pure, whatever is pleasing, whatever is commendable, if there is any excellence and if there is anything worthy of praise, think about these things. [9]Keep on doing the things that you have learned and received and heard and seen in me, and the God of peace will be with you.

Catalogs of commendable moral qualities or actions are found elsewhere in Paul's letters,[44] but none is so resonant of Hellenistic moral philosophy, especially Stoic thought, as this one. Two of the virtues named appear only here in the New Testament (*prosphilē*, "what pleases," and *euphēma* "what is commendable"). An additional two terms appear nowhere else in Paul's letters (*semna*, "what is honorable," and *aretē*, "excellence"). Some of the virtues appear rarely or not at all in the LXX, and some that do appear elsewhere in the New Testament or the LXX are there only in different forms or with rather different meanings.

---

42. Second Macc 9:27, "moderation and kindness [*epieikos kai philanthropos*]"; 3 Macc 3:15, "clemency and great benevolence [*epieikeia de kai polle philanthropia*]."

43. Both Joachim Gnilka, *Der Philipperbrief* (4th ed.; HTKNT 10/3; Freiburg: Herder, 1976), 5–11, and Collange, *Philippians*, 12–15, regard Phil 4:8–9, along with 3:1b–4:1, as belonging to a letter that Paul dispatched to Philippi subsequent to a letter that included 1:1–3:1a and 4:4–7. Koester, *Introduction*, 54, believes that it is unclear to which letter 4:8–9 originally belonged.

44. Second Cor 6:6–7a; Gal 5:22–23a.

Unlike his counseling of gentleness toward all people, there seems to be no specific reason why Paul is commending these particular qualities. His list serves to direct the congregation's attention not to special responsibilities that their local circumstances may thrust upon them, but to the broader, public setting in which moral choices have to be made and acted upon. This is the force of the rhetorically powerful, sixfold iteration of the pronoun *hosa*: *whatever* is "true," *whatever* is "honorable," *whatever* is "just," and so on. Believers are responsible for recognizing and doing *whatever* there is in the world's treasury of wisdom that can be reckoned morally excellent and praiseworthy. Here the apostle is presupposing that at least some of what is esteemed as "good conduct" in the civic community can be accepted as such also by the believing community.

This is not to say, however, that Paul regards society as itself the *source* of moral insight or ethical norms. His sharp critique of worldly wisdom laid out in 1 Corinthians (1:18–2:16; 3:18–20) is neither softened nor qualified here in Philippians. It remains the case that believers are to live as citizens who are "worthy of the gospel of Christ" (1:27). Accordingly, the apostle joins to his general commendation of the universally recognized virtues a much more specific instruction: "Keep on doing the things that you have learned and received and heard and seen in me" (4:9). The congregation has learned, received, and heard from him the gospel of Christ, and it has seen in him what it means to live in accordance with that gospel.

Doing the Good: Galatians

The appeals in Galatians 6:9–10 conclude a section of pastoral directives and exhortations that begins with an admonition about the proper use of one's freedom in Christ: "For you were called to freedom, brothers and sisters; only do not use your freedom as an opportunity for self-indulgence, but through love become slaves to one another" (5:13). Paul may have formulated some or even most of the subsequent exhortations with the special needs of his Galatian congregations in mind.[45] Yet this seems not to be the case with the two, closely related concluding entreaties, which are quite general. The subject of both is "the good," even though the apostle has employed two different Greek expressions for this, *to kalon* in verse 9 and *to agathon* in verse 10. Here, as elsewhere in his letters, he appears to use these terms interchangeably.[46]

---

45. E.g., J. Louis Martyn, *Galatians: A New Translation with Introduction and Commentary* (AB 33a; New York: Doubleday, 1997), 544.

46. This is apparent from Rom 7:18–21, and also when 1 Thess 5:21 ("hold fast to what is good [*to kalon katechete*]") is compared with Rom 12:9 ("clinging to what is good [*kollōmenoi tō agathō*]"). Moreover, both terms can be contrasted with [*to*] *kakon* (*kalon*, 2 Cor 13:7; Rom 7:21; *agathon*, 1 Thess 5:15; Rom 12:21; 13:4; 16:19; cf. 13:3 and 3:8) and *ponēron* (*kalon*, 1 Thess 5:21–22; *agathon*, Rom 12:9). Ernest DeWitt Burton, however, believes that the two are "not quite identical" in Gal 6:9–10, with *to kalon* designating "what is morally right" and *to agathon* "what is beneficial to another" (*A Critical and Exegetical Commentary on the Epistle to the Galatians* [ICC; Edinburgh: Clark, 1921], 346). Cf. the NRSV, which renders *to*

6 ⁹Let us not grow weary in doing the good [*to kalon*], for we will reap in due season, providing we don't give up. ¹⁰So then, as we have opportunity, let us work for the good of all [*to agathon pros pantas*], especially for those of the household of faith. (NRSV alt.)

A theological grounding for both appeals is given with the promise attached to the first one, that "we will reap in due season, providing we don't give up" (v. 9b, vpf). This warrant follows logically from Paul's immediately preceding admonition, that those who sow to the flesh "will reap corruption from the flesh," whereas those who sow to the Spirit "will reap eternal life from the Spirit" (v. 8). These two appeals concerning "the good," like all of the pastoral exhortations they bring to a close, presuppose that believers have been graced, through the saving death of the crucified Christ, with the liberating reality of the Spirit's empowering and guiding presence (e.g., Gal 3:1–5; 3:23–4:7; 5:1, 13–24, 25).

The first appeal offers encouragement to persist in doing what is good; the second one emphasizes both the seriousness and the scope of that responsibility. The words "So then" introduce an appeal that the apostle deems to be of fundamental importance.⁴⁷ The next phrase, "as we have opportunity" (*hōs kairon echomen*), might seem to suggest otherwise, but it actually lends further weight to the appeal. It does not mean "on whatever occasion may happen to present itself," nor is it equivalent to the expression "if possible" (*ei dynaton*), which Paul uses elsewhere (Gal 4:15; Rom 12:18). Even as employed by Aristotle, the expression refers to a time that is especially propitious for action.⁴⁸ In the present case, the key term, *kairos*, is the one Paul has just used in referring to the eschatological judgment, when it will become clear who has sown to the Spirit and who has sown to the flesh (Gal 6:7–8). Judgment, he has said, will come in "due season" (*kairos idios*, 6:9; cf. 1 Cor 4:5). When he now proceeds to apply this same word to the present, it continues to carry eschatological connotations, as it does almost always in his letters. For Paul, God's sending of his Son in "the fullness of time" (*to plērōma tou chronou*, Gal 4:4) has given the *whole* of this present time (*chronos*) the character of *kairos*. This is time that has been *claimed* as well as graced by "the promise of the Spirit through faith," which believers have come to know in Christ Jesus (3:14).

So Paul is not saying, rather generally, that "*whenever* we have an opportunity" (NRSV) we should work for the good. He is saying that precisely now, in this "meanwhile" until the Lord's return, in this time that has been both graced and

---

kalon in Gal 6:9 as "what is right"; but this could be mistaken as a translation of *to dikaion* (as in Luke 12:57; Col 4:1), which in Paul's letters has its own special semantic field. If it is deemed important to indicate that two different Greek terms are involved, then *to kalon* might be rendered as "what is morally admirable."

47. Elsewhere appearing in 1 Thess 5:6; Rom 14:12, 19.

48. Thus, *hōs kairon echontes* in Aristotle, *Politics* 5.10.31 (1312b), is appropriately rendered, "feeling that the opportunity was ripe" (Ernest Barker, *The Politics of Aristotle* [London: Oxford University Press, 1958], 240).

claimed by God's promise, believers are to be working for the good.[49] Regarding
the content of this exhortation and its function in the context, three further observations are in order.

First, it encompasses and concludes all of the preceding entreaties (beginning
with 5:13) and draws meaning from them. "The good" to which believers are
summoned is surely to be identified, above all, with love. Paul begins his appeals
by urging the Galatians to use their freedom in Christ for the purpose of serving
one another "through love" (5:13). He supports this appeal by declaring that the
whole law is fulfilled in the one commandment to "love your neighbor as yourself" (5:14, citing Lev 19:18). And he names love first when listing the fruit of the
Spirit (5:22–23). The underlying premise of this whole section, and thus of the
concluding exhortation to labor for "the good," is the conviction stated a bit earlier in chapter 5: "In Christ Jesus . . . the only thing that counts is faith made active
through love" (5:6, vpf).

Second, the exhortation to "work for the good of all" (6:10) not only gathers up
and draws meaning from the preceding pastoral directives, but also brings them,
as it were, out of church and into the public square. Now, sounding more like a
Hellenistic moral philosopher than a pastor, Paul speaks simply of *the good*. Like
his listing of representative virtues in Phil 4:8, his use of this all-encompassing
and open-ended term suggests that believers are responsible for every conceivable
kind of beneficial disposition and deed.

Third, Paul's stipulation that believers should work for the good of *all* emphatically broadens his earlier appeal that they serve "one another" through love (5:13).
The same thing happens twice in 1 Thessalonians. First the apostle prays that the
Lord enable the congregation to "increase and abound in love *for one another and
for all*" (3:12, emphasis added). Then he appeals, "See to it that no one repays anyone evil for evil; instead, seek always to do good to one another and to all" (5:15,
vpf). Also here in Galatians, the apostle seems intent on ruling out any interpretation of the love commandment that would require the "neighbor" to be a fellow believer.[50] When he adds that believers should do what is good "*especially* for
those of the household of faith," that neither rescinds nor compromises the all-
inclusive scope of his appeal (6:10, vpf). Rather, this proviso underscores the
urgency of it; it identifies the place where believers most readily can and therefore
most definitely should begin to "work for the good of all" (6:10). As J. Louis Martyn

49. Cf. Otto Merk, *Handeln aus Glauben: Die Motivierungen der paulinischen
Ethik* (Marburger theologische Studien 5; Marburg: Elwert, 1968), 79; V. P. Furnish,
The Love Command in the New Testament (Nashville: Abingdon, 1972), 101.

50. Contrast the view expressed by Karl Barth, who distinguishes between the
good that Christians are to do "to all men" (he cites Gal 6:10 and, inter alia, 1 Thess
5:14–15; Rom 12:17; Phil 4:5, 8) and *love* (*agapē*) that is directed to a "closed circle," "the circle of disciples, brothers, the saints, members of the body of Christ";
Church Dogmatics, vol. IV/2, *The Doctrine of Reconciliation* (Edinburgh: Clark,
1951), 804–5; cf. 808–9. He mentions 1 Thess 3:12 as "the one exception" to the
rule, which it confirms, that "what the New Testament calls love takes place between
Christians" (805).

has aptly said, Paul does not mean to replace the old distinction between Jew and Gentile with one between the church and the world. Instead, he understands God to be "summoning his new creation onto the world scene by calling into existence the church that exists for the sake of 'all.'"[51]

Life in the Everyday World: Romans

In Romans, attention needs to be focused not only on the famous paragraph that refers to governing authorities, but also on the larger section within chapters 12 and 13 where that passage is situated.[52] Romans 12–13 constitute a more or less self-contained unit, which is opened and closed with appeals that are so formulated as to provide an eschatological framework for the counsels that stand in between. A first group of counsels pertains to life within the believing community (12:3–13).[53] A second and larger group pertains to the community's life in the everyday world (12:14–13:7).[54]

Romans 12:1–2, Introductory Appeals

Two introductory appeals (12:1–2) presuppose everything that Paul has been saying about the gospel up to this point in the letter (*"Therefore,* I appeal to you," 12:1). They themselves lay the groundwork for the following advisories and counsels, especially those about the community's life in the everyday world.

> 12 ¹Therefore, I appeal to you, brothers and sisters, by the mercies of God, to offer up your bodies as a living sacrifice, holy and acceptable to God, which is your reasonable worship. ²And do not allow yourselves to be conformed to this age. Rather, allow yourselves to be transformed in the renewal of the mind, so that you can discern what is the will of God—the good and acceptable and perfect. (NRSV alt.)

---

51. Martyn, *Galatians*, 554.

52. An especially perceptive discussion of these chapters is offered by Walther Bindemann, *Die Hoffnung der Schöpfung: Römer 8, 18–27 und die Frage einer Theologie der Befreiung von Mensch und Natur* (Neukirchener Studienbücher 14; Neukirchen-Vluyn: Neukirchener Verlag, 1983), 96–117.

53. Alternatively, Rom 12:3–8 can be taken as an intervening paragraph between the opening, programmatic appeals of 12:1–2 and the beginning of the counsels proper in 12:9; see Walter T. Wilson, *Love without Pretense: Romans 12.9–21 and Hellenistic-Jewish Wisdom Literature* (WUNT 46; Tübingen: Mohr-Siebeck, 1991), 126–36.

54. A different analysis is offered by Kent L. Yinger, "Romans 12:14–21 and Nonretaliation in Second Temple Judaism: Addressing Persecution within the Community," *CBQ* 60 (1998): 74–96, who argues that all of the counsels in chapters 12–13 pertain to life within the church. His case is not persuasive, however; on his reading, for example, the persecutors (12:14) have to be Christians, which seems highly unlikely (he regards Paul as reflecting what victims in Rome would have felt about other Christians), and he offers no good explanation of how 13:1–7 fits in.

The first appeal is stunningly formulated. Using imagery that evokes the rituals of sacrifice as practiced by both Jews and pagans in their holiest places, Paul enlarges the concept of worship to include the believers' "life on the street." Their worship is to consist of the offering of their "bodies," which he describes as "a *living* sacrifice, holy and acceptable to God," their "reasonable worship." In Romans, the term "body" (*sōma*) stands for the whole self, which in its corporeality and creatureliness (cf. "mortal bodies," 6:12) is able to relate to the world and other selves, and which, in Christ, has been set free from the tyranny of sin and death (6:12–13). Therefore, the "living sacrifice" that is holy and acceptable to God involves putting *oneself* entirely at God's disposal. This kind of worship cannot be confined to special, sacred spaces, but must be fulfilled as well in the public sphere, the so-called secular world of the believers' everyday lives.

The second introductory appeal speaks to what is required of the believing community if its worship is to be both "public" in this particular sense and acceptable to God. Although their service of God takes place in the everyday world, believers must not allow themselves to be conformed to the values, expectations, and claims of this present evil age. Yet the apostle does not call on believers to withdraw from the world (the ascetic option), or to form an alternative society (the sectarian option), or to work toward a Christian political order (the theocratic option).[55] Rather, he issues an appeal on the assumption that, for the present, most believers remain involved in the same situation wherein they heard and accepted the gospel (cf. 1 Cor 7:17–24). But if their circumstances have not changed, *they* have been changed, and for this reason they no longer belong to the world in the same way as before.

Identifying them as persons who have been transformed by God and endowed with a "renewed" mind (Rom 12:2), the apostle summons them to the ongoing task of discerning and obeying the will of God. This appeal to *discern* God's will is misunderstood if it is taken as an appeal to "learn" or "be instructed in" a stable body of knowledge—for example, the Torah (see Rom 2:18). Paul's term (*dokimazein*) points, rather, to a process of inquiry and reflection that includes examining, testing, and appraising whatever may be alleged to be the will of God, or "the good." It therefore is difficult to imagine Paul agreeing with the proposition that "the Bible is the perfect revelation of God's will, including His perfect moral will,"[56] or with the inference ordinarily drawn from this, that the scriptural *revelation* renders *critical moral reflection* invalid as well as unnecessary. The apostle's summons is precisely to the task of Christian moral reflection. He calls on

---

55. With these three "options" I do not intend to be representing Ernst Troeltsch's typology of the sect, the church, and mysticism as "the three main types of the sociological development of Christian thought" (*The Social Teaching of the Christian Churches* [trans. Olive Wyon; Halley Stewart Publications 1; London: Allen & Unwin, 1931], esp. 328–43, 993–1013; here, 993). However, what I mean by the "sectarian option" correlates closely with his characterization of the "sect" type of Christianity.

56. From a resolution adopted by the Southern Baptist Convention in June of 1996, which urged the prohibition of partial-birth abortions.

believers, as they consider what God requires, to take continuing and careful account of the challenges, the responsibilities, and the opportunities that confront them in the public sphere.

Such challenges and responsibilities are the focus of Paul's counsels in 12:14–21 and 13:1–7. It is important to observe that these paragraphs contain no explicitly christological or soteriological language, and that such religious terminology as does appear (drawn largely from the Jewish Scriptures) would have been widely understood and appreciated in Greco-Roman society.

Romans 12:14–21, On Living Peaceably with All

12 [14]Bless those who persecute you; bless and do not curse them. [15]Rejoice with those who rejoice, weep with those who weep. [16]Live in harmony with one another; do not be haughty, but associate with the lowly; do not claim to be wiser than you are. [17]Repay no one evil for evil; take thought for what is noble in the sight of all people. [18]If it is possible, so far as it depends on you, live peaceably with all people. [19]Beloved, never avenge yourselves, but leave room for the wrath [of God]; for it is written, "Vengeance is mine, I will repay, says the Lord." [20]No, "if your enemies are hungry, feed them; if they are thirsty, give them something to drink; for by doing this you will heap burning coals on their heads." [21]Do not be overcome by evil, but overcome evil with good. (NRSV alt.)

The counsels here are only loosely connected and echo various traditions of moral wisdom known to Paul (scriptural, Hellenistic, Hellenistic Jewish).[57] Among these is one appeal that is expressed in a less traditional way than most of the rest, and probably explains the aim of the entire paragraph: "If it is possible, so far as it depends on you, live peaceably with all people" (v. 18, NRSV alt.). While "all people" would of course include all believers, outsiders are the ones especially in view. The believing community is to maintain amicable relations with the unbelieving public. It is an indication of how seriously Paul intends for this instruction to be taken that he acknowledges the difficulty of accomplishing it—"*if* it is possible." He means, in the first place, "if it is possible, so far as it depends on *you*." This shows that he is not speaking idealistically, but of what believers should try actually to achieve in their dealings even with unbelievers.[58] Behind this conditional clause there also lies, no doubt, the apostle's recognition

---

57. E.g., on nonretaliation: *Ps.-Phocylides* 77–78; *Jos. As.* 23:3, 9; 28:5, 10, 14; 29:3; 1QS 10.17; Seneca, *De ira* 2.34; Menander, *Sent.* 675; Polyaenus, *Strategems* 5.12; on rejoicing with those who rejoice: Epictetus, *Discourses* 2.5.23; on weeping with those who weep: Sir 7:34; on haughtiness: Seneca, *Tranq.* 10.5–6; on taking thought of what is noble: Prov 3:4; Philo, *Ebr.* 84; on peace: Epictetus, *Discourses* 4.5.24; *1 Enoch* 52:8–9; Seneca, *Constant.* 7.2; on conquering evil with good: *T. Benj.* 4:2–3; *T. Jos.* 17; 18:2–3; *1 Enoch* 95:5; Plutarch, *Mor.*, "On Compliancy," 13.

58. Cf. Bindemann, *Die Hoffnung der Schöpfung*, 115; James D. G. Dunn, *Romans* (WBC; Dallas: Word, 1988), 2:748.

that what circumstances and other people *do* make possible, or even attractive, may not be in accord with the will of God. To be discerning with respect both to what the circumstances allow and to what is acceptable in the sight of God requires the renewed mind and the commitment to critical inquiry for which Paul has appealed at the beginning of the chapter.

His counsel about living peaceably with everyone is complemented by instructions to bless one's persecutors, repay no one evil for evil, and leave vengeance to God (vv. 14, 17a, 19–20). In addition, there is the comprehensive admonition that closes the paragraph: "Do not be overcome by evil, but overcome evil with good" (v. 21). There are also appeals for sympathy, harmony, and humility (vv. 15–16), which most interpreters believe are directed to relationships among believers themselves, but which in this context can just as easily be understood as directed to relationships with outsiders.[59] In either case, the apostle is promoting conduct that outsiders could readily observe and would doubtless regard as praiseworthy.[60]

That Paul cares about the church's moral standing in the eyes of the world is evident in his advice, adapted from Prov 3:4 (LXX), to "give consideration to what is noble in the sight of all people" (v. 17b, vpf). Here again, the apostle assumes some measure of overlap between conduct that is acceptable to God and conduct that is esteemed in society overall. This is even clearer when he quotes the same Proverb more fully in 2 Corinthians: "We give consideration to what is noble not only in the sight of the Lord, but also in the sight of people" (8:21, vpf).

Romans 13:1–7, On Being Good Citizens

> 13 ¹Let every person be subject to the governing authorities; for there is no authority except from God, and those authorities that exist have been instituted by God. ²Therefore whoever resists authority resists what God has appointed, and those who resist will incur judgment. ³For rulers are not a terror to good conduct, but to bad. Do you wish to have no fear of the authority? Then do what is good, and you will receive its approval; ⁴for it is God's servant for your good. But if you do what is wrong, you should be afraid, for the authority does not bear the sword in vain! It is the servant of God to execute wrath on the wrongdoer. ⁵Therefore it is necessary to be subject, not only because of wrath but also because of conscience. ⁶For the same reason you also pay taxes, for the authorities are God's servants, busy with this very thing. ⁷Pay to all what is due them— taxes to whom taxes are due, revenue to whom revenue is due, respect to whom respect is due, honor to whom honor is due. (NRSV alt.)

---

59. Correctly, N. T. Wright, "The Letter to the Romans," *The New Interpreter's Bible*, vol. 10 (ed. L. E. Keck et al.; Nashville: Abingdon, 2002), 393–770; here, 714.

60. Note Plutarch's comment about the relationship between private and public morality (cited by Winter, *Seek the Welfare of the City*, 88): "Disorder in the State is not always kindled by contentions about public matters, but frequently differences arising from private affairs and offences pass thence into public life and . . . private troubles become the causes of great ones" (*Precepts of Statecraft* 825A).

Unlike the preceding paragraphs, this one is focused on a single topic. The subject here is nothing so abstract as "the nature of the state" but, more concretely, the responsibility of believers—specifically those in Rome—to be good citizens. This paragraph is formally distinct from those preceding in that Paul is now developing an argument rather than issuing counsels and directives.[61] In both cases, however, his concern is with the church's life in the everyday world. His advice about fulfilling one's obligations as a citizen can be understood as following from the general appeal he has already made, to try to live peaceably with all people (12:18). Now he indicates that "all people" includes the governing authorities—by whom he most likely means provincial and local authorities. The two conditions Paul has attached to the more general counsel—"if it is possible" and "so far as it depends on you" (12:18)—are especially pertinent when one is dealing with such officials. The apostle knows this very well from his own experience, which included imprisonments and beatings by local authorities (e.g., Phil 1:12–14; 2 Cor 11:23, 25a). Several particular points in this passage are especially important for our topic.[62]

First, Paul regards the governing authorities as having been instituted by God (Rom 13:1, 4, 6), which means that he understands their authority as *conferred*, not autonomous, and thinks of it as exercised for the specific purpose of supporting the public "good" (v. 4).[63] He explains that the authorities fulfill this function by bestowing praise on those who do good and punishing those who do evil (v. 3).[64] Here "good" is not an alternative expression for "the will of God," as in 12:2, but has the more particular sense of conduct that contributes to the well-being of the civic community—although the assumption surely is that such conduct is in keeping with the will of God. Throughout the paragraph, Paul takes it for granted that the authorities are faithful executors of the will of God, both wise and just in their administration of praise and blame. Despite his own difficulties with government officers, he does not pose or consider the question of what would be required of citizens in the event that the ruling authorities were unfaithful to their task of supporting the public good, or unwise or unjust in fulfilling it.

Second, the apostle may have something more specific in mind here than simply the responsibility of civic authorities to enforce laws and maintain public order. When speaking of the "praise" that government officers bestow on those who do the good, he employs a term often used in a technical sense of the public

---

61. Cf. Klaus Haacker, *Der Brief des Paulus an die Römer* (THKNT 6; Leipzig: Evangelische Verlagsanstalt, 1999), 264.

62. For a more comprehensive discussion of Rom 13:1–7, see V. P. Furnish, *The Moral Teaching of Paul: Selected Issues* (2d ed., rev.; Nashville: Abingdon, 1985), 115–39.

63. A strikingly different assessment of political authorities is offered in Rev 13, where they are portrayed as demonic perpetrators of evil, not guardians of the good.

64. See, especially, Willem Cornelis van Unnik, "Lob und Strafe durch die Obrigkeit: Hellenistisches zu Röm 13,3–4," in *Jesus und Paulus: Festschrift für Werner Georg Kümmel zum 70. Geburtstag* (ed. E. E. Ellis and E. Grässer; Göttingen: Vandenhoeck & Ruprecht, 1975), 334–43; here, 336–40.

recognition accorded to citizens who had in significant ways contributed to the well-being of their city.[65] Similarly, it is well attested that in such contexts the expression "to do the good" meant to perform a notable act of community service.[66] Citizens were officially honored for such acts of generosity as providing funds for the construction of public buildings, adorning or improving old ones, arranging for relief in times of famine, and contributing to the construction of roads or other public facilities.[67] The apostle's commendation of this kind of public service suggests that he knows (or assumes) that there are some Christians in Rome who have the means to provide civic benefactions on this scale.

Third, Paul indicates that believers should be respectful and responsible citizens, not just because they fear what will befall them if they are not, but also "because of conscience" (13:5). Although he regards the conscience as a faculty that can be informed by the gospel (see 1 Cor 8:1–13), he certainly does not regard it as a uniquely Christian or even specifically religious capacity. He conceives of it, rather, as the universally human capacity to recognize and reflect on moral claims with some degree of self-awareness, to experience moral obligation, and also to be tormented by moral ambiguity, afflicted by moral shame (the so-called pangs of conscience), and uplifted by moral conviction. For example, earlier in Romans he has allowed that when the Gentiles "do instinctively what the law requires," they are showing that those requirements are "written on their hearts, to which their own conscience also bears witness" (2:14–15). Thus, he now says that subjection to the governing authorities is necessary "not only because of wrath but also because of conscience" (13:5). He apparently means that both believers and nonbelievers should be able to recognize, quite apart from what is required by public laws and regulations, that fulfilling the duties of citizenship is a moral obligation ("one *must* be subject," v. 5).[68]

Fourth, for the most part, Paul has constructed and presented this argument for responsible citizenship in a way that would have been understood and affirmed throughout the entire civic community.[69] As in the preceding paragraph (12:14–21), there is not a trace of christological or soteriological language. The function of the governing authorities is identified in general terms—supporting what is good and suppressing what is evil.[70] Good citizens are to be subject to the authorities not only in order to win their praise and avoid punishment, but also because their conscience attests that it is "the right thing to do" (cf. 13:5). One need

---

65. Winter, *Seek the Welfare of the City*, 30–33; Halvor Moxnes, "The Quest for Honor and the Unity of the Community in Romans 12 and in the Orations of Dio Chrysostom," in *Paul and Hellenism* (ed. Troels Engberg-Pedersen; Minneapolis: Fortress, 1995), 203–30; here, 215.

66. Winter, *Seek the Welfare of the City*, 34–36.

67. Ibid., 37.

68. Cf. Haacker, *Römer*, 267.

69. Edward Adams, *Constructing the World: A Study in Paul's Cosmological Language* (Edinburgh: Clark, 2000), 205–6; cf. Merk, *Handeln*, 163.

70. Cf. Musonius Rufus, 96–97, ch. 15, lines 12–14, quoted above, n. 17.

not identify Paul as a Rawlsian liberal[71] (which, of course, he was not) to recognize that he is providing several "public reasons" for the conduct that he urges toward government officers. His understanding of the public good is "thin" enough to have been acceptable to most of his contemporaries, whether Christian or not.

Finally, however, underlying Paul's argument is a clear theological warrant. Believers are to subject themselves to the governing authorities because those authorities are *God's servants* (*diakonos*, v. 4; *leitourgoi*, v. 6), appointed by God to support the public good. This is why he can call for subjection to the governing authorities even in a passage that he introduces with an appeal not to be conformed to this age (12:2). *Conforming* oneself to this age means allowing oneself to be tyrannized by what the world esteems and claims, and that is clearly incompatible with putting oneself wholly at the disposal of God. But *subjecting* oneself to the governing authorities is not incompatible with serving God, insofar as those authorities faithfully discharge their responsibility to be God's agents for the common good.[72] Even so, it is still the case that the subjection Paul enjoins is provisional; like all of the conduct commended in these chapters, it takes place in the "meanwhile" of this present age. Nothing in this paragraph compromises the apostle's statement in Philippians that believers belong, not just ultimately but even now, to a commonwealth that is in heaven.

Thus, although Rom 13:1–7 is certainly one of those "elements of the Christian tradition that could offer us a more positive assessment of government and political authority" than is heard from many quarters today,[73] it is by no means an unqualified endorsement of governing authorities. This reticence is overlooked by those who, like Antonin Scalia, interpret the passage as calling for unconditional obedience to any "lawfully constituted" government.[74] In fact, Paul's counsel about being good citizens, like all of the other specific counsels in chapters 12–13, is significantly qualified by the fundamental, eschatologically oriented appeals, which not only introduce but also conclude this section of Romans (12:1–2; 13:8–14).

Romans 13:8–14, Concluding Appeals

> 13 [8]Owe no one anything, except to love one another; for the one who loves another has fulfilled the law. [9]The commandments, "You shall not commit adultery; You shall not murder; You shall not steal; You shall not covet"; and any other commandment, are summed up in this word, "Love your neighbor as yourself." [10]Love does no wrong to a neighbor; therefore, love is the fulfilling of the law.

---

71. For the views of John Rawls, see Robin W. Lovin's essay in this volume.

72. Cf. Bindemann, *Die Hoffnung der Schöpfung*, 117.

73. Jean Porter, in this volume.

74. See Antonin Scalia, "God's Justice and Ours," *First Things*, no. 123 (May 2002): 17–21; here, 18–19.

¹¹Besides this, you know what time it is, how it is now the moment
for you to wake from sleep. For salvation is nearer to us now than when
we became believers; ¹²the night is far gone, the day is near. Let us then
lay aside the works of darkness and put on the armor of light; ¹³let us live
honorably as in the day, not in reveling and drunkenness, not in
debauchery and licentiousness, not in quarreling and jealousy. ¹⁴Instead,
put on the Lord Jesus Christ, and make no provision for the flesh, to
gratify its desires.

Paul's statements here about love (vv. 8–10) lend a degree of coherence to Rom
12–13 that these chapters would not otherwise have. His call to watchfulness in
prospect of the approaching end time (13:11–14) underscores both the urgency
and the provisional character of the conduct that he has commended. Beyond
this, three special points may be noted.

First, when Paul declares that love is the fulfilling of the law, he is saying, in
effect, that love is definitive of the will of God, and thus also of "the good and
acceptable and perfect" (12:2). Ulrich Wilckens probably goes too far when he
suggests that the actual theme of these two chapters is "Love as the good."[75]
However, there is ample evidence, and not only from these chapters, that Paul
does view love as the fulfilling of the good, even as he regards it as the fulfilling
of the law.[76] Insofar as he gives specific content to the conduct that love requires,
it comes in his quotation of the four commandments, "You shall not commit adultery; You shall not murder; You shall not steal; You shall not covet" (v. 9), and in
his own formulation, "Love does no wrong to a neighbor" (v. 10). The positive
counterpart to the latter appears later in Romans (but with "the good" in place of
"love"!): "Each of us must please our neighbor for the good of building up the
neighbor" (15:2, NRSV alt.).

Second, here as in Galatians (5:13–6:10), the context requires that the counsel
of love for "one another" be understood inclusively as love for *all* others. Paul has
linked it to the preceding directive about paying "all" to whom anything is owed.[77]
He reformulates it using a generic term: "One who loves *the other* fulfills the law"
(Rom 13:8a).[78] The Greek term *plēsion* ("neighbor," 13:9) that stands in his citation

---

75. Ulrich Wilckens, *Der Brief an die Römer,* 3 Teilband, *Röm 12–16* (2d ed.;
EKKNT 6/3; Zurich: Benziger Verlag, 1989), 31. Cf. Wilson, *Love without Pretense,*
esp. 150–55, 207, identifying love (*agape*) as the theme of 12:9–21.

76. As already noted, the appeal in 1 Thess 5:15 to "pursue the good" has a parallel in 1 Cor 14:1, to "pursue love." In addition, Paul uses both terms in counsels
about "building up" others ("the good," Rom 15:2; "love," 1 Cor 8:1, etc.) and
serving the "neighbor" ("the good," Rom 15:2; "love," Gal 5:14; Rom 13:10). The
extent to which the two are interchangeable is especially apparent in Rom 12:9–21.

77. Charles E. B. Cranfield, *A Critical and Exegetical Commentary on the Epistle
to the Romans* (2 vols.; ICC; Edinburgh: Clark, 1975–79), 2:675; cf. Bindemann,
Die Hoffnung der Schöpfung, 114; Wright, "Romans," 724.

78. E.g., Joseph A. Fitzmyer, *Romans: A New Translation with Introduction and
Commentary* (AB 33; New York: Doubleday, 1993), 678.

from Lev 19:18 means simply anyone who is at hand,[79] not necessarily a compatriot or close associate. Such an inclusive interpretation is more in line with the apostle's earlier counsels about nonretaliation and living peaceably with all (Rom 12:14–21).

Finally, in 13:11–14 Paul underscores the seriousness with which the Roman Christians should take their present moral responsibilities. He stresses that the end time is ever nearer (vv. 11–12), and he issues a reminder (so it would seem) of the obligations that believers accept at their baptism, when they "put on the Lord Jesus Christ" (v. 14). This is only one of two explicitly christological elements in chapters 12–13, the other being in 12:5. The appeal to "conduct yourselves honorably as in the day" (v. 13, vpf) is a further instance of his encouraging conduct that outsiders will find commendable (cf. 1 Thess 4:12: "Conduct yourselves honorably toward outsiders" [vpf]). The several dishonorable behaviors he warns about here—reveling, drunkenness, debauchery, licentiousness, quarreling, and jealousy—were regarded as such not only by those who had "put on the Lord Jesus Christ" (Rom 13:14), but also by Greco-Roman society in general. Once more, believers are being advised, in effect, to "give consideration to what is noble in the sight of all people" (12:17b, vpf).

Paul and the Common Good

The present study does not allow us to conclude that Paul ever specifically encouraged his congregations to participate in public conversation about the common good, or even that the "common good" was, as such, a Pauline topic. It does suggest, however, that what the apostle declared about the uncommon love of God redemptively enacted in Jesus Christ nourishes a concern for the common good and opens the way for Christian participation in the public conversation about it.

First, Paul's letters reveal him to have been mindful not only of the daily risks, but also of the everyday responsibilities that believers faced in the civic sphere. This involved their dealings with unbelievers generally, including those who would do them harm because of their faith, and their dealings with public officials specifically. His view was that the present evil age is passing away (1 Cor 7:31), and that believers should understand themselves to be ultimately—and already—citizens of a heavenly commonwealth (Phil 3:20). Nevertheless, he did not consider them to be either "resident aliens" or merely "transients" in this age. He regarded believers as also, even though temporarily, citizens of the wider civic community. Hence, he addressed them as people who were in certain respects still accountable to its social and political institutions, and still responsible for contributing to the public good.

Second, the apostle's openness to the world is seen in his numerous counsels to maintain, so far as possible, cordial relations with unbelievers; and more than that, to work for their good and embrace them in love. Such counsels are not as unusual

---

79. E.g., Epictetus, *Discourses* 4.13.2, 9.

or incidental as some interpreters have represented them to be. They are present already in the earliest surviving letter (1 Thessalonians) and still in the latest (Romans).[80]

These counsels are sometimes attributed to prudential considerations (good relations would be in the best interest of the Pauline congregations and their members) or the apostle's missionary goals (a friendly public would be more open to hearing the gospel). Prudential considerations, however, are evident, if at all, only in 1 Thess 4:11–12 ("so that you may conduct yourselves honorably toward outsiders and be dependent on no one" [vpf]). And nowhere in Paul's letters does he so much as hint that doing good to unbelievers may win them over to the gospel. Clearly, the linking of humanitarian aid with evangelical outreach, adopted today by certain Christian denominations and agencies, has no precedent or warrant in the Pauline letters.[81] What his letters do encourage is the sort of action exemplified by Habitat for Humanity International. This organization identifies its work as "a Christian ministry" that is "driven by the desire to give tangible expression to the love of God through the work of eliminating poverty housing." But neither those who contribute to this effort nor those who are aided by them are required to be professing Christians, nor are they regarded as potential converts. Habitat's work is carried on "without seeking profit or interest,"— with no other objective than "that every man, woman and child should have a simple, decent, affordable place to live in dignity and safety."[82]

Third, Paul's openness to the world is also seen in a number of places—again, beginning with the earliest and continuing through the latest of his surviving letters. He has clearly presumed a significant degree of correspondence between what is recognized as "good" by society in general and what may be discerned as "the good and acceptable and perfect" will of God. This is especially clear in several instances: He speaks of conduct that will be regarded as "honorable" (1 Thess 4:12; Rom 13:13) or "noble" (2 Cor 8:21; Rom 12:17b) in the sight of everyone

---

80. See 1 Thess 3:12; 4:11–12; 5:15; 1 Cor 7:12–13, 15–16; 10:32–33; Phil 4:5a; 2 Cor 8:21; Gal 5:13–14; 6:10; Rom 12:14, 17–18; 13:8, 10; 15:2.

81. "Samaritan's Purse," for example, describes itself as "a nondenominational evangelical Christian organization providing spiritual and physical aid to hurting people around the world. Since 1970, Samaritan's Purse has helped meet needs of people who are victims of war, poverty, natural disasters, disease, and famine with the purpose of sharing God's love through His Son, Jesus Christ. The organization serves the Church worldwide *to promote the Gospel of the Lord Jesus Christ*" ("Our Mission," at www.samaritanspurse.org [emphasis added]). Similarly, on 4 April 2003, Mark Kelly of the Baptist Press reported that boxes of relief supplies being shipped to Iraq by Southern Baptists would contain "no literature of any sort," since "the inclusion of evangelistic tracts could cause the aid shipment to be rejected by authorities." But then he went on to note: "A label on the outside of each box will quote John 1:17 in Arabic: 'For the Law was given through Moses; grace and truth were realized through Jesus Christ.' It also will identify it as 'A gift with love from the Southern Baptist churches in America'" (www.bpnews.net).

82. For a full statement of this organization's motivations and objectives, see "Habitat as a Christian Ministry" at www.habitat.org.

(cf. 1 Cor 5:1; 10:32; Phil 4:5a; Gal 6:10). He directs believers to "test everything" in order to "hold fast to what is good" and "abstain from every form of evil" (1 Thess 5:21–22). He commends *"whatever"* may be affirmed as praiseworthy and so on (Phil 4:8). And he refers to "the [public] good," which governing officials have been authorized by God to serve (Rom 13:3–4). That Paul assumed a certain universal sense of what is good and of what is evil is also clear from his comments about the Gentiles, who know "instinctively" and through the witness of their conscience what God requires (Rom 2:14–15; cf. 1:20, 32; 13:5).[83]

Such passages do not contradict the apostle's view of the present age as "evil" and doomed to destruction. He did not waver in his belief that God is the source of all good, and that God's love, manifested in the saving work of Christ, is its norm. Nonetheless, and unlike many Fundamentalist Christians today, Paul was not willing to dismiss unbelievers as utterly deprived of moral wisdom and insight, or to assume that believers had nothing to learn from them.[84] For him, the process of Christian moral discernment requires believers to do more than just read their Scriptures, recall their traditions, and consult with one another. It requires them, as well, to take critical account of whatever society in general deems to be good, just, and honorable, and also of whatever it regards as evil, unjust, and shameful.

Fourth, the stance toward the world that Paul's counsels seem to encourage may be described as one of *critical engagement*. His apocalyptic theology rendered pointless any attempt to "Christianize" society (although not the missionary task of carrying the gospel "to more and more people," 2 Cor 4:15), while both practical and theological considerations ruled out the option of disengagement from the world (1 Cor 5:9–10; 7:17–24). The choice confronting believers, as the apostle expressed it in Rom 12:1–2, was not *whether* but *how* to conduct their lives in the world. On the one hand, they could allow themselves to be "conformed" to

---

83. Cf. Wolfgang Schrage, *Die konkreten Einzelgebote in der paulinischen Paränese: Ein Beitrag zur neutestamentlichen Ethik* (Gütersloh: Gütersloher Verlagshaus Gerd Mohn, 1961); idem, *The Ethics of the New Testament* (Philadelphia: Fortress, 1988), 200–201.

84. Contrast "Lex Vera—'The True Law,' A Statement of Policy and Purpose by the American Family Association Center for Law & Policy" (at www.afa.net/clp/lexvera.asp), which evidently presumes that all moral truth is found in the (Christian) Bible: "Biblical morality . . . is the morality of the Creator for mankind. To deny this is to deny the nature and being of man. It is no intrusion upon the mind for government to govern, and to teach and encourage its citizens to act, in accordance with the principles of Biblical morality. Someone's moral code must prevail in public and private affairs. . . . Our commitment is to a principled and consistent application of a Biblical worldview in opposition to the prevailing, almost universal and wholehearted commitment to relativism in law and policy that has left us a nation of brutes. Is it any wonder that we have become no better than the beasts of the forest when the 'learned' among us see man as no different than 'a grain of sand'? We are in a culture war; it is our mission to advance our principles in the courtrooms of America, as well as in legislative halls and the culture at large. We are resolute in advancing these principles, under all conditions, and at whatever cost."

the present age, recaptured by its death-dealing values and claims. On the other hand, as "transformed" persons whose minds had been "renewed" in Christ, they could apply themselves to discerning and doing what God was requiring of them within their present worldly circumstances.

Paul understood that the worldly circumstances of believers included their continuing and sometimes difficult relationships with unbelievers, the intimidation and even hostility that they experienced from the unbelieving public, and constant pressure to fulfill the social and political expectations of the civic community. He did not direct believers to withdraw from their relationships with unbelievers, or categorically to renounce their responsibilities as citizens. Rather, he charged them in all of their dealings with the world to remain faithful to the gospel. This meant embracing whatever they discerned to be in accord with the will of God, rejecting whatever they believed was not, and seeking, as agents of God's love, to "work for the good of all" (Gal 6:10).

This, one might say, is an "interactive" model for the church's moral witness in the world. On this model, the church is not conceived as "an island of one culture in the middle of another,"[85] nor is it called to be only "a countercommunity" in the world, in whose life outsiders may observe "the gospel in action."[86] According to this model, the believing community is to be a constructive but challenging presence in society, affirming what it can and opposing what it must. Thus, the citizens of God's heavenly commonwealth are understood to be called, individually and corporately, to the complex and always perilous task of bearing their moral witness precisely where they are caught up in the life of the wider civic community, and doing so as responsible members of society. They are to make the most of every social and political means that may be open to them to oppose whatever does harm and to support whatever contributes to the common good.

Such a course is fraught with many risks, and the apostle called attention to two in particular. On one hand, the church may so accommodate itself to the world that it compromises the gospel and ceases to be the body of Christ. On the other hand, whenever the church's commitment to the gospel leads it to oppose the world, it may find itself, like Paul, sharing in the sufferings of Christ (e.g., 2 Cor 1:6). Yet that, too, as in the apostle's case, becomes part of its witness (e.g., Phil 1:12–14, 29–30).

---

85. Hauerwas and Willimon, *Resident Aliens*, 12.

86. See Richard B. Hays, *The Moral Vision of the New Testament: Community, Cross, New Creation: A Contemporary Introduction to New Testament Ethics* (San Francisco: HarperSanFrancisco, 1996), 458. Concerning abortion (which he believes is all but ruled out by "the New Testament witness"), he says: "The primary task of the Christian community on this issue is to be a countercommunity of *witness*, summoning the world to see the gospel in action" (his emphasis). Hays says much the same about the church's response to other social issues; e.g., on war: "If we live in obedience to Jesus' command to renounce violence, the church will become the sphere where the future of God's righteousness intersects—and challenges—the present tense of human experience. The meaning of the New Testament's teaching on violence will become evident only in communities of Jesus' followers who embody the costly way of peace" (344).

Fifth, there are several places where Paul's encouragement of believers to love or work for the good of *one another* is at once extended or interpreted in such a way as to include *all people* as the beneficiaries (1 Thess 3:12; 5:15; Gal 5:13–6:10; Rom 13:8–10). The appeals of this type show that he made no distinction between the uncommon love of God that is constitutive of the believing community, and of which believers are agents in the world, and the love that believers are to extend to outsiders. Fundamentally, then, Paul commended love toward all people because he understood them to be *already* beneficiaries of the uncommon love of God—who "shows no partiality" (Rom 2:11; cf. Gal 2:6), and whose love has been "proved" for us "in that while we still were sinners [enemies] Christ died for us" (Rom 5:8, 10).

In summary, the apostle addressed believers as already citizens of a heavenly commonwealth and summoned them to discern and do the will of God. Nevertheless, he also counseled them to take seriously their responsibilities as members of society. He called them to recognize that this had to involve their ongoing critical assessment of society's manifold and competing claims concerning good and evil, right and wrong. And he led them to understand that what they could determine to be the will of God—as normed by the uncommon, saving love disclosed in the cross—ought to govern their conduct in relation to society at large no less than their conduct within the believing community.

Classical Voices

Introduction

Jean Porter

The common good is widely associated with Catholic social ethics. The wide-ranging essays collected in this volume make it clear that this association is too narrow. The idea of the common good has deep roots in Scripture and in the earliest theological reflection of the Christian community, and it can serve as a moral and theological ideal, or alternatively, as a fruitful provocation, in diverse theological contexts. Nonetheless, it does seem to be the case that even though the idea of the common good is more wide-ranging than we might have expected, since medieval times the explicit language of the common good has been particularly characteristic of Catholic social thought within the broad Thomistic tradition.

The three essays by Jean Porter, Dennis McCann, and Robin Lovin focus on three moments in the history of reflection on the common good, seen as a theologically informed tradition of reflection on the values and challenges distinctive to life in community. All three locate their papers within the trajectory of the Thomistic strand of the common good tradition, and all three focus to a greater or lesser degree on the political dimensions of the common good. As all three papers suggest, this convergence is by no means a coincidence. The Thomistic strand of the natural law tradition is marked by its emphasis on political life, governmental action, and the rule of law as characteristic expressions of the common good, at least when they are functioning in good order. Porter and McCann explore the history of this aspect of the common good tradition in the medieval and modern periods. Lovin draws on the thought of one of the most distinguished twentieth-century exponents of the Thomistic tradition, John Courtney Murray, to develop a constructive defense of the legitimacy of introducing religious considerations into public discourse.

"The Common Good in Thomas Aquinas," as the title suggests, examines Aquinas's own concept of the common good. As Porter observes, this concept does not play the central role in Aquinas's moral and social thought that we might have assumed, given its centrality in later Catholic social ethics. Nonetheless, when we place Aquinas within the context of contemporaneous scholastic thought, we see that this idea does play an important role for him, even though he does not develop a theory of the common good as such. More specifically, this idea emerged out of attempts by Aquinas and his interlocutors to make moral sense of the emerging structures of centralized governance and political order, the precursors of the modern nation-state. The common good offers an ideal in terms of which these institutions are justified, and by the same token it also provides criteria for evaluating their actions. So understood, the common good is closely tied to an ideal of the rule of law. The common good provides the basis for legislative authority, and correlatively, no enactment counts as binding law unless it is oriented toward the common good.

In "The Common Good in Catholic Social Teaching," Dennis McCann examines the development of the Thomistic tradition of reflection on the common good in later Catholic social thought, focusing on its expression in modern and contemporary social encyclicals. As he shows, this tradition reflects both continuities and discontinuities with medieval reflection on the common good. It remains focused on political questions and disposed toward a positive view of government and public authority. At the same time, it is more disposed toward an organic view, according to which the structures of society represent the natural expressions of human life, and for this reason, it has tended toward social and political conservatism. However, this conservative tendency has been balanced, and at some points overridden, by an emphasis on the economic dimensions of the common good. This latter emphasis has had the effect of broadening the scope of the common good, as understood in this tradition, to take in economic arrangements and activities of all kinds. As a result, the contemporary Catholic conception of the common good is broader and more comprehensive than its medieval counterpart. While this expansion can sometimes lead to a loss of focus, it also provides the breadth of scope that is necessary if the idea of the common good is to be effectively deployed in a globalized world society.

Finally, in "Public Discourse and the Common Good," Robin Lovin draws on an expansive conception of the common good to address one of the distinctive conundrums of liberal political thought. As he observes, the pursuit of the common good by political action requires public discussion. However, some philosophers within this tradition have found it necessary to place limitations on such discussions, barring distinctively religious perspectives and insisting that all arguments be based on considerations that all members of a society could share. Moreover, a number of theologians today would agree, on the grounds that the Christian ideal of communal life and practice is so radically different from any secular ideal that Christians have nothing to add to public discussion. In response to both of these views, Lovin argues that Christians can and should participate as such in public discourse, drawing on the concern for the legitimacy of law that they share with liberalism. He develops this argument by relating the political liberalism of John Rawls to the Thomistic account of the common good set forth by John Courtney Murray. Rawls suggests the possibility of a variety of concepts of public reason, including one developed from "Catholic views of the common good and solidarity." Murray, for his part, offers a differentiated account of public discourse, including the restricted political discourse that is of special concern to Rawls. At the same time, he also provides for a discussion of "affairs of the commonwealth," in which religious ideas about the common good might contribute to the further development of public reason. In this way, Lovin argues, he suggests the legitimate place that distinctively religious arguments might have in the public square. This would not be as a basis for legislation, but as a contribution to the ongoing development of shared assumptions and commitments that form the necessary context for legislation, and for public action more generally.

The Common Good in Thomas Aquinas

Jean Porter

The language of the common good is frequently invoked in theological discussions of political life, social ethics, and related topics, especially but not only by Catholic scholars.[1] Its attractions are clear. It suggests a distinctively theological approach to social issues, which nonetheless is open to other traditions and approaches, and it underscores the importance of attending to communal and public, in contrast to individualistic and private goods. Furthermore, the language of the common good suggests points of contact between theological ethics and other prominent strains of social thought in the United States, including varieties of communitarianism and recent work on civic society.

The idea of the common good can be traced most immediately to modern Catholic social encyclicals and the social ethics tradition that has developed from them. The *Pastoral Constitution on the Church in the Modern World* (*Gaudium et spes*), promulgated by the Second Vatican Council in 1965, provides what has become a classic definition of the term:

> Every day human interdependence grows more tightly drawn and spreads by degrees over the whole world. As a result, the common good, that is, the sum of those conditions of social life which allow social

1. I extend my thanks to the Center for Theological Inquiry for sponsoring the discussion group on the common good out of which this essay developed, and for their warm hospitality. Warm thanks are due also to my fellow participants in this discussion group, who have become not only stimulating conversation partners but good friends. I would also like to thank Joseph Blenkinsopp for his helpful comments.

groups and their individual members relatively thorough and ready access to their own fulfillment, today takes on an increasingly universal complexion and consequently involves rights and duties with respect to the whole human race.[2]

Within these encyclicals the common good is generally equated with a set of conditions necessary for the full human flourishing of all members of society. As such, appeals to the common good offer useful reminders of the moral priority of equality and sufficiency, but they do not do a great deal of independent theoretical work. Hence, we need to determine independently what the conditions necessary for full human flourishing are, and to resolve the hard questions about the access and distribution of these goods, in order to give content to the concept of the common good. Recent theological discussions of the common good have begun to address these questions, but there is still much work to be done along these lines.

Under these circumstances, it is not surprising that current interest in the common good should extend to the historical roots of this motif, if only to provide resources for developing a fuller concept of the common good. In particular, over the past several decades there have been a number of efforts to retrieve the account of the common good developed by Thomas Aquinas.[3] It is easy to understand why Aquinas's account would attract so much attention. In the first place, it is widely assumed, by Catholic social thinkers themselves as well as their interlocutors, that modern Catholic social thought is grounded more or less directly in Aquinas's political theory. Hence, if we want to understand the idea of the common good as expressed in modern Catholic social thought, what better way to do so than through an analysis of its original source? Furthermore, Aquinas seems to offer an entrée into a distinctively premodern approach to social ethics, attractive

---

2 . *Gaudium et spes*, 243–335, in *The Gospel of Peace and Justice: Catholic Social Teaching since Pope John* (ed. Joseph Gremillion; Maryknoll, NY: Orbis, 1976), 263, par. 26. The translation is from Abbott's standard *Documents of Vatican II*, prepared largely by Joseph Gallagher; see the note at the beginning of the text in Gremillion's version for more details.

All references to primary sources are incorporated in this chapter and with the texts cited. All translations from medieval texts are my own. Some of these are taken from passages excerpted by D. Odon Lottin or Rudolf Weigand; these references are provided in the notes. All other texts can be found in any standard critical edition of the relevant works.

3. Helpful summaries of these attempts are provided by Brian Stiltner, *Religion and the Common Good: Catholic Contributions to Building Community in a Liberal Society* (Latham, MD: Rowman & Littlefield, 1999), 83–89; and Michael Sherwin, OP, "St. Thomas and the Common Good: The Theological Perspective: An Invitation to Dialogue," *Angelicum* 70 (1993): 307–28 (Rome: Pontificia Universita San Tommaso). Sherwin's monograph is itself a retrieval of Aquinas's account of the common good for contemporary debate (as the name suggests). Stiltner offers a retrieval of the thought of Jacques Maritain, whose own work was centrally focused on retrieving Aquinas's thought.

because he seems to have avoided the flaws—individualism, a focus on rights claims, an excessive valuation of freedom—that are often attributed to modern political thought.[4] Finally, Aquinas's treatment of the common good is particularly attractive from a theological standpoint, precisely because the term seems to have theological resonance for him. In his commentary on Aristotle's *Nicomachean Ethics*, Aquinas observes that the good of the political community is said by Aristotle to be more divine than the private good of an individual, because it more closely attains a likeness of God, who is the supreme cause of all goods (50.1.1.2), and in his commentary on Peter Lombard's *Sentences*, he speaks of God Himself as a common good (*In I Sent.* 49.1.1.1 ad 3).[5]

However, when we turn to Aquinas's comments on the common good in search of a substantive account of the social good, we are likely to be disappointed. We tend to assume that because an idea of the common good, which stems from Aquinas, is central and foundational for contemporary Catholic social thought, then this idea must be central and foundational for Aquinas as well. But the texts do not bear this out. Even a quick survey of Aquinas's constructive writings will indicate the motifs he appropriates to organize his moral theory—unsurprisingly, the two most important are virtue and law—and common good is not included among them.[6] We do find frequent references to the common good throughout his writings, but he seems to appeal to it in passing, as a way of making some specific point, without offering much in the way of systematic development of the concept. The common good does not even merit a separate discussion in a specific question of either of the two great *summae*, as do (for example) the concepts of merit (*Summa theologiae* [*ST*] I-II:114 [I-II = first part of the second part]) or the right (*jus*; *ST* II-II:57 [II-II = second part of the second part]). As for the alleged theological significance of this concept, we can only say that Aquinas's explicit references to the common good do not offer a great deal of support for such an interpretation. Even the claim that the common good is more divine than the good of an individual is qualified in important ways, as we will see further on.

Nonetheless, in this essay I will argue that the motif of the common good does play an important role in Aquinas's mature moral thought. Admittedly, this motif is not central to his moral thought, in the way that it later came to be central to Catholic social thought, and he does not develop a full-scale theory of the common good per se. Nonetheless, the motif of the common good does play an important

---

4. But as I argue below, this impression should be qualified. Aquinas does acknowledge the value of individual autonomy, although not in exactly the same terms as contemporary political liberalism.

5. I take the latter reference from Sherwin, "St. Thomas and the Common Good," 310.

6. In *Summa contra gentiles*, Aquinas discusses matters pertaining to human morality under the rubric of law, which is in turn interpreted as an expression of God's providence (SCG III:114–130). In the *Summa theologiae*, we find both law and virtue as central organizing concepts. There has been much debate over the precise way in which Aquinas relates them. In my view he clearly regards law and virtue as complementary and mutually interpreting ways of understanding the moral life from a theological perspective (*ST* I-II:49, introduction).

role in his overall moral theory. It provides him with a conceptual space, as it were, for identifying a set of motivations and justifications that cannot readily be accommodated within a framework of interpersonal relationships. In other words (and I clarify this in what follows), the motif of the common good provides Aquinas with a way to speak about what we would now call "reasons of state" and to reflect on the moral differences that these make.

This brings us to a further point. If we are to understand Aquinas's account of the common good, it is necessary to place that account within the context of his immediate predecessors and contemporaries. Of course, we will better understand any aspect of Aquinas's thought once we have located it within its context, but as I hope to show in what follows, some sense of context is particularly important for understanding the way in which he uses this motif. Precisely because Aquinas says little directly about what the common good is, we need some sense of the discussion that he is presuming in order to appreciate the significance that this expression would have had for him. This context will be especially critical for our assessment of the claims made for the theological significance of the common good. Moreover, it is only through examining this context that we can get a sense of the problems that Aquinas attempts to address through his use of this motif.

Hence, in what follows I will first trace the development of the motif of the common good, or common well-being or utility, through the early Scholastic period up until Aquinas's time. Next I will consider its development in Aquinas itself, seen in light of that context. Finally, I will offer some suggestions about the continuing relevance of Aquinas's account of the common good.

The Common Good in scholastic Thought: Antecedents to Aquinas's Account

The century and a half preceding Aquinas's birth (in about 1225) comprised a period of rapid social change and institutional expansion throughout Western Europe. A society that had been predominantly rural, agricultural, and widely scattered became—to a large extent, although of course not completely—urban, mercantile, and centralized. These social changes were reflected in and further promoted by a resurgence of intellectual speculation and popular spirituality, so much so that scholars of the period commonly speak of a twelfth-century renaissance, or even a reformation. The increasing centralization and mobility of European society required and enabled institutional reforms in both church and civil society. Beginning in the late eleventh century, reforms in church law and practice began to bring major segments of life (especially marriage) under church control. The twelfth century also saw the emergence of the university system and the development of centralized bureaucracies in both church and civil society— two mutually reinforcing developments, since the universities were the training grounds for the new intelligensia required by the new church and civic societies.[7]

---

7. So far as I can determine, no historian today denies that the period from the late eleventh through about the mid-thirteenth century was a period of tremendous

Most importantly for our purposes, this was a period of rapid legal and political transformations. Throughout most of Western Europe after the collapse of the Roman Empire, both law and political relations more generally tended to be structured around interpersonal relations of authority and subordination. All this was backed up by local customs and religious doctrines and practices, which were themselves by no means clear or rigorously enforced in the earlier Middle Ages. At the end of the eleventh century, secular lawyers began to develop a system of jurisprudence through commentary and reflection on Justinian's *Digest*, through which they could review and regularize laws and develop generally recognized standards for legal procedure. Canonical jurisprudence emerged a little later, through the impetus of Gratian's analytic compilation of church law known as the *Decretum* (1140). His work quickly assumed the same foundational status as the *Digest* held in civil law, or Peter Lombard's *Sentences* held in theology. Finally, recognizable precursors to the modern state—that is to say, a political entity defined in terms of geographical boundaries and having plenary authority within those boundaries—began to emerge at the end of the thirteenth century (at least on the continent; arguably, it developed earlier in England).[8]

---

demographic and economic expansion and rapid social and institutional change. Nevertheless, there has been considerable debate over the causes and the exact character of these developments. In my own interpretation of the period, I rely especially on the following: Marc Bloch, *Feudal Society* (trans. L. A. Manyon; 2 vols.; Chicago: University of Chicago Press, 1961); James A. Brundage, *Medieval Canon Law* (London: Longman, 1995); M. D. Chenu, *Nature, Man, and Society in the Twelfth Century* (ed. and trans. Jerome Taylor and Lester K. Little; Chicago: University of Chicago Press, 1968); Giles Constable, *The Reformation of the Twelfth Century* (Cambridge: Cambridge University Press, 1996); C. H. Lawrence, *The Friars: The Impact of the Early Mendicant Movement on Western Society* (London: Longman, 1994); Lester K. Little, *Religious Poverty and the Profit Economy in Medieval Europe* (Ithaca, NY: Cornell University Press, 1978); Barbara Reynolds, *Fiefs and Vassals: The Medieval Evidence Reinterpreted* (Oxford: Oxford University Press, 1994); R. W. Southern, *Scholastic Humanism and the Unification of Europe*, vol. 1, *Foundations* (Oxford: Blackwell, 1995); Hendrik Spruyt, *The Sovereign State and Its Competitors* (Princeton, NJ: Princeton University Press, 1994), 59–150; R. C. van Caenegem, "Government, Law and Society," in *The Cambridge History of Medieval Political Thought: c. 350–c. 1450* (ed. J. H. Burns; Cambridge: Cambridge University Press, 1988), 174–210; and André Vauchez, [*Les*] *Laïcs au moyen âge: Pratiques et expériences religieuses* (Paris: Cerf, 1987).

8. Specifically, France under the royal house of the Capetians is widely regarded as the first state of a recognizably modern kind in Europe; the argument for this view is summarized by Spruyt, *The Sovereign State*, 79–80. However, van Caenegem in "Government, Law and Society," 183–92, claims that a unified national monarchy emerged in England as early as the tenth century, and that unified states began to emerge on the continent in the late eleventh century. Without attempting to adjudicate this debate, I observe that Spruyt and van Caenegem seem to be emphasizing different criteria for what counts as a state. Spruyt emphasizes territorial sovereignty, but van Caenegem emphasizes the more inclusive criterion of centralized administrative authority. And in fact, different conceptions of statehood have led to still earlier dates for the emergence of the state. For example, Barbara Reynolds (*Fiefs and*

When we examine medieval moral writings, it is clear that in this period theologians and jurists were caught up in a process of developing an adequate conceptual framework and vocabulary for dealing with these changing conditions. Indeed, not all of them realized that their inherited frameworks for thought were no longer adequate to the structures of their society. Consider, for example, these remarks by Aquinas's contemporary Bonaventure, taken from the treatise *Quaestiones disputatae de perfectione evangelica* (*DPE*, ca. 1260). Bonaventure wants to show that the practice of vowed obedience is morally legitimate; to do so, he must first argue that obedience *tout court* is in accordance with the natural law. The natural law takes on different expressions in the different conditions of human life, he says, and accordingly it can be said to prescribe obedience in three ways:

> Hence it is that the natural law prescribes filial obedience whether in accordance with the state of fallen nature, or the state of nature as first set up. It prescribes servile obedience, however, not without qualification, but in the state of fallen nature as a punishment of sin, in accordance with the prescription of the law of nations, which commands from reason and from an instinct of nature. It prescribes jurisdictional obedience in accordance with the state of nature as repaired or to be repaired, and with respect to the status of the wayfarer. . . . Therefore, in accordance with the threefold differentiation of superiority, there is a threefold mode of obedience: the first nature prescribes without qualification, because it is universal and explicit and applies to every status; the second and third, however, it prescribes implicitly and in accordance with a specific status. (*DPE* 4.1)

What is striking about this line of analysis is that Bonaventure provides little space for positive forms of authority and obedience outside the ambit of the church. Filial obedience is natural in an unqualified sense, but other forms of obedience stem from human sinfulness—either as a part of the remedy for sin, within the church, or else as a part of the punishment for sin, in secular society. Correlatively, every form of subordination within secular society, excepting only the subordination of children to their parents, is regarded a form of servitude, and by implication every corresponding relation of obedience is servile. This is a remarkably negative view of secular authority, one that leaves little room for social critique and reform in civil life. Even more importantly from our standpoint, it is an undiscriminating view. It does not allow for the distinctions among different kinds of authority and obedience that were drawn in society by this time. In particular, it does not acknowledge the then-current distinctions among free and servile forms of subordination and obedience (paradoxical though the idea of free subordination may sound to us).

Vassals) understands national unity in terms of the self-identification of a people as a nation under a monarch and claims that the nation in this sense never really went away in Europe.

Aquinas agrees with Bonaventure, and indeed with the whole Western medieval tradition, that servitude, because of its penal character, cannot be rooted in unfallen human nature but must in some way reflect human sinfulness. However, he differs from Bonaventure in that he allows for a kind of dominion and subordination that does stem from human nature and would therefore have existed even if there had never been a fall. As he explains, we speak of dominion in two senses. Understood in one way, dominion implies servitude properly so called, a relation in which the actions of one person are directed for the sake of the good of the other, the one who commands. This kind of relationship is penal (which is not to say that it implies any specific personal sin on the part of the person in a state of servitude) and would not have existed except for the fall, just as Bonaventure also says. There is, however, another sense in which we can speak of dominion and subordination:

> Someone exercises dominion over another as a free person, when he directs him to the proper good of the one being directed, or to the common good. And such dominion of a human person would have existed in a state of innocence, for two reasons. The first, because the human person is naturally a social animal; hence, human persons in a state of innocence would have lived in society. But the social life of a multitude is not possible, unless someone is in charge, who aims at the common good, because a multitude as such aims at many things, whereas one aims at one thing. Hence the Philosopher says that whenever many are ordained to one thing, there is always found one as the principle and director. . . . Secondly, because if one person should be pre-eminent over another with respect to knowledge and justice, this would be inappropriate unless it were directed towards the well-being of the other. (*ST* I:96.4; except where otherwise indicated, all subsequent references to Aquinas are taken from the *Summa theologiae*)

Hence, for Aquinas there is a kind of authority natural in the sense that it stems from uncorrupted human nature, is consistent with free status on the part of its subjects, and takes its raison d'être from its orientation to something other than the private good of the person exercising it. This "something else" may consist in the good of the person being directed—although it is hard to think of any instances of purely paternalistic authority in Aquinas, apart perhaps from parental authority itself. (Even the authority of husband over wife is exercised for the sake of the common utility of the household; see *Ad Ephesios* 50.8, commenting on Eph 5:22ff.). More commonly, it will consist in the common good, the well-being of the community as a whole. Correlatively, as we will see, the exercise of authority is legitimated (at least in part) by its orientation toward the common good.

Here we see the central elements of Aquinas's account of the common good. Most fundamentally, the common good is understood by contrast with one's private good, or with the good of an individual. As such, it provides the rationale for political authority; the ruler acts with a view to the common good, just as each person directs her or his actions in accordance with some conception of his or her private good. By the same token, the common good provides a rationale for laws, and it serves to justify the ruler in some courses of action that would be closed to private citizens. Finally, because the good of individuals is inseparable from the common good (as we will see further on), the political authority so constituted is appropriate in a community of free persons.

This account of the common good clearly implies a conception of political authority quite different from Bonaventure's. But Aquinas did not develop this account out of whole cloth. There were a number of other scholastic theologians and jurists reflecting on the new political realities of their time, and these reflections provided the elements out of which Aquinas's account was developed. In order to appreciate the significance of Aquinas's own account of the common good, we must look further at three contexts that shaped that account.

Civic Virtue and the Common Good

The first of these contexts may seem at first to have little to do with social ethics, yet it provided a set of crucial distinctions that were appropriated in subsequent reflection on the purposes of civil society. This is the context set by scholastic reflections on the virtues. In the early scholastic period, we find two contrasting approaches to the virtues, as exemplified by the writings of Peter Abelard (1074–ca.1142) and Peter Lombard (ca.1100–1160).[9] Abelard understood virtue in philosophical and more specifically Aristotelian terms, as a stable disposition that enables persons to act morally. In contrast, Peter Lombard proposed a strictly theological account of the virtues in his *Sentences*. In this work, he defines virtue as a good quality of the mind, which God brings about in us without our activity. His definition takes its terms from Augustine's writings, although the formulation is Peter's own. As he goes on to explain, God brings about virtue in the soul, while we bring about the acts of virtue through our exercise of free will in cooperation with God's grace. Hence, there can be no true virtue without grace, and by implication, there is no place in Christian theology for a distinctively philosophical analysis of the virtues.

These two approaches to virtue might seem to be irreconcilable; nevertheless, most scholastic theologians after Peter Lombard found a way to reconcile them. They did so by drawing a distinction between two different kinds of virtues, distinguished by the goals toward which they are directed.[10] Here is an explanation of the distinction by the early twelfth-century theologian Simon of Tournai:

> What are the kinds of virtue? There are two kinds of virtue, which are distinguished by their duties and ends. For if a quality constitutes the

9. I take this point, together with the summary of the contrasting views of Abelard and Lombard, from D. Odon Lottin, "Les premières définitions et classifications des vertus au moyen âge," in his *Psychologie et morale aux XIIe et XIIIe siècles*, vol. 3.2 (Louvain: Abbaye du Mont César, 1949), 153–94.

10. Ibid. Here again, I rely on Lottin.

mind in such a way as to carry out political duty for a political end, it is said to be a political virtue. By this means, citizens, even unbelievers such as Jews or pagans, are said to have virtues, if their minds are so constituted by a firm resolve directed toward the carrying out of incumbent duties in accordance with the institutes of their homeland, for the purpose of preserving and building up the republic. And political virtue is so called from a *polis*, which is a multitude or a city, because it is approved by the judgement of the multitude or the city, granting however that it is insufficient for salvation. But Catholic virtue is that which establishes the mind in a firm resolve to carry out Catholic duty for a Catholic end. By this means, the faithful are said to have virtues, if their minds are so constituted as to carry out their duties in accordance with the institutes of the Catholic religion, ultimately on account of God, that they might enjoy Him.[11]

Here we see an echo of the two loves, which, as Augustine tells us, have built two cities, the earthly and the heavenly. But unlike Augustine, Simon identifies the love animating political virtue in positive terms—it is not self-love, but love for the commonwealth, out of which men and women are motivated to act in accordance with its laws, in order to promote its well-being. By the same token, the qualities stemming from this orientation are said to be virtues, even though they are admittedly not sufficient for salvation. Hence, Simon's analysis provides a place for both of the kinds of virtues identified by Abelard and by Peter Lombard, respectively. Abelard's natural virtues are reconfigured as political virtues, whereas the virtues associated with grace are reconfigured as Catholic virtues.

Subsequently, most scholastic authors adopt this approach, even though they do not all use the same terminology. The virtues oriented toward the commonwealth are also described as civic, whereas Catholic virtues are also called theological virtues. The political or civic virtues are sometimes also associated with the traditional cardinal virtues of prudence, justice, temperance, and fortitude. The Catholic or theological virtues are associated, unsurprisingly, with Paul's list of faith, hope, and charity, although the political or civil virtues can also be transformed into theological virtues through grace. From our perspective, in any case, this line of analysis is significant because it correlates one kind of virtue, held to be genuine although limited, with the well-being of the commonwealth. The latter is construed as an end of human life distinct from salvation and, furthermore, as one that is worthy in its own right. This idea, in turn, provides the scholastics with a starting point for more directly addressing other social issues.

Theory of Law

In his essay "Government, Law and Society" the historian R. van Caenegem remarks that after the closing of the Carolingian period at the end of the ninth

---

11. Ibid., 106–9, esp. 107, from the Latin text excerpted in Lottin.

century, we see "a period of more than two centuries in which the European Continent lived without legislation. Neither kings nor princes—nor popes for that matter—issued laws, edict or constitutions containing new legal norms for their subjects."[12] Of course, there was some legal development in this period, but it took place through the almost imperceptible development of customary law.

This situation began to change in the late eleventh century, as the processes of expansion and centralization mentioned above rendered more formal legal processes both possible and necessary. At first, legal scholars looked to the judge, the agent responsible for applying the laws, to serve as the agent of change in law. This meant that the legal scholar himself, who served as the adviser to the judge, also had a role to play in shaping the law. Hence, we read the anonymous author of the legal manual *Petri exceptiones*, dating from the second half of the eleventh century, cooly announcing, "If anything useless, broken, or contrary to equity is found in the laws, we trample it underfoot."[13]

The complex centralized societies that were by now emerging in Europe, however, could not function with this degree of judicial activism. Certainly, legal scholars acknowledged the need for the exercise of equity in the courtroom, but they also came to see that judicial equity could not substitute for some kind of legislative process. Accordingly, we find both secular legal scholars and canon lawyers moving toward the development of a theory that provides criteria for the legitimacy of laws.

Hence, the so-called father of secular jurisprudence, Irnerius, writing in the early decades of the twelfth century, carefully distinguishes between the exercise of equity in the courtroom and the creation of law properly so called: "It is proper to equity simply to set forth that which is just. But it is proper to the law to set forth the same by an act of will, that is, relying on some authority."[14] Similarly, Gratian— whose systematic compilation of church canons, the *Decretum*, effectively established canon law as a discipline of study—began his work with twenty distinctions on the sources for church law, the ways in which it is established and abrogated, and the relation between church law and other forms of law. He is the first to state explicitly that positive law must be promulgated in order to be valid, adding that it must subsequently be confirmed by community observance (D.4, C.3.1).

In this period scholastic theologians also take up the topic of positive law. Albert the Great was the first to offer a definition of positive law, or *lex*. It incorporates the traditional four kinds of law: the natural law, the law of Moses, the law of grace, and the law of the members, which is the innate tendency to sin that Paul mentions in Rom 7:23 (*De bono* 5.2.1).[15] For Albert, the key to analyzing the

---

12. Van Caenegem, "Government, Law and Society," 181.

13. From the Latin text excerpted in Rudolf Weigand, *Die Naturrechtslehre der Legisten und Dekretisten von Irnerius bis Accursius und von Gratian bis Johannes Teutonicus* (Munich: Max Hueber, 1967), 23.

14. Taken from the text excerpted in ibid., 22.

15. I take this point from D. Odon Lottin, "La loi en général: La définition thomiste et ses antécédents," in *Psychologie et morale aux XIIe et XIIIe siècles*, vol. 2, *Problèmes de morale*, 1e partie (Louvain: Abbaye du Mont César, 1948), 11–47, esp. 22.

concept of law is provided by Aristotle's claim that the purpose of law is to make the members of society good. On this basis he synthesized a range of reflections on positive law drawn from Cicero, Augustine, and Gratian.

So far, we do not see the scholastics developing a theory of law with explicit reference to a notion of the common good. Yet, without doing violence to their thought, it is not hard to see how their reflections on law might be developed in such a direction. In the case of Albert in particular, the definition of law is tied to some account of the purpose for which laws are promulgated. That purpose in turn is defined by reference to the kind of society that the legislator aims to produce— a society of good persons. That being said, we must turn to another set of problems to find explicit appeals to the common welfare.

Legitimate and Illegitimate Uses of Force

As theologians and church officials attempted to regularize the theory and practice of penance, they had to address a wide range of cases in which seemingly sinful behavior would appear to be justified or even morally compelled by the situation at hand. One such set of hard cases is directly relevant to the development of an idea of the common good. These have to do with the circumstances, if any, in which someone is justified in using force, in seeming contravention of moral laws against killing, seizing another's property, and the like. More specifically, the cases that concern us here are those that were generated by judicial practice and more generally by publicly sanctioned uses of force. It was generally agreed that judges, soldiers, and public officials could do some kinds of things— killing people, inflicting bodily harm, appropriating property—that private citizens could not do. But how could these kinds of actions be justified? And what are we to make of the hard cases that arise in the contexts of public life?

One case that generated widespread attention might be described as the case of the perplexed judge. A judge is trying a capital case. The accused has been shown to be guilty by overwhelming evidence produced in a court of law; but the judge happens to have private knowledge that the person is innocent. Yet, for whatever reason, he cannot legally prove what he knows. So what should he do?

According to Philip the Chancellor, a secular theologian (that is to say, not a member of a religious order) writing in the first part of the thirteenth century, the judge in such a case would be obliged to order the execution of the accused person:

> And so a judge kills a malefactor, insofar as the law is consonant with nature considered as reason, and in this case, to kill a person would not be contrary to the natural law in this sense; however, to kill an innocent person knowingly would be contrary to the natural law, because it is contrary to that which nature, as reason, prescribes. But thus far, no prescription with respect to the purpose is involved, according to which what is forbidden might be done by the authority of a superior; the law, however, is a superior, and God is above the law. From this it follows that if a judge according to his own cognizance knows this person to be innocent,

yet the proofs are to the contrary, he will judge in accordance with the proofs. And it is not the judge who kills that person, but the law, whose minister he is, according to which one who is innocent is held to be guilty.[16]

Needless to say, most of us today would be shocked by this conclusion. But before we dismiss this text as an example of sheer bloody-mindedness, we should take note of Philip's reasoning. The judge is a minister of the law, insofar as he is a judge, and for that very reason he cannot act as a private person while exercising his office. In Philip's view, this implies that he cannot use information he has obtained extrajudicially, even for the benefit of those under his jurisdiction. What is centrally important in this situation is that the rule of law should be preserved, and this requires the judge to submerge his private identity, as it were, in the operations of the law.

We find a similar line of reasoning in the secular theologian William of Auxerre, whose *Summa aurea* was written around the midpoint of the thirteenth century. William is considering whether a royal official is bound to kill someone whom the king orders him to put to death, even though he knows that the person is innocent of any crime, and the king has given the order out of malice. In such a case, says William, the official should try to get the king to change his mind:

> But if the king perseveres, he is bound to obey. This is made clear through a similar case. For if someone, whom a priest knows to be in mortal sin, asks for the Eucharist in private, he ought not to give it to him, because he knows that he would be receiving it in a state of mortal sin. But if he should ask publically in front of the whole parish, the priest must give it to him, because if the priest refuses, he will in a sense be the betrayer of his crime, and he will be infringing the seal of the confessional, which should in no case and by no coercion be infringed. And this is on account of the common utility (*communem utilitatem*), because people would be afraid to confess their sins if the seal of the confessional could be broken. And by the same token, in the case at hand the official is bound to obey the king on account of the common utility, since without subordination and dominion there would be no way to rule the human race or a republic. (*Summa aurea* 3.25.4.3)

Again, it is the rationale for William's conclusion that I want to underscore. The official qua official is not only permitted but also obliged to do something that would be sinful for him as a private person, namely, to kill an innocent person. But for William, this conclusion is explicitly grounded in an appeal to the well-being of the community. If officials were free to act on their own private judgement, the structures of authority and obedience sustaining society could not be maintained. Again, this is shocking to our sensibilities, and rightly so—but it

16. From the Latin text excerpted by D. Odon Lottin, *Le droit naturel chez saint Thomas d'Aquin et ses prédécesseurs* (2d ed.; Bruges, Belgium: C. Beyaert, 1931), 113.

is worth remembering that public order, and a civic society existing over and above networks of personal relationships, were at this point still new and fragile achievements in most of Europe. William, like Philip before him, reflects early efforts to grapple in this context with the kinds of hard questions generated by the existence of a public order and, correlatively, the creation of public identities that are distinct from, and may be in tension with, one's private self.

Aquinas's Account of the Common Good

At this point we turn to a closer examination of Aquinas's account of the common good. In what follows I focus on the account as set forth in the *Summa theologiae*, since this will provide us with Aquinas's mature thinking on the subject. The account in the *Summa* has the further advantage of being developed within the context of Aquinas's fullest statement of his overall theology, including most importantly (from our present standpoint) his theology of virtue. We thus see here an account of the common good that has been worked out in tandem with a systematic development of wider subjects, including law, justice, and virtue, which provide that account with its necessary context.

In order to reflect the logic of Aquinas's development, we will trace his account of the common good in roughly the order in which he presents it over the course of the *Summa*. This means that the order to be followed in this section will be (roughly) the reverse of the order followed above. First we will examine Aquinas's account of the common good in the context of political authority, law, and the use of force for "reasons of state." Next we will examine his treatment of the common good in the wider context of his theory of virtue.

Political Authority, Law, and the Common Good

Aquinas's first extended discussion of the common good occurs in the *Prima pars* (*ST* I). This discussion occurs in the context of examining the conditions of life that humanity would have enjoyed in paradise, if our first parents had not sinned. While this may seem to be an abstruse subject of little practical importance, the comparison with Bonaventure indicates its significance for Aquinas and his contemporaries. In this period the natural law was frequently analyzed in terms of a historical account of the different stages of human life, the history in question being taken predominantly from biblical narratives. Within this schema, the first stage, that of unfallen human nature, is especially significant because it provides a touchstone for identifying what is proper to human nature as it would ideally be, as fully and integrally reflective of the creative will of God. By the same token, this first stage also provides a standard against which to evaluate some institutions and practices as reflecting the human nature only as distorted by sin. As Bonaventure's example indicates, the scholastics considered servitude to be natural only in this qualified sense: it reflects human nature as distorted through the effects of sin.

Aquinas also makes use of the distinction between institutions and practices that are natural to the human person in an unqualified sense, and those that are natural only in the sense of stemming from our nature as wounded by sin. As we have already observed, he accepts the consensus that servitude is natural only in this latter sense. It is all the more striking, therefore, that he also insists that there is another kind of political authority that is not equivalent to servitude, but is appropriately exercised within a society of free persons. This kind of authority is characterized by its orientation toward the common good, rather than toward the private good of the one in authority. Presumably, Aquinas says that this kind of authority is consonant with rule over free subjects, since (as he will subsequently explain) no one can attain his own proper good unless he stands in right relation to the common good (I-II:92.1 ad 3; II-II:47.10). Therefore, in a community freed from sin, governance on behalf of the common good would never be contrary to the will of those subject to its direction.

Here we see the two central features of Aquinas's conception of the common good. It is understood by contrast to private or individual good, and it is closely tied to political authority. These two aspects of the concept are connected through the analogy that Aquinas draws in I:96.4. Just as an individual directs all of her actions by reference to her good as she understands it (cf. I-II:1), so the ruler of a community directs all of the activities of the community with a view toward safeguarding and promoting its common good. What is striking about this approach to the common good, at least as seen from the perspective of later Catholic social thought, is that Aquinas says little about what the common good is, beyond drawing the parallel between private and common good. In contrast to later attempts to develop a full-scale social ethic out of the concept of the common good, Aquinas says just enough about the common good at this point to make a basic point. There is a kind of public authority that is good and natural without qualification. Later he will qualify his account of the common good in various ways, but at no point does he develop anything like a substantive account of the good society under the rubric of the common good.

Before turning to the next point at which Aquinas elaborates his conception of the common good, we should take note of one misunderstanding that frequently arises at this point. It is often assumed that Aquinas's appeal to the naturalness of political authority should be understood in Aristotelian terms, with the implication that Aquinas is defending the naturalness of existing social hierarchies. It is true that Aquinas appeals to Aristotle in order to establish the fundamental point that the human person is naturally a social animal. Nonetheless, there are critical differences between the accounts of political authority developed by each. According to Aristotle, the hierarchies actually existing in society reflect natural divisions among human persons. Only some persons are capable of rational judgment and self-control. Others lack this capacity altogether (natural slaves), or else possess capacities for judgment but not self-control (women; see *Politics* 1.4–5, 12–13). Aquinas also says that human persons are naturally unequal in their capacities for judgment and moral virtue; in fact, this provides him with one of his arguments in support of the claim that political authority would have existed in paradise.

Nonetheless, there are two critical differences between his view and Aristotle's. First, Aristotle claims that the relevant differences in rational capacity amount to differences in kind, not just in degree; there are some things that natural slaves and women are constitutionally unable to do. In contrast, Aquinas insists that all human persons possess the same fundamental kinds of capacities for rational judgment and moral action, even though some are more intelligent, or constitutionally better disposed to virtue, than others. Second, for Aristotle the relevant differences are correlated with recognizable classes of people, and they can therefore be translated more or less completely into social structures. For Aquinas, however, the differences among persons are individual differences; he does not distinguish among classes of people, some of whom are fit for rule while others are fit only to serve. Indeed, he explicitly denies that social inequality is grounded in differences of nature among human beings (I:109.2 ad 3). This is in contrast to the demons, whose hierarchical differences *do* reflect natural differences (as do the hierarchical distinctions among the angels, at least in part; see I:108.4).

The partial exception to this generalization is of course the fundamental distinction between the sexes, which Aquinas does correlate with a social structure of dominion and subordination, in considering marriage. He does say that women are generally less reasonable than men, and he justifies the dominion of husband over wife on these grounds (I:92.1 ad 2; cf. *Ad Ephesios* 50.8). Yet even this is clearly a difference of degree and not kind, since as he repeatedly reminds us, with respect to the fundamental rational nature of the human soul, there is no distinction between the sexes (I:93.4 ad 2, 6 ad 2; II-II:177.2). Moreover, the relative superiority of men over women does not apply in every case (II-II:177.2). Most significantly, he does not object to women holding authority over men in civic society, as he says in his commentary on Peter Lombard's *Sentences* (*In IV Sent.* 25.2 ad 1a). In fact, one of his treatises, the *De regimine judaeorum*, is addressed to a female ruler.

Similarly, Aquinas reinterprets Aristotle's remarks on natural slaves in such a way as to deny, in effect, that there are any such. On Aristotle's view, slaves are incapable of exercising practical wisdom or prudence (again, see *Politics* 1.4–5). Aquinas is well aware that this is Aristotle's view; and it is true, he notes, that someone in a servile or subordinate condition does not exercise prudence *as* a slave or serf. Nonetheless, because every human person possesses capacities for rational judgment and self-direction, it is proper to such persons to exercise prudence, precisely as human beings (II-II:47.12). Even more significantly, Aquinas does not follow Aristotle in saying that servitude, as such, is natural. As we have already observed, Aquinas agrees with the medieval consensus that servitude, involving dominion over a subordinate for the sake of the master, has only been introduced into human life as a result of sin. His distinctiveness lies rather in the fact that he identifies another form of authority between adults that is not a form of servitude (again, see I:96.4).

Let us return now to Aquinas's account of the common good and its relation to political authority. We noted above that Albert the Great was the first scholastic theologian to develop a comprehensive theory of law. Aquinas follows the lead of his teacher in developing his own analytic definition of law, a definition, it should be noted, that is meant to comprehend every kind of law, from the eternal

law to human legislation (I-II:90). For Aquinas, however, the key to the definition of law is not provided by its purpose in making men and women good.
Rather, he emphasizes the character of law as a norm of reason that is oriented
toward the common good (I-II:90.1–2). In order to establish the specific point
that the law is always ordained toward the common good, he turns to Isidore of
Seville, rather than Aristotle, in order to justify his analysis. This is a significant
move, in light of the fact that Isidore's writings on law drew on classical Roman
jurisprudence, which had been foundational for the twelfth century revival of civil
jurisprudence (I-II:90.2).[17] (Aquinas probably would not have been aware of
Isidore's antecedents. My point is that his theory of law draws on the same line of
thought as we find in the secular jurisprudence of the time—mediated, in the latter case, primarily through Justinian's *Digest*). At the same time, Aquinas points
out that not just any rational norm can count as a law. Rather, a genuine law can
only be established by the community as a whole, or by those individuals who
have responsibility for the community (I-II:90.3). Furthermore, he follows Gratian
in saying that a law must be promulgated in order to have force within its community (I-II:90.4). Hence, his much-quoted definition of law: "Law is an ordi-
nance of reason directed toward the common good, instituted by one who has
responsibility for the community, and promulgated" (I-II:90.4).

Three points should be underscored here. The first is that positive law takes
its point, and therefore its legitimacy, from its orientation to the common good.
It is significant that Aquinas does not follow either Aristotle or his teacher Albert
by identifying the primary purpose of the law as the inculcation of virtue. A well-
disposed body of law will have this effect, precisely because it will direct persons
to act in accordance with the common good as regulated by divine justice. In other
words, the morally salutary effects of the law are derived from its orientation
toward the common good (I-II:92.1). Moreover, for a political community to be
in good order, its rulers must be virtuous, but the subjects need only be virtuous
enough to obey the decrees of their rulers (I-II:92.1 ad 3). Second, positive law
can only be promulgated by someone who has legitimate law-making authority—and this authority stems from the legislator's responsibility to act for the
common good (I-II:90.3). The aim of the law and the ground of legislative
authority are therefore one and the same, that is, their orientation toward the
common good. Finally, not everything can be justified through an appeal to the
common good. A decree that places inequitable burdens on different persons is
unjust and therefore not a valid law, even if it is genuinely oriented toward the
common good (I-II:96.4).

So far as I have been able to determine, Aquinas is the first scholastic to link
legislative authority explicitly to the common good. Yet when we place Aquinas's
theory of law in its immediate context, it is easy to see the lines of continuity
between his theory of law and the scholastics' more general reflections on political
authority. We have already observed that for Aquinas's immediate predecessors and

17. I owe this point to Michael Crowe, *The Changing Profile of the Natural Law*
(The Hague, Netherlands: Martinus Nijhoff, 1977), 69–70.

contemporaries, certain courses of action, otherwise ruled out, can be justified through an appeal to the common good. It is easy to see how this line of analysis could be extended to cover the general authority to make laws on behalf of the community. What Aquinas takes from his predecessors and contemporaries, I suggest, is the idea of a public role. Such a role implies both a general authority to direct the community as a lawgiver, and specific powers to do some kinds of things on behalf of the community at large that would be forbidden to private citizens. Aquinas's theory of law is nonetheless innovative in articulating the link between legislative authority and the common good.

By the same token, his remarks on the powers of public officials offer the clearest indication of continuity with his predecessors and interlocutors. In defense of the common good, what can a public official do that a private person cannot do? To begin with, he can kill those who are guilty of a capital offense (II-II:64.2). It is worth noting that *only* someone who has authority for the common good may do so; a private citizen must not even kill someone who has been sentenced to death (II-II:64.3). Similarly, the soldier may kill enemy soldiers because he is acting on the authority of the ruler (II-II:64.3 ad 1). Someone in authority may also inflict the penalty of lesser bodily harm or incarceration for the sake of the common good (II-II:65.1, 3). He can, finally, seize property from the infidels, or in pursuit of a just war, or for the sake of the common good (II-II:66.8). The general principle here is enunciated at II-II:64.3 ad 3: Any private citizen may act on behalf of the common good *unless* the act in question involves harming another. But only someone who holds authority for the common good may inflict harm on behalf of the community.

In this connection, it should be emphasized that there are some things that no one, even someone in a position of authority, can do in defense of the common good. No one is justified in killing the innocent, even in defense of the common good, because "the life of the just is conserving and promotive of the common good, because they themselves are the more important part of the multitude" (II-II:64.6). More generally, we are told at II-II:68.3 that "no one ought to do harm to another unjustly, in order to promote the common good."

Virtue, Justice, and the Common Good

In the first section of this chapter, I observed that the motif of the common good, or common well-being or utility, enters scholastic moral thought by means of the scholastics' attempts to develop a comprehensive analysis of virtue and the diverse kinds of virtues. More specifically, they appeal to this motif in order to explain the difference between the theological virtues, which depend on grace, and the civic or political virtues, which do not. This line of analysis seems to have commended itself to the scholastics because it enabled them to reconcile two strands of thinking about the virtues. On the one hand, they could still endorse Peter Lombard's view that only the theological virtues can lead us directly to God. On the other hand, this approach left room to affirm that the civic virtues are genuine virtues, because they are directed to a genuine good, albeit limited and this-worldly.

In the *Prima pars* Aquinas also refers in passing to the political virtues. These, he says, are oriented toward the common good (I:60.5; cf. *De virtutibus in communi*, art. 9, distinguishing between virtues proper to the human person as a citizen of an earthly city, and virtues proper to the human person as a citizen of the heavenly Jerusalem). However, when we turn to Aquinas's systematic treatment of the virtues in the *Summa theologiae*, he seems to have dropped the category of the political or civic virtues (apart from a brief discussion at I-II:61.5), and with it, the link between this-worldly virtues and the common good. In the first place, Aquinas gives more attention than most other scholastics to the intellectual virtues, most of which have no direct moral or theological significance at all (I-II:57). More to the point (for our present purposes), when we turn to Aquinas's analysis of the virtues directly relevant to the moral life and salvation, we find that it is significantly more complex than that of his interlocutors. Aquinas presents us with not one, but two fundamental divisions between classes of virtues.

On the one hand, he distinguishes between the theological virtues of faith, hope, and charity, which have God as their immediate object, and the cardinal virtues of prudence, justice, temperance, and fortitude, which are directed toward various kinds of finite objects (I-II:61–62). On the other hand, he distinguishes between the infused virtues, which are the operative principles of grace, and are therefore bestowed on us directly by God, and the acquired virtues, which (as the name suggests) can be acquired by the human person through her own efforts (I-II:63). Moreover, these distinctions do not neatly map onto one another; the theological virtues are always infused, but the cardinal virtues may be either infused (they are all bestowed together with charity) or acquired (I-II:63.3–4). The acquired cardinal virtues are directed toward a form of happiness that is connatural to us as creatures of a specific kind. The infused cardinal virtues are directed, through charity, to the supreme happiness of direct union with God. Precisely for that reason, the acquired virtues are specifically different— different in kind from their infused counterparts (ibid.).

Thus far it might appear that Aquinas has simply dropped the link between the virtues and the common good. Yet on closer examination, we see that this is not quite true. There is a kind of virtue that is directed toward the common good, legal justice—so called because "it pertains to the law to govern in accordance with the common good" (II-II:58.5; cf. II-II:58.6). Understood in this sense, justice is said to be a general virtue because it directs the acts of the other virtues to its own object, the common good, which transcends the good of the individual toward which the other particular virtues are directed (I-II:60.3, II-II:58.5–6). In other words, justice understood in this sense is architectonic with respect to the other moral virtues, in somewhat the same way, as we learn further on, that charity is architectonic with respect to all the virtues (II-II:23.8). At the same time, legal justice is not essentially equivalent to the other virtues (even though it is also known as general justice), and it is therefore considered to be a particular virtue (II-II:58.6).

Throughout the *Summa theologiae* Aquinas's approach is to clarify and simplify the issues informing current theological speculation. Why, then, does he introduce complexity into his theory of virtue, replacing the straightforward division between political and theological virtues with a more complex twofold division? Although it would take us too far afield to attempt to answer this question completely, one part of the answer is directly relevant to the task at hand. Aquinas's more complex analysis of the virtues appears to have commended itself to him, in part at least, because it allows him to incorporate both individual and communal goods into the objects of the virtues. And this point, in turn, is relevant to the often-discussed question of whether Aquinas's analysis of the common good completely subsumes the individual good into the common good.

We have already recognized that both Aquinas himself and his interlocutors understand the common good as in contrast to the private good of individuals. So long as this motif is used to make specific points about the legitimacy of law and the scope of political authority, such a distinction between common and individual good is adequate. However, as a basis for a comprehensive theory of virtue, it seems to be overly simple. If all nontheological virtues are oriented toward the common good, what place is left for the pursuit of private and individual goods through such virtues? The very idea of the common good would suggest that individual goods of all sorts are to be subsumed under the common good, or at most are to be pursued only to the extent that they can be seen to contribute to the common good. At some points, this is exactly what Aquinas seems to say (most strikingly, at I:60.5; see also II-II:47.10). However, when we take account of his wider theory of virtue, it becomes apparent that his overall position is more complex.

When we examine his theory of virtue more closely, we see that one of the things that Aquinas's more complex analysis provides him is a space for virtues that are focused directly on private and individual goods. First and most fundamentally, the virtues of temperance and fortitude, which shape and direct the desiring and irascible passions respectively, are immediately directed toward the good of the individual and take their nominative content by reference to her overall good (I-II:60.2; 64.2; II-II:58.9–10). Second, Aquinas distinguishes between prudence simply so called, which is directed to the private good of the individual, and political prudence, which is directed toward the common good and is therefore a specifically different virtue (II-II:47.10–11). He goes on to introduce a further distinction, between regnative prudence, exercised by someone who has authority over a perfect (a complete and self-sufficient) community, and political prudence, the virtue proper to subjects considered as such, which they exercise in carrying out the directives of the ruler (II-II:50.1–2).

In this context Aquinas underscores the point that the political prudence exercised by individuals as subjects of political authority is specifically different from the form of prudence they exercise as individuals. This is true precisely because the former is directed to the common good while the latter is directed to their own private good (II-II:50.2 ad 3). As we would expect, regnative and political prudence is closely connected to justice, which (as we have seen) is linked to the common good (II-II:50.1 ad 1). In addition, Aquinas identifies a form of justice distinct from legal justice: particular justice, which rectifies our relations with other individuals and is thus directed toward individual goods other than the agent's own private good (II-II:58.8). Since particular justice concerns the person's relationships to other individuals, its actions are directed toward the common good by legal justice, in the same way as are the actions of the other particular moral virtues (II-II:58.5).

While these distinctions reflect the importance that Aquinas gives to the common good, they also suggest that for him the good of the individual cannot simply be subsumed under the common good. It is true that the agent's own private good, to which temperance and fortitude are immediately directed, is referred to the common good through legal justice (ibid.). While we can imagine conflicts between private and common good, these are forestalled, on Aquinas's view, by the fact that the individual's own private good depends on the common good in at least two ways. First, the individual depends on the community for the necessities of life. Second, since the individual can be considered as a part of a whole, she cannot attain her own good in that respect unless she stands in right relation to the whole (II-II:47.10). So far, Aquinas's analysis appears to be consistent with the view that the good of the individual is wholly subsumed in the common good. Yet if so, why does he develop a theory of virtue that is distinguished, in part, by the scope for private goods that it allows? This aspect of his analysis at least suggests that he recognizes that individual goods do have independent value.

When we examine what Aquinas says about the relation between legal justice and the other moral virtues, we see that he does indeed spell this relationship out in terms that preserve the distinctiveness and individual value of one's private, individual goods. As we observed above, legal justice is architectonic with respect to the other moral virtues: it directs their acts to its own proper object, the common good (II-II:58.6). This is possible precisely because the good of the individual can be considered to be part of the common good (I-II:60.3 ad 2). Suppose an individual acts out of temperance or fortitude in pursuit of her own private good, or aims at the good of some other individual through particular justice. Her action thus is ipso facto directed to the common good, precisely because the latter includes the good of every individual in the community (II-II:58.5). This does not mean that the act in question ceases to be an act of temperance, fortitude, or particular justice, with an immediate orientation to some private good (the agent's, or another's). The act retains its character as an expression of the particular virtue that elicits it, while at the same time it is referred to the common good through legal justice (II-II:58.6; cf. II-II:32.1 ad 2). By the same token, Aquinas observes that even though justice is the paradigmatic virtue of external operations, through which we are related to other persons, that does not mean that every exterior operation is an act of particular justice (which, as recognized above, governs the agent's relations to other individuals). This is true because the other moral virtues are sufficient to rectify the exterior actions that concern the individual herself alone (II-II:58.2 ad 4).

This leaves a great deal of room for the pursuit of purely personal goods, since someone who pursues her own genuine good is promoting the common good by that very fact. It would be easy to misunderstand Aquinas at this point. His idea of what it means to pursue one's own genuine good is quite different from modern notions of pursuing one's self-interest, one's desires, or one's economic well-being. Aquinas is not Adam Smith. But then, neither is he an advocate of a totalitarian regime, which subsumes every individual interest and desire in the community. His theory of virtue presupposes that men and women will naturally and legitimately pursue many things simply because these promote their own individual well-being. A man who temperately declines a third piece of pie for the sake of his own health and equanimity is not acting out of particular justice at all. His act is an act of legal justice only insofar as he is promoting the common good by preserving his own well-being.

The mention of particular justice brings us to a further point. Aquinas does not just distinguish the common good from the agent's own private good; he also draws a contrast between common good and the individual goods of other persons. Such a contrast is significant because even though the agent may go to great lengths to sacrifice himself for the common good, he must not sacrifice other people in the same way. This brings us back to the conclusion of the last section, where we observed that Aquinas places clear and explicit limits on the degree to which individuals may be sacrificed in pursuit of the common good. Even earlier, we recognized that even a putative law genuinely directed toward the common good is unjust and therefore invalid as a law if it places inequitable burdens on individuals. We might wish for a more extended account of what counts as an equitable division of social burdens, but at least Aquinas recognizes that individual claims to equity and fair treatment set constraints on what can be done in pursuit of the common good.

Aquinas's qualifications to the common good are significant because they indicate that the relation of dependence between individual and common good does not run in one direction only. While it is true that individual good is dependent in some way on the common good, we also see that the common good is dependent in some ways on the goods of individuals. When Aquinas says that just persons are the principal part of society, he does not mean that they are numerically superior. He means that the well-being of upright citizens is the raison d'être of a community, in such a way that a community that attacks its own citizens has undermined its own common good. More generally, the requirements that the common good be pursued in accordance with the demands of equity and justice implies that the well-being of a community is constituted, in part, by the boundaries of justice. These boundaries include fundamental norms of respect for individual well-being. Such limits, in turn, suggest that even seen from the perspective of a private person, individual good is not wholly subsumed in, or by implication subordinate to, the common good.

Reading on, we find that Aquinas does indeed qualify the supremacy of the common good in this way. The context occurs in a discussion of the excellence of virginity. Aquinas is referring to the objection that marriage, which promotes the common good, is thereby preferable to virginity, which promotes the particular good of an individual. He replies that "the common good is greater than a private good if both are of the same kind; but a private good is greater if it is better in accordance with its kind. And in this way, virginity is said to be preferred by God to carnal goods" (II-II:152.4 ad 3). This text, in turn, points us to the most significant way in which the good of the individual is not just subsumed in the common good. That is, the individual is ultimately called to a good that transcends the good of the community: union with God in the beatific vision. Of course, this means that the community cannot legitimately ask the individual to do anything that would be contrary to God's decrees (cf. II-II:104.5). But it also implies that the spiritual life of the human person falls outside the scope of the common good, and for this reason, spiritual goods can be pursued apart from the common good.

Yet at this point it might seem that we have simply reintroduced the idea of the common good at a higher level. For is it not the case that Aquinas also speaks of God as a common good, as noted above? This line of analysis seems to be reinforced by the analogy noted above between the common good, seen as the object of legal justice, and the supreme good of union with God, which is the object of charity. Yet these parallels need to be treated with caution.

We oversimplify Aquinas's view if we assume that the common good stands in the same relation to the cardinal virtues as the good of union with God stands to the theological virtues. In one sense, this is indeed a valid analogy, but the relation between the common good and the virtues is more complex than might be suggested by this point alone. In order to determine how far we can press this analogy, we need to ask how far the common good is comparable to the good of union with God, toward which we are directed by charity.

The good of union with God in the beatific vision is the supreme good that the human person—or indeed, any rational or intellectual creature—can obtain (I:12.4–5; I-II:109). It represents the greatest possible development of the powers of the human soul and fulfills every human desire and aspiration in a superlative way (I-II:3.8; *Summa contra gentiles* III:63). Because charity is directed immediately toward this mode of attaining God, it is the greatest virtue without qualification and directs all the acts of all the other virtues to its own proper end (II-II:23.8). The good toward which we are directed by charity is a common good in one sense; it is a good that can be enjoyed by an indefinite number of persons, without being in any way diminished. However, there is nothing intrinsically common, in the sense of communal, about the individual's enjoyment of the beatific vision. Because the happiness of the beatific vision is a complete good, to which nothing can be added, it is not intrinsically increased by being shared with companions, even though this fellowship increases the well-being of happiness (I-II:4.8).

These considerations rule out any simple parallel between the political common good and the supreme good of union with God. The political common good is not a particularly divinized form of temporal good, nor does it provide a special mode of access to union with God. Because the common good is the object of the virtue of justice, its pursuit can provide a framework within which to exercise the theological virtue of charity; but the same can be said for every object of a genuine virtue.

There is one respect, however, in which the parallel between legal justice and charity is particularly illuminating. Both virtues are only possible because the orientation of the will, which is the subject of both virtues, is naturally directed toward good in general (I-II:56.6). This is why the will can direct itself toward goods that transcend the individual, whether on a purely natural plane (the common good) or a supernatural plane (with God, considered as the object of a desire for personal union). For this reason, the sense that the common good has a special theological significance does not lack all grounding in Aquinas's thought. Because the common good engages the will in somewhat the same way as does God, considered as the object of charity, the former can be considered as an intimation or symbol of the latter. Even to say this much, however, takes us beyond what Aquinas explicitly says, to a consideration of the way in which we might appropriate his thought today. We now turn to that subject.

The Contemporary Significance of the Common Good

Any effort to draw out the contemporary relevance of Aquinas's account of the common good must take account of both negative and positive considerations. On the negative side, Aquinas offers us little in the way of a substantive account of what the common good is, or what the conditions for its attainment must be. Even the minimal definition offered by *Gaudium et spes*—"the sum of those conditions of social life which allow social groups and their individual members relatively thorough and ready access to their own fulfillment"—goes well beyond anything Aquinas says, and is indeed arguably not consistent with what he does say. At most, Aquinas tells us that the common good implies a respect for constraints of justice and equity, which are partially constitutive of the common good, and which therefore cannot be violated without destroying the actual common good that they are meant to secure. These are important conditions, to be sure, but they do not amount to a morally substantive theory of the common good.

And as we have seen, neither Aquinas nor his contemporaries has any interest in developing a comprehensive moral theory of the good society under the rubric of the common good. The scholastics do offer more substantive accounts of the good society, but these draw on a wide range of motifs and concepts, which are integrated in accordance with the overall aims and theoretical commitments of each author. When they appeal to the common good, or common well-being or utility, their aims are more focused. They appeal to the common good in order to draw a distinction between private or individual good on one hand, and the common good on the other, with an aim to setting forth the kinds of things that may morally be done in pursuit of the latter.

In Aquinas himself, as we have already noted, the idea of the common good is always linked to public authority in some way. This idea plays a central role in his theory of law, and he also uses it to justify courses of action on the part of public authorities that would be ruled out for private individuals. This does not mean that private individuals cannot act in such a way as to promote the common good, on his view; on the contrary, his analysis of the virtues presupposes that they can and do. But individual action on behalf of the common good is almost always tied to the activities of public authority in some way. This may be by way of contrast, as when Aquinas compares what private individuals can do in this regard with what public authorities can do (II-II:64.3 ad 3). Or it may be by way of dependence, insofar as legal justice and political prudence depend on conformity to the rule of law and the directives of public authorities (as we have seen above). He spells out the connection between common good and political authority explicitly:

> All things which belong to the moral virtues pertain to prudence, as to a director; hence it is that the right reason of prudence is contained within the definition of moral virtue, as was said above. And therefore also the execution of justice, since it is ordained to the common good, which pertains to the office of the king, needs the direction of prudence. Hence these two virtues, that is to say, prudence and justice, are most proper to the king. (II-II:50.1 ad 1)

We may be tempted to disregard these and similar texts as reflections of Aquinas's own political situation (even though he goes on to say that his analysis of regnative prudence would apply to any kind of morally legitimate rule; II-II:50.1 ad 2). Yet I suggest that it is precisely this aspect of Aquinas's account of the common good, the close connection he makes between the common good and political authority, that is most relevant to our own time. As we have already recognized, Aquinas wrote at a time when the existence of an effective, centralized public authority, executed (to a large degree) through an impersonal bureaucracy rather than through relations of personal dominion and loyalty, was still a new and fragile achievement. The language of the common good offered him one way to address these new social realities, more positive and also more flexible than the language of dominion and servitude that we find in Bonaventure.

At this point we find a relevant similarity between Aquinas's situation and our own. In the thirteenth century, centralized public authority was a new and fragile achievement. In the early twenty-first century, it is fragile again, not because it is new, but because of the tremendous centrifugal forces generated by the world economy and new technologies of communication and transportation. The strains on the modern nation-state system introduced by the forces of globalization are an old story by now, and the recent terrorist attacks on the United States have thrown the vulnerability of even the most powerful nations into sharp relief. Most significantly of all, the recent adoption of imperial policies by the United States government represents the most radical challenge to the nation-state system of international relations that we have seen since the Second World War. Even though on its face this policy may seem to represent an assertion of national power, it should be seen rather as a subversion of the critical principle of national sovereignty.

At the same time, all these forces have developed in tandem with a growing tendency among intellectuals of all stripes to denigrate the nation-state system. Many intellectuals argue that public functions should be assumed, as far as possible, by either small face-to-face communities or large-scale market forces, or perhaps both. Over the past thirty years, Christian theology, at least in the English-speaking world, has reflected this general tendency to denigrate public authority, particularly as linked to the nation-state. At its best, this tendency reflects deep and serious elements of the Christian tradition, including an abhorrence to violence and dominion in all its forms. Yet it is surely no accident that these elements of the Christian tradition have been given particular salience by the more general antigovernment orientation of the wider culture. Other elements of the Christian tradition could offer us a more positive assessment of government and political authority, and it may well be that the time has come to retrieve them.

Within this context the scholastic deployment of the idea of the common good may carry a lesson for Christian theology. As we have seen, this idea was centrally linked to emerging institutions of public authority, which it served to legitimate. This applies as much to Aquinas's use of the idea as to that of his interlocutors. Aquinas further develops it in such a way as to link the justification of public authority with some account of its scope and limits. This connection, in turn, implies that the idea of the common good is fundamentally a political idea for Aquinas and his interlocutors, which is not to deny that it is also a moral norm. More specifically, the idea of the common good developed in a context in which new forms of centralized public authority were beginning to replace older and more localized forms. The idea reflects attempts both to justify emergent public authority and to delineate the proper forms of its exercise.[18] This study further implies that the idea of the common good developed in tandem with the emergence of the modern state, which was not at the time the only form of centralized authority. But it was beginning to emerge at this point and rapidly became the dominant form of public authority.[19]

---

18. Elsewhere in this volume, William Cavanaugh argues that the modern state, and more especially the nation-state as we know it today, has been closely tied to the rise of politically sanctioned forms of violence. It is not so clear, however, that the emergence of the nation-state led to an increase in violence across the board. Almost eighty years ago, the sociologist Norbert Elias argued that the emergence of centralized authority in the later Middle Ages was one part of a far-reaching transformation in attitudes and mores, which had the overall effect of reducing private violence even as it led to the formation of warlike regimes. More recently, historians have begun to apply statistical analysis to court records and other similar documents from the medieval and modern periods, and the results of these theories seem generally to confirm Elias's thesis. More specifically, it appears that murder was much more common in Europe in the medieval period than now, and that murder rates dropped sharply beginning in the seventeenth century—about the same time as the modern nation-state system was becoming entrenched. Of course, this work is still controversial. Nonetheless, it suggests that empirical assessments of the effects of the nation-state system are difficult, and their results should be treated with caution. See Norbert Elias, *The Civilizing Process* (trans. Edmund Jephcott; rev. ed.; Oxford: Blackwell, 1994); original, *Über den Prozess der Zivilisation*, 2 vols. (Basel: Haus zum Falken, 1939). The subsequent research and reassessments mentioned are described in "Did Knives and Forks Cut Murders?" *New York Times*, May 3, 2003, A21, 23.

19. Of course, things need not have turned out in this way; that is the point of Spruyt in *The Sovereign State*. But even if public authority had taken some other

In calling attention to this connection, I do not mean to imply that the common good considered as a moral and political norm can only be applied in contexts of national policy. Yet I do think that this norm is most naturally and properly employed in broadly political contexts.[20] Furthermore, I hope it goes without saying that this approach to the common good does not at all imply that Christians should cede their moral judgments on political matters to whomever happens to be in power at a given time. At least in a democracy, the ideal of the common good would have just the opposite force. It would require all citizens to exercise the most conscientious vigilance over the policies and actions of their elected governmental officials.

At the same time, the close historical connection between the idea of the common good and the emergence of state power does at least suggest both a justification for the nation-state as it currently exists, and a set of criteria for evaluating specific nations and their policies. The key to the moral ideal represented by the idea of the common good, I propose, is its positive valuation of public authority as the guarantor of the rule of law. For all its limitations, the nation-state remains the most effective form of large-scale public authority. In particular, the principle of national sovereignty is one of the foundations for the formal and tacit structures of international law structuring relations among nations and peoples. For this reason the nation-state system still has a central role to play in securing constitutive ideals of the common good: the rule of law, and correlatively civic order and justice, on an international scale.

Of course, these observations do not imply that specific nation-states always act in accordance with the common good. Nor does it mean that the nation-state is the only form of public authority that promotes the common good, or that public authority will take this form in the indefinite future. Nonetheless, so long as the nation-state remains the most effective form of public authority, it will continue to be the most important (actual or potential) agent for promoting the common good, regionally and even globally. A commitment to the common good certainly does not require us to support the actual policies of our own or any other particular nation. Yet I would argue that (in general) it does require us to support the nation-state system and the principle of national sovereignty on which that system depends—at least, until we are sure that we have a practical, effective, and morally superior alternative to put in its place.[21]

---

institutional form—and even if it does so in the future, as it almost certainly will—the terms of Aquinas's analysis suggest that the common good will continue to be the special concern, and therefore also a criterion for evaluation, for public authority, whatever form it may take.

20. On this point I agree with James Skillen (in this volume).

21. Two qualifications are in order here. First, I endorse respect for national sovereignty as a general policy but not an absolute rule, even though I think current circumstances call for more emphasis on the policy than on its qualifications. Second, it may well be that practical and effective alternatives to the nation-state system are already at hand. If these can preserve order and justice among peoples better than

At any rate, the motif of the common good as developed by Aquinas and his interlocutors offers us a starting point for reflecting on the positive justification for public authority and the scope and limits suggested by that justification. This presupposes that public authority does have a positive and indeed indispensable role to play in promoting the common good, even in our globalized, market-driven, empowered, and threatened society. It would take a separate study adequately to argue this point. All the same, it should be clear by now that I follow Aquinas in affirming that public authority is not only a practical necessity, but also a worthy human institution, which takes its moral value from its orientation to the common good. It is not necessary to fall into the earlier mistake of elevating this common good into a quasi-divine reality, an exemplary paradigm for God's goodness, and a distinctive medium for salvific grace. In the view of Aquinas and his interlocutors, the common good is none of these things. Nonetheless, it is a worthy form of human goodness, the legitimate object of specific virtues, and therefore also an appropriate object of charity. This last point, in turn, reminds us that the ultimate significance of the common good for the Christian is bestowed through the orientation of charity. Christian charity is concerned with all aspects of human well-being because they are all of concern to the neighbor, whom we are commanded to love (II-II:59.4).

---

the current system, certainly we should endorse them. For a persuasive argument that this is indeed the case, see Jonathan Schell's two-piece article, "No More unto the Breach," *Harper's Magazine*, March 2003, 33–46; April 2003, 41–55. However, U.S. imperialism is not, in my view, plausible as such an alternative.

The Common Good in Catholic Social Teaching

A Case Study in Modernization

Dennis P. McCann

What does modern Catholic Social Teaching (CST) mean by "the common good"? This question needs to be asked because what CST means is not necessarily identical with the meanings represented in this term by medieval theologians like St. Thomas Aquinas or his later disciples in the history of Scholasticism and neo-Scholasticism. To ask what CST means by it requires, first of all, a clarification of what CST is. For purposes of this essay, CST is the body of official church teaching on political, economic, and social questions that has been regarded as an identifiable tradition since the papacy of Pope Leo XIII (1878–1903). Besides the so-called "social encyclicals" issued by Leo and his successors up through Pope John Paul II, the tradition also includes the major statements issued by various national and regional episcopal conferences. Examples are the pastoral letters of the National Conference of Catholic Bishops (NCCB) in the USA, and the documents of Vatican II (1962–65) that focus primarily on political, economic, and social questions. Numerous books and articles interpreting CST have been written by Catholic theologians and ethicists as well as by other scholars.[1] But given the limitations of space for this chapter, I restrict my analysis to formal statements of official church teaching.

Preliminary inquiries seeking to answer the question of what CST means by "the common good" yield an abundance of specific references, but only rarely do any of these approach definition. As Jean Porter has already pointed out (see page

---

1. A recent search on Amazon.com asking for books on CST, for example, yielded 29,841 entries.

94–95, Vatican II's Pastoral Constitution in the Modern World, Gaudium et Spes (1966) gives what appears to be an essential definition. The common good is to be understood as "the sum of those conditions of social life which allow social groups and their individual members relatively thorough and ready access to their own fulfillment." But this ostensibly essential definition is presented in a more or less casual aside. Paragraph 26 is part of a larger chapter, "The Community of Mankind," purporting to discern the ultimate significance of certain "signs of the times." In this case the "sign" is the fact of social interdependence and the aspiration toward global solidarity carried within it. A footnote attached to this passage refers the reader to Pope John XXIII's encyclical letter Mater et magistra (1961). There one may find not another definition, but—within a discussion of the responsibilities of public authorities—similar language linking the common good to "all those social conditions which favor the full development of human personality" (par. 65).

The lack of a tight conceptual definition of the common good does not warrant the conclusion that it is marginal to CST. The contrary impression of the common good's importance seems generally taken for granted in CST. It is explicitly reasserted by the NCCB's pastoral letter, *Economic Justice for All* (*EJA*, 1986). Here the NCCB recalls the words of Pope Pius XI, in his encyclical condemning atheistic Communism, *Divini redemptoris* (*DR*, 1937): "It is of the very essence of social justice to demand from each individual all that is necessary for the common good" (*EJA*, par. 71; *DR*, par. 51). Of course, this statement also requires further qualification, for the very same pope in *Quadragesimo anno* (1931) also memorably formulated CST's principle of "subsidiarity" (pars. 79–80). This principle set certain moral and structural limits to government intervention in the affairs of civil society, and thus galvanized Catholic resistance to totalitarianism and other extreme forms of statism. Presumably, the demands made upon "each individual" also have their moral and structural limits, especially when it is the state that is making the demands on behalf of the common good.

A preliminary inquiry into what the common good means for CST thus yields the impression that the common good is both very important, a core value indeed for this tradition, and yet resistant to tight conceptual definition. Even so, if CST is understood as a form of "critical reflection on religious [Christian social] praxis"[2] and not as a deductive system of applied moral logic, this finding would not be surprising. The current essay thus is meant not to tidy up the embarrassingly fuzzy concept of the common good, but to explore the patterns of its actual usage in representative documents of CST. The study will proceed by offering a plausible reconstruction of CST, understood as a tradition first becoming aware

---

2. Cf. Dennis P. McCann and Charles R. Strain, *Polity and Praxis: A Program for American Practical Theology* (Minneapolis: Seabury, 1985). In that work, Strain and I sought to define the genre of practical theology. A body of Christian social thought such as CST purports to be is most fruitfully analyzed within the conventions and assumptions governing practical theology generically.

of itself and later progressively adapting itself to the challenges presented by societal modernization.

Within that perspective on CST, I hope to show that the common good functions as a token of protest against certain symptoms of modernization and also as an endorsement of certain other possibilities emergent in modernization itself. In either case, whether as protest or as prayerful hope, CST's invocations of the common good call for critical engagement with modernization. This modernization is itself tacitly understood as a process whose origins, development, and inner logic, perceived as alien to the tradition, must elicit a response as if to an external stimulus. Such a perspective, I hope, will allow for a more realistic assessment of common good discourse in CST and what, if any, transformative possibilities—imperatives and virtues, as well as basic moral vision—it may yet contribute to our own search for a common good.

Use of the Term "the Common Good"

It may be useful to begin this inquiry with some statistics on the use of the term "the common good" in the major documents of CST. I subjected electronic copies of these documents to analysis by a standard word-processing program, discovered the specific citations of "the common good," and counted the number of times (No.) it is used in each document, arranged in order of publication:

No.	Document	Year
3	Leo XIII's *Libertas*	1888
7	Leo XIII's *Rerum novarum*	1891
3	U.S. Bishops' *Program of Social Reconstruction*	1919
16	Pius XI's *Quadragesimo anno*	1931
20	John XXIII's *Mater et magistra*	1961
47	John XXIII's *Pacem in terris*	1963
28	Vatican II's *Gaudium et spes*	1965
6	Paul VI's *Populorum progressio*	1967
8	Paul VI's *Octagesima adveniens*	1971
7	John Paul II's *Laborem exercens*	1981
34	NCCB's pastoral letter *Economic Justice for All*	1986
11	John Paul II's *Sollicitudo rei socialis*	1987
16	John Paul II's *Centesimus annus*	1991
12	John Paul II's *Evangelium vitae*	1995

In trying to evaluate the possible significance of these statistics, I determined that the frequency of use did not correlate with the overall size of the document. Thus, for example, although *Rerum novarum* refers to the common good 7 times, as compared to 28 citations of the term in *Gaudium et spes*, the latter at 36,668 words is not 4 times the size of the former at 14,465 words. Similarly, in the one document in CST that features the common good as its central theme, the 1996 statement of the Catholic bishops of the United Kingdom, *The Common Good and Catholic Social Teaching*, the term is used 104 times. Yet this text is no more than 10 percent larger than *Populorum progressio*, in which the term appears 6 times. Likewise, there are virtually no explicit references to the common good in other major documents that are pivotal for the church's contemporary self-understanding but not directly related to conventional questions of social justice. *Lumen gentium* (1965), Vatican II's *Dogmatic Constitution on the Church*, for example, contains not a single reference to the common good. Even more telling is the fact that there is but one citation in *Dignitatis humanae* (1965), Vatican II's epoch-making *Declaration on Religious Freedom*.

Though the common good appears frequently in the social encyclicals of John Paul II, it is extremely rare in his major statements on moral theology and theological method. There is only one citation to be found, for example, in *Veritatis splendor* (1993), and none whatsoever in *Fides et ratio* (1998). Yet both documents are invaluable for understanding the claims made for any theme in CST, including the common good, and some prior understanding of the common good is implicit in their teachings.

Thus it seems that references to the common good are neither random nor evenly distributed throughout the tradition of CST. The rest of this essay is an attempt to explain the meaning of their uses, within a general hypothesis about the impact of modernization on Roman Catholicism.

Modernization and the Development of Catholic Social Teaching

It may not have been the intention of the Protestant reformers to preside over the birth and development of modernization.[3] Yet arguably that was one major result of their attempt to rethink the underlying spirituality of the Christian life and

---

3. The view of modernization and its relationship to CST, particularly the periodization of phases in CST's response to modernization, is entirely my own; nevertheless, it has been influenced significantly by a reading of the following historical and interpretive sources: E. E. Y. Hales, *The Catholic Church in the Modern World: A Survey from the French Revolution to the Present* (Garden City, NY: Doubleday Image Books, 1960); Thomas Bokenkotter, *A Concise History of the Catholic Church* (rev. and expanded ed.; New York: Doubleday Image Books, 1990); Langdon B. Gilkey, *Catholicism Confronts Modernity* (New York: Seabury, 1975); Ernst Troeltsch, *Protestantism and Progress: A Historical Study of the Relation of Protestantism to the Modern World* (Boston: Beacon, 1958); Max Weber, *The Protestant Ethic and the Spirit of Capitalism* (Routledge Classics; 2d ed.; New York: Routledge, 2001); Jürgen Habermas, *The Theory of Communicative Action*, vol. 1, *Reason and the Rationalization of Society*, and vol. 2, *Lifeworld and System: A Critique of Functionalist Rationality* (trans. Thomas McCarthy; Boston: Beacon, 1984–87).

reform its practices, on a personal, ecclesial, and social level. The social consequences of the Calvinist reform took at least two centuries to incubate in the hos-
pitable environment of northwest Europe, particularly in Scotland, England, and
the Netherlands. Once the pattern was established there, it spread rapidly in an
eastern and southerly direction, even into territories that had remained at least
officially loyal to Roman Catholicism. The first such development occurred in
France, the so-called "eldest daughter of the Roman church." The political failure
of the Reformation in France meant that the French Enlightenment and
Revolution, the chief bearers of the ideology and politics of modernization, were
significantly more violent and anticlerical than they had been in the Protestant
countries to the north. At this stage, the Catholic church experienced modernization mainly as an external threat, still to be dealt with militarily and politically.
The alliance of throne and altar that had characterized Christendom since late
antiquity was soon disrupted by the Revolution and its aftermath in the imperial
adventures of Napoleon. Once "the grand alliance" defeated Napoleon (1815), the
"*ancien régime*" was restored, the Bourbon dynasty returned to Paris, and the pope
was once again established in Rome as ruler of the Papal States. The Restoration,
however, proved to be short-lived, and from 1830 onward the pressures toward
modernization were now experienced within Catholicism as an internal challenge.

Though modernization, from the perspective of the church's increasingly centralized administration in Rome, may thus be regarded as a form of colonization,
the colonization was at least partially successful, and to that extent a real cause for
alarm. Now the pope and his supporters had to deal with educated Catholics, particularly in France, who were adopting and adapting various parts of the program
for modernization. Their efforts first become visible historically in the development of a movement toward a Liberal Catholicism that supported dismantling
the alliance of throne and altar, reforming the church in the direction of democratic accountability, and recognizing religious liberty, or freedom of conscience,
as a universal human right. Such Liberal Catholics—laymen like Frederic
Ozanam and Count Montalembert, priests like Lammenais and Lacordaire, and
bishops like Doupanloup—met with stiff resistance. Yet generally they struggled
to retain good standing in the Catholic church, even as they attempted to reform
it. They have served as role models for reform-minded Catholics ever since.

One of the most intriguing forms of resistance to modernization within
Roman Catholicism is the rise of the modern papacy. The pope's prestige in
Europe had probably reached its lowest ebb in 1804, when Napoleon snatched
the imperial crown from the hands of his prisoner, Pope Pius VII, and placed it
on his own head. Once Napoleon had been disposed of, his enemies were out to
reverse that shameful usurpation. Ultramontanism is the resulting movement that
meant to anchor its hopes for a restoration of Europe's traditional order "across
the mountains," meaning across the Alps, in a newly clarified and strengthened
papal authority. Once again (or perhaps really for the first time) the pope would
become "the arbiter of Europe." The Catholic church would be the bulwark of
Christian orthodoxy against the spiritually and morally destructive tendencies
identified with the French Revolution.

Ironically, the eventual success of some of the Ultramontanist hopes was occasioned by the final collapse of the Papal States in 1870. In that year, not coincidentally, an assembly of bishops—which the Catholic church includes among the twenty-one "ecumenical councils" that it regards as authoritative in defining matters of faith and morals—met in Rome to solemnly define "papal infallibility." This doctrinal innovation was the claim that the pope could not make an error when teaching anything of significance in the areas of faith and morals. It provided an automatic warrant of certainty for the pope's solemn theological declarations, giving them a finality that Catholics were to accept as a condition for membership in the church. Of course, there was much skepticism about papal infallibility, especially among Liberal Catholics. But the effect of the declaration was to shore up the pope's spiritual authority over all Catholics worldwide, and thus secondarily to secure the Vatican's claim to a privileged role in shaping their social and cultural values. Nevertheless, even armed with the certification of papal infallibility, with the collapse of the Papal States the pope became "the prisoner of the Vatican." For most of the remainder of the nineteenth century, the church entered a period of self-imposed exile from European social and political affairs.

Understood as Roman Catholicism's primary mode of response to modernization, the development of CST must be seen in this historical context. Summarized schematically, there are three or possibly four phases marking the ways in which the church's central authority (the Vatican) has responded to modernization: (1) Resistance (1830–1907), (2) Critical Engagement (1891–1958), (3) Accommodation (1958–78), and then (4) Consolidation in the reign of the current Pope John Paul II, which combines elements of all three (1978–). Within this general perspective, my thesis here is that the range of meanings expressed by "the common good" are best understood, not in essentialist terms as a logical explication of what is already implicit in the concept, but in pragmatic terms. These meanings are important markers for mapping CST's own role in the church's struggle over modernization.

First I sketch the four phases before exploring more fully the meaning of "the common good" as used in the documents of each period.

Resistance (1830–1907)

This first phase begins with the emergence of the Liberal Catholic movement in France and its condemnation by Pope Gregory XVI in the encyclical letter *Mirari vos* (1832). Later the resistance is reinforced and laid out comprehensively in Pope Pius IX's *Syllabus of Errors* (1864). It is given an impressive philosophical rationale in Pope Leo XIII's encyclical *Libertas* (1888) and then specifically applied to resurgent forms of Liberal Catholicism in Pope Leo XIII's condemnation of "Americanism" in *Testem benevolentiae* (1899). The ideology of papal resistance culminates in Pope Pius X's condemnation of "Modernism" as such in *Pascendi* (1907).

Critical Engagement (1891–1958)

This second phase begins with the memorable social encyclical of Pope Leo XIII, *Rerum novarum* (1891), which defends the basic human dignity and rights of workers against the harm to which they are exposed by those who would exploit them for their own purposes. Specifically, *Rerum novarum* condemns both laissez-faire or Manchester-style capitalism and Marxist socialism; it links their errors in social analysis to their atheistic presuppositions. Though both capitalism and communism are thus condemned as modernist aberrations, this encyclical is seen as initiating the period of Critical Engagement. It moves quickly from abstract doctrinal condemnation to active engagement with the social problems—for example, unemployment, lack of education and economic opportunity—faced by ordinary people caught up in the processes of modernization. *Rerum novarum* sets the tone for the formative period in the development of CST, as seen in the work of Leo's successors, notably Popes Pius XI (1922–39) and Pius XII (1939–58). In this period CST thus confronts many of the social dislocations that modernization brings in its wake and that modernizing ideologies also seek to address. But the solutions that it advocates are typically based on the church's self-understanding of its own distinctive set of cultural values, mostly a distillation from premodern, typically medieval, Scholastic social philosophy. These teachings are still set in formal opposition to cultural values regarded as typically modern.

Accommodation (1958–1978)

The third phase covers the work of the ecumenical council, Vatican II (1962–65), and its immediate aftermath. The period is that marked by the reigns of Popes John XXIII (1958-63) and Paul VI (1963-78), the popes most immediately responsible for the church's shift in its basic posture toward modernization. When compared to certain benchmarks characteristic of the earlier phases, the change is truly breathtaking. Vatican II's *Declaration on Religious Liberty* (*Dignitatis humanae*) effectively reverses the explicit teachings of the *Syllabus of Errors*. Furthermore, the *Pastoral Constitution on the Church in the Modern World* (*Gaudium et spes*), by extending sympathy to the aspirations of modern men and women for freedom, dignity, and equality, effectively though implicitly reversed the teaching of *Libertas*. The warrant for this dramatic change, interestingly enough, is taken from a biblical verse urging the disciples of Christ to discern the meaning of the "signs of the times" (*Gaudium et spes*, par. 4). Vatican II, then, does not mean a capitulation to the forces of modernization, motivated either by exhaustion, internal weakness, or expediency. Instead, it is what John XXIII called "aggiornamento," an updating of the church's thinking about its surroundings that is meant to be as refreshing as opening a window in a stuffy room.

During this phase, CST becomes more closely identified with popular aspirations for the good life as defined in modern terms, and insists that in the onward march of social progress, no one be excluded or written off. Examples of this new

trend abound in *Gaudium et spes*, which not only calls for and models a new attitude of dialogue with atheism and other modernizing ideologies, but also accepts
a more personalistic approach to marriage and family life, at least in principle.
Similarly, *Gaudium et spes*'s understanding of the church's limited role in politics
tacitly accepts the "separation of church and state" that is a core value in one way
or another for all programs of modernization. The CST is to be implemented
through persuasion, in the give and take of public argument in genuinely open
forms of political participation, in collaboration with people and parties not necessarily committed to Catholicism as such. No longer is it to be unilaterally
imposed by governments whose policies are coordinated behind the scenes with
church teaching. In this phase, the focus of CST also shifts away from Europe and
toward a concern for the poor of the so-called Third World. Consistent with this
new focus, the church can be seen expanding its influence especially in international settings such as the United Nations, where it seeks to make common cause
with other international agencies working for social justice and peace.

Consolidation (1978–)

The current phase is the period of consolidation, retrenchment, and rethinking
that has occurred under Pope John Paul II. There is no one name that captures
the ambivalence of the church's posture toward modernization under John Paul
II. Given the pope's personal achievements as a Polish philosopher, it is no surprise that the encyclical letters that he has issued have marked an extraordinary
rise in the quality of philosophical and social analyses offered in CST's diagnosis
of a modernizing world now well launched on the path toward globalization. At
the same time, the depth of the pope's understanding of CST has also reinvigo-
rated the church's resistance to any unthinking accommodation to the intellectual
follies and social disasters that have also marked the processes of modernization.
What comes to the fore, however, are the deep differences between the pope and
some neo-Liberal Catholics, as well as partisans of various forms of Liberation
Theology, on how to interpret "the signs of the times." Under John Paul II the
aspirations of modern men and women have been subjected to more skeptical
criticism. What some would claim as a matter of human right, or as warranted by
their basic human dignity, often is rejected by the pope as morally and spiritually
decadent, inappropriate, or contrary to what he regards as the manifest will of God.
    Thus, the current pope sounds more like the *Syllabus of Errors* (1864) in resist-
ing proposals for democratizing the church's own authority structures. His own
interpretation of the human dignity and rights of women, for example, does not
warrant ordaining women to the priesthood or actively encouraging women to
take up careers outside the home. On the other hand, the pope's statements on
economic justice, such as his encyclical letter *Centesimus annus* (1993), are among
the most forceful and persuasive in the history of CST. These, at the same time,
continue the trend toward accommodation by clarifying the intent of CST toward
existing modern social systems like capitalism and socialism. The intent is not to
offer a full-blown alternative to them, but to hold out a standard of morality by

which to judge the inadequacies of both and to formulate policies of reform in both that promise to advance the common good. *Centesimus annus*, for example, moves beyond the more abstract rhetoric of evenhanded rejection of both capitalism and socialism as modernizing ideologies, and tries to show how CST can identify spiritual and moral resources for reform in either system. The document as a whole offers a program for constructive engagement in the process of globalization. It points out how globalization can be made to benefit all the people of the earth, and condemns those who would use globalization only to benefit themselves.

The legacy of this current period, so massively dominated by the opinions of Pope John Paul II, may indicate that the phases of Catholicism's struggle with modernization are not to be understood in a linear progression. If, as seems clear, some of the energy and animus of the preceding phases of Resistance, Critical Engagement, and Accommodation continue to inform CST in its current phase, then these phases must be understood as overlapping or layered like the stratification of the earth's surface. On any specific question the dynamisms identified with some earlier phase may yet burst forth to the surface and shape the church's current teaching. If this image is valid, then it suggests that the surface of contemporary CST is not likely to be consistent or smooth. What it teaches on one question, such as political and economic rights, may not easily be squared with what it does and does not teach on another question, such as reproductive rights or public policy questions associated with abortion, birth control, genetic engineering, and so on. This, in the end, may be the most obvious sign that modernization is still experienced as a form of colonization within the life-world of Roman Catholicism. For if modernization were as internal to Catholicism as it is to liberal Protestantism, such inconsistencies would be fewer and more easily dealt with. If modernization were simply internal to Catholicism's own development, CST's uses of "the common good" would either seem far less problematic than they often do, or they might have disappeared altogether.

Let us now seek to understand the uses of "the common good" characteristic of each of the four phases of Catholicism's struggle with modernization. Though each phase may be represented by a variety of documents that can and ought to be examined in any definitive study of the common good, for purposes of this essay, the analysis will focus on only one or two documents for each phase.

Phase One: Resistance (1830–1907)

The most memorable symbol of the Catholic Church's resistance to modernization, of course, is *The Syllabus of Errors* (1864) issued by Pope Pius IX. The syllabus culminates in a condemnation of the proposition, number 80, that "the Roman Pontiff can, and ought to, reconcile himself, and come to terms with progress, liberalism and modern civilization." Not surprisingly, "the common good" does not appear in the document, for its point is not to defend CST's alternative vision of our common life, but to identify and condemn heresies that have infected one or another group of Catholics. The overall impression created by the Syllabus is one of impotent rage against an impending doom. Pius IX sees the church, as embodied in his own person and office, as the innocent victim of a vast conspiracy, coordinated by the devotees of "freemasonry" who are out to destroy every last vestige of the post-Napoleonic Restoration, including the Papal States.

Pius IX's successor, Pope Leo XIII, the celebrated author of *Rerum novarum*, shared his predecessors' view of the threat that modernization posed for Catholicism. This is clear from an examination of Leo's less-renowned encyclicals written both before and after *Rerum novarum*. Examples are *Immortale Dei* (*On the Christian Constitution of States*, 1885), *Libertas* (*On the Nature of Human Liberty*, 1888), *Sapientiae Christianae* (*On Christians as Citizens*, 1890), and *Testem benevolentiae* (*Concerning New Opinions, Virtue, Nature and Grace, with Regard to Americanism*, 1899). In all of these Leonine encyclicals, though the idea itself seems to be uniquely relevant, references to "the common good" are infrequent and casual. Nevertheless, in contrast to Pius IX, Pope Leo XIII places resistance to modernization on a different footing. Instead of simply condemning various aspects of modernization, Leo sought to develop a philosophical defense of the church's self-understanding of its mission in society. His argument rests more on "right reason" as well as Scripture, rather than on direct invocations of papal authority. Leo well understood that since papal authority was crucial to the church's social mission, such authority could only be defended successfully by demonstrating its philosophical truth and social relevance.

Judged by the three occurrences of the term in *Libertas*[4] and its seven appearances in *Rerum novarum*, the meaning of "the common good" must be regarded either as more or less self-evident or so obvious to anyone familiar with Catholic social thought as to need no further explanation. Nevertheless, certain patterns are already evident in Leo's usage. *Libertas* first invokes the common good as a justification for Leo's speaking out. Civil society, he says, is threatened by the opinions of those who "imagine these modern liberties, as cankered as they are, to be the greatest glory of the our age, and the very basis of civil life" (par. 2). The liberties falsely claimed include religious freedom, freedom of the press, academic freedom, and so on. *Libertas* throughout implies that the protection of the common good is the basic task of the state. Yet its use of the term is confined to making two declarations. First, the state, "for the sake of the common good, . . . may or even should tolerate evil" so that a "greater good may not be impeded" (par. 33). Second, regardless of what form of government is adopted by a given civil society, "the Church approves of every one devoting his services to the common good, and doing all that he can for the defense, preservation, and prosperity of his country" (par. 44). *Libertas* thus seems to be saying that considerations of the common good are sufficient reason to overcome any temptation of Catholics to withdraw completely from public life when governments either are unwilling or unable to implement CST in its current requirements. This especially includes situations where the state does not secure the privileged status of the Catholic Church as society's supreme moral and spiritual authority.

---

4. The official text of *Libertas* is from the Vatican Web site: http://www.vatican.va/holy_father/leo_xiii/encyclicals/documents/hf_l–xiii_enc_20061888_libertas_en.html.

There is no reason to suppose that *Rerum novarum*[5] (*On Capital and Labor*) does anything but presuppose Leo's earlier teachings about the church's social mission even as it concentrates specifically on questions of economic justice. Indeed, *Rerum novarum* explicitly teaches that "civil society exists for the common good" (par. 51). Considerations of simple justice, however, link the specific question of labor with the common good:

> But although all citizens, without exception, can and ought to contribute to that common good in which individuals share so advantageously to themselves, yet it should not be supposed that all can contribute in the like way and to the same extent. . . . Nevertheless, it is the business of a well-constituted body politic to see to the provision of those material and external helps "the use of which is necessary to virtuous action." Now, for the provision of such commodities, the labor of the working class—the exercise of their skill, and the employment of their strength, in the cultivation of the land, and in the workshops of trade—is especially responsible and quite indispensable. Indeed, their co-operation is in this respect so important that it may be truly said that it is only by the labor of working men that States grow rich. Justice, therefore, demands that the interests of the working classes should be carefully watched over by the administration, so that they who contribute so largely to the advantage of the community may themselves share in the benefits which they create—that being housed, clothed, and bodily fit, they may find their life less hard and more endurable. It follows that whatever shall appear to prove conducive to the well-being of those who work should obtain favorable consideration. There is no fear that solicitude of this kind will be harmful to any interest; on the contrary, it will be to the advantage of all, for it cannot but be good for the commonwealth to shield from misery those on whom it so largely depends for the things that it needs. (par. 34)

Thus the common good, it seems, is not simply a political concept. It also involves economic and social goods chiefly realized through human labor, the individual's contribution to which entitles him or her to a fair share defined in terms of adequate food, clothing, shelter, and the basic requirements of bodily health that make life "less hard and more endurable."

The common good thus immediately raises questions about the just distribution of private property. While *Rerum novarum* urges economic justice, the common good does not thereby permit usurping the property of others, based on mistaken notions of economic equality:

---

5. The official text of *Rerum novarum* is from the Vatican Web site: http://www. vatican.va/holy_father/leo_xiii/encyclicals/documents/hf_l-xiii_enc_15051891_ rerum-novarum_en.html. A hard copy of *Rerum novarum* is also available in O'Brien and Shannon, *Catholic Social Thought*, 12–39. The paragraph numbering system for *Rerum novarum* in O'Brien and Shannon differs from that given in the official Vatican version quoted here.

> Most of all it is essential, where the passion of greed is so strong, to keep
> the populace within the line of duty; for, if all may justly strive to better
> their condition, neither justice nor the common good allows any indi-
> vidual to seize upon that which belongs to another, or, under the futile
> and shallow pretext of equality, to lay violent hands on other people's
> possessions. (par. 38)

The other passages in *Rerum novarum* make clear that the common good thus
presupposes an unequal or—as Aristotle would have it—a proportionate distribution of political, economic, and social goods. This is within an overall vision of a
civil society composed primarily of associations embodying what later will be
termed "solidarity" (par. 51). It also links the common good with a view of the
state that requires the state to observe certain moral limits to its own powers of
intervention, thus anticipating what later will be termed the principle of "subsidiarity" (par. 35).

Rather than providing a systematic clarification of the common good, *Rerum
novarum* uses it to map out the aspects of the question of economic justice that
specifically raise the issue of the legitimacy of private property, the responsibilities
of the state, and the limits the state must observe in the exercise of those responsibilities. Leo XIII, like a statue of the Roman god Janus, thus stands at the
threshold of CST. His writings share the characteristics of the initial phase of
Resistance to modernization, especially in their commitment to a hierarchical and
authoritarian view of civil society in which the church should continue to enjoy
its traditional privileges as the supreme moral authority. Nevertheless, Leo XIII
also provides a reasoned defense of CST and demonstrates its continued relevance
by offering new and innovative applications of key ideas like the common good
to the social evils specifically generated in the processes of modernization.

Phase Two: Critical Engagement (1891–1958)

Pope Pius XI's *Quadragesimo anno*[6] (*On the Reconstruction of the Social Order*, 1931)
seems the most illuminating representative of CST's development within the
Catholic Church's ongoing struggle over modernization. As its Latin title suggests, it is the first of the anniversary encyclicals, written specifically to commem-
orate the fortieth anniversary of *Rerum novarum*. It contains 44 specific references
to Leo XIII and another 17 that refer to him as "Our Predecessor." *Rerum novarum*
is praised for having "proved itself the Magna Charta upon which all Christian
activity in the social field ought to be based, as on a foundation" (par. 39). Indeed,
Leo's encyclical, in Pius XI's view, has inspired Catholic academicians to develop
"a true Catholic social science," whose intellectual cogency and practical efficacy

---

6. The official text of *Quadragesimo anno* is taken from the Vatican Web site:
http://www.vatican.va/holy_father/pius_xi/encyclicals/documents/hf_p-
xi_enc_19310515_quadragesimo-anno_en.html. A hard copy of *Quadragesimo
anno* is also available in O'Brien and Shannon, *Catholic Social Thought*, 42–79.

is making a significant impact not just among Catholics but also in the public arena (pars. 20–21). According to Pius XI, the various economic and social reforms instituted in Europe after World War I to a great extent coincided with policies specifically recommended by Leo XIII. The basic security concerns of workers had begun to be addressed by the postwar governments. What the Pope doesn't say is that the basic security concerns of the papacy have also been addressed, with the ratification in 1929 of the Lateran Pact with Mussolini's Fascist government in Italy. Thus *Quadragesimo anno*, the first major encyclical written after the creation of the state of Vatican City, fittingly seems to usher in a new phase, one that will be characterized by critical engagement with the political, economic, and cultural aspects of modernization.

Pius XI's reference to "a true Catholic social science" is a useful way to think about what happens to CST and the common good in *Quadragesimo anno*. The new encyclical is not merely an act of mythmaking, intended to create from Leo's "immortal encyclical" an identifiable tradition dedicated to the "Christian reconstruction of human society" (par. 147). It also seeks both to systematize Leo's teachings and to clarify them precisely at the points where there is significant controversy among Catholic activists ostensibly seeking to put them into practice. The common good, apparently, is not itself controversial. Of the sixteen passages in which the term occurs, most remain consistent with the usages already laid down by Leo XIII. They merely reiterate Leo's teachings, so that the common good, first of all, remains a bulwark against liberal (laissez-faire) interpretations of the role of the state (par. 25). The state's responsibility for the common good specifically includes determining how the acknowledged natural right to private property is to be respected and exercised, by setting limits to what is and is not permitted in the ways property owners actually use their property. The state, in short, must defend the common good against any absolutist interpretation of private property precisely in order to preserve legitimate and reasonable claims to private property:

> Yet when the State brings private ownership into harmony with the needs of the common good, it does not commit a hostile act against private owners but rather does them a friendly service; for it thereby effectively prevents the private possession of goods, which the Author of nature in His most wise providence ordained for the support of human life, from causing intolerable evils and thus rushing to its own destruction; it does not destroy private possessions, but safeguards them; and it does not weaken private property rights, but strengthens them. (par. 49)

Quadragesimo anno, in its attempt to honor Leo XIII by offering a more systematic statement of CST's vision of the social order, underscores the analogical character of the common good and the responsibilities of various members of civil society for achieving it:

> Because order, as St. Thomas well explains, is unity arising from the harmonious arrangement of many objects, a true, genuine social order

demands that the various members of a society be united together by some strong bond. This unifying force is present not only in the producing of goods or the rendering of services—in which the employers and employees of an identical Industry or Profession collaborate jointly—but also in that common good, to achieve which all Industries and Professions together ought, each to the best of its ability, to cooperate amicably. And this unity will be the stronger and more effective, the more faithfully individuals and the Industries and Professions themselves strive to do their work and excel in it.

It is easily deduced from what has been said that the interests common to the whole Industry or Profession should hold first place in these guilds. The most important among these interests is to promote the cooperation in the highest degree of each industry and profession for the sake of the common good of the country. (pars. 84–85)

Civil society thus is conceived analogically with all levels or parts or members contributing to the realization of the common good. The common good thus is the "strong bond" uniting the various members of society.

Quadragesimo anno's most interesting innovation, however, is the use of a new term not to be found in *Rerum novarum*, construed as more or less synonymous with the common good:

To each, therefore, must be given his own share of goods, and the distribution of created goods, which, as every discerning person knows, is laboring today under the gravest evils due to the huge disparity between the few exceedingly rich and the unnumbered propertyless, must be effectively called back to and brought into conformity with the norms of the common good, that is, social justice. (par. 58)

Similarly, the document states:

It is contrary to social justice when, for the sake of personal gain and without regard for the common good, wages and salaries are excessively lowered or raised; and this same social justice demands that wages and salaries be so managed, through agreement of plans and wills, in so far as can be done, as to offer to the greatest possible number the opportunity of getting work and obtaining suitable means of livelihood. (par. 74)

Social justice and the common good thus are made more or less synonymous. Since this new terminology emerges in *Quadragesimo anno*'s discussion of workers and their wages, it may be useful to ask how "social justice" differs from both commutative and distributive justice, both of which are also aspects of this question.

Commutative justice is justice in exchange relations and other forms of private transactions.[7] Commutative justice is essentially achieved when the mutual consent of the contracting parties is reasonable, uncoerced, and fair to everyone involved. Distributive justice is the responsibility of the magistrate or the state. It is the proper ordering of proportional shares of or access to public goods, carried out by the state in its transactions with the individual and corporate members of civil society. Paying my monthly Visa bill is an act of commutative justice. My employer's contribution to the Social Security fund or my neighbor's qualifying for an earned income tax credit from the federal government are acts of distributive justice. What social justice covers is the comprehensive context, the overall social order, in which the agents involved in the other two forms of justice carry on their activities along with those involved in other forms of association. This seems clear from the larger concerns animating Pius XI's discussion, for example, of wage justice:

> In the first place, the worker must be paid a wage sufficient to support him and his family. That the rest of the family should also contribute to the common support, according to the capacity of each, is certainly right, as can be observed especially in the families of farmers, but also in the families of many craftsmen and small shopkeepers. But to abuse the years of childhood and the limited strength of women is grossly wrong. Mothers, concentrating on household duties, should work primarily in the home or in its immediate vicinity. It is an intolerable abuse, and to be abolished at all cost, for mothers on account of the father's low wage to be forced to engage in gainful occupations outside the home to the neglect of their proper cares and duties, especially the training of children. Every effort must therefore be made that fathers of families receive a wage large enough to meet ordinary family needs adequately. But if this cannot always be done under existing circumstances, social justice demands that changes be introduced as soon as possible whereby such a wage will be assured to every adult workingman. (par. 71)

What makes the worker's wages a matter of social justice is the fact that in an industrial society the worker's family, in Pius XI's view, depends on them for its sustenance. If the wages on offer in the labor market force the wife and children to work outside the home just to make ends meet, such wage levels are a violation of social justice. They contribute, in Pius XI's view, to the further deterioration of the most basic institution in society, the family. The integrity of the social order thus is at stake in the wage issue, and hence it is a matter of social justice.

---

7. Cf. NCCB, *Economic Justice for All* (1986), pars. 69 and 70. The American bishops' clarification explicitly relies on Jon P. Gunnemann's essay, "Capitalism and Commutative Justice," in the *Annual of the Society of Christian Ethics* (from the 1985 annual meeting; ed. Alan B. Anderson; Washington, DC: Georgetown University Press, 1986), 101–22.

Quadragesimo anno, however, does not consistently link the common good and social justice. There are passages in which the common good occurs without any reference to social justice and, conversely, there are passages where social justice is invoked without reference to the common good. When they are linked, as in the examples just given, social justice seems to add a note of social concreteness and perhaps historicity, as well as moral urgency, that is lacking in the notion of the common good when used alone. Thus, in this new tradition of CST that Pius XI is hoping to forge from the legacy of Leo XIII, the common good remains the undefined and perhaps indefinable centerpiece in the Catholic Church's vision of the social order. Consistent with the pattern established in the work of his predecessor, Pius XI seems more interested in the concrete social consequences of recognizing the overriding priority of the common good than in fixing forever its philosophical content.

That *Quadragesimo anno* fittingly represents the new phase of Critical Engagement can be seen from the specificity of Pius XI's understanding of society and the major alternatives against which CST's vision of the social order must contend. Instead of the relatively simple polarity described by Leo XIII, according to which the church must resist both laissez-faire liberalism and radical socialism, Pius XI sees himself confronting at least four options. In addition to the two condemned by Leo, *Quadragesimo anno* specifically recognizes the development of a militant Communism, now concretely represented in the Soviet Union, and a moderate socialism, which is nonviolent and less radical in its conception of the changes needed to achieve social justice. In addition, without specifying the term "Fascism" or acknowledging the direction of Mussolini's own attempts at economic and social "reform," the encyclical speaks of the "inauguration of a special system of syndicates and corporations." This would be directed by the state in order to insure peaceful relations in industry between labor and management. "Strikes and lock-outs are forbidden; if the parties cannot settle their dispute, public authority intervenes" (par. 94). Faced with the new developments of a moderate socialism and the kind of syndicalist or corporatist order espoused by Fascism, Pius XI unequivocally condemns moderate socialism insofar as it remains truly socialist: "Its concept of society itself is utterly foreign to Christian truth" (par. 117). But he offers only muted criticism of the syndicalist order and encourages Catholic laity to engage critically with the new system:

> We are compelled to say that to Our certain knowledge there are not wanting some who fear that the State, instead of confining itself as it ought to the furnishing of necessary and adequate assistance, is substituting itself for free activity; that the new syndical and corporative order savors too much of an involved and political system of administration; and that (in spite of those more general advantages mentioned above, which are of course fully admitted) it rather serves particular political ends than leads to the reconstruction and promotion of a better social order.
>
> To achieve this latter lofty aim, and in particular to promote the common good truly and permanently, We hold it is first and above everything

wholly necessary that God bless it and, secondly, that all men of good will work with united effort toward that end. We are further convinced, as a necessary consequence, that this end will be attained the more certainly the larger the number of those ready to contribute toward it their technical, occupational, and social knowledge and experience; and also, what is more important, the greater the contribution made thereto of Catholic principles and their application, not indeed by Catholic Action (which excludes strictly syndical or political activities from its scope) but by those sons of Ours whom Catholic Action imbues with Catholic principles and trains for carrying on an apostolate under the leadership and teaching guidance of the Church—of that Church which in this field also that We have described, as in every other field where moral questions are involved and discussed, can never forget or neglect through indifference its divinely imposed mandate to be vigilant and to teach. (pars. 95–96)

Clearly, Pius XI, now secure in his sovereignty over Vatican City, hoped for a critical engagement with Italian Fascism, provided that the new order actually could deliver on its promise of greater social harmony, and that the Catholic Church's moral and spiritual authority should be respected. Perhaps, even as late as 1931, it was too early to detect the totalitarian tendencies lurking in the Fascist program of social reconstruction. As the 1930s wore on, however, Mussolini would launch a frontal assault on Catholic Action and seek to curtail the church's influence over education and virtually all phases of Italian public life. Eventually, World War II would see the church completely disengage from Fascism, as Pius XII (1939–58) encouraged the development of a new strategy for critical engagement through the formation of the Christian Democratic parties of Italy, Western Europe, and Latin America.

Phase Three: Accommodation (1958–1978)

The Second Vatican Council (1962–65), at that time at least, appeared to be, literally speaking, an epoch-making event in the history of Roman Catholicism. If so, many observers in retrospect may be tempted to think that the new epoch, alas, was of short duration. In any case, Vatican II's *Pastoral Constitution on the Church in the Modern World* (*Gaudium et spes*) still set a new tone for how CST presents itself in a world no longer resisted as alien and threatening, but embraced as, for the most part, an expression of God's continuing presence among us. There are still errors to be corrected, of course, and evils to be overcome; but the council's fresh attempt to "discern the signs of the times and interpret them in light of the Gospel" (par. 4) offers a strikingly generous and optimistic reading of humanity's increasingly global aspirations for freedom, equality, prosperity, and personal as well as social development. How, then, did this new tone affect the way "the common good" is used in *Gaudium et spes*?

One crucial indication of the new phase of Accommodation is that for the first time something like a definition of the common good is presented. As indicated early in this chapter, *Gaudium et spes* describes the common good as "the sum of those conditions of social life which allow social groups and their individual members relatively thorough and ready access to their own fulfillment" (par. 26). Further on it gives what amounts to a definition: "Indeed, the common good embraces the sum of those conditions of the social life whereby men, families and associations more adequately and readily may attain their own perfection" (par. 74). The very fact that a definition is offered at all suggests the extent to which CST, or at least the council *periti* who formulated this document, was aware that the meanings of the common good as well as other key concepts in the tradition could no longer be regarded as self-evident. Arguably, this is a crucial accommodation. It tacitly concedes that the Catholic Church no longer enjoys a monopoly on moral discourse, as if the *philosophia perennis* actually were still the common framework for thinking about the social order and its transformations. "Dialogue" in a context characterized by respect for the pluralism of religious faith traditions, ideologies, and social philosophies is the new order of the day. Evidence of this is the fact that Vatican II was the first ecumenical council recognized by the church that did *not* conclude its deliberations by issuing a list of heresies to be anathematized.

The definition also illuminates another pattern characteristic of the period of Accommodation. This is the tendency to define the common good in terms of other moral aspirations and imperatives. These come to be regarded as concrete, historical, and partial realizations of the common good, which itself remains more comprehensive, transcendent, and abstract. In *Gaudium et spes*'s definitions the common good is understood teleologically. It is what contributes to universal human, personal, and collective "fulfillment" or "perfection." "The political community exists . . . for the sake of the common good, in which it finds its full justification and significance, and the source of its inherent legitimacy" (par. 74). Given the religious ultimacy inherent in this telos, the task of interpreting the common good and mobilizing social cooperation to implement it continues to be a part of the church's own mission in the world:

> With great respect, therefore, this council regards all the true, good and just elements inherent in the very wide variety of institutions which the human race has established for itself and constantly continues to establish. The council affirms, moreover, that the Church is willing to assist and promote all these institutions to the extent that such a service depends on her and can be associated with her mission. She has no fiercer desire than that in pursuit of the welfare of all she may be able to develop herself freely under any kind of government which grants recognition to the basic rights of person and family, to the demands of the common good and to the free exercise of her own mission. (par. 42)

Further on, in chapter 4, "The Life of the Political Community," *Gaudium et spes* makes clear that the exercise of the church's responsibilities toward the common good no longer requires that it be granted a privileged status within the political community. Examples are the ill-fated Lateran Pact with Mussolini, or the system of concordats by which the church sought legal sanctions to protect its social influence in some other European nations:

> There are, indeed, close links between earthly things and those elements of man's condition which transcend the world. The Church herself makes use of temporal things insofar as her own mission requires it. She, for her part, does not place her trust in the privileges offered by civil authority. She will even give up the exercise of certain rights which have been legitimately acquired, if it becomes clear that their use will cast doubt on the sincerity of her witness or that new ways of life demand new methods. It is only right, however, that at all times and in all places, the Church should have true freedom to preach the faith, to teach her social doctrine, to exercise her role freely among men, and also to pass moral judgment in those matters which regard public order when the fundamental rights of a person or the salvation of souls require it. (par. 76)

Thus Accommodation means that the common good is still the ultimate telos of society, but it is to be pursued within the framework of a political ecclesiology strikingly different from that envisioned in the previous two phases.

As to what the common good concretely requires in the modern world, *Gaudium et spes* follows the new direction initially laid down in Pope John XXIII's *Pacem in terris*[8] (*On Establishing Universal Peace in Truth, Justice, Charity, and Liberty*, 1963), by making a top priority for the protection of human rights. Here is what was said in *Pacem in terris*:

> It is generally accepted today that the common good is best safeguarded when personal rights and duties are guaranteed. The chief concern of civil authorities must therefore be to ensure that these rights are recognized, respected, co-ordinated, defended and promoted, and that each individual is enabled to perform his duties more easily. For "to safeguard the inviolable rights of the human person, and to facilitate the performance of his duties, is the principal duty of every public authority." (par. 60)

Gaudium et spes echoes this point, though in somewhat muted terms:

> Every day human interdependence grows more tightly drawn and spreads by degrees over the whole world. As a result the common good, that is, the sum of those conditions, . . . today takes on an increasingly universal complexion and consequently involves rights and duties with

---

8. The official text of *Pacem in terris* is from the Vatican Web site: http://www.vatican.va/holy_father/john_xxiii/encyclicals/documents/hf_j-xxiii_enc_11041963_pacem_en.html. A hard copy of *Pacem in terris* is also available in O'Brien and Shannon, *Catholic Social Thought*, 129–62.

respect to the whole race. Every social group must take account of the needs and legitimate aspirations of other groups, and even of the general welfare of the entire human family. (par. 26)

The common good, in the modern world, also requires an acknowledgement of the basic equality of all men and women, and thus equality in the recognition and enforcement of their "fundamental rights" and an end to all unjust forms of discrimination:

> [W]ith respect to the fundamental rights of the person, every type of discrimination, whether social or cultural, whether based on sex, race, color, social condition, language or religion, is to be overcome and eradicated as contrary to God's intent. For in truth it must still be regretted that fundamental personal rights are still not being universally honored. Such is the case of a woman who is denied the right to choose a husband freely, to embrace a state of life or to acquire an education or cultural benefits equal to those recognized for men.
>
> Therefore, although rightful differences exist between men, the equal dignity of persons demands that a more humane and just condition of life be brought about. For excessive economic and social differences between the members of the one human family or population groups cause scandal, and militate against social justice, equity, the dignity of the human person, as well as social and international peace. (par. 29)

Here is concern for "social justice, equity, the dignity of the human person, as well as social and international peace." Clearly *Gaudium et spes* shows that specific concerns for "social justice" are to be regarded as concrete expressions of the common good.

Another that could be added to this list is the council's concern for an equitable distribution of "cultural benefits" or, if you will, a basic right to education and/or cultural and social development. In light of the "right of all to a human and social culture in conformity with the dignity of the human person without any discrimination of race, sex, nation, religion, or social condition," *Gaudium et spes* urges the following policy:

> Therefore it is necessary to provide all with a sufficient quantity of cultural benefits, especially of those which constitute the so-called fundamental culture lest very many be prevented from cooperating in the promotion of the common good in a truly human manner because of illiteracy and a lack of responsible activity. (par. 60)

This and similar passages in *Gaudium et spes* bear striking testimony to the extent to which the council meant to embrace "the joys and hopes, the griefs and the anxieties of the men of this age, especially those who are poor or in any way afflicted" as "the joys and hopes, the griefs and anxieties of the followers of Christ" (par. 1). As a result of this identification with the modern world, "common good" discourse was retained, but its use was refocused on a set of "conditions"—moral aspirations and imperatives—that had heretofore been regarded with deep suspicion within the tradition of CST. Not surprisingly, *Gaudium et spes* makes a further innovation in the use of the term, speaking hopefully of a "universal common good" (pars. 68, 84). This usage is not pleonastic. "The common good" is still an analogous term, and its meaning in the context of the nation-state must now, in the council's optimistic view, be expanded to address the aspirations of an emerging global society.

Phase Four: The Current Phase (1978–)

If *Gaudium et spes* may be taken as an early representative of the Accommodation phase in the development of CST, it might also be reckoned as some kind of high-water mark in the use of the common good. After all, the two major social encyclicals—*Populorum progressio* (1967) and *Octagesima adveniens* (1971)—of Pope Paul VI, who reigned from the Second Vatican Council to the end of the third phase, together contain fewer references to the common good (16) than *Gaudium et spes* (28), and dramatically fewer than Pope John XXIII's two major social encyclicals, *Mater et magistra* (1961), which uses the term 20 times, and *Pacem in terris* (1963), which uses it 47 times. There may be a temptation to interpret these statistics in a linear fashion, as if once the process of accommodation had begun in earnest, the common good would tend to disappear in favor of its more readily intelligible synonyms. Perhaps. But it may also simply reflect differences in education, intellectual temperament, and professional experience between Pope John XXIII and Paul VI, or at least the different concerns of their theological advisers. At any rate, the current phase of the development of CST has not witnessed the total disappearance of "the common good" from the documents, but has seen the term's meaning expanded as the church seeks new ways to address today's challenges and priorities.

The current phase of CST is dominated, to be sure, by the work of Pope John Paul II, whose achievements in the field of moral philosophy would be significant even if he had not been elected to the papacy in 1978. In his tenure at the Vatican, John Paul II has made effective use of the encyclical letter form, authorizing two major commemorative statements on the anniversaries of *Rerum novarum* (*Laborem exercens*, 1981, and *Centesimus annus*, 1991). Both of them bear unmistakable testimony to his own personal and pastoral experience in Poland. He has also begun what may have been intended as a new tradition, a commemorative encyclical (*Sollicitudo rei socialis*, 1987) to celebrate the twentieth anniversary of Paul VI's *Populorum progressio* (1967). At the same time, this phase has been marked by notable collective statements on CST from various national and regional episcopal conferences, each of which has also contributed to the rich semantic field constituted by "the common good." The difference between the current phase of CST and the previous phase of Accommodation seems to be primarily ecclesiological: *Gaudium et spes* put CST on a new footing by outlining a

program for "discerning the signs of the times" (par. 4). It was generally interpreted, consistent with other conciliar teachings, as encouraging all Catholics to
participate in the processes of discernment,[9] with the expectation that diversity in
the form of regional or local differences of perspective in CST and its application
would emerge. The current phase, however, has witnessed a reassertion of papal
authority such that the processes of discernment are now firmly under the direction of the Vatican, with the expectation that uniformity in perspective and application will be achieved and preserved.[10]

In the current phase of CST's development, the previous trends noted in the
use of "the common good" have persisted. The combined total of references to the
common good (46) in John Paul II's four major encyclicals on CST, *Laborem
exercens* (1981), *Sollicitudo rei socialis* (1987), *Centesimus annus* (1991), and
Evangelium vitae (1995), is somewhat larger than the number (28) found in
Gaudium et spes. Yet the term itself continues to function as a symbol for a cluster
of social aspirations and imperatives that may be better understood or more readily implemented in piecemeal fashion. *Sollicitudo rei socialis*, for example, suggests
the transcendent and thus increasingly elusive character of the common good: "In
a different world, ruled by concern for the common good of all humanity, or by
concern for the 'spiritual and human development of all' instead of by the quest
for individual profit, peace would be possible as the result of a 'more perfect justice among people'" (par. 10). Also noteworthy is the fact that this passage is seeking to identify the common good with Paul VI's memorable formulation in
Populorum progessio: "Development is the new name for peace." Thus, another
synonym is offered for the common good.

Among the more innovative uses in *Sollicitudo rei socialis*[11] (*On the Twentieth
Anniversary of "Populorum progressio,"* 1987) is the pope's attempt to link his

---

9. This seems to be the clear message of the Synod of Bishops' statement, *Justice
in the World* (1971), and Paul VI's *Octagesima adveniens* (1971).

10. At least two major examples of this tendency can usefully be examined: (1)
The emergence of the *Instructions on Liberation Theology* that corrected or clarified
certain theological developments and social action strategies that had been endorsed
in the documents of the Latin American Bishops Conference (CELAM). (2) The
Vatican's intervention in the U.S. bishops' development of their pastoral letter on
national defense policy, *The Challenge of Peace* (1983), which corrected or clarified
the range of policy inferences that the U.S. bishops could draw from their attempt
to honor both the just-war tradition and the witness of Catholic peace activists like
Dorothy Day. At issue was the NCCB's endorsement of the "Nuclear Freeze" movement, and recommendation in favor of a policy of "No First Use" of nuclear
weapons, both of which were out of step with statements previously made by the
German bishops, supported by the Congregation for the Doctrine of the Faith
(CDF). My own account of these controversies and their impact on CST is available
in *New Experiment in Democracy: The Challenge for American Catholicism* (Kansas
City: Sheed & Ward, 1987).

11. The official text of *Sollicitudo rei socialis* is from the Vatican Web site:
http://www.vatican.va/edocs/ENG0223/_INDEX.HTM. A hardcopy of *Sollicitudo
rei socialis* is also available in O'Brien and Shannon, *Catholic Social Thought*, 393–436.

theological understanding of "the structures of sin" in the world with "the sum total of negative factors working against a true awareness of the universal common good":

> It is important to note therefore that a world which is divided into blocs, sustained by rigid ideologies, and in which instead of interdependence and solidarity different forms of imperialism hold sway, can only be a world subject to structures of sin. The sum total of the negative factors working against a true awareness of the universal common good, and the need to further it, gives the impression of creating, in persons and institutions, an obstacle which is difficult to overcome. . . . "Sin" and "structures of sin" are categories which are seldom applied to the situation of the contemporary world. However, one cannot easily gain a profound understanding of the reality that confronts us unless we give a name to the root of the evils which afflict us. (par. 36)

Placing the common good in this theological horizon illuminates a point that in retrospect is latent throughout the history of CST: the common good is an eschatological concept. The common good in its fullness is transcendent, and will always remain at least partially unrealized, at least this side of the Parousia. The practical implication of such an eschatological concept of the common good is, arguably, to warrant CST's increasingly clear preference for reformist rather than revolutionary programs seeking economic and social justice.

If the common good is ultimately an eschatological notion whose concrete social and political content can never be determined exhaustively, then the search for what I have called "synonyms" or appropriate partial substitutes[12] is not a sign of lack of mental acuity or philosophical rigor. Instead, it is precisely what is needed if the transcendent character of the common good is to have any social relevance, to make a practical difference in how we understand and seek to change the world in which we live. Just as *Sollicitudo rei socialis* contributed to the search for appropriate substitutes by linking the common good with "integral human development," so *Laborem exercens* makes its chief contribution by linking the common good directly to John Paul II's emphatically teleological notion of human work. Once that connection is made, the common good is readily put to work to clarify the moral framework in which the state and organized labor, in the pope's view, must interact. *Centesimus annus*[13] (*On the Hundredth Anniversary of*

---

12. One could also call them "middle axioms." Cf. Dennis P. McCann, "A Second Look at Middle Axioms," in *The Annual of the Society of Christian Ethics* (from the 1980 meeting; ed. Thomas W. Ogletree; Dallas: The Society for Christian Ethics, 1981), 73–96. At that time I was seeking to understand the continued relevance of John C. Bennett's use of the term, primarily in the context of Protestant social ethics. It is clear, to me at least, that a similar need animates CST discourse seeking to interpret the concrete meaning of the common good over time.

13. The official text of *Centesimus annus* is from the Vatican Web site: http://www.vatican.va/edocs/ENG0214/_INDEX.HTM. A hardcopy of *Centesimus annus* is also available in O'Brien and Shannon, *Catholic Social Thought*, 437–88.

"Rerum novarum," 1991), besides providing a magisterial review of Leo XIII's formative role in CST, extends the common good to the concerns for preserving and enhancing the natural and social environment. In the following passage observe how priorities in achieving the common good are expected to shift as the processes of modernization continue to unfold:

> It is the task of the State to provide for the defense and preservation of common goods such as the natural and human environments, which cannot be safeguarded simply by market forces. Just as in the time of primitive capitalism the State had the duty of defending the basic rights of workers, so now, with the new capitalism, the State and all of society have the duty of defending those collective goods which, among others, constitute the essential framework for the legitimate pursuit of personal goals on the part of each individual. (par. 40)

Indeed, the common good, now increasingly thought of in universal terms, is to be commended as the guiding principle for managing the processes of globalization:

> Nor is it a matter of eliminating instruments of social organization which have proved useful, but rather of orienting them according to an adequate notion of the common good in relation to the whole human family. Today we are facing the so-called "globalization" of the economy, a phenomenon which is not to be dismissed, since it can create unusual opportunities for greater prosperity. There is a growing feeling, however, that this increasing internationalization of the economy ought to be accompanied by effective international agencies which will oversee and direct the economy to the common good, something that an individual state, even if it were the most powerful on earth, would not be in a position to do. (par. 58)

However innovative these uses of the common good, they also reveal a deep continuity in CST's understanding of political economy. Market forces alone, left to their own devices, are not likely to achieve the common good, even as an unintended benefit. Strong institutional coordination—call it, if you will, government regulation—is necessary even for any partial realization of the common good in this world.

Among the most important tendencies in the expansion of the common good in the encyclicals of John Paul II is his linkage of the common good with his understanding of what it means to be "pro-life." His 1995 encyclical, *Evangelium vitae*[14] (*On the Value and Inviolability of Human Life*, 1995), must be regarded as an integral expression of his views on CST and not just as a treatise in biomedical ethics. In it he explicitly links the common good with his increasingly critical reservations against capital punishment and his uncompromising resistance to abortion:

---

14. The official text of *Evangelium vitae* is from the Vatican Web site: http://www.vatican.va/edocs/ENG0141/_INDEX.HTM.

The Gospel of life is for the whole of human society. To be actively pro-life is to contribute to the renewal of society through the promotion of the common good. It is impossible to further the common good without acknowledging and defending the right to life, upon which all the other inalienable rights of individuals are founded and from which they develop. A society lacks solid foundations when, on the one hand, it asserts values such as the dignity of the person, justice and peace, but then, on the other hand, radically acts to the contrary by allowing or tolerating a variety of ways in which human life is devalued and violated, especially where it is weak or marginalized. Only respect for life can be the foundation and guarantee of the most precious and essential goods of society, such as democracy and peace. (par. 101)

This strong demand for moral consistency is what Joseph Cardinal Bernardin called "a seamless garment ethic." Here it is used to appeal to social activists who regard themselves as already committed to achieving the common good, but whose understanding of the circle of persons and concerns included within it is, in the pope's view, much too restricted. The universality of the common good, this pope urges, is not simply a spatial metaphor encompassing the processes of globalization; it is also temporal and serves to remind everyone of their responsibilities for all generations, past, present, and future.

Conclusion

This overlong study is meant to be methodologically innovative and to demonstrate how the interpretation of texts, particularly those embedded in a tradition that harbors a normative view of its own development, can be opened up for fresh inquiry, using electronic word-processing technologies. The substantive conclusions that this method of analysis has drawn me toward regarding the meaning of common good discourse in CST are the following:

- The common good resists essential definition, ultimately because, in CST at least, it functions as an eschatological notion, or, if you will, a limit-concept. It represents a telos, in short, that is not likely to be fully realized in history as we know it.

- Though the common good is ultimately eschatological, it has practical implications for how the social order is to be understood as to its purpose, and the roles that various primary institutions and secondary associations can and ought to play in achieving that purpose. It is, in short, a limit-concept for orienting politics, based on a proper understanding of the social order.

- Within CST's evolving vision of the social order, the common good thus serves to order ethical priorities among a number of aspirations

and imperatives that give this term its concrete meaning and resonance. Among the "synonyms" so regulated are social justice, human
rights, integral human development, the common welfare, public
good, and most recently, a preferential love (or option) for the poor.

- In light of these synonyms, CST's substantive understanding of the
  common good is warranted by a theological horizon based, to use current terminology, on a biblically oriented understanding of human
  dignity and social solidarity. These two terms are understood recipro-
  cally and can never be abstracted in the direction of either individualism or collectivism.

- The basic vision of the social order presupposed by CST's usage of
  "the common good" term seems to fluctuate between hierarchical and
  egalitarian patterns of organization. The principle of subsidiarity is
  normally invoked as the key to any coherent effort to implement the
  common good. Although it was originally formulated in hierarchical
  terms, the principle of subsidiarity can also be stood on its head, as it
  were, to argue for the primacy of human aspirations toward universal
  freedom and equality.

- Despite its openness toward egalitarian interpretation, common good
  discourse remains profoundly conservative precisely insofar as it is
  based on a distinctive conceptual logic that can no longer be taken for
  granted in our world today. In identifying the profoundly conservative
  nature of the common good, I am not thereby criticizing it or rejecting
  it. Conservative thought, left to its own devices, may inspire any of the
  following political responses—reactionary, radical, and reformist—and
  sometimes an uneasy mixture of all three. All three have their representatives in the development of CST, at least as I have understood its four
  phases. The current direction of CST's basic conservatism seems to be
  reformist, which as such may offer a useful basis for further criticism
  and reflection.

Public Discourse and Common Good

Robin W. Lovin

There would be little reason to have an idea of the common good if one could not talk about it. Public discussion is necessary to win support for the idea, to implement it, and perhaps even to understand it for oneself. So it seems perfectly straightforward to suggest that those who want to achieve the common good will want first make it the central topic of a lively public discussion. It seems too, that a democratic society with a commitment to the free expression of ideas is a place where that discussion would flourish. However, some of the most important understandings of liberal democracy suggest that such a discussion of the common good has little prospect for success and may imperil the delicate balance between freedom and order, which is key to democracy's common good in the first place. This is particularly true, these critics suggest, if the ideas about the common good under consideration are sanctioned by religious authority or derived from specifically religious ideas about human nature and the human good. If this assessment is correct, we may solve our common problems more effectively by *not* seeking the common good. The most important virtue of those who are committed to the common good may be a prudent self-restraint that refrains from introducing religion and other particularistic understandings of the human good into public discussion.[1]

---

1. Robert Audi, "Liberal Democracy and the Place of Religion in Politics," in *Religion in the Public Square: The Place of Religious Convictions in Political Debate* (ed. Robert Audi and Nicholas Wolterstorff; Lanham, MD: Rowman & Littlefield, 1997), 9–15. Audi's specific concern is the role of religious arguments in public life.

A renewed understanding of the common good in Christian theology, then, does not automatically have a place in contemporary politics. To secure that place, we must answer some questions about the risks involved in public discussion of the good, questions deeply rooted in the history of liberal democracy. This essay undertakes that task, but it does not proceed, as some contemporary theologians do, by rejecting the constraints of liberal political theory. My proposal is rather that liberal theory and the common good raise complementary concerns about our political life, and both have a place in an account of the variety of forms that public discourse takes. There have been at least two decades of charges that liberalism has robbed public discourse of meaning and countercharges that ideas about God and the good would rob it of freedom.[2] Yet, one may now conclude, that debate itself has impoverished public discourse, obsessively fixing attention on old aporias and neglecting other issues more important to the civic community. This essay will serve its purpose if the reader comes to the end ready to address those other, more important issues.

The Origins and Assumptions of Liberal Democracy

Pursuing a common good requires a degree of agreement that is rare in modern pluralistic societies. People begin with different ideas about what is good, and moral goods inspire a quality of commitment that makes compromise difficult. Often, moral commitments are also religious, which makes compromise even more difficult and may make it hard to explain the commitments to those outside the faith. When "the good" is the object of discussion, possibilities for conflict multiply and prospects for consensus shrink. The risks of violence or coercion begin to loom larger than the potential moral achievement.

For these reasons, theories of liberal democracy concentrate on minimal agreements and shared procedures, rather than common goals. Political life should be about maximizing the opportunities that individuals have to pursue their own notions of the good, rather than identifying a good that all must pursue in common.

This concern to minimize conflict over the good bears the imprint of the conflicts in which liberal democracy originated. In early modern Europe, especially in Britain and the colonies Britain founded in North America, the freedom of liberal democracy provided an alternative to the civil and religious conflicts that had divided the nation for most of the seventeenth century. John Locke and his successors envisioned a society that did not require unanimity about the good in order to maintain civil peace. In that society, people could safely make their own choices about the good. Politics could concentrate on securing them in the enjoyment of the goods they were able to choose and achieve and on settling the disputes about justice and property that inevitably arise between people who pursue their own individual good under conditions of limited resources.

---

2. The debate may be conveniently dated from the appearance of Richard John Neuhaus's indictment in *The Naked Public Square* (Grand Rapids: Eerdmans, 1984). His argument was anticipated in some ways by John Murray Cuddihy, *No Offense: Civil Religion and Protestant Taste* (New York: Seabury Press, 1978).

In that historical context, one of the greatest dangers to liberal democracy was that people with authoritarian aspirations or religious motivations would use the democratic process to reintroduce a single idea of the common good, imposing it on their contemporaries and binding subsequent generations to its ideals. Jefferson, Madison, and the other theorists of the American Revolution sought to prevent this, first by a rigorous separation of church and state, but also by devising protections against the danger that a new tyranny by the majority would replace the old tyranny by authority.

The dangers of sect and faction that Jefferson and Madison decried were no doubt real, and they continue in new forms today. The importance of this problem in the eighteenth century, however, has perhaps given it too prominent a place in subsequent democratic theory. As a result, one of the first items of business in any account of liberal democracy is to specify constraints to ensure that democratic procedures will not be used to secure antidemocratic results.

In the shaping of the American polity, those constraints took the form of individual constitutional rights. In contemporary democratic theory, they center on identifying the sorts of reasons that ought not to be offered in public discourse. A considerable literature, for example, discusses limitations on the use of religious reasons in public arguments.[3] Other philosophers develop concepts of "public reason" to set criteria that determine what arguments will be acceptable in public discourse.[4] For purposes of this essay, we may summarize the results of this development succinctly: A liberal democracy best serves the common good by refusing to make the common good the center of its political discussion.

History explains this caution, but it has led in recent years to criticisms of liberal democracy by communitarian critics who believe that the political discourse that could be sustained on these terms is too "thin" to support either identity or community.[5] The relative isolation from disputes about God and the good that first made liberal democracy attractive now becomes for some a reason to abandon it. Postmodern politics seems once again to offer the early modern choice between the good and democracy, though the choice now takes the form of abandoning liberal democracy in order to achieve the good, rather than abandoning the good in order to achieve liberal democracy.

The Common Good and Legitimate Law

It would be easy to conclude from history that liberalism is a political philosophy that excludes the good from its understanding of law and government, while

---

3. Christopher Eberle, *Religious Conviction in Liberal Politics* (Cambridge: Cambridge University Press, 2002), offers a useful overview of this discussion. He himself defends a position that is more open to religious reasons.

4. This essay will focus particularly on the concept of public reason in the work of John Rawls. See John Rawls, *Political Liberalism* (New York: Columbia University Press, 1993), 213–54.

5. Michael Sandel, *Liberalism and the Limits of Justice* (Cambridge: Cambridge University Press, 1982).

theological approaches to politics depend on it. In Thomas Aquinas, as Jean Porter notes in her essay, "the idea of the common good is always linked to public authority in some way. This idea plays a central role in his theory of law, and he also uses it to justify courses of action on the part of public authorities that would be ruled out for private individuals."[6]

Aquinas states simply that "every law is ordained to the common good."[7] A way of thinking about politics that leaves the good out of consideration could hardly produce anything that Aquinas would recognize as law. Perhaps, then, the close relationship between Christianity and liberal democracy that characterized world affairs for much of the past century rests on a mistake. Contemporary critics with clearer sight may be right in saying that liberalism's commitments to individual rights and individual judgment are, in fact, incompatible with authentic Christian faith. Perhaps, too, liberals whose first commitment is to democracy are right to suggest that beliefs about truth and the good have no place in genuinely free political choices.[8] Clearly, much about our ordinary understandings of citizenship and civic life will have to change if Christianity and democracy are incompatible ideals, if the common good and liberalism are contradictory commitments.

But these alternatives, suggested by a radically theological critique of politics and a radically political rejection of theology, may be too sharply drawn. The traditions of Christian political thought and modern liberal political theory may understand law and government in different ways, but they share a concern with the moral authority of law. Thus, both liberalism and Christian theology are concerned to justify the powers of government and to give people reasons to obey the laws under which they live. It is this question about the criterion of legitimacy by which a law is measured that the two traditions share. A comparison of the ways they answer it gives us a more nuanced way to assess the differences between them.

Conformity with the law can in some measure be secured by force, but a society will be more unified and stable if people believe that their laws make a legitimate moral claim on their obedience. By contrast, when people believe that law is arbitrary, immoral, or serves the interests of some limited group, they will try to ignore or evade it.

That is the most immediate reason why law must be "ordained to the common good." A society regulated by such laws will enjoy conditions for the good life that only a whole society can maintain and in which every member of the society has a share.[9] Over the long run, such a society may make its members better people

---

6. Jean Porter, "The Common Good in Thomas Aquinas," in this volume.

7. Aquinas, *Summa theologiae*, I-II (first part of the second part), Q. 90, A. ii.

8. For the theological critique of liberalism, see Stanley Hauerwas, *A Better Hope: Resources for a Church Confronting Capitalism, Democracy, and Postmodernity* (Grand Rapids, MI: Brazos, 2000), 27–32. For a liberal critique of theological and philosophical attempts to "re-enchant" the world of politics, see Richard Rorty, "The Priority of Democracy to Philosophy," in Gene Outka and John P. Reeder Jr., eds., *Prospects for a Common Morality* (Princeton: Princeton University Press, 1993), 269.

9. Cf. Louis Dupré, "The Common Good and the Open Society," in *Catholicism and Liberalism* (ed. R. Bruce Douglass and David Hollenbach; Cambridge: Cambridge University Press, 1994), 172.

than they would otherwise be and give them better lives than they would other-wise have. But in the meantime, that prospect gives everyone in the society good reasons to accept the constraints that law imposes. If people ask why they should obey the law, their questions can be answered by pointing to the goods the law provides. It may sometimes be necessary also to point out that the law's demands can be backed up by force, but this will never be the *only* reason why a legitimate law should be obeyed.

Aquinas accompanies this moral criterion of legitimacy, orientation to the common good, with two procedural criteria: The law must be decreed by a legiti-mate authority, and it must be promulgated in the proper form.[10] The requirements of the common good do not become law simply by being recognized as such. A legitimate ruler must make them law by decreeing them in the proper way. These procedural marks of legitimate law are, of course, rather more easily ascertained than the complex substantive requirement that the law must serve the common good. Aquinas sometimes seems to say that correct procedure is determinative for ordinary people in ordinary circumstances. If one knows that the legitimate ruler has in fact properly ordained this law, that in itself establishes a prima facie moral obligation to obey it.[11]

Nevertheless, the ordering of law to the common good precludes any claim that the ruler's authority alone is sufficient to make a legitimate law. The linking of legitimate law to a substantive judgment about the common good, especially when combined with Aquinas's teaching about the authority of conscience, creates a strong case for moral freedom in relation to political authority. "A man is bound to obey secular princes insofar as the order of justice requires it. And so if princes have a ruling power which is not just but usurped, or if they command that which is unjust, their subjects are not bound to obey them, except perhaps accidentally, in order to avoid scandal or peril."[12] There is little here to suggest the later ideas of Hobbes, who thought that the creation of government authority involves a contract in which the individual surrenders all claims against the sovereign's judg-ment, nor even to anticipate doctrines of "passive obedience" set forth by later Reformers. Aquinas's ruler, no less than Luther's, has a comprehensive power over our life and goods, but only if what the ruler commands is ordered toward a com-mon good in which we also share.

Liberalism and Legitimacy

Aquinas's political theology thus begins with the idea that legitimate law is shaped by the common good and moves cautiously toward the notion that individuals may

10. Aquinas, *Summa theologiae*, I-II, Q. 90, A. iii–iv.
11. See, for example, ibid., II-II (second part of the second part), Q. 104, A. vi. Dennis McCann's essay (in this volume) notes the persistence of this theme in con-servative Catholic social thought. Even in a democracy, this interpretation suggests, citizens should defer to the judgment of civil authorities in disputed questions about what makes for the temporal welfare of the community—for example, in the deci-sion about whether to go to war or not.
12. Aquinas, *Summa theologiae*, II-II, Q. 104, A. vi, reply to obj. 3.

make their own judgments about that legitimacy. Liberalism, by contrast, seems to begin with the presumption that whatever the people collectively decide has a claim to be legitimate law. For a particularly consistent theory of procedural democracy, that may be all that needs to be said about law and legitimacy. Upon reflection, however, the idea that popular choice alone is the criterion of legitimacy needs some qualification. Otherwise, individuals and minorities in a liberal democracy would have no protection from the arbitrary choices of a majority of their fellow citizens.

A common good precludes these arbitrary impositions by directing political choices toward a good in which everyone has a share. Liberalism, assuming that agreement on such a good is unavailable, tries to provide the same sort of constraints by rules about public debate and decision-making that require the persuasion of those on whom the law will be imposed. Of course, we cannot require that everyone actually be persuaded. That would require that all legislation be agreed unanimously. But we can insist that everyone be offered reasons that a reasonable person could understand and might reasonably accept. In the end, the law may be imposed on some who are unconvinced by the reasons that the majority offers. But that is quite different from saying that they must accept whatever the majority decides, even if the choices are arbitrary, invidious, or incomprehensible. The criterion of legitimacy in liberalism, parallel to Aquinas's requirement that the law be ordained to the common good, is this: law must be supported by reasons that are recognizably good reasons, even to those who are not in the end persuaded.

Something like this seems to lie behind the idea of public reason that is important to many recent accounts of political discussion in liberal democracy. For John Rawls, the practical problem that any liberal political discourse must solve is the irreducible pluralism of ideas about the human good. To secure general support for and participation in the political process, it must be possible for people to hold diverse and contradictory ideas without fear that their deepest commitments and values will be rejected and even forbidden by the collective decisions of their fellow citizens. Free people will not enter into a political process that might settle on a good that renders their own cherished values illegitimate. So a liberal society must employ a criterion of legitimacy based on shared, public reasons and not on shared goals. At the outset its citizens must be assured that the political framework within which they live is acceptable to their reason. When coercive rules are imposed on them, there should also be reasons that they could rationally accept. As Rawls puts it:

> Our exercise of political power is fully proper only when it is exercised in accordance with a constitution the essentials of which all citizens as free and equal may reasonably be expected to endorse in the light of principles and ideals acceptable to their common human reason. This is the liberal principle of legitimacy. To this it adds that all questions that arise in the legislature that concern or border on constitutional essentials, or

basic questions of justice, should also be settled, as far as possible, by principles and ideas that can be similarly endorsed.[13]

Rawls differs from Thomas Aquinas on several important points about the nature of political communities. What Rawls and Aquinas have in common is that each thinks it is important that people have reasons to obey the law, and indeed, having those reasons is essential for the law to be legitimate.

"Public reasons" for Rawls are in the first instance simply those reasons that give persons in a society reasons to think that the laws under which they live are legitimate. Based on his understanding of the assumptions that people in a liberal democracy must share, Rawls has an account of what kind of reasons will count as public. In his later work, however, Rawls states more clearly that public reason is not limited to the system he has set out in *A Theory of Justice*.[14] Other conceptions of justice might also be elaborated to show the sorts of reasons that people who adhere to them would regard as public. We could use that knowledge to understand what political discourse would be like for such people and to determine what laws they would be likely to accept as legitimate. Among the candidates Rawls specifically mentions for this sort of development into an account of public reason are "Catholic views of the common good and solidarity when they are expressed in terms of political values."[15]

Considering these suggestions in Rawls's later work, Paul Weithman proposes that we think of a "family of liberal political conceptions of justice."[16] There is no single, unchanging set of public reasons that governs all public discourse, but a changing set of ideas that people at any given time will accept as good reasons for the laws under which they have to live. From the standpoint of liberal political theory, it is the philosopher's task to investigate this family of ideas and make sure that the members are actually up to performing the task of legitimation that liberal democracy assigns to them. The "family of liberal political conceptions of justice" that Weithman proposes would appear to include at least Rawls's own idea of justice as fairness, a political conception of the common good, and Habermas's account of discourse and democracy (which Rawls also explicitly mentions, along with the Catholic idea of the common good). Others might also be developed. Eric Mount's essay on community suggests that participation is a criterion of justice and could be developed as a distinctive way of determining what counts as public reason. The idea of solidarity, which Rawls simply links together as "Catholic views of the common good and solidarity," might be developed independently into a concept of public reason appropriate to liberation theology.

---

13. Rawls, *Political Liberalism*, 137.

14. John Rawls, "The Idea of Public Reason Revisited," in *John Rawls: Collected Papers* (ed. Samuel Freeman; Cambridge: Harvard University Press, 1999), 582–83.

15. Ibid.

16. Paul Weithman, *Religion and the Obligations of Citizenship* (Cambridge: Cambridge University Press, 2002), 197.

Josiah Young suggests ways in which this might be done. James Skillen proposes an account of the common good that, rather like Habermas's concept of discourse ethics, provides a norm for political thinking that is implicit in the political relationships itself and independent of the achievements and failings of actual political communities. Participants in public life who followed out any of these suggestions could arrive at a workable concept of public reason that would set the terms of political discourse in the same way that Rawls's public reason does, though the terms might be different from Rawls's own.

Rawls does not suggest that these different concepts of public reason are interchangeable or equivalent to one another. Weithman describes the variety of concepts of public reason as "competing"[17] for recognition as the best account of the reasons that would be affirmed by other citizens for accepting the constraints of legitimate laws. No doubt Rawls continued to regard the political conception of justice as fairness to be superior to the others in its capacity to justify the necessary arrangements for a liberal democracy without encumbering it with additional, and possibly divisive, political constraints. Though we might expand the family of liberal political conceptions of justice beyond the few members that Rawls actually suggests, it does not seem that he thought the family was quite large.[18]

To understand why Rawls hesitates to expand the scope of public reason, it is important to remember the specific purpose that public reasons serve. They are the sorts of reasons we offer our fellow citizens when we are proposing laws under which they will have to live, assuming that we are politically successful as well as rationally persuasive to a majority of the relevant decision-makers. As we saw in Aquinas, procedural criteria of legitimacy are also important. Ideas do not become law just because they are supported by public reason. But just as the medieval prince might promulgate an unjust law and enforce it by his princely power, a democratic legislature might follow all the proper procedures in enacting a law that imposed a narrow set of rules and values on the whole population. The constraint of public reason, like the constraint of the common good on the powers of the prince, serves to prevent a process that is procedurally correct from yielding a result that is unjust.

Discussion of the common good, for Aquinas and for the theological traditions that have developed from his work, serves a great many other purposes and happens in many other contexts. Rawls's idea of public reason, by contrast, is narrowly tailored to this specific purpose. (That seems to be one reason why Rawls thinks his conception serves the purpose better than its competitors.) The constraints of public reason may prove quite restrictive, limiting people from appealing to ideas of the good and imperatives of faith that are important to them and central to their own identities. But the constraints apply only to that narrow range of discussions in which the possibility of coercion is integral to the purpose of discourse.

> It is imperative to realize that the idea of public reason does not apply to
> all political discussions of fundamental questions, but only to discussions

---

17. Ibid., 199.
18. Ibid., 198–201.

of those questions in what I refer to as the public political forum. This forum may be divided into three parts: the discourse of judges in their decisions, and especially of the judges of a supreme court; the discourse of government officials, especially chief executives and legislators, and finally, the discourse of candidates for public office. . . .[19]

In other discussions where a coercive outcome is not in prospect, the rigorous constraints of public reason do not apply. This is what Rawls calls the "background culture," with its wide array of voluntary organizations, educational institutions, civic groups, and communications media.[20] It appears that few general rules govern the offering of reasons in the background culture, and Rawls in any case does not elaborate them.

While it might be possible, of course, to set out a notion of democracy that rests entirely on public reason and prohibits mention of God and the good in public discourse, it should be clear from this study that Rawls's liberal democracy is not such a theory. Public reason, for Rawls, performs an essential but limited task.[21] His version of liberal democracy does not impose the constraints of public reason beyond those limits.

Finding a place for the common good in liberal democracy might best begin, then, by exploring possibilities that lie beyond the "public political forum." It may be that the common good has its primary role in another part of public discourse, through which it complements, rather than competes with, the role of public reason in politics, narrowly understood. To identify that other part of public discourse, we will need a more differentiated account of what Rawls treats simply as the "background culture." When we have provided that, it may be possible to see how the common good shapes an important part of public discourse and thus makes its own contribution to public reason. In this way, a law may be "ordained to the common good" even though it is supported politically by what everyone would recognize as "public reasons."

Public Discourse in the Thomistic Tradition

Thomas Aquinas, writing before the rise of parliamentary systems of government and developed systems of legislated law, does not give the same consideration to public discourse that Rawls's account of liberal democracy requires. Thomists living in a liberal democracy, however, have to make sense of its ongoing

---

19. Rawls, *Collected Papers*, 575.
20. Ibid., 576.
21. To put the point more precisely, we might say that public reason *as Rawls conceives it* performs an essential, but limited task. It should be clear from the idea of a "family" of conceptions of public reason that the idea of the common good, or the principle of solidarity in liberation theology, might generate a different account of public reason, in which public reasons would have other functions as well. Because public reason is central to Rawls's account of "public political discourse," I will generally use the term "public reason" in the remainder of this essay to mean "John Rawls's conception of public reason."

public discussion in their own terms. In a society where everyone has a share in government, the deliberative process cannot be irrelevant to the search for the common good. This connection is particularly evident in the account of public discourse developed some forty years ago by John Courtney Murray. Murray, like Rawls, developed his reflections on the liberal political system as it has developed in the United States, and for that American context he was particularly concerned to interpret the tradition of Catholic political thought derived from Thomas Aquinas.

Toward that end, Murray begins, not with a description of the goods sought in American political life, but with an understanding of its "civil argument." Civil argument is not an episodic confrontation between parties disputing specific political questions, but an ongoing process of deliberation that defines the political community. "The specifying note of political association is its rational deliberative quality, its dependence for its permanent cohesiveness on argument among men."[22]

Civil argument for Murray has three major themes:[23] *Public affairs* are matters of common concern that call for public decision and action by the government. This corresponds fairly closely to Rawls's idea of matters that get resolved in the "public political forum." *Affairs of the commonwealth* are wider concerns that "fall, at least in decisive part, beyond the limited scope of government."[24] The *constitutional consensus* provides the unity and identity necessary for the public argument to continue and develop. It is not so much a matter of constitutional documents and constitutional law (which belong to public affairs) as of the shared convictions that make those constitutions possible. As Murray puts it, "It seems to have been one of the corruptions of intelligence by positivism to assume that argument ends when agreement is reached. In a basic sense, the reverse is true. There can be no argument except on the premise, and within the context, of agreement. *Mutatis mutandis*, this is true of scientific, philosophical and theological argument. It is no less true of political argument."[25]

No doubt Murray would affirm a rational unity behind this constitutional consensus that Rawls would regard as unnecessary.[26] But Murray's intention is not to reduce the public argument to a set of propositions that could be deduced from a single, rational starting point. Murray is a moral realist at this point. The rational unity of the consensus exists independently of our knowing it. It becomes effective through the deliberative process by which we arrive at agreement about what the constitution means for the moment, in our present situation. Far from anticipating a progressive refinement of the public argument toward a final, rational order, Murray suggests that the constitutional consensus remains relevant only as long as we continue to argue about it. "Only at the price of this continued contact

22. John Courtney Murray, *We Hold These Truths* (New York: Sheed & Ward, 1960), 6.
23. Ibid., 8–10.
24. Ibid., 8.
25. Ibid., 10.
26. There appear to be functional similarities between Murray's "constitutional consensus" and Rawls's "overlapping consensus." See Rawls, *Political Liberalism*, 133–40.

with experience will a constitutional tradition continue to be 'held' as real knowledge and not simply as a structure of prejudice."[27]

Murray's interest is centered, however, on the second theme of public argument, the "affairs of the commonwealth." Here, it seems, substantive agreements on elements of the common good are achieved, tested in experience, and formulated and reformulated as public moral principles. This public argument goes on in a wide variety of cultural, religious, and educational institutions, and it often goes on quite independently of the political discussions by which some public conclusions become law.

What Murray calls "public argument" about "affairs of the commonwealth" thus appears as part of the "background culture" in Rawls's account of public reason, but it is only part of it. For Rawls, the "background culture" covers all the discussions in which the coercive power of government is not involved and in which the constraints of public reason therefore do not apply. Churches arguing about their liturgy are part of the background culture, as are theologians debating with humanists about the possibility of altruism. Debates among art critics about aesthetic theory belong to the background culture, as do debates among educators about the balance between classical and scientific learning in the secondary school curriculum. Murray's "affairs of the commonwealth" concern only the "background culture" discussions in which a substantive determination about the common good is at stake. Discussions about the common good are nonetheless public in a way that does not apply to other discourses in the background culture, such as a discussion about church liturgy, a seminar on personal finance, or a master class in piano.

This more differentiated account of the discussions that go on in the "background culture" is part of Murray's contribution to our understanding of public discourse. He draws our attention to the fact that not every determination about the common good is a matter for government action. The boundaries between these forums are not sharply demarcated. Nearly every activity that involves people in groups has some implications for the common good, and nearly every aspect of the common good raises some questions about appropriate government action. Nevertheless, with the aid of Murray's account of "civil argument," we can identify an important range of discussions that are broadly public in nature, precisely because of their substantive concern with the common good. And yet such discussions are not strictly political in a way that would lead a Rawlsian liberal to restrict their discourse within the constraints of public reason.

Beyond Liberalism and Its Critics

If public discourse is viewed as a single field of discussion in which the only important result is coercive public law, the common good and public reason become competitors for control of that discussion. If, as James Skillen suggests,[28]

---

27. Murray, *We Hold These Truths*, 11.
28. James Skillen, "'The Common Good' as Political Norm," in this volume.

law is rather the outcome of a complex of interrelated discussions, then the common good and public reason may be viewed as complementary criteria of legitimacy. The criteria are clearly different, yet it is possible for the requirements of both to be satisfied by the same outcome. In fact, that seems to be what we want from our public discourse taken as a whole, and what we should expect when it is functioning well.

It is possible, of course, to devise a conflict between the common good and public reason. Advocates of particular religious tradition could demand the adoption of their idea of the good as the basis of law for a whole society, offering as their reason only that this is the will of God. Those committed to public reason might, in turn, argue that particular views of the human good should be excluded from every public discussion, including the "affairs of the commonwealth," lest they contaminate the "public political forum" in which public reasons are brought to bear on the formulation of law. As we have seen, theologians and philosophers do, in fact, take versions of those positions in our contemporary debates about public life.[29] But those positions begin to seem extreme, and the conflict between common good and public reason begins to seem somewhat contrived. It is quite possible to imagine one person concerned about both the common good and public reason at the same time.

Nevertheless, a coherent public discourse requires more than just the absence of unavoidable conflict between these two criteria of legitimacy. It might turn out that their convergence is merely a lucky accident, so that people interested in the common good and those committed to public reason just go on talking past one another, sometimes happily turning out the same recommendations for law and public policy. To move beyond the impasse between liberalism and its critics, we must also seek connections between the different sorts of public discussion, so that each influences the other in ways that are apt to bring their outcomes together.

We should not expect the convergences to be perfect. It is easy to imagine a law or policy legitimated by reference to the common good that has not yet acquired a compelling case in public reason, or to make a public case for a law or policy that supports particular interests without connecting to any notion of the common good. The "affairs of the commonwealth" are tied to "public political discourse" by experience and history, not logic. Nevertheless, it is possible to describe how that experience has developed in modern liberal democracy.

As Murray understands that history, it yields in the "affairs of the commonwealth" a sustained and detailed discussion in which competing ideas about how to achieve the common good are tested in relationship to shared truths. Such truths hold the community together in spite of the diversity of backgrounds, religious beliefs, and loyalties that people bring with them into public life. This is an iterative or dialectical process, in which both the ideas of the good that are proposed and the fund of shared truths that the community holds in common are changed. The public consensus on these matters is therefore not static. It has a "growing edge."[30]

---

29. See above, in section "The 'Growing Edge' of Public Reason."
30. See, generally, Murray, *We Hold These Truths*, 97–123.

People who are committed to an idea of the common good seek to persuade others to it, and they sometimes use public reasons for that purpose. Ideas about the common good sometimes also change our ideas about what counts as a public reason. This essay concludes by examining each of those developments in turn.

Public Reason and the Affairs of the Commonwealth

What marks the affairs of the commonwealth off from other discussions in the broader culture is a substantive concern with the common good. That is, the purpose of the discussion is to determine the conditions for the good life that only a whole society can maintain and in which every member of the society has a share. What identifies the discussion of affairs of the commonwealth is the subject matter, what that discussion is about. Once that is clear, we are able to distinguish discussion of the affairs of the commonwealth from a number of other closely related discussions that may, in everyday experience, overlap with it and thus become conceptually confused with it.

Groups and individuals may demand general acceptance of ideas and practices that they deem essential to their own well-being. But this becomes an affair of the commonwealth only when their proposal includes a substantive claim that these ideas and practices are themselves part of the common good, or that having a society that makes a place for them is part of the common good. Bargaining for acceptance and asserting control on the basis of political or economic power fall outside of the affairs of the commonwealth, though they may be aimed at similar results as far as the parties involved are concerned. Religious witness to a way of life and the distinctive commitments that it requires is not in itself an affair of the commonwealth, though its witness may be an implicit critique of prevailing ideas about the common good. Self-expression and cultural expression are not affairs of the commonwealth, though they may imply ideas about the common good or make implicit claims that rights protecting such expressions are part of the common good. Taken together, the growing importance of some of these other forms of public expression may have crowded the discussion of affairs of the commonwealth out of public consciousness in recent years. But that gives us all the more reason to recover its distinctive characteristics and purposes.

Affairs of the commonwealth concern proposals regarding the common good. Other items of public interest or public action belong in other discussions. So those who participate here must be prepared to state their points not only in terms of self-interest, but with reference to a good in which all persons share. This provides substantive criteria by which to determine whose reasons belong in the discussion. Or rather, to put the matter more precisely, these criteria determine who is, in fact, discussing the affairs of the commonwealth and who, despite appearances, is actually discussing something else. It is vital to the understanding of the affairs of the commonwealth as a *public* forum that no one is categorically excluded from participation. But it is equally important to the integrity of the discussion that all participants recognize its defining characteristic: concern with the substantive common good.

Religious traditions and communities are important participants in the discussion of affairs of the commonwealth. Understandings of the human good are important points of continuity and ongoing discussion within the traditions, so they have something to contribute to the public discussion of these matters. Indeed, where a religious tradition is widely shared among the public, the boundary between the theological and the public discussions—always important for scholars to locate conceptually—may be difficult to fix in practice. Since the more rigorous constraints of public reason that apply in the public political forum do not apply in this discussion, it is not necessary to maintain the distinction between religious and public reasons for accepting an understanding of the common good. Nevertheless, reasons that have a clear religious particularity may undermine the case that those who use them are trying to make.

The exact role of religious traditions and arguments in the affairs of the commonwealth will differ with the occasion, and also no doubt over time, as the diversity and religious complexity of the society changes. What passes for a statement of the common good at a civic observance in a rural community with a Catholic and a Protestant church (or perhaps just one or the other!) may appear confessional in a national or global context. So, over time, religious spokespersons and their traditions become quite adept at shaping their theological contributions to the particular requirements of the affairs of the commonwealth. Religious participation in the public discussion thus focuses most often on an application of religious traditions and teaching to the particular problems that occupy the public at the moment, rather than on comprehensive claims that urge the public to adopt the tradition's view of human good as a whole. Religious and "secular" arguments for a particular element of the common good are often combined to build a more comprehensive case. Theologians learn to state their points in terms that are responsive to the questions of skeptics and critics, as well as expressive of the convictions of the faithful. In all of these ways, a religious tradition, once embedded in a particular social context, learns to be a participant in the public discussion of the affairs of the commonwealth. David Hollenbach describes this religious adaptation to the persistent questions and persuasive forms of argument that are in more general use in a society as an exercise in "intellectual solidarity."[31] It is a concern for the neighbor that goes beyond merely opportunistic use of the public forum as a place to spread religious truth.

The "Growing Edge" of Public Reason

The affairs of the commonwealth do not have the immediate relationship to government and law that Murray's "public affairs" or Rawls's "public political discourse" has. The affairs of the commonwealth would, however, become mere speculation if they did not at some point affect the making of law and policy. Murray sometimes suggests an even stronger connection between the common

31. David Hollenbach, *The Common Good and Christian Ethics* (Cambridge: Cambridge University Press, 2002), 137–70.

good and coercive law. He says that after thorough public discussion, it falls to those who understand the affairs of the commonwealth to "require" compliance with what the common good requires, and even to "require that this moral dictate be made public law."[32] Such a statement suggests a conflict with the requirements of "public political discourse." It appears that we are to move directly from the affairs of the commonwealth to legislative enactments. If the liberal criterion of legitimacy is correct, that process could yield legitimate law only if specifically religious reasons were eliminated from the discussion of the affairs of the commonwealth. Or, if everything that is ordained to the common good is supposed to become a requirement of law, we would have to be prepared to abandon the constraints of liberal political discourse.

Murray's elaboration of this understanding of the affairs of the commonwealth provides, however, for more differentiation between the discernment of the common good and the enactment of law and policy. To be sure, the Thomistic criterion of legitimacy—ordination to the common good—remains paramount, and the civil argument about the affairs of the commonwealth is the primary place where the common good is determined. The "requirement" that this determination be made law is, however, primarily a rational requirement, not a procedural one. Once the civil argument reaches a consensus on the common good, the necessary legal arrangements logically follow, and legislative action can be assumed.[33]

Murray's account of the affairs of the commonwealth in fact focuses the determination of the common good in the university, not in the legislature.[34] The public consensus on the common good is articulated by *magistri*, not *domini*. Their statement has moral authority, but it is not itself law.

Yet Murray's "university" or *studium*, of course, is an idealized body, corresponding to no actual educational institution. His political thought, as William Cavanaugh's essay reminds us,[35] is not an empirical study of American democracy, even in his own time, and his ideal is perhaps even more distant from political reality today. Murray's intent is not to offer a sociological identification of the persons best equipped to articulate the common good. "In point of principle," he says, "all one can say is that they are the men who have a 'care,' but who are not interested parties (in the usual sense of the latter phrase)."[36] His unself-conscious use of the phrase "men who have a care" is a reminder of how much we have learned since 1960 about the difficulties of identifying all the interests that are actually at play among persons who claim to have a "care" for the common good. We will take many more steps than he did to ensure that the discussion of the affairs of the commonwealth is actually open to all and that the requirement of having a

---

32. Murray, *We Hold These Truths*, 120.
33. Assuming, of course, that the legislature can be expected to act rationally. I also leave aside the important qualification that not every requirement of the common good should be made into public law. Some things are best left to private organizations or to individual conscience.
34. Murray, *We Hold These Truths*, 122.
35. William Cavanaugh, "Killing for the Telephone Company," in this volume.
36. Murray, *We Hold These Truths*, 123.

"care" does not exclude those whose grievances are more specific and whose needs are more urgent.

Nevertheless, the structure of public discourse that Murray suggests has much to commend it as an account of how moral arguments should go in a pluralistic, democratic society. He draws our attention to a distinctly public discussion of the affairs of the commonwealth within the larger background culture. His important suggestion is that the affairs of the commonwealth precede the formulation of law and policy, often by some distance in time, so that those who want to shape the growing edge of the public consensus do well to concentrate their efforts in that more open discussion. Religious ideas about the human good may not only be more welcome, but also more effective in the affairs of the commonwealth than in the public political forum.

In place of the stark opposition that some see between Thomism and liberalism, this closer comparison of the structures of public discourse in John Rawls and John Courtney Murray suggests a certain complementarity between their views. Murray traced the roots of liberalism back beyond Locke and Hobbes to the common search for peace in Augustine, and he once referred to Thomas Aquinas as "the first Whig."[37] Perhaps Rawls, with his insistence that the shape of liberal politics must be determined by public *reason* rather than by majority preference, should be known as "the last Thomist."

The differences between Murray and Rawls are real, but the boundary between the "public political forum" and a discussion of the "affairs of the commonwealth" is not as clearly demarcated in experience as the conceptual differences between them suggest. The public forum is distinguished by its concern with law and the coercive powers of government. But it is possible to talk about what the law ought to be in a forum that is more public than a confessional religious group and less political than a legislative body. The constraints of public reason would not apply in that discussion. Some proposals are put forward in legislative bodies with no expectation that they will be accepted and enacted, but rather as a means of furthering public and legislative awareness of an issue. Is the legislative discussion of those proposals strictly limited by public reason, simply because of the place where it occurs, or is that discussion more properly an "affair of the commonwealth"?

By contrast, people who initiate public discussions of issues that have wide social impact and moral resonance may find that they are propelling the society rapidly toward new laws and regulations, so that the usual distance between general public discussion and decisive political action is dramatically reduced. Rawls mentions the abolitionist movement before the Civil War and the civil rights movement led by Martin Luther King Jr. as two examples in American history.[38] In these cases, the religious appeals of the movement were intended to hasten the coming of a "well-ordered and just society in which the ideal of public reason could eventually be honored."[39] In view of their historical circumstances and the

---

37. Ibid., 32.
38. Rawls, *Political Liberalism*, 249–51.
39. Ibid., 250.

prevailing injustices in society at the time, we may conclude in retrospect that these movements did not violate the ideal of public reason, despite the religious basis for many of their public arguments.

Rawls summarizes that brief discussion with the point that "the appropriate limits of public reason vary depending on historical and social conditions."[40] One might amplify the point by suggesting that they do not vary randomly, but in such a way that transformations pushing the limits of public reason at one time become the normal requirements of public reason in the next. Public reason, as Murray might put it, has a "growing edge." We can make historical judgments about whether a claim regarding justice or the human good complied with the prevailing requirements in the past. We can even make retrospective normative judgments about specific uses of public reason, as Rawls does with the abolitionists. But in the moment, it may only be possible, with respect to a specific new and important idea, to say that we will know in the outcome whether the reasons that support it are public reasons.

Thus, we have observed a convergence between a liberal public discourse, in which public reason is the criterion of legitimacy, and a Thomistic consensus, in which the criterion of legitimacy is orientation toward the common good. This convergence suggests that those who are concerned for the renewal of American public life might well focus their attention on the discussion of the common good that lies outside the realm where reasons have to be public enough to legitimate the use of coercive force. Yet such discussion remains sufficiently public to require that the goods and goals under consideration must require the participation of all for their achievement and to allow the participation of all in their enjoyment. Such a forum is not only a place where the common good can be discussed; its existence is itself a part of the common good. The vitality of that discussion will be best served, not by determining which arguments must be excluded from it, but by ensuring that it is genuinely open to everyone's participation.

Religious groups and movements have an important stake in that discussion. It is where they hone their skills of "intellectual solidarity." The religious elements of their vision of the human good are more likely to be respectfully heard and thoughtfully considered there than in a forum where they are advocating more specific legislative or policy initiatives. Theorists and practitioners of political liberalism have a stake in it, too, because the growing edge of that discussion is where public reasons are created.

---

40. Ibid., 251.

Whose Good?
Whose Commons?

Introduction

Josiah Young

The responses of Eric Mount, Cheryl Kirk-Duggan, Josiah Young, and Milner Ball to the questions "Whose good? Whose commons?" reflect the diversity of their disciplines and scholarly passions.

In "It Takes a Community—or at Least an Association," Eric Mount argues that individualistic Americans have "better" things to do than pursue communal activities that promote neighborly bonds and "civic virtue." Where Americans assume they *are* communal—as is the case with so-called ethnic groups or religious associations—their communities advance competing claims about what is good for and common to all. Mount would like to see those partisan agendas, whether individualistic or communal, at least coalesce into associations that would overcome "exclusivism and domination" while protecting "dissent and difference." For Mount, the theological virtues of faith, hope, and charity could persuade Americans to cultivate such associations as those virtues rise above "egoism" and "tribalism" in advancing what is good for all persons and the earth itself. He also finds the philosophical virtues of justice, prudence, wisdom, and courage to be helpful insofar as ancient philosophers such as Plato have held that virtuous individuals transcend self-gratification or the narrow interests of their group in working for the good of the whole society. Above all, Mount holds that conceptualizations of the common good *must* overcome idolatry in acquiescing in the mystery of the Creator—the "Good that challenges all of our idolatries," whose good creation is the commons to which all are heir.

In "A Rose by Any Other Name," the womanist scholar Cheryl Kirk-Duggan argues that our questions "Whose good? Whose commons?" indicate that theorists of the common good have deemed some people to be bad and to embody the negative connotations of "common": *of inferior quality, less than excellent.* In the context of the United States, for example, whites have barred African-Americans, Native Americans, Hispanics, and Asians—the vulgar "commoners," as it were—from first-class citizenship, to protect it from profanation. These people of color, the commoners, have therefore been integral to the definition of first-class citizenship as they accent its positive significance. For Kirk-Duggan, difference and commonality have gone together ineluctably with tragic consequences for those whose otherness has been devalued by those in power. In appealing to Toni Morrison's novel, *The Bluest Eye*, bell hook's critical theory, and certain biblical texts, Kirk-Duggan argues that the common good must be divested of such "binary opposition" so that it might signify the inclusion of all rather than the privileging of some.

Josiah Young's "Good Is Knowing When to Stop" tackles our questions by suggesting that the concept of the common good comes to us in the twenty-first century rooted in ancient metaphysical assumptions that forbid disadvantaged people from having anything to say about their ascribed unlikeness to the Good. For Young, an African-American theologian, philosophers such as Aristotle have defined the common good in terms of the "constitutional rights" and "household justice" of elite, freeborn males. Those rulers equated their privilege with rational, immortal principles while relegating their slaves to transience and irrationality. Young finds that this early worldview has taken on racist, modern implications with the historic development of the United States: African-Americans had been excluded from *constitutional justice* for centuries. According to upholders of the common good, themselves influenced by Aristotle, blacks were disqualified necessarily from any justice but that of the master's household. In light of that sad history, Young—appealing to the insights of thinkers such as Toni Morrison and Emmanuel Lévinas—appropriates the questions "Whose good? Whose commons?" as follows: Who ultimately sanctions the masters' view of justice—Jesus Christ's God, who promises to end the master-slave dialectic once and for all, or Aristotle's Primary unmoved mover, rooted in the masters' privilege?

Milner Ball's essay, "The Common Good in Performance," attempts to persuade white Americans that their differences from Native Americans need not have been used as a foil to exclude the latter from the good. According to Ball, an attorney and an activist, it would have been good if white Americans had been receptive to the perspectives of Native Americans such as Black Elk—Lakota holy man and Roman Catholic catechist. Such perspectives would have been invaluable critiques of white Americans' privilege. Placing himself in the tradition of John Neihardt—the white writer who told Black Elk's story true to his experience of both the great injustices done to his people and their hopes to live in peace with the whites—Ball wants us to see that American freedom has hardly been for all. In making his case, Ball appeals to the incarnation: Here, the difference between God and human beings—a difference far greater than that between whites and "Indians"—has been overcome in Christ's resurrection. His nonviolent way in the world and identification with the wretched of the earth promise that the lion will lie down with the lamb in the new creation that, one hopes, is coming. If the predator will no longer devour what had been its prey, *human beings* can surely forsake their predatory ways *today*—for the common good.

Ball, Young, and Kirk-Duggan answer the questions Whose good? Whose commons? by focusing on a history that has been unfairly partial to some and ineffably damaging to others. All three scholars agree with Mount that a way out of this dilemma is to realize that God's good creation must be held in common by all and without self-serving privilege if it is to take on the character of justice.

It Takes a Community—
or at Least an Association

C. Eric Mount Jr.

What life have you if you have not life together?
There is no life that is not in community,
And no community not lived in praise of God.
Even the anchorite who meditates alone,
For whom the days and nights repeat the praise of God,
Prays for the Church, the Body of Christ incarnate.
And now you live dispersed on ribbon roads,
And no man knows or cares who is his neighbour
Unless his neighbour makes too much disturbance,
But all dash to and fro in motor cars,
Familiar with the roads and settled nowhere.
Nor does the family even move about together,
But every son would have his motor cycle,
And daughters ride away on casual pillions.
....
When the Stranger says: "What is the meaning of this city?
Do you huddle close together because you love each other?"
What will you answer: "We all dwell together
To make money from each other"? or "This is a community"?[1]

_____

1. T. S. Eliot, "Choruses from 'The Rock,'" *The Complete Poems and Plays 1909–1950* (New York: Harcourt Brace, 1952), 101–3 (used with permissions from Harcourt, Inc., and from Faber & Faber Ltd.).

T. S. Eliot's words may betray their context in the first third of the twentieth century, but they still provide a barometer of a human condition that we know all too well. The question of community in a culture steeped in individualism remains, and the burden of concerting our attention to the common good is still more than the market can bear or the state can command. Without some sense of community as a commons in which we all have a stake and of which we all have a stewardship, our quests for the common good are doomed to be bedeviled by a host of suspicions, exploited by a spate of pretenders, and seduced by a passel of idolatries. It takes a community to acknowledge a common good, and a community itself could even be designated as a common good for its members. We are faced then with the question of what makes a collection of people a community.

Common Good and Community

Even with a postmodern caveat concerning the seeming exclusivity of Eliot's claim about the church as the true community, a theologian might well begin a discussion of the common good by positing God, or whatever center of value holds people together, as the ultimate common good, with the warning that our visions of the ultimate are always at high risk for idolatry. And some believers refer to more than a commonly held faith when they speak of the commonness of God as the highest good. Free-will theists, for example, may point to the community of the Trinity as the Good in common that graciously moves to include humanity in that community. Process panentheists, in turn, may argue that God and some world, not necessarily the one we have, require each other since reality is essentially related and lured toward the good of shared enjoyment.[2] In his Judaic rendering of divine relationality, Martin Buber posits, "In the beginning is relation." He pairs our need of God with the corresponding reminder that "God needs you—in the fullness of his eternity needs you."[3]

To claim in any of these ways that life is always lived in relation to God is not to claim that Eliot's "praise of God" is necessary for life support. But it does at least suggest that life in community is not primarily an act of human invention but an actuality of our human condition, and that a community holds because it has a center or a unifying commitment. As Buber asserts, "The true community does not arise through peoples having feelings for one another (though indeed not without it), but through, first, their taking their stand in living mutual relation with a living Centre, and second, their being in living mutual relation with one another."[4]

---

2. John B. Cobb Jr. and Clark H. Pinnock, eds., *Searching for an Adequate God: A Dialogue between Process and Free Will Theists* (Grand Rapids: Eerdmans, 2000), ix–xiv. As an illustration, in his essay in this present volume (not the one edited by Cobb and Pinnock), William Cavanaugh states, "Our natural community is the Triune God."

3. Martin Buber, *I and Thou* (trans. R. Gregor Smith; 2d ed.; New York: Charles Scribner's Sons, 1958), 18, 82.

4. Ibid., 45.

The focus of this particular exploration is not the domain of theology proper but rather that of social ethics, the meeting place between theology, on the one hand, and social philosophies and sciences on the other. Theology informs the particular form of societal claim advanced here, but similar claims could grow from other backing. It is also fair to say that even communities claiming grounding in Christian faith may contradict these very claims.

Four characteristics or criteria for determining whether a society is also a community are offered by economist Herman Daly and theologian John B. Cobb Jr. Both are Christians who believe that "human life is lived most richly and most rightly when it is lived from God and for God."[5] (1) Membership in the society must contribute to the self-identity of the person, but not necessarily totally define it. (2) Members should participate extensively in the decisions that direct the community's life. (3) The whole society assumes responsibility for the entire membership. (4) The diverse individuality of each member is respected.[6]

These features of community are not limited to small face-to-face communities although such communities may enjoy certain advantages in the realization of them. Indeed, there are intimate collectivities that exhibit identity constriction, participation exclusion, responsibility evasion, and diversity suppression. No matter how large or small the community in question is, the realization of community in this normative sense is a matter of degree rather than total fulfillment. Where these ingredients are sufficiently present to qualify a society as a community, it makes sense to say that the very community that is present is a commons in which the members have a stake and toward which they have an obligation.[7]

Using the example of the village commons where people could graze their sheep without cost and might jeopardize the commons by inordinate grazing, ecologists have taught us to think of the earth's air, water, and other shared resources as a commons that is imperiled by private abuse. Neva Goodwin, an ecological economist, has also suggested that we think of a "global human commons." This commons is found in institutions built and shared by people who represent the whole human family and even the entire ecosystem, rather than the particular interests of a certain business, government, or other institution.[8] For its membership, any community is a commons. That commons is a common good, and that community's life entails a process of continuing exploration of what the common good entails. As the Catholic Bishops of Appalachia have stated in "At

---

5. Herman Daly and John B. Cobb Jr., *For the Common Good* (Boston: Beacon, 1989), 394.

6. Ibid., 172.

7. In the present volume: Robert Jenson's argument regarding God as the common good acknowledges that the common good of a community is inseparable from the community that seeks it but emphasizes the independent reality of that good as well. Also related to this point is Cheryl Kirk-Duggan's treatment of bell hooks, who presents a community as a collective good in itself.

8. Neva R. Goodwin, "Introduction—Global Commons: Site of Peril, Source of Hope," *World Development* (January 1991): 1–15 as summarized in *A Survey of Ecological Economics* (ed. Rajaram Krishnan, Jonathan M. Harris, and Neva R. Goodwin; Washington, DC: Island, 1995), 323.

Home in the Web of Life," "the common good" is another way of stating the principle of community.[9] For the commons and the common good to have global reach, it follows that the community must also have global reach.

Community in Question

Definitions of community that require only a shared commitment to a common history, identity, and set of values and what Amitai Etzioni calls a web of criss-crossing "affect-laden relationships"[10] lack some of the moral safeguards built into the Daly-Cobb proposal. And even in their case, the prophetic, biospheric vision that informs their view of the person-in-community is the only sure brake against idolatrous slippage.

Josiah Young's chapter in this volume shows how Aristotle's version of the common good privileged an elite few and relegated women, children, and slaves to separate forms of justice. The Third Reich and the Ku Klux Klan have advanced their versions of the common good and no doubt considered that they had the community to go with it. Along with Josiah Young's essay, Milner Ball and Cheryl Kirk-Duggan, also in these pages, bear dramatic witness to ominous renditions of the common good that have reflected and perpetrated marginalization and dehumanization in the cases of Native Americans and African-Americans respectively. Some group's notion of the common good probably informed the tribal massacres in Rwanda, the ethnic cleansing in Bosnia and Kosovo, and the elimination of education for girls in Afghanistan under the Taliban. The blood curdles at the fanaticism that has its identity defined by only one narrow community and therefore lacks the perspective to see totalitarianism and terrorism for what they are.[11] Theocratic impositions of ideological uniformity should occasion healthy disrespect for both states attempting to be churches and churches trying to run states. Even under religious auspices, the collective egotism that Reinhold Niebuhr would not let us overlook can gild concerted selfishness with a patina of nobility that can fool the best of us.[12]

There are also objections to the facile use of the term *community* that are rooted in justifiable human preference as well as lamentable human perversity. Martin E. Marty uses the porcupine argument, which he borrows from Arthur Schopenhauer and Michael Oakeshott. The imagined colony of porcupines appreciates each other's company to weather the winter cold, but objects to each other's prickliness when those others get too close. "Civil association" operates on the porcupine model of desirable closeness and distance, while "community"

---

9. Catholic Bishops of Appalachia, *At Home in the Web of Life* (Webster Springs, WV: Catholic Committee of Appalachia, 1995), 32.

10. Amitai Etzioni, *The New Golden Rule: Community and Morality in a Democratic Society* (New York: Basic Books, 1996), 127.

11. Michael Walzer, *Thick and Thin: Moral Arguments at Home and Abroad* (Notre Dame, IN: University of Notre Dame Press, 1994), 98–99.

12. Reinhold Niebuhr, *Moral Man and Immoral Society* (New York: Charles Scribner's Sons, 1960).

implies a less prickly communion that is cemented by love rather than enabled by less intense middle-range sentiment or affection.

Marty makes "association of associations" the preferred way to see our American republic and traces it to Johannes Althusius, the early seventeenth-century Calvinist political philosopher. He prefers this translation of the usual "community of communities," a term also used by Daly and Cobb, because a community would imply more of a creedal bond and more personal intimacy than an association. Marty not only doubts that our nation has a common creed; he also dislikes the efforts of those who try to enforce one. He is much more comfortable with the model of many citizens sharing their stories in a conversation about the common good than with a push toward an imposed, unified common good under the banner of a reigning ideology or civil religion. Both visionaries of national unity and sectarians of national fragmentation are conversation stoppers—the first because they know the answers in advance, and the second because they do not think that the other groups even understand the questions that their own tribe is asking.[13]

Marty's fears are not unfounded, nor is his impatience with facile talk of community where any that exists is not visible to the naked eye. Depending on one's definition, talk of biotic community, global community, European community, national community, the Christian community, the "religious" community, the African-American community, the Chicago community, or the Kentucky community can be highly problematic. And one need not focus on questionable claims about big communities. Even community talk about small colleges, towns, and families can strain credulity at times. If the bar is set high enough, one begins to think that true community is as rare as Gideon Bibles in brothels.

Despite considerable sympathy for Marty's conversational rendition of the "struggle for the common good" and a ready admission that "association of associations" cautions us against naïveté as surely as it cushions us against nationalisms of the worst kind, I resist giving up the language of community in seeking the common good. If the nature of the unity we seek makes generous allowances for the prickliness of difference and the plight of the powerless, we can make community-building a prime expression of concern for the common good. Properly understood, a community is itself a common good, and it need not be oppressive and monolithic. Remembering the porcupines, we might venture that in today's world it is always winter, and that we need each other for survival, but that we need to make allowances for prickliness. One can accept Glenn Tinder's denial that no historical institution "can be purely and simply a community" without believing that community is nothing more than "a tragic ideal."[14] Those institutions can be goods held in common, even if no one of them should define the common good for all other institutions. Herein lies James Skillen's objection, explained in his essay in this volume, to making the political common good in complex societies all-consuming because "political authority cannot be omnicompetent." It remains,

---

13. Martin E. Marty, *The One and the Many: America's Struggle for the Common Good* (Cambridge: Harvard University Press, 1997), 19–23, 118–29.

14. Glenn E. Tinder, *Community: Reflections on a Tragic Ideal* (Baton Rouge: Louisiana State University Press, 1980), 2–4.

nevertheless, that we Americans are all part of a commons, "the public-legal community," for which we should be seeking the common good.

The challenge in our time is to stretch the reach of the commons and the membership of the community to the boundaries of the biosphere, while nurturing the particular communities of greater personal intimacy and creedal thickness that teach us to live in community and foster respect for difference and uniqueness. For example, Lisa Cahill's social ethic of the common good aptly argues for an "institutional component" that will extend a "Christian ethic of compassion and other-concern" to "distant persons and communities." "This institutional extension of co-responsibility with and for other human beings in concentric and overlapping communities from local to global," she writes, "is the essence of social ethics."[15] Such extension is a task for both religious and political communities, but religious communities should have an impetus toward universal community that political institutions notoriously lack. That religious communities become co-opted by nationalism and consumed by institutional self-preservation does not cancel the universal mandates that are constitutive of their stated identities. In this expansive and intensive endeavor, the definition of community offered by Daly and Cobb can serve as a safeguard against exclusivity and domination and as a protection of dissent and difference. Their criteria can be helpfully augmented by the normative language of solidarity, sufficiency, sustainability, and subsidiarity found in recent Catholic and Protestant social teaching.[16]

Identity in Community

First, then, is the issue of self-identity. This fundamental question explores the extent to which we understand personal identity as inseparable from community membership. Is it not in the covenantal ties of some community that we discover our identities? The second question, also fundamental, challenges the narrowness of identity definitions that totally submerge us in either tribal or broadly societal—even global—identifications.

---

15. Lisa Sowle Cahill, *Family: A Christian Social Perspective* (Minneapolis: Fortress, 2000), 131.

16. Subsidiarity can be tracked back to *Quadragesimo anno* of Pius XI (1931). Participation and solidarity figure prominently in *Economic Justice for All*, the pastoral letter of the National Conference of Catholic Bishops on the U.S. economy (1986). The language of sustainability and solidarity and the pairing of participation and sufficiency are found in *Restoring Creation for Ecology and Justice*, adopted by the 202nd General Assembly of the Presbyterian Church, USA, in 1990 (Louisville, KY: Office of the General Assembly). The document refers to previous joint statements of two General Assemblies (1981) that presented three norms appropriate to an ethic of ecological justice—sustainable sufficiency, participation, and justice. The 1990 statement presents participation and sufficiency as the best expressions of justice "for our time" (p. 22). These norms are also found in documents of the World Council of Churches, for example, the fact sheet of the Ecumenical Team at the World Summit on Sustainable Development in Johannesburg, 2002. To be specific, the statement indicates that "sustainable communities" should include respect for diversity, equity, full and meaningful participation, mutual accountability, solidarity, sufficiency, and subsidiarity.

In the first instance, we are talking about solidarity, whether we define ourselves in community or in isolation from it. And the solidarity of which we speak
is considerably more than liberalism's "mutuality of rights."[17] In *Democracy on
Trial,* Jean Bethke Elshtain speaks of the "civic identity" of democratic citizenship, the sense that we are all in it together. She believes that it will require a new
social covenant to repair the fragmentation that we now feel.[18] This question of
self-identity for Americans is posed for Michael Walzer in the context of a double pluralism—of groups and of individuals within and divorced from groups. In
what he calls "perhaps the most individualist society in human history," the pre-
dominant lean is away from cultural association and identity in the pursuit of private happiness and economic survival/success. Eschewing a sense of belonging,
Americans tend to seek help from ethnic, racial, and religious associations only as
a last resort and with no intention of incurring membership costs. In sum, "footloose individuals are not reliable members."[19]

Mirroring Walzer's lament about footloose individuals are the numerous diag-
noses of the decline of "civil society" in America. Civil society includes the family
and all of the voluntary associations that give people a sense of belonging that neither the market nor the state can provide. Robert Putnam's 1995 article "Bowling
Alone" documents the decline of association in our nation and with it the deval-
uation of our social capital.[20] When critics began to cite soccer leagues and the
data Putnam used proved to be misleading, he had to return to the drawing board;
but more survey data surfaced to show that Americans were indeed turning away
from all forms of social interaction, not just from civic groups and bowling
leagues. Attendance at public meetings and participation in volunteer organizations was clearly down. He admitted that membership in environmental groups
and organizations like the AARP was up, but the rise was mainly in check-writing
and not in level of association with other members.

It is noteworthy that Putnam moved to writing about "Bowling Together"
soon after the events of September 11, 2001. Basing his observations on a 2001
survey (conducted from mid-October to mid-November) of many of the same
people polled in the summer and fall of 2000, he found "a more capacious sense
of 'we' than we have had in the adult experience of most Americans now alive."
With a definite foreign enemy and an experience of common suffering, we were
suddenly drawn to collective sacrifice by "a powerful idea of cross-class, cross-
ethnic solidarity." The survey found much greater trust in political institutions,

---

17. Also in the present volume: Such a minimal understanding is what James
Skillen's essay finds wanting in Alan Gewrith. Dennis McCann's conclusion to his
essay concerns the biblically oriented reciprocal terms "human dignity" and "social
solidarity" in Catholic social teachings and their distance from both individualism
and collectivism.

18. Jean Bethke Elshtain, *Democracy on Trial* (New York: Basic Books, 1995), 31.

19. Michael Walzer, *On Toleration* (New Haven, CT: Yale University Press,
1997), 100–102.

20. Robert Putnam, "Bowling Alone: America's Declining Social Capital,"
Journal of Democracy (January 1995). A book by the same title followed.

even including a dramatic burst of enthusiasm for the federal government. It also found greater trust in our neighbors and more cooperation with them to solve problems without any attendant rush to join civic organizations. In these responses Putnam saw a window of opportunity for the affirmation of membership in a national community, but the moment needed to be seized or the reawakened sense of solidarity would be lost.

Without more active civic education in our schools and elsewhere, our sense of solidarity was not going to make the gains in social justice that followed the national bond produced by World War II. At the time when he reported on the survey, he felt that the replenished "wells of solidarity" remained untapped.[21] One thinks of the *New Yorker* cartoon that appeared some weeks after September 11, showing one subway rider saying to another, "It's hard, but slowly I'm getting back to hating everyone." Our pervasive disconnection from nature, kin, the larger American society, and the global society dies hard. And the national conflicts about war with Iraq, civil liberties, patriotism, environmental protection, the social safety net, and tax policy on the heels of the rank-closing that followed the events of 9/11 soon belied our protestations of national solidarity.

Putnam's initial claim about the decline of social capital was not, of course, a new one. The civil society crisis was already getting considerable attention before he wrote, and a decade earlier the Robert Bellah team had diagnosed the American malaise caused by the dominance of expressive and utilitarian individualisms over civic and biblical individualisms in *Habits of the Heart*.[22] They found that language about the public good had become a second language and that civic virtue had become a lost art.

The response to September 11 was also not the first qualifier of Putnam's claims about "Bowling Alone." Alan Wolfe's Middle-Class Morality Project, reported in *One Nation, after All* (1998), was one notable challenger. It found more community than Putnam allowed, for one reason because Americans' community identification now revolved around the workplace, which had allegedly become our most important public sector, more than around civic organizations. Wolfe also cautioned that Putnam might have idealized a previous version of the public world that was, in fact, dominated by men. Nevertheless, even if the decline has been overestimated, there is a sense in which the instrumental ties of the workplace are not an adequate substitute for the loss of such ties as neighborhood affiliations that has been brought about because everyone is working too hard.[23] From a more recent vantage point, we can see that workplace security and loyalties have been taking a beating. A sense of community in companies has generally declined in "the new economy."[24]

---

21. Robert Putnam, "Bowling Together," *American Prospect*, February 11, 2002, 20–22.
22. Robert N. Bellah et al., *Habits of the Heart: Individualism and Commitment in American Life* (Berkeley, CA: University of California Press, 1985).
23. Alan Wolfe, *One Nation, after All* (New York: Viking, 1998), 260.
24. Robert B. Reich, *The Future of Success: Working and Living in the New Economy* (New York: Random House, 2000), chs. 4–5, esp. pp. 84, 87–88; Gloria

The continuing expressions of alarm have been notable, Putnam or no Putnam. Michael Sandel has bemoaned our loss of a public philosophy and of "narrative resources" that enable us to find common identity in a common story and common purposes.[25] Elshtain laments the loss of "a vast network" of "sustaining and supporting civic institutions: churches, schools, and solidaristic organizations, such as mothers' associations," which nested the family, which in turn nested the child who was being nurtured for citizenship in a "densely textured social ecology."[26] *The State of Disunion: 1996 Survey of American Political Culture* found a widening gap between public and private destinies, relatively low levels of general political participation, and a significant drop in levels of membership in civic and political groups other than religious ones.[27] Both this survey and the Middle-Class Morality Project found a culture that values individual rights and personal judgments over the common good or bonding commitments.

Regarding our second question about narrow community identity, stated above, Martin Marty plots a course between the patriotic "totalists," who would impose a single national identity, and the parochial "tribalists," who espouse the separatism of "identity" politics. One wants a societal definition of the common good that is set in stone; the other despairs of discovering any common good not dictated by those who are dominant in society and therefore pushes the pursuit of group interest from a base of parochial separation. In our nation's "struggle for the common good," we do well to avoid the acceptance of a single version of it, but we do worse to abandon the common conversation in continuing pursuit of it.[28]

Against this backdrop of lamentable disaffiliation, it is troubling to find that our level of societal tolerance (Americans' highest good, according to Wolfe) may also have declined as our intensity of affiliation has gone down. It turns out that an active "civil society" is no guarantee against narrowness, bigotry, and group idolatry. Our group identifications in civil society do not automatically tilt us toward altruistic care for those beyond the bounds of our in-groups. Our groups can be as self-interested and self-indulgent as ourselves. As Cahill labels it, a "double dynamic" is often at work in our communities, taking us beyond ourselves but further shutting us off from outsiders.[29] She finds Wolfe also overly trusting that recovery of civil society will tend us toward altruism rather than self-interest writ larger.

H. Albrecht, *Hitting Home: Feminist Ethics, Women's Work, and the Betrayal of "Family Values"* (New York: Continuum, 2002), 108–9.

25. Michael Sandel, *Democracy's Discontent: America in Search of a Public Philosophy* (Cambridge, MA: Belknap, 1996), 351.

26. Elshtain, *Democracy on Trial*, 6.

27. Lawrence E. Adams, "Christians and Public Culture in an Age of Ambivalence," *Christian Scholar's Review* (Fall 2000): 18, 28–29. James Davison Hunter and Carl Bowman of the University of Virginia directed and published the study. Its findings included: "Less than 10 percent are involved in civic, political, professional, and other organizations." William Cavanaugh's essay cites further the variety of points on the political spectrum from which the laments about the decline of civil society have come.

28. Marty, *The One and the Many*, 10–23.

29. Cahill, *Family*, 11.

Finding identity and empowerment in community would supposedly start with family, but we know that most home fires only burn now in the microwave, the facilitator of individualized, domestic fast food. Even strong families can be more ingrown than contributory to the common good, and many a voluntary association is likewise culpable. One challenge before us entails finding ways for various levels of government, education, religious community, and workplace leadership to foster community in their spheres, in families, and in the rest of civil society. The churches and other religious communities should feel this challenge acutely, but state action need not be antithetical to the flourishing of civil society. In Walzer's words, "Group life won't rescue individual men and women from dissociation and passivity unless there is a political strategy for mobilizing, organizing, and if necessary subsidizing the right sort of groups."[30] Just how this mobilizing might work and what would make a group "the right sort" would need clarification to allay some fears, as the debates about Charitable Choice and the role of faith-based organizations in welfare reform illustrate.[31]

In itself, trying to find identity in community membership arising from a sense of belonging at the level of family or voluntary association or workplace is elusive enough. But many invocations of common-good language now attempt to extend our sense of belonging beyond the bounds of more immediate, localized expressions of community to national, international, and even biotic community. The challenge of close-knit solidarity is accompanied by the challenge of universal inclusion or scope. As indicated by Cahill's "double dynamic," there are at least two presumptions at work in debates about how allegiance to the national community, the church universal, global community, or biotic community relates to our allegiances to home, particular church, and interest group. Walzer sees both a tension and a continuity between particular interests and common interests, but he is hopeful about what he sees as a tendency of engaged men and women to become more widely engaged. Involvement and commitment in connection with one group tends to spill over, he believes. Security in one's more tribal affiliations can ready one for coalitions with other communities and even openness to claims of universal community.[32]

Cahill sees the tendency pulling in the other direction. In the tension between particular interests and common interests, collective egotism tends to narrow rather than broaden one's identifications and loyalties. She is less sanguine about the expansion of concern to a larger common good. She acknowledges that "real compassion, altruism, and self-sacrifice without hope of gain" may at times be achieved among groups and not just among individuals. Yet she cautions, "Compassionate action of a group beyond its own sphere of 'belonging' is virtually

---

30. Walzer, *On Toleration*, 111.
31. For an exploration of the pitfalls of Charitable Choice along with the possibility of other forms of state encouragement and church-state cooperation through 501 (c) (3) organizations and tax and other incentives, see Fred Glennon, "Blessed Be the Ties That Bind? The Challenge of Charitable Choice to Moral Obligation," *Journal of Church and State* (Autumn 2000).
32. Walzer, *Thick and Thin*, 81–82.

always mixed in motivation and never extends far or lasts long."[33] Therein lies the challenge to the churches and other religious communities to model communities of universal reach as well as particular intimacy.

Will only the consciousness of global interdependence prompt more universal community identification? Will we come to see ourselves as part of a biotic community, for instance, only if we consider our own survival and that of our children and grandchildren threatened if we do not? Or will an encompassing center of value stretch our vision of the common good? Bruce Grelle observes that any group that gains intellectual and moral leadership in a society without exercising coercion to gain or keep it has to appeal to broad and disparate interests and is therefore stretched toward at least lip service to a larger common good.[34] H. Richard Niebuhr made a related claim that groups gain and keep people's loyalties by elevating values or causes that supposedly transcend the narrow boundaries of that group and tend to push toward universal community.[35] It may take both a normative pull and a pragmatic push to stretch us out.

Building identification with community is critical for any ethic of the common good, and identification with more than one community serves to deliver us from the uncritical allegiance to one that risks a fanatic's lack of perspective. Religious communities have spawned scary expressions of fanaticism and narrowness. Nevertheless, at their best, these communities can combine the draw of "a living Centre" (Buber), the closeness of an intimate fellowship, and the reach of a global concern. The biblical covenant tradition, for example, at its best combines the tightness of covenant or collection of covenants among the people of God with an expansiveness that has universal scope. From the indicators cited above, it appears that local religious solidarities are exceptions to the drift toward disaffiliation, but they are often not exemplary at creating a sense of civic identity or helping people form a public philosophy. Involvement in a faith community and civic engagement have, for many, become alternatives rather than mutually reinforcing commitments.

The possibilities for religious communities to build members' sense of community extend beyond particular religious communities to interreligious dialogue. As Daniel Maguire observes, "All religions consider egoism and an absence of any sense of *the common good* and human solidarity."[36] Religions typically speak in expansive terms about a message with universal import and about human ties that transcend narrow identifications. Even in their significant differences, they should be able to converse about the common good. This dialogue can model the conversational approach to the common good, one that regards the continued discussion as a common good in itself and does not aim at total unanimity as the desideratum of the dialogue. In this volume, Milner Ball's treatment of "translation," as practiced

---

33. Cahill, *Family*, 15.

34. Bruce Grelle, "Scholarship and Citizenship: Comparative Religious Ethicists as Public Intellectuals," *Explorations in Global Ethics* (ed. Sumner B. Twiss and Bruce Grelle; Bounder, CO: Westview, 1998), 56–57.

35. H. Richard Niebuhr, *The Responsible Self* (New York: Harper & Row, 1963), 87.

36. Daniel C. Maguire, *Sacred Energies* (Minneapolis: Fortress, 2000), 38.

by Black Elk, and its advance over the logic of conversion shows how, in dialogical translation, a third reality can emerge that is a common good in performance.

Religious communities have created and exacerbated conflict, but they also have possibilities for expanding our sense of a shared global commons and a global common good. Bruce Grelle writes hopefully, "The interfaith movement is one of the few places in contemporary society where it is possible to employ a moral language of universal interests and the common good while recognizing and even celebrating the irreducible plurality of religious, social, and cultural life."[37]

Participation in Community

The second community criterion is participation. The broader meaning of participation goes beyond explicit participation in decision-making to the requirements of community membership. What does it take for persons and for the entire biotic community to have a place at the table, to have a voice, to be able to sustain life, to be full members of the community, to receive consideration in quests for the common good? *Gaudium et spes*, from Vatican II, defines the common good as "the sum of those conditions of social life which allow social groups and their individual members relatively thorough and ready access to their own fulfillment."[38] Such conditions characterize a community because they enable full participation in common life. We can call this norm "justice" or "equity" because it targets the distribution of rights and freedoms in society and seeks to assure all members of equal opportunity to realize their possibilities. We can also call it "sufficiency" because it addresses the minimal requisites for full community membership. Liberals and communitarians alike may be able to find common cause here if they can see individual rights and freedoms, on one side, and community well-being, on the other, as potentially complementary rather than antithetical.

In *Development as Freedom*, Amartya Sen speaks of what is required in a particular setting to enable people to realize their capabilities as free agents. He is claiming that deprivation of capabilities is more inclusive than income deprivation. The freedom to pursue and to achieve is more than the negative freedom of protected rights. It includes what is necessary for human development. It requires the removal of major sources of freedom denied. Different times and places will require different guarantees to enable people to be full participants in their segment of the human community. The list of what is needed does not stop with essential material goods, but extends to political participation and spiritual enrichment. Poverty is thus reenvisioned as "capability deprivation."[39]

---

37. Grelle, "Scholarship and Citizenship," 56.

38. Second Vatican Council, *Gaudium et spes: Pastoral Constitution on the Church in the Modern World* (7 December 1965), in *Catholic Social Thought: The Documentary Heritage* (ed. David O'Brien and Thomas A. Shannon (Maryknoll, NY: Orbis, 1992), par. 26. In the present volume see also Dennis McCann's observation about the absence of a consistent definition of "the common good" in Roman Catholic social teaching.

39. Amartya Sen, *Development as Freedom* (New York: Alfred Knopf, 1999), introduction.

To insure full community membership, making everyone a consumer is not enough. However, anyone not a potential consumer is not a full participant. To Walzer, for example, in America "unemployment is probably the most dangerous form of dissociation."[40] And, of course, not just any job assures full participation in a workplace community, in a society's economic life, and in both domestic and political life beyond the job. Participatory, secure, meaningful, safe, and sustainable work is different from a mere job.[41]

In addition, we must ask not only whether individuals are enabled to enjoy full participation but also whether families are. In Lisa Cahill's words, what is needed is what "makes it possible for all families to participate in the common good of society and for women and men to be equal participants in family and social life, including economic life."[42] Other groups are equally needful of participatory possibilities.

Some members of both the human community and the larger biotic community will not be able to speak for themselves as participants, but that does not mean that their welfare is not "on the table" when community conversation about the common good takes place. For example, families, advocates, or sensitive health professionals may represent nursing home residents who are incompetent. Sometimes participation takes the form of a recognized accountability to neighboring forms of nonhuman life or generations unborn that cannot speak for themselves.

What the European Union calls "transparency" suggests a minimal level of participation since people are not apt either to voice dissent or to keep significant silence if they are not entrusted with knowledge of what is going on. Some understandings of our global economy would imply or insist that questions about full participation will take care of themselves if the earth has a common market since more and more people will benefit from more and more economic growth. When we talk about the common good and a global commons and the possibility of global community, however, we are neither talking about bread alone nor settling for a persistent underclass as either inevitable or necessary to drive the engine of economic progress toward a common market's good. Participation means sufficiency translated as having the requisites for seizing fair opportunity as well as seeking personal fulfillment, justice as having a place and a portion at the table, and freedom as being empowered for agency.

Responsibility in and for Community

Participation means more than just gaining a place at the table where benefits are distributed and the decisions are made. It includes the third measure of community—

40. Walzer, *On Toleration*, 105.
41. Advisory Committee on Social Witness Policy of the General Assembly Council, *God's Work in Our Hands: Employment, Community, and Christian Vocation* (Louisville, KY: Office of the General Assembly, Presbyterian Church USA, 1995), 10–11. Full, fair, sustaining, and participatory are the characteristics of "good work" as outlined in the policy statement.
42. Cahill, *Family*, xii.

taking responsibility for all of its members. The issue is not merely entitlement but obligation and accountability. Elsewhere in these pages, Patrick Miller effectively captures the reciprocal responsibility implied in the Decalogue. Israel's covenant was not only a bond between God and the people; it included all the nations in the scope of concern, and it involved covenants between every Israelite and every other Israelite. If we are members one of another, we are not only owed participation; we are also obligated to extend our care to the entire community and to extend community beyond the narrow reaches of our particular interests.[43]

By contrast, Wolfe's Middle-Class Morality Project found a sense of responsibility that sounded more philanthropic than covenantal. People should look out for each other and care about each other, it seemed, but people are only responsible for their own fate. "Morality Writ Small" is one of Wolfe's chapter titles. His subjects were suspicious of grand-design moralities promulgated by church or state, and they were convinced that we do best morally with those closest to us.[44]

With the global reach that we have been suggesting, what the Catholic Bishops of the Columbia River Watershed Region call repeatedly "concern for the common good and the good of the commons" takes in all of humanity and the biosphere.[45] The bishops speak of their watershed as a sacramental commons and seek to heighten responsibility for all of the human and nonhuman members that constitute that commons. There are communities that do assume responsibility for all of their members. But in our fractured world, it is often hard to sell the breadth of responsibility that is implied by language about a national community, a regional community, a global community, or a biotic community. Public responsibility is often equated with state responsibility and therefore viewed with skepticism. But why cannot government enable assumption of responsibility by numerous institutions instead of always being viewed only as a substitute, and a poor one at that? After all, what other institutions are vested with assuring universal coverage and enlisting universal support? Beyond the nation-state, we continue to search for institutional carriers of large-scale public authority that can match the power of global corporations without attempting an omnicompetence that poses forbidding hazards.

When we consider responsibility that stretches beyond our own generation to the next, beyond our own species to the others, beyond the success of our own corporate interests to the state of the world, the norm of sustainability commends itself. The Ecumenical Team of the World Council of Churches at the Johannesburg Summit cautioned that sustainability has often been paired uncritically with growth and development. "Sustainable growth" can prove to be a contradiction in terms and a cover for making a safe environment for corporations

---

43. Also in the present volume: Prophetic attention to those denied justice is treated forcefully by Jacqueline Lapsley in her chapter. Young's essay highlights the stark contrast between Aristotle's rule of the master and Martin Luther King Jr.'s "beloved community," with its responsibility for the least.

44. Wolfe, *One Nation, after All*, 266–67.

45. Catholic Bishops of the Region, *The Columbia River Watershed: Caring for Creation and the Common Good* (Seattle, WA: Columbia River Project, 2001.

and investors "the real priority." Building "sustainable communities" should be the primary goal.[46] Responsibility for all members of the global family means accountability for long-term consequences and far-flung lives.

Here and there hints of global community and a global common good peep through the pavement over which the economic juggernaut rolls. Pharmaceutical companies make AIDS drugs available at cut rates to impoverished African nations. Nations agree to emissions reduction in response to climate change. Disparate parties sit down to contemplate the future of the Columbia River watershed. Governments come together to create an International Criminal Court. International aid flows to earthquake victims. Debts of impoverished nations are forgiven. And international peace keepers go to Kosovo.

The failures of international community and of respect for the global commons, of course, make a much longer list. Our own nation's holdouts on the International Criminal Court, the Kyoto Treaty, the International Bill of Rights for Women, and the Convention on the Rights of the Child are telling reminders that reductions in national sovereignty sell poorly to powerful states that want to be able to act unilaterally.

Who or what will teach our families, our governments, our economic institutions, our religious organizations, and various other voluntary associations to enlarge their sense of responsibility? What can expand our sense of community and of the common good? Religious communities, families, schools, governments, media, workplaces, and nongovernmental organizations can teach civic virtue of the broadest sort if they are shown the way and accept the task. Religious visions that encompass the whole human family as an actual or potential community and that view the biosphere as a sacred commons have a golden opportunity. Clashing crusades could be the ugly alternative.

Diverse Individuality in Community

Our fourth criterion is the respect for the diverse individuality of each member. When we think in terms of "communities of communities," we can extend that respect for individuality to respect for particular communities within larger communities. Pluralism need not be the ruination of national or global community efforts. Difference need not be submerged if there is healthy dialogue about the common good. "Commons sense" need not mean that particularity and uniqueness are stampeded by common consent.

Addictive organizations squelch bad news and screen participants from straight talk that might undermine the hegemony of the powerful. In contrast, healthy communities find ways to hear disparate voices into speech even when they may be disinclined to speak up.[47] Healthy communities do not aim to eliminate

---

46. World Council of Churches, "Sustainable Communities—People and their Livelihoods," a fact sheet, Johannesburg, 2002.

47. "Hearing into speech" is an expression that I first read in Nelle Morton's *The Journey Is Home* (Boston: Beacon, 1985), 41, 55–66.

pluralism or individuality. Democracy needs controversy, and surely its presence does not preclude community.

One of the marks of life in covenant as presented in the Bible is that argument and struggle are not eliminated. Abraham, Jacob, Moses, Job, and even Jesus present a trust that is more than subservient obedience. They take issue, they complain, they seek to change what God seems intent on doing, and at times they succeed.

Toleration of difference can rise to several levels.[48] Grudging tolerance is a far cry from affirmative tolerance that regards the building or sustaining of community as a common good that is enhanced and not diminished by avowals of particularity and uniqueness and not discouraged by argument. The common story that bonds a community can include a vision of hospitality to plural stories. True dialogue means that the participants need not have common agreement in advance and that they need not become clones or facsimiles in the end. As Patrick Miller observes about Israel in these pages, the discernment of the common good is a continuing quest. Robin Lovin's article, also in this volume, makes a similar point about the public forum as a dialectical process.

Coercion happens when we no longer have a common stake in some good that is worth preserving or promoting and no longer share any vocabulary to continue the conversation. If we recognize that we share an ecological or international or national or ecclesiastical commons, for example, we may stay at the table "for good." Far too many of our community identifications pit "us" against "them." What keeps us together may be only a common enemy. Efforts to include the other, even all others, within the reach of our commonality attempt to substitute vis-à-vis for versus. The faces of the " vulnerable other" (Lévinas) then become a presence that cannot be ignored, no matter how different the others are.[49]

A principle from Catholic moral teaching that illumines this fourth criterion is subsidiarity. It involves respecting possibilities for various communities, levels of government, and sectors of society to serve the functions that they can most appropriately and effectively discharge. Families should be allowed and encouraged to do what they can do best as long as they are able. By the same token, environmental problems can seldom be addressed simply by neighborhoods, or local communities, or even single nations. A larger commons calls for the attention of representatives of a larger community. That level of address doesn't mean that local input and local ownership of the concerted efforts are not crucial; it only means, for example, that the protection of human dignity worldwide requires global human rights efforts by a global community. That global community may express itself, however, through the particular communities of nongovernmental organizations that make up a global civil society.[50]

48. Walzer, *On Toleration*, 10.

49. Emmanuel Lévinas, *Totality and Infinity: An Essay on Exteriority* (trans. Alphonso Lingis; Pittsburgh: Duquesne University Press, 1966), 34, 38, 80, 173, 213, 295.

50. Ronnie D. Lipschutz, "Reconstructing World Politics: The Emergence of Global Civil Society," *Millennium: Journal of International Studies* (1992): 389–420; Paul Wapner, *Environmental Activism and World Civic Politics* (Albany: State University of New York Press, 1996).

With respect to each of the four criteria, we end up with destructive tensions that demand discernment and choice—between atomistic individualism and solidarity, between idolatrous solidarity and universal solidarity, between participation and exclusion, between narrow interest and sustainability, between uniformity and diversity. We also encounter creative tensions that need perpetuation—between individuality and solidarity, between freedom as autonomy and freedom as sufficiency, between sufficiency and sustainability, between diversity within unity and diversity in subsidiarity. The task is to be able to make distinctions in the first instance and to sustain the creative tensions in the second. What is at stake is a matter of character, of conscientious sensitivity, of virtue.

By Virtue of Commons Sense

Ability to tell the difference, to draw distinctions, to strike a balance, to maintain creative tension is the bailiwick of virtue. Dealing with the tension between private interest and the public good is the purview of civic virtue (Montesquieu) or public-spiritedness (William F. May).[51] It takes character to build community, but even more fundamentally, it also takes community to build character. If civic virtue is to flower, it will happen not merely by the invocation of criteria or principles of community, but by the nurturing of "habits of the heart" (Tocqueville) that are sensitive to what solidarity, sufficiency, sustainability, and subsidiarity mean in practice. In community we learn that personal welfare is dependent on the general welfare and that our own good is inseparable from the common good. We learn commons sense. Such an understanding of democratic citizenship is what Bellah and his associates called "the uncompleted American quest" to realize the vision of the founders.[52]

What light does this rendition of civic virtue shed on other virtues? What virtues correspond to the principles of identity/solidarity, participation/sufficiency, responsibility/sustainability, and diversity/subsidiarity? As Jean Porter's treatment of Thomas Aquinas in this volume helpfully explains, justice is the virtue that directs other virtues toward the common good and links the individual good to the good of the whole. There may also be more to say about the civic sentiments of the other virtues. For example, what William May calls practical wisdom or discernment keeps simple prudence from shrinking to shrewdness because it deals with ends as well as means and connects private goods to the common good.[53]

---

51. William F. May, *Testing the Medical Covenant: Active Euthanasia and Health Care Reform* (Grand Rapids: Eerdmans, 1996), 74–79; idem, *Beleaguered Rulers: The Public Obligation of the Professional* (Louisville: Westminster John Knox, 2001), 10–12, 132–34, 173–74. Without using the term "civic virtue," Victor Furnish's chapter in the present volume traces a support for responsible citizenship in Paul's writing, a feature that has often been neglected.

52. Bellah et al., *Habits of the Heart*, 252.

53. May, *Testing the Medical Covenant*, 46; idem, *Beleaguered Rulers*, 172.

Courage and temperance also take new forms when the common good is not ignored in the pursuit of personal goods. The actions of firefighters and other public servants at the World Trade Center and the Pentagon after the 9/11 attack exemplified risk-taking as civic virtue. Their actions exceeded the calculus of pain justifiable for personal gain and reasserted our commonality in self-sacrificial and heroic fashion. Temperance too involves not only taking good care of ourselves with the result that we are better able to help others. It also knows its limits in a world of limited resources. In ecological perspective, gluttony is not just injurious to my health; it also is injurious to our commonwealth.[54] What is more, the actions of certain Enron, WorldCom, and other corporate officials were intemperate not simply because they were failures of self-control but also because they took hundreds of people down to financial ruin by being "on the take."

The theological virtues likewise have a civic sense—not simply because they can transform the cardinal virtues, but because they prompt action for the common good. Instead of sinking to demonization of the other, faith risks openness to the other, which is essential to community formation. It also keeps promises to the other, which is essential to community sustenance. Hope sees beyond the failures to envision and attempt the common good, looking to the possibilities involved in continuing conversation and to the future generations that expand the commonality we should espouse. Love involves the compassion that cares beyond calculated personal benefit and affirms beyond comfortable social similarity. At best, faith, hope, and love are public-spirited.

If we are to find identity in community connections that expand our sense of solidarity beyond the confines of collective egotism, we shall need a temperance that can accept limitations. We shall require a form of courage that can risk hospitality to strangers and a practical wisdom that knows which end is up. Above all, we will have to internalize a sense of justice that insists on the well-being of community and not mere equal opportunity to pursue self-interest.

If we are to make possible and embrace full participation in community life where all have what is needed to take part fully, we shall need to regard with temperance the limits that others' sufficiency may place on our surplus of privilege and power. We shall need to hang tough with courage in efforts at institutional change, to discern the situational demands of sufficiency with prudence, and to order and provide the places at the table with justice.

If we are to advocate community responsibility for and by all members that sustains us all over time, we shall need to take on Sallie McFague's ecological discipline "to think of everyone and everything all together."[55] That discipline will require a temperate respect for the global commons, a courageous advocacy for the

---

54. Robin Lovin, *Christian Ethics: An Essential Guide* (Nashville: Abingdon, 2000), 71, treats this fitness to meet others' needs. Wendell Berry, in his 1978 commencement address at Centre College, discusses gluttony in similar terms.

55. Sallie McFague, *Life Abundant: Rethinking Theology and Economy for a Planet in Peril* (Minneapolis: Fortress, 2001), xiv.

voiceless, a discerning development of public policies, and a justice that leaves no one behind.

If we are to respect diverse individuality in each community and among our communities, allowing each to flourish to its capacities and in its obligations, we shall need the communal and institutional temperate self-denial to accord to other communities and institutions their share. We shall require courage to see difference as the occasion for covenant instead of the signal for combat. We shall rely on wise discernment to develop partnerships where there might have been zero-sum power struggles. And we shall practice the public-spirited justice that combines insistence on recognition and protection of individual and group rights with recognition and pursuit of individual and group responsibilities.

The communities that inspire and model these virtues will be those familial, religious, educational, occupational, and political associations that are loyal to inclusive centers of value and not just hostile to common enemies. They will be hopeful about the possibilities of social change and not cynical about every encouraging word. And they will be compassionate in their affirmation of all the membership of the biotic community. They will engender commons sense. The church as the Body of Christ should be an exemplary community in this respect and not allow itself to be a colony of either the nation-state or the market, as William Cavanaugh cautions in these pages.

Conclusion: Idolatry and the Common Good

As John Cobb has pointed out, the major ways in which we have sought to unify ourselves in the West during the Common Era have all had both constructive and destructive elements and have produced both good and bad consequences. "Christianism" was finally undone by the seventeenth-century wars of religion. Nationalism was indicted because of the Third Reich and the Holocaust. Economism is far from being done for, but it is leading toward social and ecological disaster if present trends continue. And the recently emergent earthism can be flawed by its own kind of indifference to the population thinning of plague and natural disaster and the sufferings of individual lives.

Every one of these isms has had an implicit or explicit commitment to a common good with some positive effects, although the victims and the ignored of those visions have only the scars and the graves to show for those visions. William Cavanaugh's chapter provides a trenchant tracing of nationalism's perils. However, its claim that the nation-state is "simply not in the common-good business" fails to acknowledge some of the positive possibilities that constitutionalism has opened up, even in the modern nation-state. Governmental action on behalf of expanded civil rights in our nation is a case in point. Also in this volume, Lovin, McCann, Porter, and Skillen hold out more hope in this respect without harboring illusions about virtues of nationalism or righteousness of the nation-state. Earthism is a sorely needed corrective to the perils of economism's single-minded pursuit of economic growth; yet it too is an idolatry when compared to the kingdom of God, even if it should be the idolatry of choice for our time because it affirms biotic community.[56]

We are driven back, therefore, to the linkage between true community and the praise of God that Eliot articulated. Not all of our religious communities are theistic, and the theistic ones do not have a monopoly on all truth. In fact, the most sinister idolatries can parade under the banner of religion. Nevertheless, we need communities that reach beyond exclusivity, that mutually correct fanaticism, that extend participation by enabling human flourishing, that stretch responsibility with global reach, and that respect difference and individuality instead of pitting us against them. If we are to have such communities, we shall need continuing correction of our vision of the common good by the summons of a common sense, or commons sense, the call of a Good that challenges all of our idolatries and includes the well-being of a universal, biotic community. It is incumbent on us to see and to act in virtue of this commons sense.

The presence of such commons sense in a society provides a corrective to idolatries of every sort without promoting the conversion of the state into a church. It models community of a thicker kind without discounting the importance of a continuing conversation about the common good with people informed by different stories. (As a haunting contrary example, Milner Ball warns in these pages that the United States has no narrative that includes Native Americans.) If community as understood here is itself understood as a common good, it can be an uplifting ideal and not merely a tragic one. If participation in community is a human birthright, the freedom to do so should be everyone's entitlement. If freedom makes our association or community membership in any particular grouping voluntary and not mandatory, our struggle for the common good is covenantal and not organic. No version of collective good should legitimate discounting the welfare of part of the whole or ignoring minority voices. Lockstep collectivities are not only out of touch with the pluralism and mobility of a shrinking globe. They also hold under suspicion the very difference that is requisite for covenant and for the ongoing dialogue about the universal common good found in the best of covenants. If the covenants we make with each other as communities are inclusive and not exclusive, they will give us a good in common. They will promote a continuing conversation in perpetuity, one in which one story never rules out all others and in which we can find words to talk with each other because of our commons sense.[57]

---

56. John B. Cobb Jr., *Earthist Challenge to Economism: A Theological Critique of the World Bank* (New York: St. Martin's Press, 1999). The challenge to idolatry carries the transcendent dimension in my own chapter in a manner similar to what eschatology does in this volume's essays by Robert Jenson, Max Stackhouse, and Josiah Young. Also here, Patrick Miller gives considerable weight to idolatry, but concludes on an eschatological note. My own treatment of hope and my references to the common good as an unfolding and unfinished process have eschatological implications.

57. In this volume Max Stackhouse's chapter entertains the hope that an open global interreligious dialogue will reveal to all of the partners the superiority of Christian revelation, but he seems not to want an accompanying demise of the other stories involved in the dialogue.

A Rose by Any Other Name?

Deconstructing the Essence of *Common*

Cheryl A. Kirk-Duggan

Stories, in sacred and popular culture, relate lived experiences, prophetic imaginations, and tensions around commonality and difference: Who is included? Who is excluded? Shakespeare tells stories through plays (comedies and tragedies), conjuring nostalgia and commonality when speaking about the shared smell of a rose, regardless of its name.[1] Jesus tells stories in parables. A parable, an extended simile, compares a point of commonality (that which is similar, thus, simile) between two different things to demonstrate and teach that point—a lesson transferred from one realm of experience to another. A parable, an analogy that uses comparison to illumine something unknown, compares the unknown with something that is known or familiar. Jesus used brief stories that ring true to life, comparing the point of commonality between two unlike things. The known or the common reveals the unknown, the different. Jesus used parables, an indirect methodology, to teach, sometimes reversing ordinary values.[2] While Jesus waxes eloquent in short tales about values and life in God's realm, Toni Morrison tells riveting stories in novels.

---

1. Shakespeare, *Romeo and Juliet*, act 2, scene 2, lines 43–44:

   What's in a name? That which we call a rose
   By any other name would smell as sweet.

2. Bruce M. Metzger, et al., *The Bible through the Ages* (Pleasantville, NY: Reader's Digest Association, 1996), 160; Vergus Ferm, *The Encyclopedia of Religion* (Secaucus, NJ: Poplar Books, 1945), 560; http://www.discipleship.net/parables.htm.

Morrison's first novel, *The Bluest Eye*,[3] conveys the story of an eleven-year-old girl, Pecola Breedlove, the protagonist, who wants what she does not have or share in common with little white girls, whom everybody loves: blue eyes. Pecola and her family incarnate and broadcast difference. In her quest for beauty and acceptance, society constantly bombards Pecola with signals that foster existential angst and belief in her own ontological difference as ugliness. In the stories of Jesus and Morrison, themes of common and difference emerge, conflict, and can act as foils for each other.

When the term *common* modifies a particular concept, ideology, or place, many English-speaking adults assume that *common* has a certain meaning. The term common appears throughout our thought, as a qualifier of reality, signifying a quality from the ordinary and universal to the vulgar or coarse.[4] I find the term *common* to be problematic; when the term is used in relationship as "common good," it seems impossible to redeem *common* in a way that is not exclusive of something or someone. Using *common* for a particular community implies inclusion of the many, whereas systemic and institutional exclusion for particular persons is the norm. A quick jaunt back into United States history since 1620 provides numerous incidents where particular actions obliterated commonality amid the populace by intentionally spreading smallpox, inducing alcoholism, championing lynching, and condoning slavery. Those in power disregarded the notion of Gen 1:26, where God created all humanity in God's image and named those creatures good—an engagement of active, loving relationship. In exegeting the term *common good*, the biases of the one who decides what is the common and what is the good usually mean that what is common is actually unique and thus different. Those systems include some in "common" and exclude others, and invite an exploration of the dynamics of difference toward a concrete meaning of *common*.[5] To the extent that the very diverse term *common* suggests general or universal agreement, we must then ask who says so. Womanist theological ethics insists on that question, to sensitize us to social location and the power dynamics behind every claim about what is good for everyone.

My essay explores selected theological, ethical, and biblical implications of the term *common* over against a notion of difference from a womanist perspective. After briefly reviewing my understanding of womanist theological ethics, I explore the general meaning of *common* and interrogate the place of *difference* in the thought of cultural anthropologist René Girard and the literary and cultural critic bell hooks. I do this to construct my understanding of *common* emerging

---

3. Toni Morrison, *The Bluest Eye* (New York: Penguin/Plume, 1970).

4. In daily parlance, the terms *common* denominator, *common* ground, *common* law, *common* market, *common* place, *common* sense, *common*weal, *common*wealth, and *common* good—all denote the sense of a shared space, shared goals, and familiar territory.

5. While our working group focused on and deconstructed notions of the larger question of "the common good," I find it imperative to wrestle with some of the submerged, societal, and systemic assumptions we have around the term *common*.

from their work. This follows with an analysis of two narratives, Toni Morrison's *The Bluest Eye* and the Beatitudes in Jesus' teachings (Matt 5:3–12), where I use my gleanings from Girard and hooks to explore the difference-commonality dialectic. These gleanings are shaped by a notion of *imago Dei* emerging from Gen 1, with the created difference in Gen 2–3 between male and female allowing for the known ambiguity around gender. Then I move toward a constructive, liberatory, pedagogical notion of the meaning of *common*, toward one that can theologically modify a notion of "the good."

Womanist Theological Ethics

Womanist theological ethics–the study or discipline of God-talk amid human behavior, meaning, and values—emerges out of the experience of African-American women. Womanist theory and praxis analyze human individual and social behavior and the related value systems, in concert with the purpose of exposing injustice and the special malaise caused by complex, multiple oppressive uses of power. Womanist thought does this social analysis in relation to a sense of the divine. *Womanist*, derived by Alice Walker[6] from the term *womanish*, refers to women of African descent who are audacious, outrageous, in charge, and responsible. A womanist emancipatory theological ethics embraces hope, engenders mutuality and community, and honors the *imago Dei* in all persons. Womanist theological ethics builds on the essential goodness of humankind and focuses on liberation amid personal, societal, and theological-ethical fragmentation. This womanist manner of seeing questions issues pertinent to quality of life and stewardship, critiques decision making; and asks how these inquiries affect and are affected by the related social, political, economic, religious, and cultural environment. Womanist thought includes but is not limited to issues in theology (identity, sacrality, subjectivity, spirituality, power), Bible and/or other sacred texts (authority, characters, language, rituals, history), ethics (value, behavior, visibility, integrity, praxis), and context (authority, culture, aesthetics, ecology, community). I appreciate interreligious sensibilities and embrace new avenues of possibility and communal solidarity, toward reformation that champions immediacy, inclusivity, and justice.

Womanist methodology is critical for analyzing the concept of common, for it asks questions that often disappear in general discourse. For example, issues of patriarchy and white privilege need to be explored to champion fully the freedom, dignity, and justice of *all* people. Much of the rhetoric on common and common good makes assumptions that suggest a normative reality that may exist for most middle-class, Anglo-Saxon, Protestant, male landowners. They were the beneficiaries of common equality in 1776, when Thomas Jefferson wrote in the Declaration of Independence that "all men are created equal." While liberatory in theory as it broke the bonds with England, in praxis the declaration embodied the

---

6. Alice Walker, *In Search of Our Mother's Gardens: Womanist Prose* (New York: Harcourt Brace Jovanovich, 1967, 1983), xi.

hypocrisy of pronouncing white men free by natural right while decimating Native Americans and keeping African-Americans enslaved. In this society the inherent and systemic class, sexual orientation, gender, race, age, ability, and ecology oppression begs for womanist analysis, toward discerning what, if anything, is common in an oppressive milieu. I continue my investigation with an assessment of the term *common*.

Common: An Ordinary Term

Common originates from the French *commun*, the Latin *communis* from *con-* + *munis*, "ready to be of service." The term common pertains to a community at large, as a whole, the public, as in "to work for the common good." *Common* points to "a sense of belonging equally to" or "shared equally by two or more," thus signifying joint or common interests and a sense of mutuality. *Common* means available, not unprecedented; inclusive; something held in union with others; that which is human, belonging to humanity; something we all have together; of ordinary rank, quality or ability, not distinguished by superiority of any kind; shared realities. *Common* also concerns what is known to the community, as "a common nuisance" or "standard," or in "common procedure." *Common* means belonging to, or shared by two or more individuals or things or by all members of a group, as in "a common acquaintance," or "buried in a common grave." *Common* pertains to what is prevalent and widespread. What is common occurs frequently or habitually; it is usually something that is widely known or ordinary, as in the common or generic "kitchen sink." The term *common* means belonging equally to two or more mathematical entities, as in triangles with a shared base. To be common also means not having a special or unique designation, status, or rank: for example, "a common sailor." *Common* infers that something or someone is not distinguished by excellence, advanced, or striking characteristics, but is dubbed average, such as "the common height." *Common* signifies occurring or appearing frequently, something familiar, a common sight. *Common* indicates something that is widespread or general, as in "common knowledge." *Common* implies that one should conform or subscribe to accustomed criteria, as in "common decency."

Sometimes what is common has a mediocre or inferior quality or second-rate status, as in "common folk," who are plain and unsophisticated. *Common* implies unrefined or coarse in manner, which may also imply popular, vulgar, or unsophisticated, particularly denoting behavior or class status; it also indicates that one is falling below ordinary standards. The commons pertains to a common political class of people, a political class composed of commoners, or the parliamentary representatives of this class. The commons also depicts an area of land, usually in a centrally located spot, allegedly belonging to or used by a community as a whole. In the northeastern United States, where the so-called commons existed, not every person who lived in the area had access to it, was invited to use it, or could assume the privilege of participating at the commons. The commons was often a place where people gathered to pasture cows, but it could also be a place for political gatherings. In Anglo-American property law, the commons referred to an area of land for use by the public. The term originated in feudal England, where the waste or uncultivated land of a lord's manor could be used for pasture and firewood by his tenants.[7] *The commons* denotes the legal right of a person to use the lands or waters of another, as for fishing, or a building or hall for dining, characteristically at a university or college. Often, however, that deemed commons has not been a place of engagement for the many but the few. While the praxis of commonality seems problematic, linguistically there seems to be more consent.

Common designates nominal relations by a single linguistic form that in a more highly inflected language might be denoted by two or more different forms: common gender, or common case. As stated earlier, *common* has many synonyms. When thinking of common as ordinary, it pushes conformity, or a type of regular ordering of things. *Plain* usually suggests homely simplicity, as in "a plain dress." The concept of the familiar emphasizes the fact of being generally known and easily recognized, as "a familiar tune" or "melody." *Popular* pertains to something that is prevalent among people in general, often in contrast to upper classes or special groups, or to something that is accepted by the masses, as in "popular music." A negative or derogatory connotation of *common* is that which uses common or vulgar language or taste.

There is no single understanding of the term *common* itself, which then raises the question of the possibility of a lived reality of common good. Nevertheless, other essays in this volume attest to the long history of the concept of "common good" in law, religion, and philosophy. Accepting this legacy, I wonder if many of us have a superiority and supersessionist attitude in the ethos of middle-class, Western Christianity, an attitude making it impossible to embody fully the notion of common or the common good. Following the encumbered, contestability of this term, I struggle with its inherent ambiguity and privilege. Ambiguity does not, however, connote uselessness or dismissal. Deconstruction of privilege comes later. In the spirit of creative engagement, as "faith seeking understanding," I offer my working definition of common: "shared, ordinary, mutual communal engagement." Toward deconstructing an understanding of *common*, as the modifier of good in the work of this volume, I explore a dialectic of commonality and difference.

How does one relate difference to that which is common? How does a sense of shared commonality relate to inherent difference? Do we have room for the legion of differences that exist in public discourse? How do differences relate to the good? Are differences really the problem, or is it our responses to difference? Can a shared understanding help us deal with those who are different? How can one deal with the dialectic of common and difference that permeates culture? We now turn to these questions in the theory of Girard and hooks.

Girard and hooks: Difference and Commonality

The literary critic and cultural anthropologist René Girard declares, "Persecutors are never obsessed by difference but rather by its unutterable contrary, the lack of

---

7. "Commons," *Encyclopedia Britannica* (Encyclopedia Britannica Premium Service, 30 March 2003; http://www.britannica.com/eb/article?eu=25383).

difference."[8] Does the absence of difference, or that which is common, perpetuate persecution? For Girard, the import of difference is integral to "violence and the sacred theory,"[9] from which emerges his understanding of mimesis. Mimesis,[10] imitation, is vital for the way we know and learn—our epistemology. Mimetic desire occurs where two or more people desire the same person, thing, place, or status. Mimetic desire involves the imitation by the model/rival and the subject/disciple. The model/rival may ban the subject/disciple from obtaining the object of desire. This desire leads to rivalry: several parties want the same object. For Girard, mimetic desire and its resulting ritualized conflict resolve and contain the resulting violence via the scapegoat.[11] That is, a dominant group identifies and kills a victim, enacting a catharsis that produces social camaraderie so that the crowd/perpetrators begin to understand the experience religiously—the intersection of religion, violence, and culture. For the crowd, the scapegoat becomes the perpetrator, which affords intensified passion and calm, moving the crowd from a violent catastrophe into peaceful harmony. Successful scapegoating often depends upon the victim's invisibility. Scapegoating, a result of mimetic desire and violence, often helps shape social order and stabilizes relational differences. The conflict, chaos, and confusion of bad mimetic desire sets up a particular social order of power that violates, that privileges some and hurts others.[12] Many think that difference is the target of persecution, yet in some systems of prejudice, people exact hatred for the *absence* of difference, not because of the difference itself. The dominant group can define themselves and find internal unity by identifying a vulnerable group as "other," because of expressed differences (such as ability, gender, class, race, age, or sexual orientation), making persons vulnerable and visible. This results in heightened violence and monstrous doubles.

Mimetic desire leads to a monstrous double where an individual can press beyond her/himself toward a desire that the subject/disciple copies from the model/rival. One values the desired object because someone else desires it. Soon, one wants to be like the other; thus, rivalry produces the double bind. In extreme

---

8. René Girard, *The Girard Reader* (ed. James G. Williams; New York: Crossroad/Herder, 1996), 116.

9. See René Girard, *Violence and the Sacred* (Baltimore: Johns Hopkins University Press, 1977).

10. Critics use "mimesis" to describe relationships between art and nature, art and reality, or the relationship that governs the work of art as nonimitative or pre-Platonic mimesis [ecstatic play], or Platonic mimesis.

11. See René Girard, *The Scapegoat* (trans. Yvonne Freccero; Baltimore: Johns Hopkins University Press, 1986); also see my full treatment of this concept in *Misbegotten Anguish: A Theology and Ethics of Violence* (St. Louis: Chalice, 2001), chapter two.

12. Mihai Spariosu, ed., *Mimesis in Contemporary Theory: An Interdisciplinary Approach*, vol. 1, *The Literary and Philosophical Debate* (Philadelphia: John Benjamins Publishing, 1984), i–iii, 88–100; Burton Mack, "Introduction: Religion and Ritual," in *Violent Origins: Walter Burkert, René Girard, and Jonathan Z. Smith on Ritual Killing and Cultural Transformation* (ed. Robert Hammerton-Kelly; Stanford, CA: Stanford University Press, 1987), 11.

cases, one wants to become the other. Unknowingly, the closer the imitator (the disciple) gets to obtaining the object, the greater the hostility of and rebuke by the one imitated (the model). The imitator assumes that s/he ought to value the object of desire, but discovers that the closer one comes to acquiring the object, the greater the rejection by and animosity of the one being imitated.[13] The human mind looks for changes and affirms substitution and progress. With the double bind, a subject cannot accurately interpret the double command from the other person: as model, "Imitate me"; but as rival, "Do not imitate me."[14]

Doubling violates differences between people and makes them sensitive to deception and lies.[15] Desire never gets what satisfies it and never creates impartiality or mutuality: some dominate, and others are dominated. The truth of the situation, the source of relevance (mimetic desire), is concealed. The mutual attraction within their imitative interaction generates the kind of paralysis where the model wants to be autonomous, but is attracted to the model/oppressor. S/he wants what the oppressor has: power, status, fullness of being, and so on. So how is it possible for us to imitate those we hate without hating ourselves? First, the model wants to be model but defies anyone who imitates too well. The disciple wants to be autonomous from the model, but wants the model's independence. The disciple experiences an external prohibition or double bind (from the model) and an internal prohibition or double bind (from within himself or herself). Viewing these two kinds of double binds exposes the complex nature of scapegoating: the intricate motives, self-deception, gist of power, source of valuation, risk of violence when social groups vie for dominance and/or independence, and the impact of difference.

Ultimately, violence occurs as individuals and groups struggle to be different. Increased similarities create societal confusion. Yet through their struggles, people end up looking and acting more like one another. Does this resulting sameness indicate commonality? Shared sensibilities do not necessarily indicate mutual communal engagement. Someone(s) who exhibits difference is vulnerable and often ends up being the focus of a group's consolidated effort to define themselves and those deemed other, by turning against those who cannot react. Thus, a group establishes itself by psychologically or physically eliminating or ousting those who are different. Lynching (or stoning to death in the ancient world) is the classic act of collective violence.[16] What emerges is a parallel and common experience of victim and perpetrator, signaling conflictual difference, often resulting in a horrific pathology or mass hysteria—an excuse to sin.

---

13. Mack, "Introduction," 8–9.

14. René Girard, *Things Hidden Since the Foundation of the World: Research Undertaken in Collaboration with Jean-Michel Oughourlian and Guy Lefort* (trans. Stephen Bann and Michael Metteer; Stanford, CA: Stanford University Press, 1987), 291; see also 294–98, 305.

15. René Girard, *"To Double Business Bound": Essays on Literature, Mimesis, and Anthropology* (Baltimore: Johns Hopkins University Press, 1978), 46.

16. Conversations with Diana Culbertson, Professor of Literature, Kent State University, Summer, 1995.

The Girardian scapegoat mechanism, then, helps us see that mimetic rivalry shapes human behavior as we work to rationalize violence through religious practice and myth. If we see our complicity within society, then we can no longer remain ignorant to the innocence of the victim. For Girard, religion exposes violence, while the unconscious hiding of violence and the desire to avoid violence produces religion. A society tries to sustain differences and limit rivalry through its myths, taboos, and prohibitions, even though violence and chaos have existed from the foundation, the beginnings of the world.

The repeated symbolic murder or maiming is ritual sacrifice. Ironically, the victim of the sacrifice and the murder becomes the savior figure, the cause of the peace, even though the murder occurred because the victim was accused of perpetuating societal chaos. Girard names the system of ritual murder and expulsion "the sacred." For Girard, "sacred" equals violence, because when a culture or a religion starts with a sacrifice, a killing, it begins with violence, the worse side of religion. Sacrifice helps maintain the system of differences, as violence emphasizes the differences within society,[17] within a group. Without a mechanism for regulating or transcending mimetic desire, one would be in total societal chaos.

Girard contends that every individual in every culture thinks of oneself as different, and views these differences as indispensable and justifiable. The differences that cause one to select a particular victim result from the differences outside of the particular system. These external differences exact terror because the differences disclose the truth, relativity, morality, and fragility of the system.[18] Much of Girardian mimesis seems to be bad mimesis, but Girard agrees that good mimesis can occur. Theophus Smith's notion of mimetic intimacy, a good mimesis, gratifies desire, embraces the other, and experiences mimetic transformation.[19] Mimetic desire becomes creative as a good mimesis[20] takes the form of community and channels human behavior and desire to benefit self and others. Perhaps difference that honors creativity and produces good mimesis is a point of departure for a healthy sense of common good.

For Girard, difference is a tool of illumination, a category of subjectivity and personal identity. Difference is relational, has ramifications for all criteria examined in demographics; and is an arbiter of peace; its absence exacts violence. Girardian theory as a lens through which to view the twenty-first-century human condition can reveal the following about what is common: societal injustice and conflict, with a few wielding the most power in a patriarchal, hierarchical milieu. Most societal groups experience desire and learn through imitation. Systems are made up of people, subject to ambiguity and a negation of difference. Most

17. Paul Dumochel, ed., *Violence and Truth: On the Work of René Girard* (London: Athlone, 1988), 54–55; see also Mack, "Introduction," 4, 6.

18. Girard, *The Girard Reader*, 115–16.

19. Theophus H. Smith, "King and the Nonviolent Religion of Black America," in *Curing Violence: Religion and the Thought of René Girard* (ed. Theophus Smith and Mark I. Wallace; Sonoma, CA: Polebridge, 1994), 230–51.

20. James G. Williams, "Sacrifice, Mimesis, and the Genesis of Violence: A Response to Bruce Chilton," *Bulletin for Biblical Research* 3 (1993): 34–36, 32–39.

persons and groups need to be unique and in relationship. That which is common involves shared human relationships of diverse access. This makes much of what could be common, rare, and uncommon. The critic bell hooks explores the notion of desire as she "teaches to transgress," where she embraces difference and views what is common as dynamic.

In her work of liberatory pedagogy and cultural analysis, bell hooks's goal is an education for critical consciousness, particularly black, revolutionary, critical consciousness that affords one strategic posture nurturing revolutionary self-determination. hooks begins her work with class analysis to deconstruct all oppression: pro-capitalism, racism, sexism, patriarchy, imperialism, colonialism, and the related materialism and consumerism. She comprehends and critiques all forms of domination, including nationalism, which undermines revolutionary struggle. hooks has framed her pedagogical and cultural analysis with feminism. Following the commitment of liberationist pedagogue Paulo Freire's notion of educating for freedom and her childhood experience of liberatory education, hooks extols the import of education for critical consciousness and for liberation. Freire's notion of conscientization—engagement and critical awareness in the education process—illumined the disparities and shortcomings of the banking method of teaching and learning. The resulting mutuality of labor by all, by teacher and student engaging in contemplation with labor, undergirds hooks's strategy of a revolutionary classroom: a radical life of empowerment.

Together Freire and Buddhist philosopher Thich Nhat Hanh help hooks connect her thinking about the development and engagement of the mind with wholeness toward life, for learning as spiritual practice. Central to this praxis is the valuing of every person's experience. hooks's pedagogical philosophy honors the fears of teachers when one challenges them to expand and include multiculturalism or other strategies in their teaching repertoire. Many teachers will feel ill at ease when challenged to examine their own hegemonic biases, passivities, and political systems. Ultimately, hooks wants to create a pleasurable democratic setting in the living laboratory of the classroom, where all participate out of a responsibility to contribute. Despite limitations in the classroom, the gift and opportunity to work on behalf of freedom make it a locus of possibility.[21] hooks creates a learning community in her classroom where everyone can participate and receive the offerings of knowledge that reverberate within the classroom of mutuality—the interplay, interdependency, and love.

hooks contends that building a community of teaching/learning together with praxis and theory requires a passion focused in eros, in love. Such love as a motivating force opens the way for critical engagement, and for people to think about thinking about knowledge—particularly in categories like class, race, age, and gender—in different ways, and thus subsequently to live differently. Here difference connotes an openness toward inclusiveness and transformation. This openness lessens the exercise of multiple oppressions and presses for a shared common

---

21. bell hooks, *Teaching to Transgress: Education as the Practice of Freedom* (New York: Routledge, 1994), 14, 36–37, 39, 51, 207.

experience of invited participation that embraces difference in spite of fear, ignorance, or hate. Philosophically, resistance emerges because of the preponderance
of Western dualism, which fosters a mind-body split amid the legacy of erasure,
repression, and denial of our physical, sensual, sexual selves. A healthy eros-based
pedagogical strategy invites one to engage in critical thinking and knowledge
gathering as an embodied holistic person: an act of subversion, to help participants know in deeper and more profound ways. This kind of imaginative learning can be frightening and also fulfilling. Such revolutionary and philosophical
pedagogy creates an opportunity for inclusive kinds of bonds between teachers and
students. As opposed to mentoring the particular student under the so-called
model of objectivity, it is germane to liberatory pedagogy to honor, embrace, and
empower every student, engaging all students and faculty as teacher/learners.
Given the newness of these strategies, one would need to teach about how one
appropriately expresses care and love in the classroom.

Liberatory pedagogy based in love is an opportunity for authenticity and self-
actualization that appreciates and honors difference, and it invites the body and
mind together to know and feel desire.[22] hooks wants to help people construct
identity politics as a strategy for liberation rather than exclusion or domination.
Aware of binary opposition in the classroom, she notes that such insider/outsider
dynamics are a part of cultures of domination and oppression. Colonialized and
oppressed peoples do not need such tools in the classroom, because the educational system is one part of systemic domination. For hooks, the role of the
teacher/learner is to use pedagogical strategies that nonhierarchically acknowledge everyone's experience and knowledge, and thus to remove the students' need
to be competitive, because all speaking and knowing is valued. Students are less
likely to need to promote their own exclusivist, essentialist viewpoints when they
know their professors will not privilege a particular way of knowing.[23] That is,
professors honor the articulation of difference, expressed as varied experiences,
epistemologies, and communities of learning.

hooks likes to foster "communities of resistance," where people who share similar values and concerns team up to build a collective arena for communicating
specific ideas, habits of being, values, and so on. Within these communities, language—thoughts and words—disrupts and lodges in our memory. When one
uses language to oppress, dominate, or malign, hooks calls for communities of
resistance to restore intimacy, to hear and empower those who have been trauma-
tized. Rebellion occurs when the oppressed are required to use a language that was
formerly not theirs. Such rebellion resists domination and makes room for those
who dominate to listen in new and different ways, toward transformation.[24] hooks
thinks that amid diverse interests in a particular community, the community itself
is a communion of the whole, a collective good, creating an ethos that can result
in a common good. hooks exposes the ethics of individualism that has harmed

---

22. Ibid., 191–99.
23. Ibid., 82–84, 88.
24. Ibid., 167–71.

social movements in U.S. society. "I think that it's one thing to enjoy the good life and to enjoy beauty and things, and another thing to feel like you're willing to support the killing of other people in other countries so that you can have your fine car and other luxuries."[25]

For hooks, part of the task for the community is to grow stronger in communion. Genuine community often emerges out of solidarity and making connections with those with whom easy kinds of connection do not seem to be forthcoming, out of dialogue. People make useful interventions, create new languages, decenter traditional modes of authority, and rupture the boundaries of fields and disciplines of study toward a pedagogical and daily experiential realm of liberatory praxis. Such processes have accompanying struggles and matters of agency and power.[26] hooks argues that there are ways people may find commonalty and solidarity via an emotional connectedness, as well as through identity politics. One vista of connectedness might involve desire, an intersection of our collective yearning and longing.

Distinguishing between love and desire, hooks views desire as opportunity, as a potential place, site, or catalyst for configuring the roots of community bonding, out of human difference. The categories of desire are quite fluid. Given the significance of the human mind in the construction of desire, we may be able to alter our consciousness and thus alter the makeup of our desire. Tensions often develop over the questions and limitations of identity politics. Unaware of the specific organizing principles, it becomes difficult to help people organize politically for the rights of others. Significantly, we must embrace different ways of organizing, of coming together on issues not central to our own well-being. hooks notes that either we develop different principles for political consensus building, or we end up with a ghettoization instead of a collectivity around particular collective concerns.[27]

Difference for hooks is a place of celebration, interrogation, liberation, and transformation. This realm presses one to honor everyone's gifts, graces, realities, and particularities, without fear, envy, or malice. All arenas of life, including the classroom, become living laboratories for questioning, investigating, and analyzing while appreciating ambiguities as well as what is holy and sacred. The process of such honor and query is the place of freedom in love. Operating in love lets one experience hopeful change. Following hooks, *common* is that which exists in communion and true community. *Common* involves those dynamics that help us form true bonds, when we communicate on a transcendent, inclusive level. What is common includes diversity and emerges out of diversity. To be common is to experience and know simultaneously the ordinary within the extraordinary. What is common is dynamic, healthy, inclusive, and meaningful.

In sum, that which is common or, in my words, "shared, ordinary, mutual communal engagement," building from the notion of difference in Girard and hooks,

---

25. See http://www.zmag.org/zmag/articles/dec95hooks.htm.
26. hooks, *Teaching to Transgress*, 129–31.
27. See http://www.rescomp.wustl.edu/~ripple/issues/9.2/bell.html.

requires a dynamic, dialogical relationship that honors healthy mimetic desire toward communion. A holistic view of common requires naming injustice and oppression, having a shared notion of power, and appreciating what is unique in each individual and in every group. To be common is to be free. Ergo, my question is, "How then can or does one maintain difference in the quest for that which is common?" One place to test Girard's and hooks's notions of difference and the derivative notions of commonality or the common as praxis is in the stories of Morrison and Jesus. This will help us move toward constructing a theological ethic of commonality.

The Narratives

Morrison's The Bluest Eye

The Bluest Eye is poignant, compelling, and illuminating about the tension and conflicts between that deemed different and that deemed common. In Morrison's consummate macroscopic vision, we experience difference, tragedy, dissonance, racism, sexism, and patriarchy run amuck, all framed by chapter headings that draw on excerpts from the Euro-American, middle-class Dick-and-Jane readers to create a variation of the theme of hegemonic commonality. For hooks and Girard, Dick and Jane symbolize white privilege, the crowd, the model, the oppressor. Pecola and her family are scapegoats, disciples, the other. The mimetic triangle involves the model (majority culture), the disciple (the Breedloves), and the object (acceptance, love, and freedom). When the triangle collapses, the resulting double bind produces incarnated ugliness.

The concept of ugliness is the metaphor for ostracized difference—all the self-loathing, pain, deceit, hatred, and crippling codependency, rooted in racism, that exist within the Breedlove family. Ironically, their name indicts their shortcomings, for the family breeds hate, not love. The ugliness, one marker of self-hatred, is a dialectical mark of difference: it sets them apart, making them unique, while also setting them up for tragedy, pain, oppression, and ridicule. The implied pedagogy is not education for freedom in love, but education for oppression and persecution. The story echoes the mantras of ugliness and hatred, rooted in United States soil: the ugliness of white privilege, intraracial racism, and external racism personify the ugliness that traps, defiles, and kills Pecola, psychologically and spiritually.

Pecola Breedlove searches for her self by pursuing the beauty that she knows she can possess if she acquires blue eyes. Her deep, pathological desire for the bluest eyes becomes obsessive. Set as a female *Bildungsroman* (psychological novel), Pecola's misguided quest for "shared, ordinary, mutual engagement" results from her distorted cosmology as a pubescent African-American female in the United States.[28] Her worldview depicts a cultural disfigurement that connects

---

28. Phyllis Klotman, "Dick-and-Jane and the Shirley Temple Sensibility," in *"The Bluest Eye" Black American Literature Forum* 13 (1979): 123–25; here, 123.

physical beauty with virtue and ideas of love as necessary prerequisites to romance.[29] Her difference disavows and truncates any potential for commonality. The symphonic pieces of her world evoke a symphony of blue-eyed blondness. Pecola's answering solo is the wailing fugue of dissonant, unskilled players. No maestro conducts her, no one teaches her, nor do her peers play with her. Her melody is a symphonic dirge of dissonance. The cacophonous dissonance symbolizes Pecola's dysfunctional family and a world that denies her meaning, health, love, understanding, security, and any shared differences and commonalities, even before her birth.

Pauline, Pecola's mother, could not deal with the difference or commonality in her world or Pecola's world. So she fantasizes in the world of the cinema, where she envisions and fashions her in-vitro daughter to fit her mirage of white beauty signified on the silver screen. Cholly, Pecola's father, fashions a free-spirited, discordant song that kills. Unloved and mortified as a young teen, Cholly loved Pecola enough to hold her, with an embrace that violated her, impregnated her, which led to her descent into schizophrenic oblivion. The harmony created by the Breedloves is misunderstood and becomes an "aesthetic of transgression" that idolizes one ideal of beauty[30] and breeds hate, which annihilates any modicum of common good, and instead celebrates individual and communal destruction. Their hateful counterpoint determines that every family member will have a pathology, as the family's self-destructive ethos manifests ugliness. The blackness and poverty surrounding the Breedlove family is common, but their ugliness is unique; it incarnates and yet transcends difference. For Morrison, it brings "anonymous misery."[31] Ugliness surpasses and goes deeper than any perceived physical description by others. Ugliness is the Breedlove's metaphor for existence. As song, their lives of ugliness praise nothingness; as petition, their ugliness moans "I am victim." As proclamation, their ugliness suffocates them as "judged and damned." The ugliness embodied by Pecola's family makes them outcasts and offers Pecola no sustenance, relatedness, commonality, or appreciation for her difference, only scorn. As Morrison's narrator tells us:

> No one could have convinced them that they were not relentlessly and aggressively ugly. . . . The father, Cholly['s], ugliness . . . was behavior, [and] the rest of the family . . . wore their ugliness, put it on, . . . although it did not belong to them. . . . You looked at them and wondered why they were so ugly; you looked closely and could not find the source. Then you realized that it came from conviction, their conviction.[32]

---

29. Barbara Christian, "Community and Nature: The Novels of Toni Morrison," *Journal of Ethnic Studies* 7 (Winter 1980): 65–78; here, 69, 73.

30. Shelley Wong, "Transgression as Poesis in *The Bluest Eye*," *Callaloo* 13 (1990): 471–81; here, 474.

31. Morrison, *Bluest Eye*, 39.

32. Ibid., 38–39.

Their ugliness sanctions that Mrs. Breedlove wears ugliness as martyrdom, to the point that her difference means she never belongs anywhere and her dreams have long since died.[33] Son Sammy uses ugliness to instigate pain as a source of empowerment that includes self-destruction. Pecola uses ugliness to shield herself from the scrutiny of others,[34] relinquishing any sense of connectedness or commonality. This conviction of ugliness distorts reality, devalues humanity, and fosters self-hatred and hopelessness. The subsequent self-hatred, addictive behaviors, and catalytic societal prejudices and commodification anesthetize people to their own cultural heritage and drive them to violence and rage. Pecola's parents' pathologies echo the obsessions of larger society. Her parents' imprisonment to their difference projected through their ugliness so destroys themselves and their reality that they taunt each other. They become psychologically and physically abusive to the point that they drown in enraged depravity.[35] Their mimetic, sick desire for the unobtainable and their pathological hate of themselves creates individual and communal pain; it provokes idolatry at the altar of fictionalized physical perfection. The addicted symphonic voices that orchestrate blonde, blue-eyed concertos and masterworks explode any hope for mutuality and assimilation toward social progress.[36] They do not have room for hooks's liberatory pedagogy, nor can they desire it, for their hope and imagination have shut down. Pecola's pathology leads to a lone voice of bruised and broken difference, wailing and playing the blues. Pecola, finally, is a scapegoat to the nth power, for all in her immediate society, black and white. No one could love Pecola because in all of Lorraine, Ohio, the idealistic primer *Dick and Jane* signified the white norm for beauty, thus obliterating a healthy aesthetic of difference, blurring the lived reality of racial diversity, denying the commonality of humanity, and eventually catapulting Pecola into madness.

Pecola wants to know love, but her pathological milieu dictates that values break down and love transmutes into hatred; the difference-commonality dialectic obliterates Pecola and makes her powerless. Because she has nothing in common with the Dicks and Janes of the world, she cannot succeed in a middle class Anglo-Saxon myth and milieu—the marker that determines who names and experiences the common in the United States as concretized by elementary school reading texts. Pecola, in her dejected devastation, is powerless; she has no ability to name, define, and perceive reality.[37]

---

33. Ibid., 110–11.
34. Ibid., 39.
35. Ibid., 42.
36. Rosalie Baum, "Alcoholism and Family Abuse in *Maggie* and *The Bluest Eye*," *Mosaic* 19 (Summer 1986): 91–105; here, 91–93, 99; Denise Heinze, *The Dilemma of "Double-Consciousness": Toni Morrison's Novels* (Athens, GA: University of Georgia Press, 1995), 24, 29, 69; Terry Otten, *The Crime of Innocence in the Fiction of Toni Morrison* (Columbia, MO: University of Missouri Press, 1989), 12–13.
37. Cynthia Davis, "Self, Society, and Myth in Toni Morrison's Fiction," in *Toni Morrison* (ed. Harold Bloom; Modern Critical Views; New York: Chelsea House, 1990), 7–26; here, 7.

Pecola knows that she has no worth, no value, no love, and is not lovable. Her mother and other black and white adults appear to love only white blue-eyed children, but not Pecola. Pecola's idolatrous worship of Shirley Temple, the icon for blonde hair and blue eyes, brings no blessing or atonement, no understanding of what is common or different: her fractured fairy tale ends in tragedy. With naive adoration and reverence, Pecola yearns for blue eyes. She desires the difference she believes will make her transcend her status of blackness and ugliness, making her beautiful, and therefore common. Perhaps blue eyes will make her parents different, too.[38] Pecola and her mother—victimized and made inferior because of their black difference, by a society that venerates whiteness—equate blackness with evil.[39] The unloved, isolated mother gave birth to an isolated, unloved daughter. They both embody the ugliness of victimized sexism, classism, and racism inflated and internalized so that they do not have to include their blackness in what is deemed common. When Pecola takes action toward her transformation, she does so through a charlatan, a "Reader, Adviser, and Interpreter of Dreams," an insipid, ego-centered, obsessive-compulsive con man. He is popularly known as Soaphead Church (because of his hairstyle and his training for ministry) and as Elihue Micah Whitcomb, whose difference the narrator captures: "Celibacy [is his] haven, silence a shield."[40]

Church, "whose business is dread,"[41] desires things and despises people, and he is pedophilic in nature. He abhors flesh and fixates on the bodies of those least offensive: children. Actually wishing that he could really grant Pecola's wish to have blue eyes, he nevertheless uses her to get rid of his landlord's sick dog. Church tells Pecola that if the dog changes (for which he gives her poisoned meat to feed the dog), her eyes will become blue. The dog gags in agony and dies. The little pregnant, surprised Pecola walks away down the street believing her eyes are now blue.[42] At the end of the day, Soaphead Church knows he is different, far from common, and blames God for all of the pain and wrongs of the world. We learn about his understanding of theodicy:

> He was aware, of course, that something was awry in his life, and all lives, but put the problem where it belonged, at the foot of the Originator of Life. He believed that since decay, vice, filth, and disorder were pervasive, they must be in the Nature of Things. Evil existed because God had created it. He, [*sic*] God, had made a sloven and unforgivable error in judgment: designing an imperfect universe. Theologians justified the presence of corruption as a means by which men strove,

---

38. Morrison, *Bluest Eye*, 47.
39. Carole Gerster, "From Film Margin to Novel Center: Toni Morrison's *The Bluest Eye*," *West Virginia University Philological Papers* 38 (1992): 191–99; here, 194–95.
40. Morrison, *Bluest Eye*, 165.
41. Ibid., 172.
42. Ibid., 173–76.

were tested, and triumphed. . . . God had done a poor job, and Soaphead suspected that he himself could have done better. It was in fact a pity that the Maker had not sought his counsel.[43]

This ugliness is misbegotten anguish.[44] The related spiritual, physical, psychological, and philosophical lynchings of one's racial/ethnic, gender, and class group by another is misbegotten anguish. Such spurious deceptive discord bifurcates, violates, and causes death. Such misbegotten anguish, such evil, is a global phenomena and is not unique to the external and internal racism felt by persons of African descent. Toni Morrison just illustrates it exceptionally well. As Pecola's life spirals beyond her dysfunctional family to insanity, we see the levels of pathology created by the dominance, disdain, and demonization of difference, and the negation of commonality. Good mimesis and education in freedom for love are nonexistent. Pecola cannot and will not know the privilege of commonality, nor the celebration of difference. Those living in Lorraine, Ohio, cannot create community with Pecola, so she cannot experience communion by connecting with power that brings about equity and healing, and thus having access to life itself.

In sum, Morrison illustrates the devastation that occurs when commonality requires sacrifice, a scapegoat, and thus mimetic violence as religion. Difference is the site of ridicule, external and internal oppression, objectification, violence, callousness, ignorance, fear, naïveté, and desperation. Aesthetically, in *The Bluest Eye*, Morrison shows what happens when "racial beauty [is a reaction] . . . against the damaging internalization of assumptions of immutable inferiority originating in an outside gaze, . . . [how] the demonization of an entire race could take root inside the most delicate member of society: a child; the most vulnerable member: a female."[45] When difference is obliterated and commonality so removed, one self-destructs and spirals down into insanity. There all love, freedom, and hope are lost. Could a Pecola have heard a place of resonance in Scripture? Could she have found some hope if her cosmology and her gaze had been fixated on texts other than Shirley Temple's blue eyes?

Scriptural Text

Matthew 5 is a curious, outrageous text when listening for difference and commonality. This text embraces the dialectic apparent in Girard, hooks, and Morrison. The Beatitudes detail who is not included and honor difference, as they press one to shift toward inclusion. Jesus establishes parameters in which human beings are to relate to those often excluded from common existence.[46] After his wilderness experience, Jesus' speech invites us to deal with a setting where Jesus

---

43. Ibid., 172–73.
44. See my recent work *Misbegotten Anguish*, 27.
45. Ibid., 210.
46. Author's phone conversation with Rev. Dr. John Randle, Oakland, CA, March 30, 2003.

recites the law to a group of people who are different in some respects and share a common sociocultural status in another.

The overall Matthean text shows Jesus as fulfilling Jewish messianic expectation, with a strong emphasis on Jesus' continuity with Jewish tradition, in his retention and interpretation of pentateuchal law. Matthew locates the church within the context of Israel's salvation history. The church is a place of much difference and diversity within the common understandings of what the church is, what it ought to do, what it believes, and who is welcomed. Some scholars view Matthew as a Christian manual that teaches Jesus as Israel's royal Messiah, from birth to resurrection. The Sermon on the Mount (with some parallels in Luke's Sermon on the Plain) sets the tone for the rest of the Gospel, and it highlights the role of the law and the fulfillment of Hebrew prophecy. Jesus acts like a Pharisee in addressing law from a spiritual perspective. The author depicts Jesus as a new Moses and teaches about the nature of God's rule and the behavior pleasing to God. Law is a way of life guiding the attitudes and actions of those who seek to please God. Therefore the *basileia*, or kingdom, law is consistent with Judaism. After his resurrection, Jesus' earthly mission to the Jews becomes a mission to all, not to a privileged group. Theologically, Matthew highlights persons removed from religion and political power in Roman and Jewish systems, those who symbolize difference rather than commonality, those not citizens. And, this Gospel critiques structures that cause social oppression or domination, that denigrate difference.

With life as dichotomy, those blessed for everything from being poor in spirit and mourning to the pure in heart and the persecuted will receive reward, will be a part of hooks's community of learning in love as resistance. Those "blessed" by God are offspring of fugitives, the disenfranchised, the Girardian subject/disciples; they are without true freedom and are often persecuted as scapegoats. All who suffer will receive a reward, consequently reversing the bad mimesis and canceling the scapegoating mechanism. Thus, others are invited to let go of position and elitist place: the model, those with hegemonic power antithetical to inclusiveness, healthy dialogue, and appreciation of the other. We recognize the rhetoric of blessedness, the issues that particularly confront women in interesting proprietary ways—adultery and divorce—and the underlying questions about economics, eschatology, and politics that span race and gender. These press the reader to take serious note of the questions of the common and the different. Certainly, Jesus' reversal of the value system by blessing those who are hurting and poor presses us to deal with the reality of difference, for this text privileges those often deemed as other, outsider, and outcast. These statements or Beatitudes were, in the words of Eugene Boring, originally "a wisdom form filled by early Christianity with prophetic eschatological content. . . . [Here is] not practical advice for successful living, but prophetic declarations made on the conviction of the coming-and-already-present kingdom of God."[47] Because they are revered and preached by

---

47. Eugene Boring, "Matthew," in *The New Interpreter's Bible*, vol. 8 (Nashville: Abingdon, 1995), 177.

many, it is particularly fitting to wrestle with the Beatitudes in thinking through a notion of common good.

These prophetic utterances make objective claims emerging out of divine activity, not subjective claims per se. As ethical exhortations, they inspire the engagement toward practice. Many prophets saw these beatitudes as pronouncements of blessedness to persons focused on the future actuality of God's rule. Hearing the pronouncement becomes an invitation to perform, for outsiders and insiders to do the work. The distinctive blessings indicate an empowerment and an ultimate intimacy with God, blurring the lines between difference and commonality among indwellers of the kingdom of heaven. The blessed inherit and find comfort, satisfaction, and mercy, for they shall see God. There is an alliance with those persecuted and oppressed in other ways, which signals that the problem is not the end of the story. There is hope, joy and gladness, and ultimately one is a blessing to God, by being a light to the world. Here difference is the locus of those who will be blessed, those usually deemed marginal. Sacrifice is not significant to Jesus' agenda for living out of God's *basileia*, or rule, for the poor. Thus, Girardian scapegoating is not a virtue. Blessedness accords its own eschatological reward.

For one to be in right relation, then, one works with Franz Fanon's "wretched of the earth." One need not be ashamed of this difference. Instead, one can embrace these differences, because Jesus pronounces these blessings with authority, framed by God's *basileia*. In working through this pericope, we see that those who are blessed share a common categorical identity that is different from those who already have, and who do not believe. When enough groups begin to embrace enough differences, does one not then move toward a working, inclusive notion of common? Is this not so even if it only means that more voices will be heard at the table, and broader questions will be asked to make sure the common good is really common?

When reviewing these narratives and the difference-commonality dialectic, we ultimately must ask, "How does one do justice to the common good amid difference?" Clearly, the alleged separate but equal practices of Jim Crow and forced, legal segregation in the United States proved that often separate is far from equal. Often those who experience equality, those deemed to be in common, those who are included, are those with privilege. In the practice of justice, then, how do we deal with the commonality-difference dialectic? Does it matter that the question of common good is one of theological ethics more so than that of law? Biblically speaking, one can propose the *imago Dei* as a metaphor for commonality, and the delineation of gender in creation as a symbol for difference. According to Gen 1, God created humanity and pronounced them "good!" In Gen 2, God creates *'ādām*, the earth creature or (in this account) male, and Eve, the female from the earth creature's rib. Structurally, then, what is common and different is our incarnated existential goodness, by divine design.

To be created as *imago Dei* means to be created in the image of God, to be engaged in active, loving relationship with God and each other. Acknowledging the *imago Dei* within all humanity, by definition, would make us avoid performing or allowing destructive acts to our physical space, using language to kill, taking our world for granted, taking more than we give back, always measuring progress in dollars and clout. Certainly, we would avoid worshipping a god who does not love us.[48] This Deity in Gen 1–3 is not Aristotle's unmoved mover, but a personal, vital God. Embracing humanity as incarnated, *imago Dei* invites an eschatological environment of holistic dimensions and creates a grassroots-to-global awareness of the ripple effect generated by human actions. Thus, rather than extract an eye for an eye, one is moved to plant a tree when someone is cruel to our loved ones or us.[49] We see the essence of God, knowing that these are glimmers of what and who God is: unconditional love.

Unconditional love means loving each other just the way we are. Unconditional love does not manipulate or disappear because another person does not act the way we want. Unconditional love does not say, "I will love you if . . . ." Conversely, unconditional love does not mean unconditional control or passive-aggressive oppression. Unconditional love means loving God, one's self, and others. Unconditional love means to be in relationships that embrace respect, mutuality, growth, and peace; that celebrate the truly organic sense of what is common and different. Unconditional love means engaging in good mimesis and a liberatory life that honors the gifts of what is common and what is different in appreciation, without fear, oppression, or hegemony. Avoiding abusive, death-creating encounters, and appreciating the aesthetics and the loves of eros, *filia* (friendship), and agape from God as incarnated in humanity—all signal the freedom to embrace and be included in what is dialectically different and common. This is not a reductionist tact, but rather an invitation to see how complex reality and humanity are. Such an invitation and plea, if you will, calls for us to operate from a notion of justice when discerning the place of commonality and difference in all decision making of who gets to sit at the table. This process is essential for situations where what is common for a particular group and what is different (because it could impede the group, such as a six-foot-tall person hoping to be a jockey) can be processed in a respectful, nonoppressive manner. A process that entertains this complexity in its formulation means that we can engage each other with dignity and respect; with care and consideration, whatever the levels of difference and commonality.

Roses by Any Other Name, or Dandelions That Choke

A rose is a rose is a rose. Roses are popular flowers that signify care and love and adoration. Dandelions, while their greens are nutritious in salads, remain a general garden variety of weed that can grow beyond three and four feet in height in the right environmental conditions. Weeds, like other plants, give off oxygen, which we as humans need; weeds are like roses in needing soil and are different

---

48. "The Auburn Lecture: A Day with Alice Walker," the second annual Auburn Lecture at Union Theological Seminary, April 25, 1995.
49. Ibid.

in that they often choke the grass. Roses can signal the distinctiveness of difference and the commonness of the divine aesthetic in all of nature. Girard, hooks, Morrison, and Jesus provide clues as to the continuum, the dialectic shared by difference and commonality.

Girard views difference as a means to see, be a self, claim identity, be relational; and work for peace; its absence exacts violence, and what is common is mimetic desire. For hooks, difference is a place of celebration, interrogation, liberation, and transformation; what is common must embrace that difference. Both paradigms honor difference and do not explicitly ask the question of commonality. When the difference fails to exist, both systems implode. The Beatitudes and *The Bluest Eye* demonstrate why it is important to hold the two concepts in tension. Does difference require commonality, or does commonality require difference? Moreover, how can one involve both in healthy community? These polar opposites usually coexist as they resonate with one another. There is still a danger when applying the notion of difference, if difference is not respected and commonality becomes a scapegoat for a blasé attitude: "I have mine. You get yours the best way you can."

Morrison portrays the devastation that occurs when difference is the site of ridicule, external and internal oppression, objectification, violence, callousness, ignorance, fear, naïveté, and desperation. Her protagonist so yearns for being included in the common that the quest for commonality disintegrates. In the Beatitudes, difference occurs as one experiences life in relationship, aware of the poor in the largest sense and treating them as neighbor. Sociohistorical and anthropological realities tell us that human life has many variations. Some are privileged, some are oppressed. In concert with societal experience, the gifts of human freedom to make certain choices, along with those issues that remain beyond our control, illustrate difference on a personal level. Commonality exists in the very being of our humanity, as homo sapiens, illustrated in the biblical text and the novel. That beingness involves particular needs along with some wants and desires that transcend culture. Critical to experiencing difference is a sense of immediacy, of being in awe of the gift of life, in trust. Certainly, in the Beatitudes Jesus' reversal of the value system by pronouncing blessing on those who are hurting and in poverty presses us to deal with the reality of difference. This text privileges those often deemed other, outsider, and outcast and presses toward a hopeful common experience of eschatological hope.

The work of theorists Girard and hooks and reflection on the two narratives indicate that what is at stake is the appreciation of the difference-commonality dialectic. The review of uses of the word *common* shows that it has a continuum of meanings: many are not inclusive, and others are clearly negative. Based upon gifts and sensibilities, there will be times when to be common is to be exclusive, to relate to those who only share a particular skill or interest. Thus, not everyone desires to become or has the gifts to be a hockey player, a visual artist, or an engineer. Not all persons can sing in an opera; many cannot sing the blues. While persons in either group share many things in common, those who could not sing or who disliked both kinds of music would not be included in the "common good" of opera or blues. Difference is a part of discerning what is common.

   Aspiring to a sense of *common* as "shared, ordinary, mutual communal engagement" in lived community is a complex venture, one that ought not to be abandoned because of its difficulty and tendency toward exclusiveness. When reviewing the basic tenets for human flourishing, there are certain elements that transcend class, gender, sexual orientation, race, ability, and age. Respect is one such characteristic. Appreciating the long heritage of the concept of *common good*, let us remember that in the best possible worlds recorded to this time in history, many people have not been included; many differences have been shunned and scorned. At the end of the day, a common good that espouses such exclusiveness actually creates as many problems as it solves. At the same time, there are times when, by definition, a particular group must be limited in membership, given the focus of the particular organization. At best, a holistic sense of the common good sees the many layers of complexity within the common, and moves toward being careful about parameters and expectations. Such a reading notes the particularity of their group without needing to oppress others, and does not pretend that their sense of commonality is more global than it really is. Not every rose remains beautiful; not every dandelion chokes the grass from which it springs.

"Good Is Knowing When to Stop"

Dénucléation and the End of Privilege

Josiah Young

Aristotle's *Nicomachean Ethics, Politics,* and *Metaphysics* are early sources of the idea of the common good. The *Nicomachean Ethics,* for instance, asserts that "the things that tend to produce virtue . . . are . . . prescribed by the law . . . with a view to . . . the common good."[1] While it is surely good to attain the good for a single man, "it is finer and more godlike to attain" the good "for a nation or for city-states."[2] In part, the common good disposes people "to do what is just and makes them act justly and wish for what is just,"[3] especially "in relation to our neighbor."[4] For Aristotle, justice takes on different forms with respect to the neighbor. Political justice, "found among men who share their life with a view to self-sufficiency," is for "men who are free and either proportionately or arithmetically equal."[5] There is another "justice" for those who fall outside that category—the wives of free men, their children, and natural slaves. A wife enjoys "household justice," which is analogous to the justice of free men, the *citizens* entitled to political justice.[6] Children and slaves are entitled to the "justice of a master and that of a father." Aristotle explains:

---

1. Aristotle, *Nicomachean Ethics,* in *The Basic Works of Aristotle* (ed. Richard McKeon; New York: Random House, 1941), 1005.
2. Ibid., 936, 1.2 (1094b).
3. Ibid., 1002, 5.1 (1129a).
4. Ibid, 1003 (1129b).
5. Ibid., 1013, 5.6 (1134a).
6. Ibid. (1134b).

The justice of a master and that of a father are not the same as the justice of citizens, though they are like it; for there can be no injustice in
the unqualified sense towards things that are one's own, but a man's
chattel, and his child until it reaches a certain age and sets up for itself,
are as it were part of himself, and no one chooses to hurt himself (for
which reason there can be no injustice towards oneself). Therefore the
justice or injustice of citizens is not manifested in these relations; for it
was as we saw according to law, and between people naturally subject to
law, and these as we saw are people who have an equal share in ruling
and being ruled. Hence justice can more truly be manifested towards a
wife than towards children and chattels, for the former is household justice; but even this is different from political justice."[7]

But is there any such thing as the justice of a *master*? Doesn't this distinction
between political justice and household justice make the *common* good a tad solip-
sistic? Was it really true that the "natural slaves" were content with their lot as slaves?

The *Politics* accounts for their contentment with the notion that a certain
necessity has made some "to be slaves and others to be masters: the one practic-
ing obedience, the others exercising the authority and lordship which nature
intended them to have."[8] If the master were to abuse this relation, he would harm
both parties; yet this view hardly reflects the *slave's* perspective. He or she is but
an appendage of the master—a "living but separated part of his bodily frame."[9]
Aristotle claims that the two—"slaves by nature" and "freemen by nature"[10]—are
friends: They would be nemeses only if the master were so unjust as to mistreat
his property—but that would be tantamount to his cutting off his own hand.[11] Yet
what would the slaves say about such friendship? What would the natural slave
say about the rule of the master?

Aristotle has said that the master's rule is not a "constitutional" rule.
Constitutional rule signifies "a government of freeman and equals." To emphasize his
distinction between the constitutional rule and the rule of a master, Aristotle argues
that the "master is not called a master because he has science, but because he is of a
certain character, and the same remark applies to the slave and the freedman."[12] In
short, the science of the master flows from his bloodline; and the same applies to the
slave—with the result that the slave's science boils down to "servile branches of
knowledge." The master need "only know how to order that which the slave must
know how to execute."[13] In managing his property in that way, the masters are
free to "occupy themselves with philosophy or with politics," for the common good.[14]

---

7. Ibid., 1013–14.
8. Aristotle, *Politics*, in *Basic Works*, 1134, 1.6 (1255b).
9. Ibid.
10. Ibid.
11. Ibid.
12. Ibid., 1135.
13. Ibid.
14. Ibid.

Aristotle's *Politics* explores the master's rule, and by implication his political justice and constitutional rights, in terms of the unequal relations within the soul itself. "One part naturally rules, and the other is subject, . . . the one being the virtue of the rational, and the other of the irrational part."[15] The soul is the unity of the rational and the irrational, which are hardly on the same level. Analogously, the freeman, the rational part, "rules over the slave after another manner from that in which the male rules over the female, or the man over the child. . . . For the slave has no deliberative faculty at all; the woman has, but it is without authority, and the child has, but it is immature."[16] (At least women and children can think: The slave has no deliberative faculty *at all*. What would account for such privation?) Aristotle makes a similar argument in the *Nicomachean Ethics* (1138b.5–10):

> Metaphorically and in virtue of a certain resemblance there is a justice, not indeed between a man and himself, but between certain parts of him; yet not every kind of justice but that of master and servant or that of husband and wife. For these are the ratios in which the part of the soul that has a rational principle stands to the irrational part; and it is with a view to these parts that people also think a man can be unjust to himself, viz. because these parts are liable to suffer something contrary to their respective desires; there is therefore thought to be a mutual justice between them as between ruler and ruled.[17]

One also finds this analogy between the household and the rational soul in the *Politics* (1254b). Here, though, the relationship between the master and the slave is likened to that between the soul and the body as well as the unequal parts of the soul itself.

For Aristotle, God or intelligence, qua monotheism, establishes the common good through free men. Indeed, "an entire political and metaphysical program" underlies this monotheism as an ultimate principle.[18] Consider the *Metaphysics* (11.10.1076a), in which Aristotle rejects the view that "the universe [is] a mere series of episodes" because such a view would "give us many governing principles." If a most primary substance governs the world, its economy accounts for why "the world refuses to be governed badly."[19] Aristotle clinches his point by quoting the *Iliad*'s Odysseus: "The rule of the many is not good; let one be the ruler."(Or in the words of a reader-friendly translation: "Too many kings spoil a nation! One king's enough for me, and why? He gets the right from God on high!"[20] But does *God* empower such monism or powerful men?)

My problem with Aristotle's perspective is heightened by the fact that American slaveholders used his views to support the chattelization of my ancestors. Hugh

---

15. Ibid., 1144, 1.13 (1260a).
16. Ibid.
17. Aristotle, *Nicomachean Ethics*, 1022.
18. Walter Kasper, *The God of Jesus Christ* (New York: Crossroads, 1991), 292.
19. Aristotle, *Metaphysics*, in *Basic Works*, 888.
20. Homer, *The Iliad* (trans. W. H. D. Rouse; New York: Signet, 1966), 26.

Thomas's massive *The Slave Trade* points out how slavery's advocates were partial
to Aristotle's view that "the use of domestic animals and slaves is about the same;
they both lend us their physical elements to satisfy the needs of existence"[21] (referring to *Politics* 1.5.1254b). David Brion Davis's Pulitzer-prize-winning *The Problem
of Slavery in Western Culture* discusses Aristotle's influence in the chapter entitled
"Slavery and the Meaning of America": "Despite a common recognition that
bondage was an unnatural and unsatisfying condition, there had been no moral
influence to overcome the specious arguments of Aristotle, who had confused
nature with the actual institutions of the city-state, and had provided sophisms for
all future apologists of slavery."[22]

In my view, Aristotle's alliance of nature and state is the key to evaluations of
his concept "the common good." The master narrative is tolerated as a sufficient
exemplification of what is good for all. Can I, however—one formed by the civil
rights and black power movements and a progeny of the survivors of the Middle
Passage—ignore this imperious dimension of the genealogy of the common
good? Aren't there other ways to conceptualize the theological implications of the
common good besides the way rooted in the *Iliad*? Can we envision a common
good that eschews Aristotlian-like privilege?

In what follows, I will explore those questions with the help of Jürgen
Moltmann, Emmanuel Lévinas, Toni Morrison, W. E. B. DuBois, and Martin
Luther King Jr. Moltmann's theology of the cross challenges the notion that an
impassible deity is the ultimate cause of the common good established through
the masters' justice and their slaves' acquiescence in it. For Moltmann, God has
undermined the "master-slave" dialectic in *suffering* Jesus' slavelike aporia (Mark
15:34).[23] In acquiescing in Jesus' mortification, God has absorbed unjust relationships and the enmity that arises from them by taking such division into the divine
life—thereby transforming tragic existence into a new creation. Lévinas's conceptualization of God also runs counter to Aristotle's sense of the theological implications of the justice of a master: Not unlike Moltmann's God, Lévinas's God comes
to mind in relation to human wretchedness rather than impassive Substance.[24]

---

21. Hugh Thomas, *The Slave Trade: The Story of the Atlantic Slave Trade,
1440–1870* (New York: Simon & Schuster, 1997), 28.
22. David Brion Davis, *The Problem of Slavery in Western Culture* (New York:
Cornell University Press, 1966), 18.
23. See Jürgen Moltmann, *The Way of Jesus Christ* (Minneapolis: Fortress, 1993),
173, 168: "The Father 'gives up' the Son that through him he may become the
Father of all those who are 'given up' (Rom. 1.18ff.). This transforms the 'almighty
Father' too; for Christ was crucified in the weakness" of God (2 Cor 13:4).
Regarding Jesus' slavelike aporia, Moltmann writes that "Jesus died the death of . . .
a slave in the Roman Empire" and so "shared the fate of these enslaved people."
24. See Emmanuel Lévinas, "A Religion for Adults," in *Difficult Freedom: Essays
on Judaism* (trans. Se·n Hand; Baltimore: John Hopkins University Press, 1997),
19, summing up his point: "The relationship with the Divine crosses the relationship with men [and women!] and coincides with social justice, . . . [which] epito-
mizes the entire spirit of the Jewish Bible."

Toni Morrison challenges the view that slavery is ever just and theologically sound. Within the context of the United States, she argues compellingly that it is time to stop advancing perspectives that equate God with the master's rule and render the slaves' suffering invisible. DuBois's scholarship on the Reconstruction complements Morrison's perspective. King's sermons on the theological implications of the civil rights movement complement the views of Moltmann and Lévinas.

Every thinker—whether European or African-American—challenges the Aristotelian notion of a common good based on "a permanent group hierarchy that is believed to reflect the laws of nature or the decrees of God."[25] In referencing these thinkers, I do not seek to demonize Aristotle, as if he and the Greeks were solely responsible for the historic tendency to conceive of the common good in ways that privilege some and subordinate others. The problem is found among just about all people.[26] Still, the fact that the Western nations root themselves in the Greek thinkers goes a long way toward accounting for my focus on Aristotle.

Moltmann and Lévinas: Being-for-Another

In his *God for a Secular Society*, Jürgen Moltmann asserts that Aristotle's *Nicomachean Ethics* signifies these principles: "Like is known by like," and "Like draws to like."[27] For Moltmann—and this is nothing new to those versed in Aristotle—the philosopher holds that the "deity is one, indivisible, immovable, impassible and hence perfect."[28] Through entelechy and *eros*, the deity brings about an analogous sameness qua the male-run state. Here, then, "correspondence in epistemology"— remember the hierarchical relations within the soul—and "homogeneity in sociology" (the way those internal relations are mirrored in a male-dominated society) mean that friendships among free males *actualize* "the Good . . . at which all things aim" more so than any other friendships.

According to Moltmann, Aristotle's monotheism has misinformed the Western theologians who have distorted Jesus' witness to God in favor of an unmoved mover.[29] Moltmann argues that this monad "is a 'loveless Beloved.' If he is the ground of the love (eros) of all things for him (*causa prima*), and at the same time his own cause (*causa sui*), he is the beloved who is in love with himself; a Narcissus in metaphysical degree: *Deus incurvatus in se*."[30] For Moltmann, however, the biblical God is not a Single Being but triune: perichoretically *differentiated—*

25. George M. Fredrickson, *Racism: A Short History* (Princeton: Princeton University Press, 2002), 6.

26. See Orlando Patterson, *Slavery and Social Death: A Comparative Study* (Cambridge: Harvard University Press, 1982).

27. Jürgen Moltmann, *God for a Secular Society: The Public Relevance of Theology* (Minneapolis: Fortress, 1999), 135.

28. Jürgen Moltmann, *The Trinity and the Kingdom* (San Francisco: Harper, 1991), 194.

29. Jürgen Moltmann, *The Crucified God: The Cross of Christ as the Foundation and Criticism of Christian Theology* (Minneapolis: Fortress, 1993), 26–27.

30. See Moltmann, *The Crucified God*, 222.

ubiquitously present in the Spirit and human in Christ. This triune God is stead-
fast love, but mutable for the sake of creation. God's mutability is seen in
Moltmann's Christianization of the Lurian notion (from Isaac Luria) of *zimsum*
(concentration/contraction, withdrawal into the self)[31] and also in his sense of the
Spirit-filled kenosis of Son, through whom the Creator/Father overcomes transience and evil. Moltmann thus contrasts his triune, crucified God—whose
pathos is mirrored in the suffering of the mortified Son (Mark 15:34)—to the
traces of Aristotle's unmoved mover, as found in Augustine's *ad extra* axiom and
the Cappadocian sense of the godhead's ineffable nature.

For Moltmann, then, the Gospels and selected emphases in Paul witness to a
God who is not preoccupied with himself but with "the others, the weary and
heavy-laden, the humiliated and insulted, the dying and the grieving."[32] If this
God, Jesus' God, informs conceptions of the state as the common good, hierarchical social relations are leveled. No one group actualizes the common good. It
is rather the case that the common good "is constantly in process and is only comprehended by participatory, dialectical thought." Such a view of the common good
has a sacramental dimension insofar as human communities that strive to embody
it are "synecdochically . . . real presences of [God's] coming omnipresence."[33]

Emmanuel Lévinas also suggests that the "like-knows-like" principle—as in
Aristotle's view of "men who are free and either proportionately or arithmetically equal"—brings God "into the course of being" in contrast to the biblical
God. According to Lévinas, the Bible's God "signifies in an unlikely manner the
beyond of being or transcendence."[34] Taking his cue from the Hebrew Bible's
focus on responsibility for the widow and the orphan, Lévinas holds that "the
idea-of-the-Infinite-in-me—or my relation to God—comes to me in the concreteness of my relation to the other, . . . in the sociality which is my responsibility for the neighbor."[35]

---

31. Moltmann, *The Trinity and the Kingdom*, 111: "The Father, through an
alteration of his love for the Son (. . . through a contraction of the Spirit), and the
Son, through an alteration in his response to the Father's love (. . . through an inversion of the Spirit) have opened up the space, the time and the freedom for that 'out-
wards' into which the Father utters himself creatively through the Son. For God [the
Father] this utterance means an emptying of himself—a self-determination for the
purpose of a self-limitation. Time is an interval in eternity, finitude is a space in infinity, and freedom is a concession of eternal love. God withdraws himself in order to go
out of himself. Eternity breathes itself in, so as to breathe out the Spirit of life. . . .
The self-determination of the Father, the Son and the Spirit takes place; and this self-
determination, as self-limitation, means making room for creation and making possible the liberty of the non-divine image of God in God."

32. Jürgen Moltmann, *Experiences of God: Ways and Forms of Christian Theology*
(Minneapolis: Fortress, 2000), 58.

33. Moltmann, *The Crucified God*, 337.

34. Emmanuel Lévinas, *Of God Who Comes to Mind* (trans. Bettina Bergo;
Stanford, CA: Stanford University Press, 1998), 56.

35. Ibid., xiv.

Lévinas's view of God thus differs from theologians who, influenced by Aristotle's entelechy and eros, have opted for an "egology": "the essentially self-sufficiency of the same . . . egoism."[36] Lévinas's critique of "egology" substantiates my suspicion that Aristotle's unmoved mover signifies privilege, *leisure*—"the pleasure of the best man," which "springs from the noblest sources."[37] Aristotle's view that "the state or political community . . . aims at good in a greater degree than any other, and at the highest good,"[38] would not, then, signify the work of God, but the *comfort* of certain kinds of men. According to Lévinas, therefore, "Behind theory and practice there is enjoyment of theory and practice: the egoism of life. The final relation [in Aristotle's notion of the common good] is enjoyment, *happiness*"[39]—*the pleasure of the best man*. Contesting that "egology," Lévinas holds that goodness, that is, God, runs deeper than the noble man's happiness. Nonpaternalistic responsibility for the other—a call to responsibility—is "older" and truer to goodness than the ego-centered psychology that has become "God" and the foundation of a certain common good.

In part (and to the ire of certain feminist thinkers), Lévinas derives that claim from the basic reality of maternity.[40] As he put it in his *Otherwise than Being*—which reinterprets Plato's view that the Good is otherwise than being—the Good is "a modification of maternity": the "gestation of the other in the same, . . . the restlessness of someone persecuted, . . . the groaning of the wounded entrails by those it will bear or has borne."[41] "Someone persecuted" signifies an individual's suffering over his/her nonegoistic responsibility for the welfare of the vulnerable Other—whose want is conceptualized in postmodern terms as "proletarian destitution."[42] Lévinas sense of the organic relationship among people thus differs from Aristotle's in that the purpose of Lévinas is to deprivilege the theory of the transcendent monad—qua the apotheosis of privileged males. "Maternity" symbolizes that the Other rather than the Same is analogous to God. Apophatically, this maternal ethic brings the Bible's Creator to mind. That is, "the oneself cannot form itself; it is already formed with absolute passivity": The unborns' dependency on their mothers—who represent all of us—is not unlike creation's dependency on the Creator. Both dependencies signify "an irrecuperable time which the present, represented in recall, does not equal, in a time of birth or creation, of which nature or creation retains a trace, unconvertible into a memory."[43] For

---

36. Emmanuel Lévinas, *Totality and Infinity: An Essay on Exteriority* (trans. Alphonso Lingis; Pittsburgh: Duquesne University Press, 1998), 44.

37. Aristotle, *Politics*, 1307 [1338a].

38. Ibid., 1127.

39. Lévinas, *Totality and Infinity*, 113.

40. For instance, see Stella Sanford, "Lévinas, Feminism and the Feminine," in *The Cambridge Companion to Lévinas* (ed. Simon Critchley and Robert Bernasconi; Cambridge: Cambridge University Press, 2002), 139–60.

41. Emmanuel Lévinas, *Otherwise than Being, or, Beyond Essence* (trans. Alphonso Lingis; Pittsburgh: Duquesne University Press, 1998), 75: "alterity in the same"; for more on this point, see 67, 105.

42. Lévinas, *Of God Who Comes to Mind*, 13.

43. Lévinas, *Otherwise than Being*, 104–5.

Lévinas, therefore, when the concept of God is made bigger, more mysterious or enigmatic than the unmoved mover—when God's "transcendence turns into my responsibility . . . for the other" rather than the self—then we discover the "good-ness of the Good."[44]

Lévinas defines this goodness as *dénucléation*: "a vulnerability and a paining exhausting themselves like a hemorrhage, . . . the passivity of being-for-another, which is possible only in the form of giving the very bread I eat."[45] Here, then, the common good is not found "in elevated feelings, in 'belles lettres,' but . . . in a tear-ing away of bread from the mouth that tastes it, to give it to the other. Such is the coring out (*dénucléation*) of enjoyment, in which the nucleus of the ego is cored out."[46] Lévinas suggests that the Christians who "opened their hearts" and risked their own lives to help Jews escape the extermination camps exemplify this cor-ing out.[47] Here, to borrow from Richard Cohen's foreword to *Otherwise than Being*, the "denucleating" self suffered on account of *the suffering* of the other" and thus exemplified an "ethical exorbitance.[48]

An ego cannot rest while the Other suffers, and so *dénucléation* is akin to *insomnia*—an ethical vigilance "disturbed in the core of its formal or categorical *equality* by the *other*, which tears away at whatever forms a nucleus, a substance of the Same." According to Lévinas, "The irreducible categorical character of insomnia lies precisely in this: the Other is in the Same and does not alienate the Same but awakens it."[49] To what? To an "extraordinary commitment" that "calls for control, a search for justice, society and the State, . . . thought and science, commerce and philosophy, and outside anarchy, the search for a principle."[50] What is this principle? Responsibility for the Other rather than deification of the Self.

Lévinas flushes this principle out compellingly in his essay "Peace and Proximity." Here, explains one source, "Lévinas does not want to reject the order of political rationality and its consequent claims to universality and justice; rather, he wants to criticize the belief that *only* political rationality can answer political problems and to show how the order of the state rests upon the irreducible ethi-cal responsibility of the face-to-face relation."[51] If, then, the conceptualization of the common good is rooted in "our" Greek heritage, "this heritage needs to be

44. Lévinas, *Of God Who Comes to Mind*, 69.
45. Lévinas, *Otherwise than Being*, 72.
46. Ibid., 64. Ostensibly, *dénucléation* could divest oppressed persons of the will to struggle against their subordination. I find, though, that Lévinas directs the call to *dénucléation* to powerful persons who are bolstered by the social arrangements that privilege them. They, rather than the wretched of the earth, can *afford* to share their bread with the "Other."
47. Lévinas, *Difficult Freedom*, xiii–xiv.
48. Lévinas, *Otherwise than Being*, xiv.
49. Emmanuel Lévinas, "God and Philosophy," in *Emmanuel Lévinas: Basic Philosophical Writings* (ed. Adrian T. Peperzak, Simon Critchley, and Robert Bernasconi; Bloomington, IN: Indiana University Press, 1996), 132.
50. Lévinas, *Otherwise than Being*, 161.
51. Emmanuel Lévinas, "Peace and Proximity," in *Basic Philosophical Writings*, 161–69; 161, source quoted.

supplemented by a biblical tradition . . . rooted in the acknowledgment of . . . responsibility to the other. It is in no way a question of moving from the paradigm of Athens to that of Jerusalem but rather of recognizing that both are simultaneously necessary for the constitution of a just polity."[52]

For Lévinas, a just polity is moved by "a remorse nourished by the memory of colonial wars and of a long oppression of those who were once called savages, of a long indifference to the sorrows of an entire world."[53] These sorrows, to which a certain common good has been largely indifferent, signify what Lévinas calls the *face*. The face raises "at once the temptation to kill and the call to peace, the 'You shall not kill.'" That biblical injunction raises "the responsibility of the ego for an other."[54] Given the fact that Lévinas lost his parents and siblings during the Holocaust,[55] one can understand why he writes that a just state ought to be edified by such faces. The state ought to operate with the realization that the common good is no "natural and anonymous legality governing the human masses, from which is derived a technique of social equilibrium, placing in harmony the antagonistic and blind forces through transitory cruelties and violence." Such "a State delivered over to its own necessities . . . is impossible to justify." Lévinas would like to believe—and so would I—that the call to *dénucléation* can enrich the common good through persons able to respond to the Other as an equal rather than an inferior. Without the "insomnia" of such persons, we would, Lévinas argues, have to be content with "the simple subsumption of cases under a general rule, of which a computer is capable."[56]

Lévinas concludes his essay with his sense that "extravagant generosity of the for-the-other" grounds the state (that is, the common good). The common good would thus be based on a "reasonable order, ancillary or angelic, of justice through knowledge, and philosophy here is a *measure* brought to the infinity of the being-for-the-other of peace and proximity, and is like the wisdom of love."[57] I take Lévinas to mean that if God gives rise to the love of wisdom, to virtue and justice, especially political justice, then the citizens of the common good ought to be, like the angelic hosts, dedicated to peace and justice—for all.

I do not agree with Lévinas's claim that "God never takes on a body, . . . never becomes, in the proper sense of the word, a being."[58] Yet I do find that Jesus' God brings to mind "a vulnerability and a paining exhausting themselves like a hemorrhage, . . . the passivity of being-for-another"—rather than the immutability of substance.[59] It seems to me, then, that God is bringing about the common good

---

52. Ibid., 162.

53. Ibid., 163.

54. Ibid., 167.

55. See Lévinas, *Difficult Freedom*.

56. Lévinas, "Peace and Proximity," 169.

57. Ibid.

58. Emmanuel Lévinas, *Alterity and Transcendence* (trans. Michael B. Smith; New York: Columbia University Press, 1999), 169.

59. Lévinas, *Otherwise than Being*, 72; consider Moltmann, *Crucified God*, 244–25, arguing that the hemorrhage of the Son is the perichoretic counterpart of the coring out of the Father.

through a certain *dénucléation* rather than privileged leisure. How *good* it would be to stop deifying privilege, qua the rule of the master. How wise "to seek the 'origin' of the word of God, the concrete circumstances of its signifying . . . in the face of the [abject] other."[60]

Morrison, DuBois, and King: Changing the System

If one can accept Lévinas's circumlocution for God "as the primordial dative of the *for another*, in which a subject" cores out his or her "kingdom of identity and substance"[61] in responsibility to "those who were once called savages,"[62] how might God call the privileged to *stop* subordinating the Other in the United States? In what sense is the Good attained in knowing when to stop the perpetuation of privilege akin to Aristotle's "constitutional rule"?

Toni Morrison's Baby Suggs, a character in her Pulitzer-prize-winning novel *Beloved*, suggests how.[63] Baby Suggs's Cincinnati home, 124 Bluestone Road, had been a place where she

> loved, cautioned, fed, chastised and soothed. Where not one but two pots simmered on the stove; where the lamp burned all night long. Strangers rested there. . . . Messages were left there, for whoever needed them was sure to stop in one day soon. Talk was low and to the point— for Baby Suggs, holy, didn't approve of extra. "Everything depends on knowing how much," she said, and "Good is knowing when to stop."[64]

Good is knowing when to stop signifies more than her motherly wisdom on plain, nonpretentious living (as in Lévinas's maternal ethics—"the one-for-the-other" rooted in "feminine alterity.")[65] Loving, cautioning, feeding, chastising, and soothing her people, Baby Suggs undermines the privileged sociality and epistemology in question. As the "origin of the word of God, the concrete circumstances of its signifying . . . in the face of the [abject] other," she teaches her community, which called her "holy," how to overcome the slaveholders:

---

60. Lévinas, *Alterity and Transcendence*, 175. With theological accents that I find edifying, Moltmann (*Way of Jesus Christ*, 244) riffs off Lévinas in asserting that we indeed discover the word of God "in the discovery of others, the pain which their difference causes, and our own preparedness to let ourselves be changed through this encounter. Our knowledge of ourselves develops in our . . . emptying of ourselves in confrontation with the other."

61. Lévinas, "God and Philosophy," 144.

62. Lévinas, "Peace and Proximity," 163.

63. Toni Morrison's *Beloved* is rooted in an historic event—the Margaret Garner case. See William L. Andrews and Nellie Y. McKay, eds., *Toni Morrison's Beloved: A Casebook* (New York: Oxford University Press, 1999), 21–36. *Beloved* takes off from Garner's tragic response to slavery.

64. Toni Morrison, *Beloved* (New York: Knopf, 1987), 87.

65. Lévinas, *Totality and Infinity*, 155.

They do not love your flesh. They despise it. They don't love your eyes; they'd just as soon pick 'em out. No more do they love the skin on your back. Yonder they flay it. And O my people they do not love your hands. Those they only use, tie, bind, chop off and leave empty. Love your hands! Love them. Raise them up and kiss them. Touch others with them, pat them together, stroke them on your face 'cause they don't love that either. *You* got to love it, *you!*[66]

Baby Suggs thus teaches her folk another spirituality (one older than the *Metaphysics*, to allude to Aristotle and Lévinas). Her imperative is not for one to love oneself as the image of God qua primary substance, but to love the deprivileged *Other* in the self.

Baby Suggs's daughter-in-law, Sethe, having run way from slave-state Kentucky in 1855, joins her at 124 Bluestone. When Sethe's owner, "schoolteacher," comes to reclaim her and her children under the authority of the Fugitive Slave Act (1850), Sethe tries to kill her children to liberate them. She only has time to kill her firstborn daughter, the "crawling-already?" girl, for whom the novel is named. Morrison reveals that Sethe's infanticide is the act of an unselfish mother—a claim that makes Lévinas' notion of *dénucléation* tragically compelling.[67] What drives this mother to such unselfishness is constitutional rule: the Fugitive Slave Act. In the immediate aftermath of the infanticide, Baby Suggs begs God's pardon—"Lord, I beg your pardon, I sure do"—since she believed she had betrayed her own wisdom: "Good is knowing when to stop." With much pain and suffering, she must have believed that her "call"—"Love your flesh"—had incited "God's" wrath. Was God punishing her for miseducating her people to love themselves far more than the free men, the exemplars of political justice and the enforcers of the rule of the household, would allow? "God puzzled her and she was too ashamed of Him to say so." Baby Suggs's life had been intolerable and had exhausted her. So she went to "bed to think about the colors of things,"[68]

until the afternoon of the last day of her life [ca. 1864] when she got out of bed . . . and announced . . . the lesson she had learned from her sixty years [as] a slave and ten years free: that there was no bad luck in the world but whitepeople. "They don't know *when* to stop," she said, and returned to her bed, pulled up the quilt and left them to hold that thought forever.[69] [emphasis added]

Sethe went too far—she didn't know when to stop—but neither did "schoolteacher" and the law that upheld his "justice."

---

66. Morrison, *Beloved*, 88.

67. See Carl Plasa, ed., *Toni Morrison, Beloved* (New York: Columbia University Press, 1998), 35.

68. Morrison, *Beloved*, 177.

69. Ibid., 104.

W. E. B. DuBois complements and foreshadows Morrison's work in his classic text *Black Reconstruction*. DuBois argues that African people made a massive contribution to the Union's victory: Slaves who had once worked behind Confederate lines joined the Union forces to serve the Union as farmers, servants, spies, and soldiers. They helped turn the tide of the war.[70] Still, the North betrayed the blacks by withdrawing Union troops and aborting Reconstruction, effectively handing blacks over to a South averse to sharing political justice with them. According to DuBois, then, "One reads the truer deeper facts of Reconstruction with a great despair" because the nation missed an opportunity to dismantle privilege in significant measure. It failed to see that "the rich world is wide enough for all, wants all, needs all." That humane ethic would have gone a long way—would have "set the strife in order, not with full content, but with growing dawn of fulfillment." Instead, the North and South upheld a notion of the common good that deified white privilege.

In setting the post-Reconstruction context for that apotheosis, DuBois observed:

> A [school] teacher sits in academic halls, learned in the tradition of its elms and its elders. He looks in the upturned face of youth and in him youth sees the gowned shape of wisdom and hears the voice of God. Cynically he sneers at . . . "niggers." He says that the nation "has changed its views in regard to the political relation of races and has at last virtually accepted the ideas of the South upon that subject. The white men of the South need now have no further fear that the Republican party, or Republican Administrations, will ever again give themselves over to the vain imagination of the political equality of man.[71]

DuBois spent his life trying to teach others how to stop the common good as "*the gowned shape of wisdom, . . . the voice of God*"; or as the *Politics* has put it, "the pleasure of the best man," which "springs from the noblest sources."

DuBois held that the disabilities of segregation could be overcome if blacks would strengthen their institutions. "Instead of letting this segregation remain

---

70. W. E. B. DuBois, *Black Reconstruction in America: An Essay toward a History of the Part Which Black Folk Played in the Attempt to Reconstruct Democracy in America, 1860–1880* (New York: Atheneum, 1962), 121: "Freedom for the slave was the logical result of a crazy attempt to wage war in the midst of four million black slaves, and trying sublimely to ignore the interests of those slaves in the outcome of the fighting. Yet, these slaves had enormous power in their hands. Simply by stopping work, they could threaten the Confederacy with starvation. By walking into the Federal camps, they showed to doubting Northerners the easy possibility of using them as workers and as servants, as farmers, and as spies, and finally, as fighting soldiers. And not only using them thus, but by the same gesture, depriving their enemies of their use in just these fields. It was the fugitive slave who made the slaveholders face the alternative of surrendering to the North, or to the Negroes."

71. Ibid., 728.

largely a matter of chance and unplanned development, and allowing its objects and results to rest in the hands of the white majority or in the accidents of the situation, it [his plan] would make the segregation a matter of careful thought and intelligent planning on the part of" African-Americans.[72] Such organization, which DuBois conceived in socialist terms, would force the dominant conception of the common good to expand its boundaries. DuBois's goal, then, was not to fortify two common goods, but to use the one—*Love your hands!*—to humanize the other. He wanted the black community to survive and revolutionize a system. "Rail if you will against the race segregation here involved and condoned," writes DuBois, "but take advantage of it by planting secure centers of Negro cooperative effort and particularly of economic power to make us spiritually free for initiative and creation in other and wider fields, and for eventually breaking down all segregation based on color or curl of hair."[73]

DuBois thought the black church would play a special role in breaking down segregation if the black intelligentsia were more involved in the life of the church. In other words, DuBois thought that a black church bereft of its most educated persons was left with an ecclesiology handed down to blacks by their Anglo-Saxon masters. This ecclesiology has been somewhat Africanized through the continuum of slave religion. Yet the ecclesiology itself was for him fairly useless without the imperative to confront and change for the better a system based from its inception on the protection of the rights of free white males.[74] DuBois thought it imperative for blacks to see the direct relation between their "pie-in-the-sky" religion and socioeconomic marginalization.

The ministry of Martin Luther King Jr. represents a certain fruition of DuBois's argument. On the one hand Dr. King was quite early disaffected by what he deemed the unsophisticated histrionics of the black church; on the other hand he emulated erudite black clergy such as Benjamin E. Mays, former president of the Morehouse College. These reactions exemplify DuBois's speculation that only leadership such as King's could move the black church to broaden the application of American democracy. I see striking parallels between the two men's conceptions of an alternative to what I have referred to as the Aristotelian-based

---

72. W. E. B. DuBois, *Dusk of Dawn: An Essay toward an Autobiography of a Race Concept* (New Brunswick, NJ: Transaction Books, 1984), 199–200.

73. Ibid., 215.

74. DuBois's argument complements Orlando Patterson's view that American Protestantism has privileged whites. The Aristotelian-like axiom that one caste has been "elected" to rule women, children, and slaves surfaces in the distinction between the eschatological city of God—where God is no respecter of persons—and its this-worldly analogue, in which racial distinctions are counted as penultimate matters that pale beside the heavenly "reality." According to Patterson, then, white Americans have used the concept of the *civitas Dei* to dissimulate their most hallowed value—privilege. The eschatological "solution on the part of a monotheistic slaveholder class" worked—and its legacy continues to work—because of a "hegemonic imposition of a rigid dualism in the socioreligious ideology." See Orlando Patterson, *Slavery and Social Death: A Comparative Study* (Cambridge: Harvard University Press, 1982), 72.

common good. Both were drawn to socialism, sought solidarity between African-Americans and Third-World people, and tried to direct the spiritual resources of the black community toward the dismantling of privilege. But whereas DuBois sought the common good in terms of Marx and a retreat from white America, King—edified by the example of Jesus—sought the common good through a liberal Christianization of Gandhi's nonviolent praxis. King valued Gandhi's exemplification of *satyagraha*—soul-force, or love-force (holding onto Truth)—and *ahimsa* (the principle of nonviolence).

King's appropriation of *satyagraha/ahimsa*, an ancient spirituality, to be sure, resembles Lévinas's notion of *dénucléation*, or "insomnia." The affinity is precisely this: for both men, the ethical self is responsible for the other. The other is not simply the indigent, oppressed, marginalized others, but also the well-heeled and prosperous ones as well, who must come to see the selfishness of their ways for the sake of justice. "The foundation of consciousness is justice," writes Lévinas.[75] And one goes to great personal lengths to effect such justice in a given context. Justice, argues Lévinas, thus involves "the risky uncovering of oneself, in sincerity, the breaking up of inwardness and the abandon of all shelter, exposure to traumas, vulnerability."[76] During the civil rights movement, which sought to establish a certain common good, the cost such trauma exacted on the black community is observed in King's eulogy for the little girls killed in the bombing of the Sixteenth Avenue Baptist Church in Birmingham, Alabama, in 1963. Delivering their eulogy, King expressed his hope that the "spilt blood of these innocent girls may cause the whole citizenry of Birmingham to transform the negative extremes of a dark past into the positive extremes of a bright future."[77] He sought to explain that their deaths were part of the cost of the struggle for a common good qua "a vulnerability and a paining exhausting themselves like a hemorrhage, . . . the passivity of being-for-another."[78] In part, their deaths helped to liberate the Other from selfishness and hatefulness.

The affinity between Lévinas's notion of *dénucléation* and King's legacy can also be seen in his sermon "The Drum Major Instinct." It concludes with Dr. King's remarks about how he wanted to be remembered—as one who tried to feed the hungry and clothe the naked, who tried "to give his life serving others." King based his sermon on Mark 10, which brings to mind something else Lévinas wrote: "The Other . . . is situated in a dimension of height and abasement—glorious abasement; he has the face of the poor, the stranger, the widow, and the orphan, and, at the same time, of the master called to invest and justify my freedom." Thus, the destitute—the stressed-out Vietnamese, the black urban underclass—call us to realize that their abjectness is simultaneously a great moral height. The

---

75. Lévinas, *Otherwise than Being*, 160.

76. Ibid., 48.

77. Martin Luther King Jr., "Eulogy for the Martyred Children," in *A Testament of Hope* (ed. James M. Washington; New York: Harper & Row, 1986), 222.

78. Lévinas, *Otherwise than Being*, 72.

poor are like towering sovereigns who define the meaning of freedom, which is forfeited unless we respond to their needs (Mark 10:21).[79]

When construed christologically, this means that the common good, or what King called "Beloved Community," is brought about through a responsibility to the least of us—a responsibility that differs radically from Aristotle's rule of the master. Here, the very abasement of the least of us (Mark 10:14) is, in truth, height, as revealed in Jesus Christ, the "master" crucified as a slave. King made precisely that point in his sermon. In a nutshell, Jesus was undermining the Romans' aggressive and narcissistic understanding of greatness and revealing the Son of Man's pacific and humble exemplification of greatness (Mark 10:25–45)— "a vulnerability and a paining exhausting themselves like a hemorrhage, . . . the . . . being-for-another, which is possible only in the form of giving the very bread I eat."[80] And let us not forget a place "where not one but two pots simmered on the stove; where the lamp burned all night long," and where "good is knowing when to stop."[81]

Moltmann: Hope for a Coming Common Good

We enter the twenty-first century still steeped in a conception of the common good that privileges the upper echelons of society and brings Baby Suggs's exhaustion to mind. Consider the plight of African-Americans: The Thirteenth, Fourteenth, and Fifteenth Amendments to the U.S. Constitution have given all Americans rights that—given the seminal role of the civil rights movement in reestablishing those rights—have made us more citizen than slave. Today, moreover, middle-class and upper-class blacks, however troubled by racism's persistence, share in America's wealth and prestige. A few—the Colin Powells, the Condoleezza Rices, the Bill Cosbys, the Earl Graves, the Vernon Jordans—have a bit of power. Too many blacks, however, continue to be locked into the cellar of society, where they are the victims of injustice. They are without work and any real power. They have no significant presence in circles where society's policies are determined. Their powerlessness is due to the fact that the government is committed to privileging the privileged. Despite the examples of Martin Luther King Jr. (his *dénucléation*) and Emmanuel Lévinas (his "insomnia"), I doubt that most beneficiaries of privilege will core themselves out and level the playing field.

I have come, therefore, to appreciate Jürgen Moltmann's "eschatological millenarianism"—however problematic from certain perspectives[82]—as a powerful

---

79. Lévinas, *Totality and Infinity*, 251.

80. Lévinas, *Otherwise than Being*, 72.

81. Morrison, *Beloved*, 87.

82. See Richard Bauckham, "The Millennium," and Miroslav Volf, "After Moltmann: Reflections on the Future of Eschatology," both in *God Will Be All in All: The Eschatology of Jürgen Moltmann* (ed. Richard Bauckham; Minneapolis: Fortress, 2001).

"hope" for a common good that is the antithesis of the rule of privilege in history. Moltmann provides no details about this new millennium's socioeconomic arrangements. The fate of our institutions—legal, educational, commercial—does not appear to concern him as much as the Parousia does. Brought about by the Parousia, the new millennium would be the messianic prelude to the universal restoration of all things rather than a mere political alternative to the prevailing state of the world.

The high mark of the Parousia—the resurrection *from* the dead as seen in terms of 1 Cor 15:21–23—would also bring about a remarkable change in those who are not destined to die (in the sense of 1 Cor 15:51 or 1 Thess 4:17).[83] Both events would occur in the Spirit's life-giving, end-time power to bring about a complete and indestructible peace with nonhierarchical justice all over the world. According to Moltmann, then, the Parousia will alter the character of time itself, which, he offers, "is determined by . . . the presence or absence of God—that is to say, by the different modes of his presence in time." Since "the presence of Christ in the life-giving Spirit" determines the present, one "expects a future of Christ in the resurrection from the dead and in the 'giving life to our mortal bodies' (Rom 8:11)."[84] One thus expects that life will no longer wane—that all will savor "the felicitous moment" unceasingly.[85] Liberated from the deep anxieties and conflicts integral to death[86]—and en route to the resurrection *of* the dead—the future would bear "the impress . . . of Christ's . . . kingdom" rather than his struggle.[87]

---

83. Jürgen Moltmann, *The Coming of God* (Minneapolis: Fortress, 1996), 82. See as well James D. G. Dunn, *The Theology of Paul the Apostle* (Grand Rapids: Eerdmans, 1998), 294–315. Moltmann appears to eschew the notion of a "rapture" that would save only some of the living. His hermeneutics is explained by his theology of the cross: "The *Christian* doctrine about the restoration of all things denies neither damnation or hell. On the contrary: it assumes that in his suffering and dying Christ suffered the true total hell of Godforsakenness for the reconciliation of the world, and experienced for us the true and total damnation of sin. It is precisely here that the divine reason for the reconciliation of the universe is to be found. It is Christ's descent into hell that is the ground for the confidence that nothing will be lost but that everything will be brought back again and gathered into the eternal kingdom of God. *The true Christian foundation for the hope of universal salvation is the theology of the cross, and the realistic consequence of the theology of the cross can only be the restoration of all things*" (*The Coming of God*, 215). If the millennium corresponds to that end, would the Parousia involve the "terrible decree"?

84. Moltmann, *The Coming of God*, 200.

85. Ibid., 200. As Moltmann puts it in *The Spirit of Life* (Minneapolis: Fortress Press, 2001), 40: "Eternity is found in the depths of the experienced moment, not in the extension of time."

86. Moltmann, *The Coming of God*, 91: Sin is not the cause of death; the inverse is the case. "The frailty of the temporal creation of human beings is like a detonator for the sin of wanting to be equal to God and to overcome this frailty. Death is only the consequence of sin inasmuch as sin exists because of death: we cannot endure mortality, and by killing we can make other people die. The vulnerability of creation-in-the-beginning makes the act of violence possible."

87. Moltmann, *The Coming of God*, 200.

Would not such a future vindicate Lévinas's sense that we are to be responsible to and for the Other? In the future, however, the pain and the "hemorrhaging" integral to the assumption of such responsibility today would pass away because "proletarian nakedness" and destitution would be no more. In my view, such a future would also substantiate Lévinas's claim that "the abstract idea of God . . . cannot clarify a human situation. It is the inverse that is true."[88] The human situation that clarifies the idea of God, and the idea of the common good that flows from it, is rooted in Moltmann's theology of the cross, the event of *dénucléation* in God. Here, the suffering of the Messiah—"the bread of life" given from the "mouth" of God through the Spirit—unveils, apocalyptically indeed, the nonhierarchical relationships in God and transvalues the concept of the common good to mean equality in diversity rather than sameness of substance or consciousness.

In one of his essays Moltmann criticizes Aristotle's principle of sameness. It "is only when we men and women become wholly godless in the sense that we dispense with self-deification or presumptuous pretense of resembling God, that we can perceive the wholly other reality of the true God; and conversely, where we experience the wholly other God, we can dispense with our anxious and aggressive 'God-complex,' and become true human beings."[89] Or as Lévinas has put it, "To posit the transcendent as stranger and poor one is to prohibit the . . . relation with God from being accomplished in the ignorance of [people] and things. The dimension of the divine opens forth from the human face. . . . [God's] very epiphany consists in soliciting us by . . . destitution in the face of the Stranger, the widow, and the orphan. . . . God rises to . . . supreme and ultimate presence as correlative to the justice rendered to" others.[90] For the sake of the common good that I hope is coming—a common good distant from Aristotle's—let us be good and stop narrowing commonality to power and might and privilege.

88. Emmanuel Lévinas, "Transcendence and Height," in *Basic Philosophical Writings*, 29.

89. Moltmann, *God for a Secular Society*, 148.

90. Lévinas, *Totality and Infinity*, 78.

Common Good in Performance

Milner S. Ball

Here I recall an episode from our past that revolves around an act of terrorism. It is less the event than what becomes of it that has moment for common good in the present: Forty years on, a victim reaches out to a person from the victor's side and tells him a story. It is the story of a vision and the vision's matrix, the community and way of life that were destroyed. The telling and the hearing of the story become a joint venture, and a new reality—a translation that overcomes loss and victory—emerges from the earlier, violent collision between the one world and the other.

I begin with the story, the storyteller, and the translation. I offer the latter as a performance of common good accompanied by faith and hope. Then I turn to the theology and politics in the achievement.

There is contemporary urgency in these things. A good that includes some but excludes others is not common, is scarcely good, and may be self- as well as other-destructive, as in an America that was half-slave and half-free. The same may be true, too, when inclusion is offered to others but only on condition of their colonization, as happened and continues to happen in America's relation to Native America.

From time to time, prophets and poets have suggested that failure to confront and redress the treatment of the original inhabitants would lead to its repetition in progressively more destructive forms.[1] Some saw a replay of the Indian wars in

---

1. In the nineteenth century, John Beeson hoped to persuade Americans that, unless they recognized and redressed their aggression against Native Americans, they would be condemned to repeat it in progressively more destructive forms. He apparently convinced Lincoln that the Civil War was an "extension of the unneighborly,

the war in Vietnam.[2] And it fell to the *New York Times* to note that the cavalry rode again in Iraq.[3] The Seventh Cavalry that George Custer led to defeat at the Battle of the Little Big Horn advanced through the Iraqi desert in "subdivisions calling themselves Apache and Crazy Horse."[4] Airborne support for ground troops was available from Apache and Kiowa helicopters and Tomahawk missiles. If we have been repeating the Indian wars, the story, the storyteller, and the translation that are the subject of what follows hold promise for release from the burden of continuing to do so.

The Story

Black Elk was a Holy Man of the Lakota (Sioux). He was born on the Plains in 1858. At the age of nine he received a great vision. *Black Elk Speaks* is the story of that vision, the duty that accompanied it, and the life of those whom it would animate. John Neihardt published it in 1932.[5]

Black Elk told Neihardt that it had taken a long time to "make words for the meaning" of the vision. Eventually "these things . . . remembered themselves. . . . It was as I grew older," he said, "that the meanings came clearer and clearer . . . and even now I know that more was shown to me than I can tell."[6]

He *could* tell how a white cloud had caught him up and carried him to "where white clouds were piled like mountains on a wide blue plain." Then "suddenly there was nothing but a world of cloud" and a great white plain amid snowy mountains, and he saw legions of horses wheeling and dancing in formation.[7] One cloud became a tepee with an open rainbow door, and in council within sat the six Grandfathers—the powers of the four directions and of the sky and earth. In elaborate ritual turn, each bestowed a gift.

---

un-Christian, and destructive practice which for generations had been operating against the Aborigines." See Francis Paul Prucha, *The Great Father* (Lincoln: University of Nebraska Press, 1984), 468. Richard Slotkin, in his *The Fatal Environment* (New York: Atheneum, 1985), provides an extended examination of progressive, twentieth-century repetition of the Indian Wars. See also Carol Bly, *Letters from the Country* (New York: Penguin Books, 1981), 4. Aggression against Native Americans is embedded in our art: in film in the figure of John Wayne and in Ft. Apache as a police station in the Bronx. It is a subject of short stories like William Faulkner's "The Bear" and Peter Taylor's "The Old Forest"; and of novels, notably Herman Melville's *Moby Dick*.

2. See, e.g., Slotkin, *The Fatal Environment*, 16–18.

3. Michelle O'Donnell, "Rich in Glory and Agony, the Cavalry Rides Again," *New York Times*, Sunday, March 23, 2003, News of the Week in Review, p. 5, col. 1.

4. Ibid.

5. Some of the material on *Black Elk Speaks* was originally published as Milner Ball, "Budding Translation," *Michigan Law Review* 99 (2001): 1265.

6. Nicholas Black Elk and John Neihardt, *Black Elk Speaks: Being the Life Story of a Holy Man of the Oglala Sioux as Told Through John G. Neihardt* (Lincoln: University of Nebraska Press, 1979), 49.

7. Ibid., 22.

The fourth Grandfather, of the south, gave him the power to make his nation live. This power took the form of a red stick that sprouted and branched and was then filled with leaves and singing birds. In the shade beneath it, Black Elk momentarily glimpsed "the circled villages of people and every living thing with roots or legs or wings, and all were happy."[8] Then he looked down to earth "and saw it lying yonder like a hoop of people, and in the center bloomed the holy stick that was a tree, and where it stood there crossed two roads, a red one and a black." The former was good, and the latter the way of trouble and war.[9]

He saw the future. He saw that his nation would walk the black road and that its hoop would be broken. He saw that the tree would die. He saw that he would then be called upon to repair the nation's hoop: He was to set the stick at the center of the hoop. He was to make it bloom and make the people live and walk again the good red road.

This vision and Black Elk's life would be intertwined. He grew up in a world of games, hunts, ceremonies, and war with the tribe's enemy, the Crow. The first sign of forthcoming trouble with another enemy was a Custer expedition into the Black Hills. The soldiers found gold. More white people (*wasichus*) arrived, followed by hostilities. Black Elk took part in the initial skirmish when he was thirteen. He took his first scalp in the battle against Custer at the Little Big Horn. On that day he thought of his vision, and as he did so, it gave him strength.[10]

The victory was short-lived. Black Elk's nation started down the black road. They lost the Black Hills. The *wasichus* lured Crazy Horse into Soldiers' Town for talks and killed him. The Oglala, Black Elk's particular Lakota community, fled to Canada when he was fifteen.

The vision burdened him, but he also felt its power grow as the nation declined. When and how, he wondered, would he "bring the hoop together with the power that was given . . . and make the holy tree to flower in the center and find the red road again."[11] The burden and the power grew into a compelling fear. When the fear at last overwhelmed him, Black Elk sought relief from a medicine man, who proscribed a cure: "You must do your duty and perform this vision for your people upon earth."[12]

Black Elk's vision must be danced and sung into this world. So began a series of community performances that reenacted first one part of the vision and then another. The Horse Dance inaugurated the series, and as Black Elk and the assembled company of horses and riders performed, the vision came to him again.

---

8. Ibid., 28.

9. Ibid., 29.

10. Ibid., 110. Because Standing Bear and Iron Hawk were older than Black Elk and therefore had richer memories of the events, they do most of the talking about the battle. The term *wasichu* or *wasi'chu* can be translated as "takes the fat" or "greedy person."

11. Black Elk and Neihardt, *Black Elk Speaks*, 147.

12. Ibid., 161.

Performance gave him a better understanding of the vision and a power that enabled him to heal the sick. Even so, although he could cure individuals, he could not revive his nation. The nation's condition grew disastrously worse. The Oglala returned from Canada and descended to the reservation. "Everything the Power of the World does," Black Elk observed, "is done in a circle," but on the reservation the people were made to live in square houses.[13]

The *wasichus* destroyed the last of the bison herds. Hunger and despair ruled Indian country. Black Elk felt the power of the vision grow, but he was powerless to channel it into the renewal of his nation. In 1886 he joined Buffalo Bill Cody's Wild West Show and traveled east. He would explore the *wasichu* world. He hoped to find sources for a better way for his people. He discovered none in New York and none in Europe during his sojourn with the show.

He returned home in 1889 and was caught up in the messianic Ghost Dance movement, a powerful attraction to those in despair. Black Elk participated enthusiastically at the start and received another vision. But soon he came to view this vision as false and to understand the Ghost Dance as a diversion from the duties of his true vision. Instead of producing salvation, the Ghost Dance provoked official United States suppression.

December of 1890 brought scant food and bitter cold. Police killed one leading holdout, Sitting Bull. And then Big Foot, desperate and desperately ill, gave up resistance and came in to the Pine Ridge Reservation with his band of four hundred starving and freezing people.

Soldiers went looking for the new arrivals. Black Elk heard rifle and cannon fire begin at Wounded Knee on the morning of December 29. He mounted his horse and raced to the site. There he came upon soldiers firing into a gulch:

> Dead and wounded women and children and little babies were scattered all along there where they had been trying to run away. . . . Sometimes they were in heaps because they had huddled together. . . . Sometimes bunches of them had been killed and torn to pieces where the wagon guns hit them. I saw a little baby trying to suck its mother, but she was bloody and dead.[14]

Black Elk wanted revenge. He wanted to kill *wasichus*. The next day he joined a firefight that forced the soldiers to retreat. Black *wasichu* reinforcements arrived, the tide of battle shifted, and the U.S. troops prevailed. "And so it was all over," he said. "A people's dream died there" with the butchered women and children.[15] There would be no revenge. There would be no nation. "It was the nation that" died.[16] Black Elk had at last encountered an enemy who would stop at nothing. There could be no common good.

---

13. Ibid., 194.
14. Ibid., 258.
15. Ibid., 270.
16. Ibid., 180.

The Book

Perhaps Wounded Knee was too much for Black Elk. Perhaps the nightmare overwhelmed the vision. Perhaps he was stunned into silence, "frozen in a single moment of despair."[17] Perhaps not. Perhaps in his subsequent "daily life as a patriarch, rancher, . . . and community elder . . . he made a successful life for himself and his family"[18] and simply found no need or occasion to speak. In any event, forty years later the vision reasserted itself and led him to deliver it and the story of his life to Neihardt in a series of interviews attended by tribal friends and ceremonies.

Black Elk Speaks is Neihardt's account of these sessions. At their conclusion, Black Elk said he hoped to stand a last time on the Black Hills' Harney Peak, the center of the world to which the spirits had taken him in his great vision. Neihardt arranged the trip. At the summit Black Elk sent his frail voice in search of the Great Spirit. He remembered his vision. He prayed for his people, for the reconstitution of their hoop, and for their return to the good red road.

The vision had always been forward-looking. It was always opening out, being grown into, becoming danced and understood.

On Harney Peak, as he had done before, Black Elk referred to himself as "a pitiful old man" who had "done nothing" with his vision.[19] Raymond DeMallie suggests that this theme is a type of Lakota ritual attitude, "for the efficacy of prayer depended upon making oneself humble and pitiable before the powers of the universe."[20] In the course of telling his story, Black Elk had said that the visions and ceremonies made him "like a hole through which the power could come to the two-leggeds. If I thought that I was doing it myself, the hole would close up and no power could come through."[21] To give voice to sorrow, humility, and despair is to make oneself an opening.

The vision characteristically achieves its greatest realization of power in the powerlessness of the person. So it was from the start. The vision first came to Black Elk when he was "lying like dead."[22] And then, at the end, at Wounded Knee, when he raced toward the gunfire, he rode unarmed except for a ceremonial weapon. "I carried only the sacred bow of the west that I had seen in my great vision."[23] In that encounter with the unthinkable, he led a charge that drove the soldiers from their slaughter in the gulch. "I just held the sacred bow out in front of me with my right hand. The bullets did not hit us at all."[24]

This protection was the last manifestation of the vision's efficacy—unless the book itself is another.

------

17. Roger Dunsmore, "Nicolaus Black Elk: Holy Man in History," in *A Sender of Words* (ed. Vine Deloria Jr.; Salt Lake City: Howe Bros., 1984), 155.

18. Raymond DeMallie, "Introduction," in *The Sixth Grandfather* (ed. Raymond DeMallie; Lincoln: University of Nebraska Press, 1984), 57.

19. Black Elk and Neihardt, *Black Elk Speaks*, 273; see also 180, 270.

20. Ibid., 56.

21. Ibid., 205.

22. Ibid., 48.

23. Ibid., 256.

24. Ibid., 258.

Roger Dunsmore observes that Black Elk does not arrive "at the *Truth*" but is instead "deeply involved in not knowing, and confronts the risk that when he gives his vision away it will be ignored, misunderstood, or misused."[25] When he committed his vision to John Neihardt, Black Elk disclosed to outsiders sacred knowledge that had life and truth in the protected, private space of his community. He could not know what effect his doing so would have on either the vision or himself. Both might die: "I have lain awake at night worrying and wondering if I was doing right; for I know I have given away my power when I have given away my vision, and maybe I cannot live very long now. But I think I have done right, . . . for I know the meaning of the vision is wise and beautiful and good."[26]

In hesitance and doubt, but also in hope, relying on the power of its images and words, he released the vision into the becoming a text. The concluding prayer from Harney Peak, addressed to "Grandfather, Great Spirit," carries the petition: "It may be that some little root of the sacred tree still lives. Nourish it then, that it may leaf and bloom and fill with singing birds."[27] His telling the vision to Neihardt may be read as his way of planting it and so of fulfilling his duty to set the stick he was given in the center of the hoop.[28] It may be read as a sign of hope for common good.

In Black Elk's world, visions and words are given for the community and are not appropriable by any one member. Like any other gift, a vision is to be given away. It must continue to move. Individuality is valued, but as Lewis Hyde observes, individuality in a gift-giving economy takes expression "in the right to decide when and how to give the gift. The individual controls the flow of property away from" rather than acquisitively toward herself.[29]

To non-Indians, "Indian giver" can be a term of disparagement. An Indian giver makes a present and then takes it back. But in an economy like that of the Lakota, Hyde points out, "the gift must always move."[30] It may be returned to the giver but is enhanced if it is passed on to someone else. Indian giving is an expression of relatedness and circularity, an affirmation "that all are relatives in the great hoop of the world."[31]

The dedicatory page of *Black Elk Speaks* carries a statement from Black Elk: "What is good in this book is given back to the Six Grandfathers and to the great men of my people."[32] By taking the form of English writing, the vision enriches a widening circle of others.

"I was seeing in a sacred manner the shapes of all things in the spirit, and the shape of all shapes as they must live together like one being," Black Elk says. "And

25. Dunsmore, "Nicolaus Black Elk,"145.
26. Black Elk and Neihardt, *Black Elk Speaks*, 206.
27. Ibid., 274.
28. Harney Peak, where Black Elk stood in his vision, was the center of the world. "But," he said, "anywhere is the center of the world." Ibid., 43 n. 8.
29. Lewis Hyde, *The Gift* (New York: Vintage Books, 1983), 79 n*.
30. Ibid., 4.
31. Dunsmore, "Nicolaus Black Elk," 157.
32. Ibid., v.

I saw that the sacred hoop of my people was one of many hoops that made one circle, wide as daylight and as starlight, and in the center grew one mighty flowering tree to shelter all the children of one mother and one father. And I saw that it was holy."[33] It was a vision of common good.

The Common Good in Translation

Black Elk was highly selective in deciding when and to whom he would give the story. When he did speak, his storytelling became a community event, and Lakota friends joined in the labor of narration.

We cannot know the precise relation between what they said and what John Neihardt published. Black Elk knew little English. Neihardt knew little Lakota. Translation required difficult negotiation between two worlds. In the Lakota world, the word is powerful, and performance is essential, for there is no writing and hence no literature and no concept of literature. The speaking had to travel between Lakota orality and Western textuality. It made the journey from Black Elk, who told the vision, through his son Ben, who repeated in English the words his father uttered, then through John Neihardt's daughter Enid, who took stenographic notes and produced a reordered transcript, and then through Neihardt, who wrote from the transcript and made alterations suggested by his own memory of the sounds and silences in the event, by his poet's gift for working words, and by Black Elk's singular openness to him.[34]

Nice attempts at sorting out exactly whose speech the book is are foreign to the subject and its performance. Once Black Elk told the story, the only fault in the hearer would lie in arresting its movement to others. *Black Elk Speaks* advances the vision's long, rare journey. Black Elk received the gift and circulated it, and so then did Neihardt. The result is a jointly achieved success of translation.

Translation that works serves generally as an image for a politics of just relationships. As James Boyd White says: "To attempt to 'translate' is to experience a failure at once radical and felicitous: radical, for it throws into question our sense of ourselves, our languages, of others; felicitous, for it releases us momentarily from the prison of our own ways of thinking and being."[35] To translate is not to pick up words from one language and drop them into another. Translation that works necessarily entails both deficiencies and exuberances, both the loss of some meaning from the original and the gain of some meaning available only in the other language.[36] The result is a third reality that did not exist before. The new

---

33. Ibid., 43.

34. Raymond DeMallie's *Sixth Grandfather* includes the transcript, an account of the interviews and the ceremonies and events in which they took place, and details about Black Elk's relation to Neihardt. See also the preface and appendixes to Black Elk and Neihardt, *Black Elk Speaks*, xv–xix, 277–99.

35. James Boyd White, *Justice as Translation* (Chicago: University of Chicago Press, 1990), 256.

36. Ibid., 235–36 (developing an insight of José Ortega y Gasset, a philosopher of revolution).

reality does not destroy, absorb, or replace the original or the differences between languages. Translation, White concludes, is "a set of practices by which we learn to live with differences," and good translation "proceeds not by the motives of dominance or acquisition, but by respect."[37]

If we take translation in this generous, political sense, the particular labor of Black Elk and John Neihardt may be understood as the performance of an alternative to American acquisitive dominance and Native American resistance or assimilation. As in the early iconography of America provided by Edward Hicks's paintings, *The Peaceable Kingdom*, so also in *Black Elk Speaks*: differences between Native America and America abide in the text, but they lie down together in a new reality without sacrifice of their integrity. It is common good in textual performance.

Black Elk and Christian Faith

I noted that Black Elk may not have been stunned into a defeated silence by Wounded Knee and instead may have afterward made a success as patriarch, rancher, and community elder.[38] There is a critical omission from this list of his roles: "catechist."

Black Elk Speaks covers the period from Black Elk's birth in 1862 to the Wounded Knee massacre of 1890. John Neihardt first met Black Elk in 1930. Nothing is said about the intervening forty years and of Black Elk's life between the ages of 27 and 67. In that meantime the Lakota holy man had apparently been silent about his vision. He had become a Roman Catholic. Black Elk was baptized in 1904 and was given the name Nicolas.[39] And then he became an active catechist of the church.

His turn to the church had been in preparation for some years. When he joined Buffalo Bill's Wild West Show to explore the eastern United States and Europe for possible sources of power for his people, his exploration included examination of Western religion. The show required all performers who became part of the troupe to be of the same religion, and that apparently meant baptism into the Episcopal Church.[40] A chaplain accompanied the show, and in a letter home, Black Elk wrote of "remembering God."[41] In another letter, written after his return, he quoted from a Dakota translation of the Bible.[42]

The details of Black Elk's determination to be baptized as a Roman Catholic are unclear.[43] About the aftermath of this baptism, it has been variously suggested

---

37. Ibid., 257.
38. DeMallie, *Sixth Grandfather*, 57.
39. Ibid., 14.
40. Ibid., 10.
41. Ibid., 8.
42. Ibid., 19.
43. See ibid., 14–15; Michael Steltenkamp, *Black Elk: Holy Man of the Oglala* (Norman: University of Oklahoma Press, 1993), 29–43.

that he gave up his old Lakota beliefs, worked out a union of the two, or integrated them in some way.[44] It is clear both that he subsequently led an active church life as a catechist and that he never repudiated his vision, his prayer on Harney Peak, or the book dedication to the Six Grandfathers.

James Clifford notes that accounts of conversions as surrendering traditional ways and religion "usually reflect a wishful evangelism." In fact there is "almost never a radical either-or choice." And in situations of unequal power, "the familiar response of colonized persons is outward agreement and inner resistance." Clifford is careful to note that he does not wish to question the genuineness of conversion but "only to caution against the either-or logic of conversion as seen by the outsiders whose accounts dominate the written record."[45]

Black Elk was a teacher in the church and a Holy Man in his tribe. After his baptism he discontinued some of his earlier practices as a medicine man, but he did not repudiate the Lakota vision or the core celebrations.[46] Apparently he neither found that his conversion trumped his prior life as a Lakota nor felt a syncretist's need to confect a synthesis of whatever he wished to extract from Christian and Lakota ways. After he gave his vision new life by releasing it into American literature, he continued as before to teach the Roman Catholic faith. If there was tension between the integrity of the vision and the integrity of the faith, he would live in it.

I believe this to be the creative tension, within an individual, of the lion lying down with the lamb. As an exemplary church elder, Black Elk was engaged in translating his Christian faith in his Lakota life. This is as an open-ended process, at least as much so in a life as with a text. A standard version of a translated text will have a revised standard version and then a new revised standard version. At different times and in different contexts in the course of his long life of exploration, Black Elk would have experimented with different terms, struck different balances, and tested new possibilities. Like any translator, he would make continuing judgments about what was *juste* in his performance and what was not, about what worked and what was good. His life may be understood as fulfilling his catechetical responsibilities: It is a positive example for American as well as Native American Christians who daily set about to live their faith and who seek common good.

---

44. For a sampling of various suggestions, see Raymond DeMallie, "John G. Neihardt's Lakota Legacy," in Deloria, *Sender of Words*, 100, 123–24; DeMallie, *Sixth Grandfather*, 25–28, 71; Carl Starkloff, "Renewing the Sacred Hoop," in Deloria, *Sender of Words*, 159, 160, 167; and Steltenkamp, *Black Elk*, 42–159.

45. James Clifford, *The Predicament of Culture* (Cambridge: Harvard University Press, 1988), 303.

46. The matter is not free of difficulty and has stirred controversy. For a sampling of different points of view on the subject, including Neihardt's omission of reference to Black Elk's role as a catechist, see, e.g., DeMallie, *Sixth Grandfather*, 8–28, 58–67, 71–72; Steltenkamp, *Black Elk*, 24–28, 44–77, 79–142, 154–66.

The Church and Common Good

The confession of faith we make within the gathering of believers establishes the ground for embracing differences, including differences in religion such as any that may exist between Western Christianity and Lakota spirituality.[47]

We believe that God the Father is the Creator and therefore the sovereign over nations and their gods. Patrick Miller carefully and insightfully notes that, although marginal to its main emphasis, Deuteronomy does sound a distinct theme of "God's other stories," the stories "of God's redemptive work in behalf of other nations," even among the Philistines.[48] Israel's own God apportions to all nations their territories and their gods. They are members of God's order. Although Israel is not to worship these other gods, they nonetheless serve "as center of value and meaning for other nations" and "have their place" in the story of God's universal rule.[49] "Israel's story, Israel's way with the Lord," Miller observes, "cannot violate the stories of other peoples and their way with the Lord."[50]

We believe that God the Son is the Redeemer to whom "nothing human was alien"(Bonhoeffer).[51] In the Jewish tradition, Israel's story includes the stories of other nations, but Paul Lehmann pointed out that the church has assumed that "the Christian Story requires or implies an indifference to or a disregard or rejection of other stories, . . . as though exclusiveness were the criterion of its particularity."[52] The contrary is true: "The Christian Story, faithfully and responsibly told, moves from its divine-human center of freedom and fulfillment to its circumference, from which nothing human is excluded."[53] That story bespeaks "God's concern for *all* humanity," and it arouses in believers "a willingness to listen to the stories of other faiths . . . from the conviction that [their] own faith 'is the defender of life' wherever, however, and by whomever lived."[54]

---

47. In this present volume, see the treatment of Phil 4:5a and Rom 12:14–21 in the essay by Victor Furnish, as well as Max Stackhouse's remarks on evaluating world religions in his essay.

48. Patrick Miller, "God's Other Stories: On the Margins of Deuteronomic Theology," in *Israelite Religion and Biblical Theology* (Journal for the Study of the Old Testament: Supplement Series 267 (Sheffield: Sheffield Academic Press), 593.

49. Patrick Miller, *Deuteronomy* (Interpretation: A Bible Commentary for Teaching and Preaching; Louisville: John Knox, 1990), 229.

50. Miller, "God's Other Stories," 599. On "other" cultures and peoples loved of God, see Jacqueline Lapsley's discussion of the place of Nineveh in the Jonah story, in her essay in this volume.

51. Dietrich Bonhoeffer, "Christ the Center," in *A Testament to Freedom* (ed. Geffrey B. Kelly and F. Burton Nelson; San Francisco: HarperSanFrancisco, 1990), 117ff.; here, 127.

52. Paul Lehmann, "The Indian Situation as a Question of Accountability," *Church and Society* 75 (January–February 1985), 51ff.; here, 59.

53. Ibid.

54. Nancy Duff, *Humanization and the Politics of God* (Grand Rapids: Eerdmans, 1992), 172, stating the theology of Paul Lehmann and James Cone.

We believe that God the Holy Spirit is active among all people. According to John Calvin, God the Holy Spirit is not only the "secret energy" that particularly illuminates the minds and opens the hearts of believers,[55] but also "the general power" that animates and supports all mankind."[56] The Spirit is therefore to be celebrated as actively present in the world in all men and women and not only in the church among believers. That presence would be denied if, instead of attempting to discern and give thanks for the Spirit in others, Christians were to engage in the coercive evangelism that Dietrich Bonhoeffer described as "attempt to impose the Gospel by force, to run after people and proselytize them, to use our own resources to arrange the salvation of other people."[57]

Unsurprisingly then, in light of the church's creedal commitments, Augustine's classic vision of the heavenly city—his portrayal of common good from the church's perspective—celebrates and embraces difference: "The heavenly city . . . calls citizens out of all nations, and gathers together a society of pilgrims of all languages, not scrupling about diversities in the manners, laws, and institutions whereby earthly peace is secured and maintained. . . . It is therefore so far from rescinding and abolishing these diversities, that it even preserves and adapts them, so long as no hindrance to the worship of the one true God is thus introduced."[58]

Translation is the action in this city. It is the contextual, tensile politics in the new reality of lying down together. Black Elk and *Black Elk Speaks* are examples of it.

Perhaps they are more than good examples. Perhaps they are bearers of the word of God. Karl Barth is a help here, not least because he grounds his appreciative readiness for the world in the exclusivity and priority of Jesus Christ. His notion of "secular parables" is particularly apt.[59]

Barth understands that humans have no natural capacity for true knowledge of God. They can know and speak truly of God only if God enables them to do so. The word of God thus relativizes all human words.[60] Even the words of the Bible and the church are not bearers of the word except as they are made so through empowerment by their subject. What the Word does for the words of

---

55. John Calvin, *Institutes of the Christian Religion* (trans. John Allen; 2 vols.; Grand Rapids: Eerdmans, 1949), 1:589 (3.1.1). Paul Lehmann drew my attention to this possible connection between Calvin and Native America. See Lehmann, "The Indian Situation," 58–59.

56. Calvin, *Institutes*, 1:590 (3.1.2): "Hence the Spirit is called 'the Spirit of holiness,' not only because he animates and supports us by that general power which is displayed in mankind, and in all other creatures, but because he is the seed and root of a heavenly life within us." See also 2:561–64 (4.14.8–10).

57. Dietrich Bonhoeffer, *The Cost of Discipleship* (trans. R. H. Fuller; New York: Macmillan, 1959), 165.

58. Augustine, *The City of God* (trans. Marcus Dods; New York: The Modern Library, 1958), 696 (19.17).

59. Barth takes up the question in Karl Barth, *Church Dogmatics*, vol. IV/3.1, First Half (ed. G. W. Bromiley and T. F. Torrance; Edinburgh: T & T Clark, 1961), 86–135. See also the helpful discussion of the subject in George Hunsinger, *How to Read Karl Barth* (New York: Oxford University Press, 1991), 224–80.

60. Hunsinger, *How to Read Karl Barth*, 245.

the Bible and the church, his Word can do for the words and events of the world. They, too, may be made to speak the Word.[61] "In the world reconciled by God in Jesus Christ, there is no secular sphere abandoned by Him or withdrawn from His control, even where from the human standpoint it seems to approximate most dangerously to the pure and absolute sense of utter godlessness. If we say that there is, we are not thinking and speaking in the light of the resurrection of Jesus Christ."[62]

Believers must therefore be prepared to receive signs and attestations of the lordship of Christ from the secular world and its events.[63] They must eavesdrop on the world, the theater of God's glory.[64] They must listen for what the Word may say to them to challenge or gladden them, to remind them that the church is not Atlas bearing the burdens of the world on its shoulders.[65]

Barth identifies God's uses of the words and events of the world to speak the Word as "secular parables."[66] Jesus' parables are their prototype. In his hands in the Gospel texts, everyday life and familiar stories become what they were not before: "the being, words and activities of labourers, householders, kings, fathers, sons, etc., become real testimony to the real presence of God on earth."[67] This is so in the biblical texts, and it is so in the world.

Perhaps it is so of Black Elk and the translation of his story. Black Elk may have told his vision to Neihardt as an act of cultural preservation, or of resistance to colonialism, or of resistance to his own giving up. But after years of exploration as a Holy Man and then after more years of reflection as a catechist, he may well have told the story of his Lakota vision as an act of Christian faith. He may have discerned a parable in the vision and its translation. That he and many other members of the church in Native America became Christians is an affirmation of the power of God to cause even the words of European colonizers to speak the Word and to cause even the ears of those whom they oppressed to hear it, as miraculously also happened in the relation between free white enslavers and their African victims. Not knowing what Black Elk intended but knowing the power of God with language, we may find that *Black Elk Speaks* is a parabolic bearer of the Word.[68]

---

61. Barth, *Church Dogmatics*, 3/1:112.
62. Ibid., 118. This is not a statement of triumphalism; see 97–98.
63. Ibid., 124.
64. Ibid., 117.
65. Ibid., 114–15.
66. Ibid., 115.
67. Ibid., 113.
68. Barth said that assessment of whether words or events have been made the Word must proceed with great caution but also with full confidence in the sovereign presence and power of the Word in the world; ibid., 124. He suggested four criteria for making the judgment: (1) Agreement with Scripture, not some confirmation in a particular biblical text but harmonization with "the whole context of the biblical message" (ibid., 126); (2) A relation to the "historic dogmas and confessions of the church" (ibid.); (3) Demonstrated effectiveness in the world (ibid., 127); (4) The bearing of both affirmation and denial to the church, "a summons to faith and a call to repentance" (ibid., 126–28). I believe that both the text *Black Elk Speaks* and Black Elk's life satisfy all four criteria. I do not argue the case here, and in any event, the judgment is for a community and not an individual to make.

In any event, the vision Black Elk received combined with the nightmare he witnessed at Wounded Knee—both in the heartland of America—yield a Native American perspective that transcends the American polity from below as well as from above. And in *Black Elk Speaks* John Neihardt "exceeds his tradition for a moment and makes the moment live forever thereafter."[69] We may therefore justly anticipate receiving from it acute human insight if not also the word of God for the common good.

American Secular Politics

Black Elk Speaks is the triumph over Wounded Knee in American literature that we await in American politics. It offers both hope for the common good that our politics can become, and a remonstrance against what it presently is.

Tribes are in one sense firmly resident within the United States and in another radically outside it.[70] Like Hermes, they may travel back and forth between worlds. American assumptions about Native Americans are shaped by a few, basic American stories in which tribes "are always either dying or surviving, assimilating or resisting." But James Clifford observes that tribes may in fact be "sometimes separate and 'Indian,' sometimes assimilated and 'American,' and their history may be a series of cultural and political transactions, not all-or-nothing conversions or resistances."[71]

The Hermetic life of tribes, the in-between where translation ought to occur, has been costly to Native America. Clifford cites as an example the 1978 case of *Mashpee Tribe v. New Seabury Corp.*[72] In that case the ownership of land at issue turned on the validity of a nineteenth-century conveyance by the Mashpee to non-Indians. But the issue of whether they could litigate it depended on proof that they were a tribe and therefore a legal person. After a jury trial, the judge decided that the tribe did not qualify. The judge and jury did not accept the tribe's oral history. As Clifford puts it, the Mashpee failed in the "contest between oral and literate forms of knowledge," where "the written archive" trumps "the evidence of oral tradition."[73] He concludes that the judgment depended on a shared culture, and a "shared culture and its commonsense assumptions" were precisely what was at stake.[74] The Mashpee "could not be seen for what they were and are,"[75] and the story they told about themselves could not be heard. They were forced to live and act "between cultures in a series of ad hoc engagements."[76]

69. N. Scott Momaday, "To Save a Great Vision," in Deloria, *Sender of Words*, 37.
70. See Clifford, *Predicament of Culture*, 339 n. 5.
71. Ibid.
72. *Mashpee Tribe v. New Seabury Corp.*, 427 F. Supp. 899 (D. Mass 1978).
73. Clifford, *Predicament of Culture*, 339.
74. Ibid., 329.
75. Ibid., 336.
76. Ibid. In this present volume, see also essays by Cheryl Kirk-Duggan with comments on insider/outsider dynamics, and by Josiah Young on treatment of privilege, dénucléation, and the other.

This failure of translation is a mark of colonialism and a denial of common good, imposing one reality upon another instead of composing a new, third one. After Wounded Knee, a U.S. agent concluded that the slaughter had been a good lesson. It taught Indians, he reported, that it is dangerous to oppose "the law of the Great Father."[77] The Mashpee were not subjected to raw violence in New Seabury, but the dominant culture was imposed on them. The case of *Mashpee* taught them that it is exhausting, expensive, and fruitless to engage "the law of the Great Father."[78]

Americanization, Past and Present

"Americanization" of Native Americans has long characterized U.S.-tribal relations. Throughout the nineteenth and twentieth centuries, congressional statutes as well as presidential-administrative policies typically lurched back and forth between the attempted destruction of Indian Nations and support for their self-determination. These approaches were never reconciled, and their contradictory effects are actively preserved in twenty-first-century law. Colonialism has always been the basso continuo underlying the diverse themes, and it cannot support common good.

For the last three decades, the colonial office has passed from the U.S. Congress and the executive branch to the Supreme Court.[79] The Court chose to play a different role in the beginning, or close to the beginning. In 1831, when the tribes initially attempted to gain entry to American law, the Court turned them away. The Cherokee sought the protection of law against the state of Georgia's aggression. In *Cherokee Nation v. Georgia,*[80] the Court found that the Cherokee were a nation but said that, for this reason, because they were neither a state nor a foreign nation, the U.S. Constitution gave them no standing to bring their case before the Court. Like the Mashpee a century-and-a-half later, they could not be translated into American law.

---

77. *Commissioner of Indian Affairs Annual Report*, 412 (report of J. George Wright, Rosebud Agency, August 27, 1891); quoted in Allison Dusias, "Ghost Dance and Holy Ghost: The Echoes of Nineteenth-Century Christianization Policy in Twentieth-Century Native American Free Exercise Cases," *Stanford Law Review* 49 (1997): 773, 799.

78. Cf. William Cavanaugh's discussion of the nation-state and *e pluribus unum* in his essay in this volume.

79. On the historical, conceptual background of colonialism in law, see Robert Williams, *The American Indian in Western Legal Thought: The Discourses of Conquest* (New York: Oxford University Press, 1990). On colonialism in present law, see Philip Frickey, "A Common Law for Our Age of Colonialism: The Judicial Divestiture of Indian Tribal Authority over Nonmembers," *Yale Law Journal* 109 (1999): 1; idem, "Marshalling Past and Present: Colonialism, Constitutionalism, and Interpretation in Federal Indian Law," *Harvard Law Review* 107 (1993): 381–440; here, 381.

80. *Cherokee Nation v. Georgia*, 30 U.S. (5 Pet.) 1 (1831).

The following year the Cherokee cause came to the Court again. This time the Court granted standing because the case was brought by a non-Indian surrogate, Samuel Worcester, an American missionary to the Cherokee. Since he was a U.S. citizen, his grievance could be heard. In his name the Cherokee won a great victory. Georgia had sought to apply its law to Worcester's activity within the borders of the Cherokee Nation. In *Worcester v. Georgia*[81] the Court held that the state's claim of jurisdiction over Indian country was unlawful, and it gave a strong, clear statement of Cherokee nationhood and sovereignty. It was an opening to exploration of a noncolonial common good.

For several reasons, however, that triumph came to nothing. The tribes were soon forcibly removed along the Trail of Tears, and the South was ethnically cleansed of them.[82] Even so, the Court had offered such protection as it could and in this way aligned itself with the tribes, if only symbolically.[83] It had paid them respect.

The modern court has abandoned that strategy for one chiefly of aggression. The tribes continue to win occasional, important victories in the Court, but even these may be hollow, as *Worcester* proved to be and as the modern case of *United States v. Sioux Nation of Indians*[84] exemplifies.

In *Sioux Nation* in a failure of translation, the Court upheld a judgment awarding the Sioux compensation for the taking of Black Elk's beloved Black Hills. However, most of the Sioux have refused to accept the money, which they regard as no substitute for the return of the land they seek. Their lawyers had not told them that money damages would extinguish their title. When the clients realized what would happen, the Oglala and Rosebud Tribes attempted to halt the claims and fired the lawyers. The lawyers pursued the claims nonetheless and entered a settlement without their clients' knowledge and against their will. The courts rejected subsequent attempts by other lawyers to win redress.[85]

Typically, as in *Mashpee*, Indian Nations do not win even hollow victories. The Supreme Court continues to reduce tribal reservations, resources, jurisdiction, and power.[86] It characteristically attributes responsibility for this colonizing action in the present to past events that never occurred. Notorious examples of this maneuver are

---

81. *Worcester v. Georgia*, 31 U.S. (6 Pet.) 515 (1832).

82. William McLoughlin's *Cherokee Renascence in the New Republic* (Princeton: Princeton University Press, 1986) offers a comprehensive account of the Cherokee and what happened to them.

83. Justice Stephen Breyer reads *Worcester* and the events that followed it as a "sad, premonitory tale" and notes that the only winner was the Supreme Court; "For Their Own Good," *The New Republic*, Aug. 2, 2000, 32, 39.

84. *United States v. Sioux Nation of Indians*, 448 U.S. 371 (1980).

85. See Steven Tullberg and Robert T. Coulter, "The Failure of Indian Rights Advocacy," in *Rethinking Indian Law* (ed. Committee on Native American Struggles, National Lawyers Guild; New York: National Lawyers Guild, 1982), 51, 53–54; Curtis Berkey, Robert Coulter, and Steven Tullberg, "Written Communication to the United Nations Commission on Human Rights," in ibid., 141, 152–54.

86. See, for example, *South Dakota v. Yankton Sioux Tribe*, 522 U.S. 329 (1998).

furnished by two cases, *Tee-Hit-Ton Indians v. United States* in 1955,[87] and *Oliphant v. Suquamish Indian Tribe* in 1978.[88]

In the first, the Court ruled that the United States did not have to pay the Tee-Hit-Ton the compensation for taking their property that the Fifth Amendment requires. It declared that "after conquest" Indians were left with only a right of occupancy of their aboriginal lands, and that this occupancy did not amount to a property right. But the Tee-Hit-Ton had not been conquered. They were first "conquered" by the Supreme Court's performative utterance in the 1955 opinion. As Nell Jessup Newton says: "The only sovereign act that can be said to have conquered the Alaska natives was the *Tee-Hit-Ton* opinion itself."[89]

The date of the case is significant. One year after the Court had offered the hope of common good to African-Americans with *Brown v. Board of Education*,[90] it aggressively denied that hope to Native Americans.

In the *Oliphant* case, then Justice William Rehnquist held that Indian tribes do not have jurisdiction over non-Indians who commit crimes in Indian country. He said they lost jurisdiction when they were "incorporated" into the United States. But no such incorporating event had occurred. As was true of the "conquest" of the Tee-Hit-Ton, the "incorporation" of the Suquamish took place only in the writing of the opinion. This performance of incorporation denies the possibility for performing a translation in which Native America and America form a new, third reality.

The Court continues to strip tribes of their sovereignty. Its 2000–01 term was one of the most devastating in decades.[91] It does not replace savagery with law; it destroys Native American law with American law.[92]

Neither Americanization nor Native-Americanization

Notwithstanding the deployment of law as an instrument of Americanization, tribes resort to law and even continue to appeal to the Supreme Court. These appeals to the Court and other appeals to the American people can be read as appeals to common good. For the last decade, the Court has decided against tribes in some 80 percent of the cases. The tribes know in advance that they will likely lose. Of course, they are often dragged into court against their will, but sometimes they initiate suits notwithstanding sound legal predictions of loss. They do win

---

87. *Tee-Hit-Ton Indians v. United States*, 348 U.S. 272 (1955).

88. *Oliphant v. Suquamish Indian Tribe*, 435 U.S. 191 (1978).

89. Nell Jessup Newton, "At the Whim of the Sovereign: Aboriginal Title Reconsidered," *Hastings Law Journal* 31 (1980): 1215, 1244.

90. *Brown v. Board of Education*, 347 U.S. 483 (1954).

91. *Nevada v. Hicks*, 69 U.S.L.W. 4528 (2001), is the most astonishing. It held that there is no tribal court jurisdiction over a tribal member's claims that state agents violated his tribal and constitutional rights in his home on reservation land.

92. Robert Cover uses the term "jurispathic" as a description of such action; Robert Cover, "The Supreme Court 1982 Term: Foreword: Nomos and Narrative," *Harvard Law Review* 97, no. 1 (1983): 4–68.

rare, surprising victories, but expectation of winning cases does not always appear to be dispositive of Native Americans' determination to bring them.

There are other explanations of the phenomenon. The determination to litigate is captured in part in the explanation Al Smith offered for his own decision to continue with *Employment Division v. Smith*,[93] the appeal to the Supreme Court in a case arising out of Oregon's penalization of his use of peyote in a ritual of the Native American Church. Smith was put under intense pressure from every side to accept a proposed settlement that offered him almost nothing. After a long, troubled night, he determined that he would not do so.

> "In the wee hours in the morning here, it came to me," he said later. "Your kids are going to grow up and the case is going to come up one of these days and someone will say, 'Your dad is Al Smith? Oh, he's the guy that sold out.' My kids are going to say, 'That's my dad, all right.'
>
> "I'm not going to lay that on my kids. I'm not going to have my kids feel ashamed. Even if we lose the case, they are going to say, 'Yeah, my dad stood up for what he thought was right.' So I got a couple of hours of sleep. I phoned [my attorney] and told him, 'Well, let's go to court.'"[94]

Standing up for what they think is right is one explanation of why tribes go to court notwithstanding the very high probability of loss. Another has to do with exhaustion of judicial remedies as prerequisite to a greater appeal. When the courts finally closed their doors to the long, hard-fought Sioux claim for land (the hollow victory mentioned above), Tim Coulter described the result as a "Pyrrhic loss": "We made a strong record of the tribes' opposition. . . . We are in an unassailable political position. No one can say that the Sioux voluntarily surrendered their legal claims to the land. They did all they could. . . . So we can say: 'Give the land back.'"[95]

This appeal beyond the courts is made not only through litigation but also through employing other forms of law such as treaties. The tribes know the unreliability of treaties with the United States. Congress can always violate or nullify them at will, and it has done so. For example, when Congress flagrantly violated the 1867 treaty of Medicine Lodge—and ostensibly violated the requirements of due process, just compensation, and morality as well—tribes sought judicial relief. The Court said that Congress had plenary authority over the matter and that the congressional exercise of power in the circumstance was not subject to judicial control.[96] Congress could do what it wished.

---

93. *Brown v. Board of Education*, 347 U.S. 483 (1954).

94. Garrett Epps, *To an Unknown God: Religious Freedom on Trial* (New York: St. Martin's, 2001), 204.

95. Milner Ball, *The Word and the Law* (Chicago: University of Chicago Press, 1992), 52.

96. *Lone Wolf v. Hitchcock*, 187 U.S. 553 (1903).

However some treaties do have present validity that the Court will vindicate, and tribes have used them effectively both in litigation and in negotiation.[97] But there seems to be a broader purpose in Native American quotation, citation, and display of treaties and the accompanying wampum belts,[98] especially in the instance of the broken treaties and breaks in the covenant chain represented by the belts. The tribes thereby keep before the people the solemn promises America has made and has often refused to keep. They keep before us the promise of common good.

If the tribes act out of convictions both that their cause is just and that they must make a higher appeal beyond the Supreme Court, they appear also to believe that vindication is not limited to the present or the foreseeable future, and that it may require preparation now for response generations hence. In response to the question of why his Pueblo had gone to court in the face of the overwhelming possibility of loss, an elder said: "The Spanish were here, and it was a long time before they left. You have been here only a couple of centuries. We can wait." They can see common good over the horizon.

What the Indian Nations await and actively pursue is the equivalent of what Black Elk and John Neihardt achieved, translation in the American polity—translation, not unidirectional imposition; common good, not imposed "good." Although the courts of the United States have not done so, the courts of the Navajo Nation have demonstrated that translation is possible and can produce a new reality advantageous to both sides.

Navajo courts employ applicable United States federal law but also their own, consisting of tribal law and customs. They employ Navajo along with American law in an Anglo-based system.[99] They have long engaged in practices that Americans were slow to employ and have now hurried to develop: alternative dispute resolution, fitting victim compensation, ways other than imprisonment for dealing with offenders, and the like. Tom Tso, former Chief Justice of the Navajo Supreme Court has observed that: "Navajos have always understood these concepts. We could have taught the Anglos these things one hundred and fifty years ago."[100]

---

97. See *Minnesota v. Mille Lacs Band of Chippewa Indians*, 119 S. Ct. 1187 (1999) (hunting, fishing, and gathering rights); *County of Oneida v. Oneida Indian Nation*, 470 U.S. 226 (1985) (title to land).

98. See, e.g., G. Peter Jemison and Anna Schein, eds., *Treaty of Canandaigua* (Santa Fe: Clear Light Publishers, 2000).

99. See, e.g., *Means v. District Court, Chinle Judicial District*, 26 Ind. L. Rep. 6083 (Navajo, 1999); *In Re Certified Question II: Navajo Nation v. MacDonald*, 16 Ind. L. Rep. 6086 (Navajo, 1989). See also Robert Yazzie, "Hozho Nahasdlii—We Are Now in Good Relations: Navajo Restorative Justice," *St. Thomas Law Review* 9 (1996): 117.

100. Tom Tso, "The Process of Decision Making in Tribal Courts," *Arizona Law Review* 31 (1989): 225.

American Religious Politics

The United States' colonizing aim was stated as "Americanizing" the tribes, but that was only half of the statement. The express policy in the nineteenth century was said to be "Americanizing and *Christianizing*" the tribes.[101] In fact, the alliance of political with religious aggression had begun much earlier.

Already in the 1630s, before the Fundamental Orders of Thomas Hooker's Connecticut could be adopted, the settlers believed it necessary first to dispatch the Pequot tribe.[102] In the decisive event, instead of attacking the Pequots' fortified main village, they mounted a surprise attack on Mystic, a Pequot town occupied by women, children, and old men. They did so with troubled consciences, apparently relieved in advance by consultation with their chaplain. They surrounded the village, set it ablaze, and slaughtered all who fled. A modern account proposes: "The virtual annihilation of the Pequot tribe by the Connecticut Congregationalists in this brief war proved the superiority of the Puritan over the heathen."[103] The way was cleared for the Fundamental Orders, which begins: "Forasmuch as it hath pleased the Almighty God by the wise disposition of his divine providence so to Order and dispose of things . . . ."[104]

The later policy of Americanizing and Christianizing was implemented through less violent means: governmental cooperation with Christian missions, support of sectarian schools, and apportionment of federal Indian agencies among Christian church groups.[105] Churches took on specific governmental, Americanizing functions.[106]

But even good intentions and less violent means sometimes resulted in destruction rather than colonization. Propagation of Christendom among Native Americans led to a perceived need to eradicate their religion.[107] In 1883 the Courts of Indian Offenses were established for the specific purpose of suppressing religious practices such as the sun dance.[108] Putting down the Ghost Dance was one of the causes of the 1890 massacre at Wounded Knee.[109] The General

---

101. See Prucha, *Great Father*, 29–31, 141–47, 289–92 .

102. For the account on which I rely, see Francis Jennings, *The Invasion of America* (Chapel Hill: University of North Carolina Press, 1975), 189–220. See also Cavanaugh's discussion of state-making and war in his essay in this volume.

103. Mary Jeanne Anderson Jones, *Congregational Commonwealth, Connecticut, 1636–1662* (Middletown, CT: Wesleyan University Press, 1968), 67–68.

104. Mary Jeanne Anderson Jones, ed., *The Fundamental Orders of Connecticut* ([Hartford:] U.S. Constitution Bicentennial Commission of Connecticut, 1988), 55.

105. Prucha, *Great Father*, 141–42, 147, 286, 289–92, 398, 488–519.

106. Ibid., 482.

107. Baptisms, Paul Lehmann remarked, took on the character of a Christian equivalent to collecting scalps; Paul Lehmann, "The Indian Situation," 58.

108. See Secretary of the Interior, *Regulations of the Indian Office* (Washington, DC: Government Printing Office, 1904), 102–3 (banning the sun dance, "all other similar dances and so-called religious ceremonies, and practices of medicine men"). See also Prucha, *Great Father*, 646–49.

109. See Black Elk and Neihardt, *Black Elk Speaks*, 248–55.

Allotment Act of 1887—by which the tribes lost 138 million acres, two-thirds of their then remaining lands—was inspired by the Americanizing-Christianizing project. The act was intended to end tribal culture, including tribal religion. It had no legitimating basis in the Constitution but did enjoy the enthusiastic support of Christian groups.[110]

The United States' formal attempt to Americanize and Christianize Indian Nations did not end until 1934.[111] Nonetheless, effects of the prior policy continued. Federal and state laws still hindered the free exercise of Native Americans' religion by, for example, denying access to or disturbing sacred sites, restricting use of ritual substances, and interfering with ceremonies.[112]

The Supreme Court carries forward the underlying mission of Christianizing the tribes as well as Americanizing them. In the 1988 case of *Lyng v. Northwest Indian Cemetery Protective Association*,[113] the Court held that a road could be built through National Forest lands that tribes regarded as the center of their world. The Court knew that construction would devastate belief systems and religious practices essential to the tribes' life. In 1990, *Employment Division v. Smith*[114] approved Oregon's penalization of the religious use of peyote in the Native American Church.

Justice Antonin Scalia's fortunes indicate that the modern, judicial version of Christianizing the tribes will continue into the foreseeable future. Justice Scalia authored the *Smith* opinion. On that occasion he had the support of the majority of the Court, but in subsequent cases his colleagues began to turn away from him. Garret Epps notes that Scalia came to portray himself as a lonely religious dissenter: "'We are fools for Christ's sake,' he said in a 1996 speech. 'We must pray for the courage to endure the scorn of the sophisticated world.'"[115] With the election of George W. Bush as president, his prayers were rewarded. Scalia is no longer scorned and need no longer play the alienated dissenter. "For Bush and the GOP," Epps says, "Scalia and his four conservative colleagues [are] now the cavalry."[116]

The tribes have developed effective modern defenses that can sometimes neutralize the impact of losses the Court inflicts on their religion. The Court in *Lyng* refused to stop construction of the devastating National Forest road. In response, tribes mounted a campaign, generated favorable public attention, directed it effectively at the White House, and won President Clinton's signature on an executive

---

110. See Prucha, *Great Father*, 617–65, 670–71.

111. The Indian Reorganization Act was passed in 1934, and in that year John Collier, the Commissioner of Indian Affairs, issued a circular, "Indian Religious Freedom and Indian Culture,"calling for "the fullest constitutional liberty [for Indians], in all matters affecting religion, conscience, and culture" (ibid., 951–54).

112. See Senate Report no. 95-709, 95-2, serial 13197-1, pp. 3–4.

113. *Lyng v. Northwest Indian Cemetery Protective Association*, 485 U.S. 439 (1988).

114. *Employment Division v. Smith*, 494 U.S. 872 (1990).

115. Epps, *To an Unknown God*, 241.

116. Ibid.

order directing federal agencies to protect Native American sacred sites.[117] So far, the road has not been built through the area in dispute. Not yet.

A second success followed the *Employment Division v. Smith* approval of penalizing sacramental peyote use. Native American Church leader Reuben Snake undertook a successful lobbying action aimed at Congress and achieved by statute the protection that the Court refused to grant.[118] Now states must respect participation in Native American religious rituals.

Conclusion

Assaults on Native America and its culture run counter to the exceptional examples of missionaries like Samuel Worcester (of *Worcester v. Georgia*) and his colleague Elizur Butler who carried the gospel to the Cherokees and who became critical to defending their culture, and like Jeremiah Evarts who was secretary of the missionary board with whom Worcester and Butler were affiliated and who led the national campaign of conscience against removal of the Cherokee[119]; and like the Jesuits who were missionaries to the Lakota in the late nineteenth and early twentieth centuries and who helped to preserve and nourish Lakota ways[120]; and like the Presbyterians whom Cecil Corbett, the distinguished Nez Perce/Choctaw clergyman from the Nez Perce Reservation in Idaho, credits for helping supply tribes with the means to read and write in their own languages.[121]

These were exemplary of Christian service in the biblical tradition. Even so, missionary traffic between America and Native America like politics and the translation of texts has been largely unidirectional, from the former to the latter. And often with this traffic have gone Western cultural accretions that the bearers of the gospel thought were necessary accompaniments of their message requiring that those to whom they preached abandon cultural practices and beliefs the bearers judged incompatible with their own.

The movement has been one-way because non-Indians have generally not gone into Indian country in expectation that tribes have significant theological or political contributions to make to an American common good—no listening for the word of God as that word may be parabolically borne by tribal life, no attempting to discern the promising strength of tribal forms of politics that took root here long before the coming of Europeans and that, in the meantime, have remarkably adapted, survived, grown, and been renewed. Tribalism has been viewed as a lower form of Western society that must be cured (Americanized and Christianized) before it can contribute to politics or theology.

---

117. Indian Sacred Sites, 61 FR 26, 771 (May 24, 1996).

118. The American Indian Religious Freedom Act Amendments of 1994. 42 U.S.C. 1996 amended, adding new sec. 3.

119. Prucha, *Great Father*, 200–13.

120. See Ross Enochs, *The Jesuit Mission to the Lakota Sioux: Pastoral Theology and Ministry*, 1886–1945 (Kansas City, MO: Sheed & Ward, 1996).

121. Cecil Corbett, "Theology, Law, and American Indians," *Church and Society* 75 (January–February 1985): 7.

Black Elk and *Black Elk Speaks* transform the movement from unilateral export of goods to the expansive circulation of gifts. When Black Elk spoke the vision, he addressed his own people, affirming for them something of the value and beauty of their identity. His story has been received in Indian Country as a defining theological statement, "a North American bible of all tribes" (Vine Deloria).[122] But Black Elk also spoke to the former enemy, reaching out across forty years and the terror of Wounded Knee. And John Neihardt—together with the others who participated in the labor—received the gift and gave it the new reality of a Native American-to-American translation, with the added value of wider circulation among Americans as well as Native Americans.

Their performance offers promise and instructive direction to us.

The Good of Not Doing Good

Black Elk and the risks he took are central here, but John Neihardt and the example he set also deserve attention. Notably, Neihardt did not enter Indian country to help Black Elk. Non-Indians have often gone to tribes stirred more by feelings of benevolence toward Indians than by hate, fear, or greed. But, as William Stringfellow warned, the desire to help another runs the "peril of tyrannizing the one of whom it is said he is being helped," because the reason for doing good to the other is the justification of the doer, and the measure of success is "how far the one who is being helped becomes like the one who is helping him."[123] American Christians' self-sacrificial determination to expand into Indian country the reach of a good they regarded as common has repeatedly turned out badly for the tribes, sometimes catastrophically so. One surge of Western benevolent paternalism became "an ethnocentrism of frightening intensity."[124] It is costly to Native Americans to be made objects of Americans' earnest desire to satisfy their own needs.

A Justly Joint Enterprise

If Neihardt did not go intending to do good, neither did he go with a discernible intention to exploit. He did not mine Indian memory for monetary or personal gain, and none followed. One reads in his work a regard for the value of tribal culture that is free of impulses to ingratiate, alienate, or romanticize. With reciprocating dignity, Neihardt received Black Elk's gift for what it was and on the terms, at the time, and in the manner chosen by the giver. The work of giving, accepting, and translating was of necessity a mutually respectful enterprise, a joint rather than an imperial venture.

---

122. Vine Deloria, "Introduction," in Black Elk and Neihardt, *Black Elk Speaks*, xiii.

123. William Stringfellow, *A Private and Public Faith* (Grand Rapids: Eerdmans, 1962), 69.

124. Prucha, *Great Father*, 610.

Acceptance

The history of the majority's relation to tribes is replete with images of American impotence: It is said that the triumph of Western civilization over tribal ways of life was inevitable; that manifest destiny could not be resisted; that the westward move of non-Indian population was an overpowering flood. These are assertions that events, systems, and institutions were beyond our control. They are a device for avoiding responsibility as though we were powerless to do otherwise. American aggression against tribal sovereignty continues, more subtly to be sure, but still destructively. This is our American doing—now, in the present—and we are responsible for it. Tribes suffer, but so does the United States. It suffers the burdening need to continue refighting the Indian Wars.

From the practice of repentance the church has long known that the acceptance of responsibility is a liberating start toward empowerment. Repentance is or requires an unsettling of the person, of the routine, of received attitudes. As W. H. Auden says about all progress, it "depends upon the experience in which life and one's nature are called into question."[125]

Following James Boyd White, I have suggested that translation provides this kind of questioning of our sense of ourselves, of our languages, and of others. It thus releases us from imprisonment in our own modes of thinking and being. *Black Elk Speaks* is exemplary of this art and promise of translation. And it offers, too, an invitation for others to join in the work. An obituary for federal Judge Frank Johnson of Alabama celebrated the decisions he made during the civil rights movement and described him as one of the "courageous men and women asking Americans to decide what kind of people they wanted to be."[126] *Black Elk Speaks* concentrates this question as the tribes have been asking it all along, from the beginning and about the beginning, in the present and about the present. This is not a forlorn attempt to relive the past. It is to offer a present, freeing gift. It is to press the question of our common good: What kind of people America is today and hopes to be tomorrow.

By questioning the foundations and what has been settled for in the meantime as common and good, Native Americans invite Americans to join with them in the work of a new political translation that offers progress toward "liberation for reconciliation" (Lehmann).[127] John Neihardt began, as he had to, by listening. Tribes speak today with many, diverse, and sometimes conflicting voices that make understanding difficult. Neihardt's example becomes all the more instructive. Lacking command of the Lakota language, he listened carefully and attentively before he could understand.

---

125. W. H. Auden, *Lectures on Shakespeare* (ed. Arthur Kirsch; Princeton: Princeton University Press, 2000), 179.

126. Robert McFadden, "Frank M. Johnson Jr., Whose Rulings Helped Desegregate the South, Dies at 80," *New York Times*, Obituaries, July 24, 1999, A15, col. 1. On the need for strong public authority and for a fresh look at its grounding, see Jean Porter's essay on Thomas Aquinas, in this volume.

127. Paul Lehmann, "The Indian Situation," 63.

Community, Society, and Politics

Introduction:
Community, Society, and Politics

James W. Skillen

The phrase "common good" covers a multitude of sins as well as a host of constructive and even redemptive ambitions, admonitions, and anticipations. The concerns of the next four essays have to do chiefly with the relation of social diversity to a highest, or broadest, or ultimate community that can be considered truly common and capable of representing or realizing the common good.

James Skillen contends that when the words "common good" are used as a standard or norm for human action, they serve preeminently as the standard for a just political community. In this regard, humans are hearing God's call to do justice to all, a call that simultaneously militates against any tendency toward political totalitarianism. A just political community, by its very constitution, must protect the many nongovernmental responsibilities people have. For artists to be free to pursue art, for engineers to do their engineering, for scholars to carry out their scholarship, for businesses to produce goods and services, and for families to enjoy domestic tranquillity—for all this to happen, there must be a public-legal order that assures equal protection and treatment for citizens who all share in the public commons.

Consequently, careful attention to the building of just states and just international organizations for the common good should draw together people of diverse faiths, vocations, and cultures in a common task, precisely in order to make public room for everyone to contend peacefully with one another over their different views of what constitutes a healthy "commons." Skillen grounds his argument for the *political* common good of highly differentiated societies in the biblical illumination of human historical development in God's creation—the common context for all of humanity.

Max Stackhouse takes the quest for clarity about the common good to the global level. Globalization is now a fact of life as well as a normative challenge to peoples in every corner of the world. Yet globalization is not a one-dimensional, reductionistic process. It is a process that develops through the continued differentiation and integration of multiple spheres of human responsibility. No single institution in one sphere of life, says Stackhouse, "is capable of manifesting the common good unless it is formed into a community of commitment that seeks not only its own good but federates with other institutional spheres to form a network of communities committed to a wider justice." Religion lies at the root of life in all of its complexity and certainly is at the root of the differences and agreements among the peoples who are shaping the interdependent societies of our day. A Christian contribution to the healthy shaping of the global commons begins with the recognition of the messianic claims of Jesus Christ in inaugurating the kingdom of God—a kingdom that is both at hand and still anticipated in its eschatological fulfillment of God's creation. This eschatological definition of redemption, says Stackhouse, "trumps and transforms every naturalist teleology or humanist contract or every hostile critique of culture, and thus reorders the decisive concept of what is common and what is good." This is the vision that can guide us to respect and nurture the legitimate diversity of life—especially human social life—in this world while also capturing it in its true unity as God's creation.

William Cavanaugh challenges the idea that the modern state is a contributor to the realization of the common good. Common-good language arose before the formation of the modern nation-state, Cavanaugh explains, and the latter represents a territorial centralization of the use of force that inevitably serves the interests of a government or state, not the common good. The state came into existence to allow princes to wage war; thus, it is not a product of society, but rather the creator of a new kind of society that tries to absorb society into itself. In its liberal version, the modern nation-state pits sovereign individuals against one another and then claims sole authority to protect them from one another. The nation-state has thus positioned itself "as the sole source of law, . . . as the guarantor of property and inheritance rights," and much, much more, says Cavanaugh. Consequently, the common good will not be achieved through the nation-state.

To properly identify and realize the common good in our shrinking world, Cavanaugh argues, the church must come into its own as *ekklesia*—the full public community it claims to be. In the process, the church needs to "demystify the nation-state and treat it like the telephone company"—a provider of goods and services, but not an institution to be trusted with the responsibility to define or maintain the common good. The church is not just one association among many in a liberal society, "but participates in the life of the triune God, who is the only good that can be common to all." The church therefore "needs to take seriously its task of promoting spaces where participation in the common good of God's life can flourish."

Robert Jenson agrees with Cavanaugh that "only the triune God perfectly satisfies the notions of polity and of a polity's common good." The modern state or even an international society cannot represent that ultimate common good but can only, at best, be an analogy of God in his triunity. Too often a state's claim to represent the common good amounts only to the representation of a "common interest" that brings people together. There may be many such communities of interest, and not all are without moral claims upon us, says Jenson. Yet any earthly polity that analogically points to the common good of the divine polity must always be recognized as less than ultimate. This judgment arises from a Christian view of history: God's creation is a history on its way toward the climax of the story God is telling (creating). What is crucial for Jenson, then, is the eschatological kingdom of God, to which the other authors also point. Yet, as Jenson puts it, the kingdom is the polity of the triune life of God, and "entry into the Kingdom of God must somehow be entry into a polity that God himself is in himself." The only nonanalogical common good, therefore, is the triune God. Jenson concludes, "This God is the final if usually unacknowledged object of the love that unites all other polities: the one tag of Augustine that everyone knows, that our hearts are made for God and find rest only in him, applies not only to persons but also to communities."

The Common Good
as Political Norm

James W. Skillen

Introduction

The thesis of this essay is that the phrase "the common good," when used as an ethical call to action or standard for human responsibility, is preeminently a call or standard for the exercise of political responsibility. The phrase is sometimes used by family members, university administrators, labor union leaders, or any number of others who bear responsibility for a particular community or organization. In these instances, however, "the common good" means something quite different for the university than it does for the family or the labor union because it will be qualified differently by the educational, familial, or laboring purpose of that entity. Furthermore, it is apparent that the common good of any one of these institutions or associations does not constitute the common good of all of them together or of everyone in society or the world. In today's highly differentiated societies, the all-inclusive, common institutions are the political-legal ones.

To say that the phrase "the common good" should be used specifically as normative political speech, however, raises important questions. What do we mean by the political? If the common good is the standard for a universal good or for the most extensive and inclusive good, does that mean the political community should subsume, subordinate, or dissolve all other goods in itself? An affirmative response to this question sounds totalitarian and thus quite negative—an affirmation of injustice. To reject political totalitarianism, however, is to raise the question of whether there can be a truly *common* good that is, at the same time, restricted in some way. That, in fact, is exactly what I want to argue: The political common good as standard or norm is the opposite of an all-dissolving, omnicompetent, totalitarian norm. This is true because a political order whose government acts (or tries to act) with omnicompetent authority undermines the very possibility of realizing the common good. The reason is that the normative question about the common good arises only because there are many things about human life in society that are uncommon, or not held in common, or for which everyone does not bear common responsibility. Not everyone belongs to a university; no family embraces everyone; only a relatively few workers belong to labor unions. The common good, then, refers to some kind of normative universality that can be realized only through the simultaneous recognition and affirmation of a diversity of nonpolitical responsibilities in a differentiated society. That is why "affairs of the commonwealth," as John Courtney Murray argues (see Robin Lovin's essay in this volume), will always include concerns that fall "beyond the limited scope of government." Nevertheless, the very question of what falls outside the limited scope of government necessarily involves the question of how public law and authority should recognize and deal with that which is nongovernmental. Jean Porter claims that Thomas Aquinas "is the first scholastic to link legislative authority explicitly to the common good," and that in Aquinas's writings "the idea of the common good is always linked to public authority in some way." If she is correct, then the argument of this essay may be seen as a continuation of her argument.[1]

Historically speaking, the challenge of, and often the fight for, achieving the common good arises as a struggle over how to govern diversified and differentiating societies, or societies that are in conflict with one another. That struggle over how to govern everyone, or how to make peace between two governments that govern the commons of two different territories, is precisely a political-legal struggle. Typically, all such governing efforts have been sufficiently unjust toward one or more groups, classes, races, nations, or religions that the struggle never ends. The struggle often becomes warfare (as William Cavanaugh emphasizes in his essay in this volume) because authority to govern the commons depends on the ability to enforce laws that hold for everyone within the same territory—the commons for which the common good should be sought. The purpose of the fight may be to liberate one group from another's oppressive rule, or to overthrow a government, redefine it, or limit it in some way. The struggle may be over the method of changing governments, or about gaining popular representation, or about establishing a formal judicial system. But by its very nature, the administration and control of the territorial commons is political in nature. Any talk of the common good, therefore, must deal with the character and purpose of political order.

The struggle to advance or protect the common good shows that what is at stake is the relation of the political to what is not political. Securing the commons for the good of all does not dissolve everything that is uncommon among people but instead draws people together in a common purpose that will uphold them in their full and diversified humanity, which includes many uncommon responsibilities. The quest for a delimited, or nontotalitarian, common good, consequently,

---

1. See Jean Porter's contributions to this volume, the introduction to "Classical Voices," and "The Common Good in Thomas Aquinas."

will demonstrate its normative success by constituting (and typically constitution-alizing) a governed political community. This community will be oriented (by "constitutional consensus," as Murray would say)[2] toward the establishment of justice for everyone in the territory, including protection of all the responsibilities that do not inhere in the internal jurisdiction of the state. Central to the realization of the common good, in other words, is the doing of justice—public justice. Giving to each its due—or doing right by each person, responsibility, institution, nonhu-man creature, and the environment—is thus constitutive of the common good.

If, in the course of history, a political community does not increasingly become defined or delimited in its own identity as a community of public justice—a *commons* in which the same standards of justice hold for everyone in the territory—then it cannot realize or represent the common good. In differentiated societies in our highly complex world, there is no way to do justice to all people and institu-tions in a common territory without delimiting (constitutionalizing) the respon-sibility that government has for the public-legal commons. This delimiting is in contrast to the wider range of responsibilities that people bear in all other kinds of relationships and institutions. Apart from clarifying the peculiar terms on which government in the political community has universal (but not omnicom-petent) authority to enforce justice for all, governance of the commons will move toward either anarchy or totalitarianism.

Now, it is certainly possible not to speak of "the common good" as a norm for human action but rather as a statement of fact or ideal: "The common good will be achieved when everyone has enough to eat and all can develop their talents." "The common good is constituted ultimately by God's governance and love of the whole creation." "The common good will be realized when the proletarian revo-lution has succeeded." "The common good is most fully realized when a genuine philosopher king rules a well-ordered polis." "The common good is evident when all peoples recognize and kowtow to the Son of Heaven in the Middle Kingdom." These statements may be truths (or errors) of faith. They may represent trust-worthy or untrustworthy theology, ideology, or metaphysics. Yet by themselves they do not clarify or stipulate the direction and dimensions of human responsi-bility. What should Socrates or Plato do if Athens is not properly governed? Does Marx's vision simply state the inevitable fate of history, or does it entail the call for a vanguard of the proletariat to try to speed up history by forcing the revolution? How should all people in the world get enough to eat? If God gov-erns and loves the whole world, how does that implicate and specify a range of human responsibilities?

The deepest convictions and beliefs people have about the meaning of life cer-tainly guide and shape their understanding of their responsibility. In this regard, it makes quite a difference whether people believe that China is the Middle Kingdom; or that Muḥammad is the final prophet; or that the proletarian revolu-tion will usher in the "new man" in a communist society; or that, with liberal democracy, humans have reached the end of history. And if the deepest convictions

---

2. See Lovin's essay in this volume.

by which people live represent radically different ideas of what constitutes the *common* good, then we should not be surprised to find that different ideas of the common good may have little in common and may drive people into conflict with one another (see the essays in this volume by Milner Ball, Cheryl Kirk-Duggan, Josiah Young, and William Cavanaugh). But the question is whether the normative demands of justice for a political commons arise only from subjective experience and construction or, instead, hold an obligation for humans regardless of their positive or negative responses to those demands.

In his book on the topic, David Hollenbach works with at least three different meanings of the common good.[3] In the first instance, he means a factual condition or experience, as when he refers to Ignatius Loyola's conviction that the common good is the good of the whole of humanity,[4] or when he refers to "the minimal level of solidarity required to enable all of society's members to live with basic dignity."[5] In the second place he speaks of a "shared vision" or *idea* of the common good—something that he thinks may now be "eclipsed" by "the reality of pluralism" in the modern West.[6] And third, Hollenbach speaks of the "common good" as a normative truth—"a truth about the human good that must be pursued and that makes a claim on the minds and hearts of all persons."[7] All three of these meanings seem to be held in equivocal tension in the following sentences. The interaction of faith and reason, says Hollenbach, "calls Christians both to remain faithful to the distinctiveness of the gospel and simultaneously to recognize that their faith in God calls for the use of human intelligence to discover the common bonds that make an inclusive human community possible. To declare that such intellectual solidarity is unattainable would be to maintain that the idea of the common good is a utopian fantasy as well."[8] The "distinctiveness of the gospel" is the normative truth that lays claim to minds and hearts. "Common bonds" make possible an experience of the common good. And "intellectual solidarity" is the source of a shared idea or vision of the common good.

The argument of this paper is that the common good is a trans-subjective *norm* for political responsibility rather than, first of all, a common experience or a shared idea. Historically speaking, human experience of a genuine common good has been rare indeed. Moreover, there is little evidence of sufficient intellectual solidarity among all people to generate a shared idea of the common good. Consequently, if actual experience or intellectual solidarity is taken to be the ground of the norm "common good" or "public justice," then the call to realize it will never be generated, never heard, and never adequate to expose our injustices and refusals to obey its demands. My argument is that the very possibility of contention over the common good arises from the inescapable norm-responsive

3. David Hollenbach, SJ, *The Common Good and Christian Ethics* (Cambridge: Cambridge University Press, 2002).
4. Ibid., 5–6.
5. Ibid., 192.
6. Ibid., 9, 13.
7. Ibid., 157.
8. Ibid., 158.

character of human existence. That is why even when humans do not agree universally on the idea of the common good and do not experience truly universal common bonds, we still cannot escape the demands of justice that call us to account—that call us to keep on trying to realize the common good.

None of us, then, is free to assess, from a position of neutrality, the vast array of experiences and ideas about the meaning of life before we enter the world we might prefer. There is, and forever will be, no neutral terrain on which to stand to negotiate agreement on an idea of "the common good" or to create the "common bonds that make an inclusive human community possible" *before* we assume responsibility for thinking about and shaping society.[9] It may be easy enough to state the obvious truth that everyone on earth shares the same atmosphere, or that a nuclear war could endanger us all, or that the world's peoples are becoming increasingly interdependent. All of this may press upon us and feed a sense of urgency to act in order to try to preserve what we all share in common, but it does not specify who or which institution is responsible to act in accord with this or that standard. This is the context in which we take up the task of trying to clarify the meaning of the common good as political norm. Before we start, we already know that our best and most convincing contribution may not lead to a consensus, much less to an actual advancement of the common good.

Views of the Commons and of the Common Good

The Biblical Heritage

From a biblical point of view, "the commons" is surely God's entire creation, the good of which only God can oversee and assure. That is why the Bible's portrayal of human responsibility is set in the grand covenantal context of creation (Gen 1–2; Ps 8; Acts 17:24-31). It is also why no one other than the Creator God may be acknowledged as the ultimate reference point of human authority and responsibility (Exod 20:1-11; Deut 5:1-15; 1 Cor 15:20-28). This is what God taught Israel in releasing them from Egyptian bondage and giving them the commandments, as Patrick Miller details in his essay.[10] This is why Israel was to have no

---

9. In my estimation, this is the approach John Rawls takes, but of course, he cannot achieve his aim without assuming—quite nonneutrally—the legitimacy of a great deal of Kant's moral philosophy.

10. Miller puts emphasis on the Decalogue as the clarifier and stipulator of the way humans should fulfill their diverse responsibilities to God and neighbor. I would place greater emphasis than he does on the creational origin and foundation of these responsibilities and the fact that marriage and other human relationships are *presupposed* in the giving of the Decalogue. Emphasizing creation-order normativity from the start opens the way to a more definite comparison of the Decalogue and the "natural law" because God's norms hold for everyone created in the image of God. The Decalogue (and also Israel as God's specially covenanted community) can then be seen as representing a creation-order rearticulation, recall, and saving recovery. In this regard, see the end of Miller's essay as well as Jean Porter's essay, both in this volume.

other gods and why the early Christians refused to acknowledge the Roman emperor as the divine-human concentration point of all authority on earth.

Yet, if the commons is God's single creation, under God's governance, what normative guidance does that offer humans with regard to their responsibility for the common good? On biblical terms, it seems to me, the broadest statement we can make in response to this question is that humans—throughout all their generations, with all the gifts and responsibilities God has given them—share *in common* the responsibility to steward one another and the entire creation to the glory of God. At the moment we say this, however, we must, on biblical terms, immediately begin to differentiate the variety of God-given responsibilities that humans hold across generations and within any current generation. Parents are called to care for children and the good of their families; farmers and shepherds to steward land, plants, and animals; elders in the gate to settle disputes and make judgments for the good of the whole city; boards of trustees to uphold the good of their diverse institutions; and priests, pastors, elders, deacons, and bishops to nurture the faithful for the good of the entire people of God and their service to one another and to the world.

Governing authorities in Israel were never commissioned with total sovereignty but only with authority to administer justice for the nation in accord with the covenant. God was Israel's only *total* Lord and King. In this regard, Jeremiah presents a stark contrast between God's approval of Judah's King Josiah, "who did what was right and just . . . [and] defended the cause of the poor and needy," and God's rejection of Josiah's son, King Shallum, "who builds his palace by unrighteousness, his upper rooms by injustice" (Jer 22:11-17).[11] And how is the degeneracy of Israel's kings and other authorities to be explained? Why is it, according to Jeremiah, that God is bringing judgment down on Israel? "Because they have forsaken the covenant of the LORD their God and have worshiped and served other gods" (22:9). The context of any and all human authority and responsibility on earth, in other words, is God's covenant, whether with Israel or with all nations. Biblically speaking, Israel is not the only nation "under God." The sovereign God above all nations puts Egypt's pharaoh in his place and tells the kings of Tyre and Sidon when their time is up. Daniel reports the consequences of Nebuchadnezzar's descent into insanity and subsequent recovery to the point where he could acknowledge and praise the God who transcends even the vast Babylonian Empire. The dominion of the Most High, confesses Nebuchadnezzar, "is an eternal dominion; his kingdom endures from generation to generation" (Dan 4:34). Whether the earth's rulers recognize it or not, they govern on God's covenantal conditions: the Most High "does as he pleases with the powers of heaven and the peoples of the earth" (4:35).

The biblical, covenantal framework is, according to Daniel Elazar, the real root of all constitutional specification of Western polities, which emerged gradually from medieval political and legal developments. Today, most Americans may think of the United States Constitution simply as that which sets limits to government

---

11. All Scripture is quoted from the NIV: New International Version.

over against the freedom of the people, who remain the republic's true sovereigns. Others may emphasize constitutional limits in relation to each person's freedom to associate in families and churches and other organizations. But the idea of constituted or chartered limits to government—the idea of a specified (not total) grant of political authority—goes back to covenantal foundations defined by God's ultimate sovereignty. "There is no 'state' in the Jewish political tradition," says Elazar.

> The contemporary Hebrew term for state, *medināh*, refers to a political unit with its own jurisdiction (*din*) within a larger entity, or a province. . . . In fact, the Jewish political tradition does not recognize state sovereignty in the modern sense of absolute independence. No state—a human institution—can be sovereign. Classically, only God is sovereign and He entrusts the exercise of His sovereign powers to the people as a whole, mediated through His Torah-as-constitution as provided through His covenant with Israel.[12]

The fulfillment of all earthly covenants in Jesus Christ, as the New Testament conveys this, does not challenge this basic orientation of the earlier Scriptures. At the foundation of the church is Christ's postresurrection announcement that "all authority in heaven and on earth has been given to me" (Matt 28:18). Christ is not only Lord of the church but also King above all kings. As the song at the beginning of the letter to the Colossians puts it, the one who is "head of the body, the church," is also the one by whom "all things were created" and in whom "all things hold together," including thrones and powers, rulers and authorities (Col 1:15-20).

From the New Testament's perspective, it is also apparent that human responsibilities under God are multiple, with no institutional concentration point on earth: Spouses are responsible to one another in love. Parents are responsible for their children. Employers are obligated to those who work for them. Pastors, prophets, elders, bishops, deacons, and others have been called to care for the church. And governing authorities, who do not bear the sword in vain, are responsible both to God and to those who are subject to them for common justice. As Victor Paul Furnish shows from Paul's letters, the responsibilities of citizenship and public office in this age are not off-base to Christians even if their approach should be one of "critical engagement."[13] Precisely because of God's uncommon love revealed in Christ, Furnish says, the believing community is not only allowed but mandated to work for the common good through political means. In all arenas of human life Christians may and should bear responsibility, recognizing as Israel did that no human office or position of authority is ultimately sovereign.

---

12. Daniel J. Elazar, *Covenant and Polity in Biblical Israel* (vol. 1 of *The Covenant Tradition in Politics*; New Brunswick: Transaction, 1995), 442–43. See Miller's comments on this topic.

13. See Furnish's essay in this volume.

Clearly this view of life meant that Christians would have to adopt a stance of critical engagement with respect to the Roman imperium, which claimed an authority that Christians believed was held only by Christ, the mediator of all divine authority to earth.[14] With hindsight, therefore, we cannot be surprised by the long Western struggle between ecclesiastical and imperial authority and the gradual differentiation of many other human responsibilities from the jurisdiction of these two.

The preliminary conclusion we can draw from this impressionistic sketch is that long before the kind of societal differentiation we experience today, the biblical, covenantal tradition laid a foundation for the *differentiated* specification of "political" or public-legal governing authority under God alongside many other kinds of responsibility. The unity of the entire human commons is found in its dependence on the Creator God, a commons that only God can govern. Within the realm of human responsibility, governance for the sake of the common good must be conducted as a delimited public-legal responsibility that recognizes and upholds other kinds of human responsibility. Because of the huge influence of the Christian tradition in the West, we should not be surprised by the extent of the influence of the covenant idea in shaping modern constitutionalism, public legal systems, international covenants, civil society, and other features of open, pluralistic societies.[15]

There have been many critics, including Machiavelli, Nietzsche, and most recently Robert Kaplan, who have argued that Christianity provides no foundation for political virtue. They claim that this is so because it celebrates the meek and aims only for the "moral conquest of the world"[16] rather than for the enforcement of law against crime and aggression in order to protect the innocent. This, I would contend, represents a fundamental misconception of Christianity.

Platonic and Aristotelian Conceptions

Of course, Israel and the Christian tradition have not alone shaped our ideas of, and struggles over, the commons and the common good in the West and throughout

---

14. See N. T. Wright, "Paul and Caesar: A New Reading of Romans," in *A Royal Priesthood: The Use of the Bible Ethically and Politically* (ed. Craig Bartholomew et al.; Grand Rapids: Zondervan, 2002), 173–93.

15. In addition to Elazar's four volumes on the covenant tradition in politics, there are source materials and additional historical insights on the impact of covenantal thinking on politics in Oliver O'Donovan and Joan Lockwood O'Donovan, eds., *From Irenaeus to Grotius: A Sourcebook in Christian Political Thought, 100–1625* (Grand Rapids: Eerdmans, 1999), esp. part 5; David Novak, *Natural Law in Judaism* (Cambridge: Cambridge University Press, 1998); William R. Everdell, *The End of Kings: A History of Republics and Republicans* (2d ed.; Chicago: University of Chicago Press, 2000); Daniel J. Elazar and John Kincaid, eds., *The Covenant Connection: From Federal Theology to Modern Federalism* (Lanham, MD: Lexington Books, 2000); and Eric Voegelin, *Israel and Revelation* (vol. 1 of *Order and History*; Baton Rouge: Louisiana State University Press, 1956).

16. Robert D. Kaplan, *Warrior Politics: Why Leadership Demands a Pagan Ethos* (New York: Random House, 2002), 77.

the world today. Surely the impact of Greek philosophy has been huge. The very language of "politics" and "polities" derives from the Greek (and now English) word *polis*. For Plato and Aristotle, the polis represented the fullest, most complete realization or maturation of human nature, of human potential. The polis— the political community—is the rational moral whole of which all other human associations and functions are parts. In fact, the polis is "man writ large"—reason governing the will that controls the passions, parallel to philosophers governing the military and administration, which control slaves and other laborers. We cannot yet speak here of a fully *differentiated* political "common good," because everything comes to fruition in the polis as parts of one whole. The polis is an educational, military, economic, and religious totality in which friendship, family, law, rationality, and communal self-sufficiency all find their fulfillment in accord with an ultimate political norm. This is one of the reasons why any talk today about the common good as a norm for *political* responsibility can be dangerous; in origin the polis represented an all-encompassing social whole, not a differentiated community of public law and governance.[17]

Both Plato and Aristotle struggled with the seemingly irrational rise and fall of regimes and polities, and with how a wise man ought to grasp philosophically what a good polis ought to be even when living in a malformed or unjust polis. Plato's academy and Aristotle's lyceum emerged as schools designed to guide the quest for wisdom through a disciplined rational ascent, which would prepare wise political leaders who had grasped the essential truth about what a polis ought to be. The emergence of those academic communities might lead us to think that perhaps philosophy rather than political community represents the highest realization of human potential. Certainly it is philosophy, not the polis, that survived after Alexander and then the Romans eventually took political control of the Mediterranean region and its city-states. Yet neither Plato's nor Aristotle's political philosophy transcended the confines of the polis, because philosophy for them achieves its best in shaping a well-ordered polis.

With respect to the historical shaping of the commons and the idea of the common good, polis-thinking obviously contributes something quite different than does the biblical covenant tradition to an idea of the "common good." In

---

17. Aristotle has a more differentiated idea of the polis than does Plato, however. Aristotle, for example, challenges Plato's reduction of the family to political purposes. Aristotle sees the polis more as an aggregate of different kinds of associations. Nonetheless, the polis is for Aristotle still the rationally realized whole of human life. According to Aristotle, "It is true that unity is to some extent necessary, alike in a household and a polis; but total unity is not. There is a point at which a polis, by advancing in unity, will cease to be a polis: there is another point, short of that, at which it may still remain a polis, but will none the less come near to losing its essence, and will thus be a worse polis. It is as if you were to turn harmony into mere unison, or to reduce a theme to a single beat. The truth is that the polis, as has already been said, is an aggregate of many members; and education is therefore the means of making it a community and giving it unity." Aristotle, *The Politics* (trans. Ernest Barker; Oxford: Oxford University Press, 1946), 51 (2.5.14–15).

Greek thought, there is no transcendent Creator God to establish the norms of the polis; instead, humans realize it through a natural reasoning and shaping process. Ultimate rationality—the pure reason of Aristotle's unmoved mover—may serve as the guiding end or purpose of life, which explains why philosophers should govern. But in the idea of the polis, God does not rule the earth and establish covenants that articulate different kinds of human accountability to God. The polis is a totality, a hierarchy in which everything finds its meaning in relation to the political whole. In that respect there is an earthly concentration point of power and authority in a single jurisdiction, even if that power and authority are to be judged and qualified by standards that are somehow rationally transcendent. Slaves, women, and children are all subordinated to the rational-political whole as less human than mature men, and the best principles for governing the polis are determined by the rational discernment of wise rulers. From such experience there could not have emerged a constitutional struggle with an independent church, whose originating authority comes from outside the polis.

Greek political philosophy might have remained mere philosophy or disappeared altogether after the Macedonian and Roman Empires triumphed over the Greek city-states. However, there was a strong cultural Hellenization of the expanding Roman Empire. Neoplatonism had a big impact on the early church fathers, including Augustine, and Thomas Aquinas made much use of Aristotle. Thus, the construction of Christendom out of a collapsing Roman Empire and resulting feudal system owes a great deal to the classical as well the biblical tradition.

From Christendom to the Modern State

In view of the essay by Porter and the first part of the essay by Cavanaugh in this volume, relatively little needs to be said here about the medieval period and particularly about the importance of Thomas Aquinas for our topic. As Porter shows, it was from the eleventh through the thirteenth centuries after Christ that tremendous social, political, legal, and ecclesiastical changes were taking place, requiring new efforts to account for the differentiation and integration of society. By the thirteenth century the Roman Catholic Church was essentially functioning as the widest, largest integrator of social and political life in the European world. Political authorities were diffuse and of many kinds. The spiritual sword held important sway over the control and use of the earthly sword. Consequently, earthly society was generally understood to be constituted by reference to the higher authority of the church.

For Aquinas, the ultimate end of human life is not found or achieved naturally, rationally, and politically. Human creatures, as the Bible and the church teach, are the image of God and are destined ultimately for communion with God and thus for a supernatural end. This world is not simply formed matter, in the classical sense, but is God's creation. Disciplined rational ascent will lead to God, though not to everything God has to reveal. Aquinas's qualification and transcendence of classical authorities in a society that had long since burst the bounds of the polis can be understood only in the historical context of the Christianization of the old

Roman Empire. Humans have an ultimate destiny beyond life in this world, but all of earthly life should be ordered in a political and ecclesiastical harmony that prepares us for and leads us to our true end. All human deeds "originate from our last end," according to Aquinas, and that end is happiness, the chief happiness being the vision of God.

If ultimate happiness is to be found in the vision of God, a person's earthly happiness is to be found, in part, through a common happiness, the common good of a justly ordered political society. For Aquinas, since individuals are part of the life of the community,

> it must needs be that law properly speaking deals with this subordina-
> tion to a common happiness. Thus Aristotle, having explained what he
> means by "legal," mentions the happiness of the body politic when he
> says in the *Ethics* (1129b17) that "we call those acts legally just that tend
> to produce and preserve happiness and its components for the political
> community," the perfect community, according to the *Politics* (1252a5),
> being the state ([Aquinas,] *Summa theologiae* 1a.2ae.90.2).[18]

Despite the reference here to Aristotle, Aquinas was not a politically reductionistic thinker about society in the way Aristotle was. Nor did he and his contemporaries develop "a comprehensive moral theory of the good society under the rubric of the common good," according to Porter. Nevertheless, the language of the common good did offer Aquinas a way to address the new social realities of his day, a way that was "more positive and also more flexible than the language of dominion and servitude that we find in Bonaventure." Aquinas was, in other words, pushing beyond the boundaries of "virtue ethics" in the classical sense, and beyond a narrow range of ideas about subordination and obligation as the glue of a social order. He articulated the rudiments of a legal and institutional norm that obligates both governments and citizens within a political order—an order that arises not simply because of sin but because of the broad needs of a complex human society as such. The idea of a normative common good calls political officials to exercise a responsibility for the political community, which has its own raison d'être. "What Aquinas takes from his predecessors and contemporaries," says Porter, "is the idea of a public role, which implies both a general authority to direct the community as a law-giver, and specific powers to do some kinds of things, on behalf of the community at large, which would be forbidden to private citizens."

There is, for Aquinas, more to the identity of persons and their responsibilities than can be comprehended by the political community. The obligation of government officials to pursue the common good "in accordance with the demands of equality and justice implies that the well-being of a community is constituted, in part, by the boundaries of justice, which include fundamental norms of respect for individual well-being. These limits, in turn," Porter continues, "suggest that even seen from the perspective of a private person, individual good is not wholly subsumed in, or by implication subordinate to, the common good."

---

18. In O'Donovan and O'Donovan, *From Irenaeus to Grotius*, 342.

Aquinas recognizes different kinds of human virtue that are realized differently, each according to its kind. Thus, he says, "Virtues are specifically differentiated according to their objectives," all of which "involve the private good of the individual person or the common good of the people."[19] "There is no virtue of which some activity cannot be enjoined by law." Yet it is also the case that "human law does not enjoin every act of every virtue, but those acts only which serve the common good, either immediately, as when the social order is directly involved from the nature of things, or mediately, as when measures of good discipline are passed by the legislator to train citizens to maintain justice and peace in the community."[20]

With respect to the diversity of human virtues, Porter explains, "Aquinas distinguishes between prudence simply so called, which is directed to the private good of the individual, and political prudence, which is directed toward the common good and is therefore a specifically different virtue." With respect to the political relationship between governing officials and citizens or subjects, Aquinas "goes on to introduce a further distinction, between regnative prudence, which is exercised by someone who has authority over a perfect (that is to say, a complete) community, and political prudence, the virtue proper to subjects considered as such, which they exercise in carrying out the directives of the ruler." If Porter is right, then we find here in Aquinas the beginning of a specification of the "common good" as a differentiated norm of justice for the political community. This norm is in distinction, from, as well as in relation to, the nonpolitical responsibilities that belong to human creatures who have a wide range of responsibilities from and to God.

John Calvin, arguably the most politically influential Protestant Reformer, was influenced in his legal studies in Paris and Orleans by all of the same classical authors that influenced Aquinas and later ecclesiastical and legal authorities. Yet he developed his idea of the civic polity in the historical context of the newly emerging nation state and the splintering of medieval Christendom. With the "pluralizing" of states and churches, there was an even greater need to justify the differentiation of human responsibilities and institutions. Political responsibility, for Calvin, was above all a differentiated institutional calling from God. Returning emphatically to the biblical idea of covenant and to the Augustinian conviction that God ordained political authority because of sin, Calvin nonetheless grounds his political ethics in equity and the law of nations, not narrowly in the law of Moses.[21] The ceremonial and judicial laws of Israel are no longer binding, but the law of equity (both natural and biblical) still holds for all nations

---

19. Ibid., 348; Aquinas, *Summa theologiae*, 1a.2ae.96.3.

20. Ibid.

21. John Calvin, *Institutes of the Christian Religion* (ed. John T. McNeill; trans. Ford Lewis Battles; 2 vols.; Philadelphia: Westminster, 1960), 2:1500: "It is a fact that the law of God which we call the moral law is nothing else than a testimony of natural law and of that conscience which God has engraved upon the minds of men. Consequently, the entire scheme of this equity of which we are now speaking has been prescribed in it. Hence, this equity alone must be the goal and rule and limit of all laws" (4.20.14).

regardless of how diverse their constitutions may be. According to Guenther H. Haas, Calvin "uses equity to harmonize the Second Table of the [Mosaic] law with the righteousness of Christ, thereby upholding the unity of the covenant in the law of Scripture. Equity has a key role in expounding the commandments of the Second Table, and in applying them to the diverse situations of social life."[22] In Calvin's view, equity "directs the implementation of love" in the sense that love of neighbor requires justice—the giving to each his due. "Equity calls believers to show the same love, compassion and self-sacrifice to others that God has shown to them in Christ."[23]

According to Haas, "equity" is the key to understanding Calvin's ethics, including his political ethics. Calvin uses "equity" in the last three of the following four senses that had developed from the classical tradition and had been drawn together by Aquinas: equity as (1) rectification of positive law where it is defective, (2) natural law, (3) justice as interpretive principle of law, and (4) the benign interpretation of law tempered by mercy and clemency.[24] In this sense, there is continuity from Aquinas to Calvin, but with the accent by Calvin on the creation-order norm of equity rather than on a naturally realized virtue. However, even with this contrast of accents, there is not as complete an opposition, it seems to me, as the one drawn by Ralph C. Hancock between Aristotle and Calvin.[25] According to Hancock, the

> linking of political virtue with what is truly best in man is wholly foreign to Calvin's thought. A complete severance of political virtue from the highest excellence of which man is capable follows from Calvin's refusal to understand political order as determined by an end accessible to man. . . . Calvin emphatically distinguishes office from man: all authority resides finally not in any human being but in a divine calling. . . . It is misleading to liken the virtue of the Aristotelian aristocrat to the political calling or "gift" of the Calvinist official. The man of virtue embodies the good which he represents; the official is a conduit of the will of God, which he cannot possibly embody.[26]

The contrast between Aristotle and Calvin is, indeed, one of fundamentally different perspectives on the meaning of life and on confidence versus lack of confidence in the potential of human beings, in their present state, to realize the end for which God created them. For Calvin, political community under government is not the highest original end of human life to be realized through the rational

---

22. Guenther H. Haas, *The Concept of Equity in Calvin's Ethics* (Canadian Corporation for Studies in Religion; Waterloo, ON: Wilfrid Laurier University Press, 1997), 124.

23. Ibid., 123.

24. Ibid.

25. Ralph C. Hancock, *Calvin and the Foundations of Modern Politics* (Ithaca, NY: Cornell University Press, 1989), 67ff.

26. Ibid., 68.

rule of some humans over others. Instead, government is given on account of sin and disobedience, a disobedience that brought the breakdown of a potentially harmonious human community in the first place. Sin, however, does not destroy God's laws for creation, including the law of equity for the nations, but only makes humans blind and disobedient to it. In a fallen world, God has ordained government as an act of common grace for an important role in upholding creation and the equitable protection of every neighbor for the good of all. Calvin does not have a low view of human responsibility, including political responsibility, exercised through a variety of callings from God. Nor does Calvin start with a disconnection between human persons and the end for which God created them, as Hancock implies. Rather, he takes seriously the disconnection that has come because of sin and that would remain forever but for the grace of God.

Seen from this vantage point, the responsibility to which God graciously calls government officials is, for Calvin, not far from what Aquinas calls "regnative prudence." Magistrates are supposed to fill their office in imitation of the justice of God by exercising complete impartiality toward every subject, promoting "brotherly love (*fraternum amorem*) among those over whom they rule by serving them."[27] This is an articulated norm of how governing officials should seek the common good. And Calvin calls citizen-subjects to the exercise of "political prudence" (Aquinas's phrase) by submitting themselves to the magistrates as representatives and ministers of God. "Such submission is necessary for there to be the practice of justice (*suum ius*) in society."[28] The political order that binds believers and unbelievers together is thus for the common good of all, but it by no means exhausts the moral responsibilities of individuals, families, and other institutions. It is one among many callings God has given men and women for their earthly well-being and the glory of God.

Aquinas, without giving up Aristotle's ethics altogether, reaches beyond the limits of classical virtue ethics toward a more institutional differentiation of the political sphere of responsibility. Then Calvin, in the spirit of Augustine, carries forward Aquinas's delimitation of the political realm in a way that, in the end, takes almost complete distance from Aristotle. Calvin also demands a greater degree of clarity about the differentiated purpose and limits of the covenanted polity.

This is an appropriate place to make a brief comment about Islam, which presents yet a different idea of the commons and the common good. On the one hand, not unlike Christianity and Judaism, Islam speaks of the one God's (Allah's) universal rule over one creation and of a final judgment of all. The universal "commons" is God's creation, and no human authority bears responsibility for the creation as a whole. Islam is clearly an all-encompassing religious way of life predicated on the sovereignty of God. The world, however, is divided in a territorial way between *dar al-Islam* (Arabic, meaning "house of Islam") and *dar al-harb* ("house of war"). The *dar al-Islam* is the territory in which God is acknowledged and obeyed and thus justly ordered in peace. The *dar al-harb* is the territory of

---

27. Haas, *The Concept of Equity*, 111.
28. Ibid.

conflict outside or beyond the *dar al-Islam*. Inside the *dar al-Islam*, there is essentially one law, that of God's revealed will in the Qur'an (or Koran). The *dar al-harb* is that territory in which God has yet to be acknowledged and obeyed. There appears to be no Qur'anic way to think about a political *territory* in which the common good of both Muslims and non-Muslims can be sought and upheld if the rule of that territory is not in accord with the Qur'an. In fact, true commonality will appear only when the people of the *dar al-harb* have acknowledged Allah, at which point there will be only the one *dar al-Islam*.

Within classical Islam, both Sunni and Shi'ite, the *dar al-Islam* has been understood as a single community without jurisdictional differentiation of "ecclesiastical" and "political" institutions. A separate "church" institution with its own canon law, for example, did not emerge in the Muslim world over against political authorities with their own claim to authorization from God. Nor did the different juridical schools of Qur'anic interpretation constitute institutional counterweights to those who governed, unless the governing authorities were not upholding Islam. Thus, the idea of a specified, differentiated human office that bears political responsibility for the common good, independent of the various uncommon responsibilities that people bear, does not have a classical Muslim foundation. Whether Islam in the contemporary world will develop pluralist ideas of society is one of the key questions of our day.[29]

Modern Synthetic Ideas

Finally, with an equally brief sweep, we consider ideas of the common good that have arisen in the West since the sixteenth century. We particularly notice those that have focused on limiting political power and those that have aimed either to extend or to eliminate it.[30] The Marxist idea of a communist revolution that puts an end to the need for states; nationalistic totalisms that aim to coordinate all human energies for a single national glory; and anarchist ideas that aim to eliminate political authority altogether—all of these exhibit the second tendency to extend or to eliminate political authority. None of them yields an idea of the common good. Instead, each inspires a movement that is supposed to eventuate in the elimination of anything that is uncommon.

Anarchism might appear to be the opposite, the refusal to have a commons at all, and yet its universalistic leveling orientation refuses to make room for any uncommon associational structure or political authority. There must be a single

---

29. See Nazih Ayubi, *Political Islam: Religion and Politics in the Arab World* (New York: Routledge, 1991); James Turner Johnson, *The Holy War Idea in Western and Islamic Traditions* (State College, PA: Pennsylvania State University Press, 1997); Bernard Lewis, "The Revolt of Islam," *The New Yorker*, November 19, 2001, 50–63; and Diana L. Eck, *A New Religious America* (San Francisco: HarperSanFrancisco, 2001), 222–93.

30. On modern ideologies, see the excellent new book by David T. Koyzis, *Political Visions and Illusions: A Survey and Christian Critique of Contemporary Ideologies* (Downers Grove, IL: InterVarsity Press, 2003).

"commons" defined by anarchy, in which there is no *communal* good. Nazism and communism, by contrast, have arisen in societies where scientific, technological, industrial-economic, and academic institutions had, to some degree, already differentiated under law. Yet the goals of these ideological movements are so reductionistic that the "good" they have in mind could be achieved only at the expense of everyone and everything not controlled by a single authority. Or, to state it more accurately in terms of historical reality, the "common good" that is sought by these ideologies is the good chiefly of those in power, who claim to represent the fated destiny (or vanguard) of all human history. All other humans are mere means toward the destined end.

Looking beyond the primary European impact zones in the world, we may wonder how Western Marxism could have had such a strong influence in China in the twentieth century. In pre-Maoist China a ruler claimed authority as the earth's central mediator and representative of heaven: the Son of Heaven with the mandate of heaven. In this respect, the political realm did not become differentiated from other realms and certainly did not recognize independent authorities outside its jurisdiction. Of course, Maoist totalitarianism, exercised through party control, had a character quite distinct from the more subtle, intricate, and scholar-administered Confucian empires of earlier eras. But Maoism did feed on the earlier patterns of close, organic, societal integration. Family, friendship, scholarship, worship, and "public governance" were organically integrated under one high authority. In much the same way that Greek philosophy was confined to polis-thinking, Confucian scholarship was confined, as Sze-kar Wan explains, by the "celebrated totalism" of "Chinese cosmo-ethical thinking [which] begins with the cultivated self and expands outward to include family, community, nation, and finally the cosmos. This is the famous eight steps in *Daxue* (*The Great Learning*)."[31]

Modern movements that have focused chiefly on limiting political power and authority have typically faced the challenge of trying to specify those limits. This is where many of the covenantal, constitutionalizing influences have been felt all the way up to the UN's Human Rights Declarations and the Geneva Conventions on warfare. However, under the impact of liberalism, most developments of this kind have chiefly emphasized government's noninterference with individual freedom and the protection of individual rights. Ideals of individual freedom that are not anarchistic have thus been tied closely to government as the means of upholding those rights. The meaning of the commons as a differentiated political *community* with its own identity has been difficult if not impossible to articulate on

---

31. Sze-kar Wan, "Christian Contributions to the Globalization of Confucianism (beyond Maoism)," in *Christ and the Dominions of Civilization* (ed. Max L. Stackhouse with Diane B. Obenchain; vol. 3 of *God and Globalization*; Harrisburg, PA: Trinity Press International, 2002), 205. See also Eric Voegelin, *The Ecumenic Age* (vol. 4 of *Order and History*; Baton Rouge: Louisiana State University Press, 1974), chap 6, "The Chinese Ecumene," 272–99. Even today, with its opening of capital markets and entrance into the World Trade Organization, China faces a real challenge of deciding whether (and how) to recognize the differentiation of independent corporations, universities, nonprofit organizations, and religious bodies.

liberal terms. Consequently, within the now widely accepted Western idea of the open society, the "common good" becomes identified as (or with) little more than national pride, economic prosperity, or a war against terrorism.[32]

Consider, for example, the contrasting but not altogether contrary views of Alan Gewirth, a University of Chicago philosophy professor, and Michael Novak, a senior scholar at the American Enterprise Institute in Washington, DC.

Gewirth believes he can build an idea of community and even of the common good from the starting point of autonomous, rational individuals. Universal human rights are his primary means of construction: "Each human must respect the rights of all the others while having his rights respected by all the others, so that there must be a mutual sharing of the benefits of rights and the burdens of duties." The requirement of mutual respect, says Gewirth, amounts to a principle of solidarity. "By the effective recognition of the mutuality entailed by human rights, the society becomes a community. So the antithesis between rights and community is bridged."[33] From my point of view, the moment of truth in Gewirth's argument is the fact that the modern, differentiated political order is, among other things, an institution of public-legal rights protection. However, Gewirth provides no basis for differentiating the political "community" from any other institution that autonomous individuals might construct. Politically speaking, in other words, no community exists except the "mutuality of rights," and that mutuality, with its sense of solidarity, depends on the willingness of each individual to accept the burdens of the duties toward other individuals. Consequently, in Gewirth's thinking there is no differentiated communal basis for the specification of a limited political commons, even though the enforcement of rights protection requires a very specific authority that can impose its will on supposedly autonomous individuals. For Gewirth, there are only human rights, which are both mutual and egalitarian in their universality.[34] On these terms, even though everything is supposedly common, there is no community except in the mutual recognition of human rights. As Gewirth explains in his argument against communitarians, his "emphasis on human rights is not only compatible with, but requires a conscientious concern for, the common good, where 'common,' from its initial distributive meaning, takes on also the collective meaning of the community that is constituted by and is the protector of human rights."[35] For Gewirth, then, wherever and whenever autonomous individuals refuse to recognize a mutual obligation, there is no commons; and wherever and whenever reasonable individuals choose to use collective means to uphold their mutuality in rights, there is no limit to the commons.

---

32. The best liberal effort to do justice to political community in a differentiated society is, in my opinion, William A. Galston, *Liberal Pluralism: The Implications of Value Pluralism for Political Theory and Practice* (Cambridge: Cambridge University Press, 2002).
33. Alan Gewirth, *The Community of Rights* (Chicago: University of Chicago Press, 1996), 6.
34. Ibid., 6.
35. Ibid., 93.

Michael Novak's initial point of departure is quite different from that of Gewirth's. Novak starts not with the rights of autonomous individuals but with a Catholic vision of the transcendent destination of the human person: "God is the universal common good not only of humans but of all created things."[36] The dignity of the person is to be found in each person's responsibility before God, and that calls for the exercise of each person's practical rationality. When a person acts "with reflection and choice—acts, that is, *as a person*—the personal good and the common good tend to coincide," says Novak.[37] The person is more than an individual, and cooperation in love leads to the creation of various kinds of institutions. However, Novak admits, there is "a serious problem in learning what the common good is."[38] Why a problem? Because the modern tendency, he believes, has been to reduce the person either to a "self-enclosed individual" or to an "unfree collectivism."[39] Novak is especially opposed to the tendency toward collectivism, through which an institution assumes power to decide, from the top down, what the substantive common good of all persons in their entirety should be.

Novak is strong in recognizing that the common good cannot be achieved if everything that is uncommon is reduced to a single good or eliminated altogether. He wants full recognition of the nonpolitical associations and communities of human life that also represent the flourishing of responsible persons. Yet in his aim to avoid collectivism and totalitarianism, Novak nearly, if not completely, eliminates the political community as an authoritative institution responsible for a definite, differentiated, common public good. "Not by politics alone is the common good publicly promoted," he writes.[40] It is almost as if Novak fears that any authoritative public body responsible for the commons will inevitably try to act in an omnicompetent fashion, violating the nonpolitical responsibilities of persons. Instead, he wants the political community to be defined only in a procedural way that sets down the rules for individual and associational interaction in freedom. The political common good is something that will arise almost inadvertently or unintentionally from the actions of responsible persons. This is much like Adam Smith envisioned the "common wealth" being achieved as an indirect result of individuals each seeking their own economic interests in free exchange.[41] This is the only way to respect the practical rationality of free persons, says Novak. "In sum, the new concept of the common good pushes us beyond a simple reliance upon authority that defines for all the substantive good, and turns us instead toward achieving the rules that make an open society possible."[42]

On the one hand, Novak accepts the differentiation of society into many different kinds of institutions and associations, because this legitimately expresses

---

36. Michael Novak, *Free Persons and the Common Good* (Lanham, MD: Madison Books, 1989), 30.
37. Ibid., 32.
38. Ibid., 34.
39. Ibid., 35.
40. Ibid., 137.
41. Cf. Ibid., 83–87.
42. Ibid., 142.

the practical responsibility of free persons. Yet, instead of recognizing the political community as having its own differentiated, specifiable sphere of responsibility to uphold the common good of the political community, Novak seems to believe that such an idea is too substantive. It gives too much authority to political officials, for they will then be tempted to act for the total good of all persons in all respects. An authoritative—but nontotalitarian—public-legal integration of citizens in a political community does not seem to be possible, in Novak's scheme of things. He tries to marry the liberal tradition and the older Thomist tradition, but liberalism triumphs in the attempted synthesis. While granting that political authority is essential if government is to act on behalf of the people, Novak defers, in good liberal fashion, to democratic procedures rather than attempting to articulate norms for the political common good.[43] While he does not want to subordinate government to ecclesiastical authority, he does move quickly to relativize, and thus limit, the political commons by pointing beyond it to eschatological expectations of fulfillment. The complete common good cannot be achieved in this age, he says, and in this way he emphasizes that the common good cannot be achieved "by politics alone."[44]

Seeking the Common Good

Gewirth is correct, I believe, that sharing in the burdens of achieving human rights for everyone is part of what constitutes political responsibility. And Novak is correct that the ultimate or comprehensive common good of all people in all respects cannot be achieved by politics alone. But neither of these positions is adequate to answer the question of responsibility for the political commons and of the normative identity of the political community. We may well agree that human rights protection is part of that responsibility, and we may also simultaneously agree that politics is not everything. Then we are still left with the question of what constitutes an all-inclusive territorial community for which humans do bear actual, specifiable, public-legal responsibility. The answer to that question, it seems to me, is the public-legal community—the political order—which today is expressed in nearly two hundred separate states and in a variety of public-legal international institutions. In the future, and even now, they require better and stronger institutions of transnational governance.[45] In all of these instances, the

---

43. Ibid., 184.

44. Ibid., 121, 186–87.

45. I agree with Max Stackhouse's emphasis in this volume on the importance of upholding the diverse institutional and individual vocations of societies around the world as the process of globalization intensifies. Globalization increases the demand for a pluralist understanding of human responsibilities in the context of growing demands for international as well as domestic justice. The need for international and even transnational public-legal institutions in a shrinking world will not meet with justice if the boundaries of the responsibilities of such institutions are not drawn clearly enough to uphold the responsibilities of other governmental and nongovernmental institutions.

responsibility being exercised (whether well or poorly) is that of enforcing public law for everyone in the territory being governed. In a world of conflicting human aims and ideals in which violent aggression has always been evident, there can be no attempt to seek the common good that is not backed by authority to enforce common law. Enforced order that is neither just nor recognized as legitimate by those subject to it will, of course, amount to nothing more than anarchism, authoritarianism, or totalitarianism. Real debates about the common good, therefore, must be about the good and just order that ought to be enforced, and that is where all the questions about the specifiable identity and limits of the political community come in.

The greatest contemporary innovation in constructing a political commons that will transcend the boundaries of separate states is the movement of the European Union toward ever increasing integration. In that context, many ideas of covenant, federation, subsidiarity, civil society, nationalism, and religious freedom are in play. The participants are trying to define not only the procedures and institutions of European governance but also the nature and limits of the specifiable responsibility and purpose of those institutions. What the European experiment also shows is the multiplicity of ideas people hold about the standard of "the common good." Christian democratic ideas and influences were highly significant in the early stages of European integration at the end of World War II, and before that, Christianity had a long historical influence in Europe. Nevertheless, it seems to me that relatively little creative Christian political thinking is being generated in the current European context.[46]

The concern about political integration, intertwinement, and interdependency exists far beyond Europe, of course, whether in various international bodies or in the attempt to find ways to stop internecine conflict within and across borders of certain states. Whether the concern is with building a just state or building a just international order, the question of the common good comes to the fore with respect to both its universal scope and its differentiated and limited responsibility to implement and uphold a just commons.

The inescapable human quest for the common good is rooted, I believe, in the very character of God's creation and of our human calling in it. The realization of our humanness through the exercise of many kinds of God-given responsibility manifests a wholeness and integrality that demands justice for all and thus the realization of the common good of all. Moreover, it is a quest that must ultimately be oriented toward the service and praise of the God in whose image we have been created. With the historical unfolding and ever-increasing differentiation of

---

46. The most significant Christian contribution to the European federation debates of which I am aware is the study (with recommendations) released in 1999 by the Christian Democratic Appeal (CDA) of the Netherlands entitled "Public Justice and the European Union, a Christian Democratic View of the Nature and Tasks of the European Union," available electronically (www.cda.nl). The most influential European Christian-democratic thinker in the middle of the last century was undoubtedly Jacques Maritain. See, for example, his *Man and the State* (Chicago: University of Chicago Press, 1951).

our multiple talents and responsibilities, however, the demands of the common good to which humans must respond require ever more clearly differentiated institutionalization. The possibility of realizing the common good in any society or in the world today thus requires the exercise of a particular kind of responsibility that is increasingly differentiated from, and impartial toward, every other kind of responsibility. We notice the historical differentiation in some parts of the world of the political community, the res publica, from land ownership and economic position, from membership in a community of faith, and from ethnic, racial, and gender identities. Such change actually gives evidence of the normative human calling to set political authority apart from all other authorities. The purpose of the differentiation is precisely so that everyone can share in the welfare of the commons, made possible by the enforcement of impartial territorial law and order.

To argue for differentiated specification of the political common good is not to argue for a disconnection and isolation of different spheres of responsibility. Obviously, there cannot be a differentiated political commons apart from its public-legal *integration* of all the spheres of responsibility that are uncommonly exercised. Moreover, the normative exercise of each of our diverse human responsibilities contributes to the full realization of human community, including the political community. But it is not the task or purpose of the family, the university, the corporation, or the medical center to administer and enforce the laws that aim to uphold the common good of all. Thus, the political commons must be differentiated from everything that is not political at the same time that it serves as the public-legal integrator of a whole society.[47] Ultimately, of course, from this point of view, part of what allows for the specification and limitation of the jurisdictional competence of human government is the fact that God alone rules over and holds together the whole creation. Only by God's grace will the whole creation receive its fulfillment in the city of God.[48]

---

47. More of this argument for pluralism is developed in my *In Pursuit of Justice: Christian-Democratic Explorations* (Lanham, MD: Rowman and Littlefield, 2004); and James Skillen and Rockne M. McCarthy, eds., *Political Order and the Plural Structure of Society* (Atlanta: Scholars Press, 1991). See also, most recently, my "Pluralism as a Matter of Principle," a response to David Little's "Conscientious Individualism: A Christian Perspective on Ethical Pluralism," both in *The Many and the One: Religious and Secular Perspectives on Ethical Pluralism in the Modern World* (ed. Richard Madsen and Tracy B. Strong; Princeton: Princeton University Press, 2003), 257–68.

48. Both my agreements and disagreements with the eschatological realization of the common good as articulated by Robert Jenson in this volume are evident in James W. Skillen, "Living in Tune with Christ's Supremacy," in *Politics and Public Policy: A Christian Response* (ed. Timothy J. Demy and Gary P. Stewart; Grand Rapids: Kregel, 2000), 71–80; idem, "The Revelatory and Anticipatory Character of Politics," in *Signpost of God's Liberating Kingdom* (ed. B. J. van der Walt and Rita Swanepoel; Potchefstroom, South Africa: Potchefstroom University, 1998), 59–70; and idem, "Cry for Justice, Hope for Shalom," in *Setting the Captives Free* (ed. Don Smarto; Grand Rapids: Baker Books, 1993), 129–39.

To make this kind of Christian confession in connection with an attempt to articulate a normative political perspective brings us back to Robert Kaplan. He has charged that real politics and the use of force require a "pagan ethos" and cannot be sustained by a Christian ethic. His contention is that if the American Empire is to survive and succeed in the world today, it requires leaders with a pagan ethos who will keep their Christian values (if they have them) tucked carefully away in private. Kaplan's reasoning depends on a peculiar, modern interpretation of Christianity as a religion that has a private ethic but not a public ethic. Kaplan sides with Machiavelli, for example, who "preferred a pagan ethic that elevated self-preservation over the Christian ethic of sacrifice, which he considered hypocritical."[49] Machiavelli's virtue is public, says Kaplan, "whereas Judeo-Christian virtue is more often private virtue."[50] Progress, as Machiavelli recognized, "often comes from hurting others," so we "have to recognize that while virtue is good, outstanding virtue can be dangerous."[51] A little later in his book, Kaplan allows that there can be an "overlap" of Christian and pagan virtues. This overlap is in part because of the influence of Cicero and Plutarch on the Christian West, and in part because some Christians, such as Richelieu, Bismarck, and Reinhold Niebuhr, simply became realistic about politics. "What all these men were groping for," says Kaplan, "was a way to use pagan, public morality to advance—albeit indirectly—private, Judeo-Christian morality."[52] Nevertheless, real progress in politics has come in "the evolution from religious virtue to secular self-interest."[53]

Kaplan's idea of historical progress from religion to secular self-interest is an odd one, given that his book is a Renaissance-like attempt to revive a pre-Christian (and thus presecular) pagan view of life. The wise men of ancient Greece and Rome and China to whom he calls us back were quite religious in their own ways, though not Judeo-Christian. The main problem with Kaplan's argument, however, is that he fails to appreciate the significance of the Christian contribution to the differentiation of society and the process of structuring constitutional political communities (see especially the essays by Dennis McCann, Robin Lovin, Eric Mount, and Jean Porter in this volume). Certain pietist, monastic, and pacifist strains of Christianity have indeed relinquished or turned against political life and government's responsibility to enforce law.[54] And there certainly is the firm Christian renunciation, enjoined by Jesus, of any effort to try to establish God's kingdom by force, or to exercise personal vengeance against

---

49. Kaplan, *Warrior Politics*, 52.

50. Ibid., 56.

51. Ibid., 77.

52. Ibid., 109.

53. Ibid., 112.

54. The work of John Howard Yoder, Stanley Hauerwas, and Richard Hays along this line has become highly influential in our day. For a critique of the pacifist argument as a biblical argument, see James W. Skillen and Keith J. Pavlischek, "Political Responsibility and the Use of Force: A Critique of Richard Hays," *Philosophia Christi*, ser. 2, vol. 3, no. 2 (2001): 421–45; and James W. Skillen, "Civic-Minded and Heavenly Good," *Christianity Today*, November 18, 2002, 50–54.

enemies, or to organize human vengeance against others. But the biblical context for such an approach to life is God's ordination of government for the purpose of protecting the weak, encouraging the good, and exercising retributive justice as an expression of God's judgment, not human vengeance (e.g., Rom 12:9–13:7). In contrast to both Kaplan and pacifist interpretations of the biblical texts, therefore, I would argue that a Christian pattern of life both entails and requires a public ethic specifically for political responsibility.

The very differentiation of society, to which we have referred, has led to the specification of the political community as a limited one of enforced law for the commons. This is in distinction from the responsibilities of parents, church leaders, educators, and corporate managers, who are not permitted to use force in the exercise of their duties. A Christian ethic belongs not only to the nonpolitical spheres of responsibility. Nor would it be legitimate on Christian grounds to argue that a Christian family ethic, or schooling ethic, or business ethic, or ecclesiastical ethic ought to be held out as the norm for political life. Niebuhr and many other Christian ethicists have made the mistake of projecting an ideal of Christian love that was too narrow and could have little or no bearing on the "realist responsibilities" of government. Suppose, however, that in keeping with the full biblical ethos and its profound illumination of normative justice, we both reject Christian imperialism of earlier eras and accept the principle that the political order should be an all-inclusive, differentiated, civic community. Then from a Christian point of view, the political community properly bears the responsibility to use force for the protection of the innocent, the punishment of criminals, and the defense of the entire commons from unjust aggression. Such an exercise of responsibility is fully compatible with the neighborly love called for by the Christian gospel. It is precisely what is necessary to make possible an open society for the free and nonviolent exercise of familial, economic, scientific, artistic, and other responsibilities. In fact, I would contend, it is precisely the Christian ethos that can articulate the firmest criteria for the limitation and just use of force (as in the just-war doctrine, civil rights, and more). These are limiting criteria that a "pagan ethos" does not offer. Moreover, these criteria, which are public and not private, allow for and encourage the legitimation of just government instead of undermining government's responsibility to uphold the common good by means of the wise and just control of force.

A Christian understanding of the political common good will certainly lead to conclusions that conflict with those of Robert Kaplan. The state as an institution will not be seen as an end in itself, to which everything and everyone else must be reduced or expended. A Christian view of human society and political order offers a larger, wider understanding of human life under God. But the larger Christian view upholds government's God-ordained responsibility to protect the commons. In the face of unjust acts, and particularly violent acts, governments must be prepared to respond retributively and even defend against unjust aggression. Kaplan, as well as "Christian" imperialists and pacifists, it seems to me, have it wrong about Christianity and the common good. It is precisely this debate over what constitutes the common good in our day that demands a fresh and creative Christian engagement.

The Common Good, Our Common Goods, and The Uncommon Good in a Globalizing Era

Max L. Stackhouse

While the concept of "the common good" clearly signals a sociopolitical arena of ethical debate and action, it is not always clear what the source and norm of the obligation to seek it is, what is genuinely common, and what is truly good. The idea, of course, has precedents in premodern theories of natural teleological ends and of ancient republics. Echoes of those views remain with us, but they have been modified by two sets of modern influences. One is the liberal political-economic theory that comes from (now) secularized forms of Anglo-American natural theology.[1] The second finds its roots in the continental traditions of state-ordered confessional dogmas in which national policies were established to regulate the whole and foment solidarity among the people. Those policies subjected religion to princely power in ways that led, after secularization, to statist forms of socialism and fascism.[2]

---

1. This history, with roots especially in Anglican doctrines of natural theology, has recently been traced by the Canadian scholar A. M. C. Waterman, in a series of articles now edited into *Political Economy and Christian Theology since the Enlightenment: Essays in Intellectual History* (New York: Palgrave Macmillan, 2004). See, for examples, his "'New Political Economies' Then and Now: Economic Theory and the Mutation of Political Doctrine," *American Journal of Economics and Sociology* 63, no. 1 (January 2002): 13–51; and "'Christian Political Economy' and 'Philosophic Radicalism,'" *Annals of the Society for the History of Economic Thought* 41 (May 2002): 1–14.

2. See, for example, Bernard J. Diggs, *The State, Justice, and the Common Good: An Introduction to Social and Political Philosophy* (Washington: Scott Foresman, 1986); Patrick Riordan, *A Politics of the Common Good* (Washington: Institute of Policy Administration, 1988); Mark Lutz, *Economics for the Common Good* (New York: Routledge, 1999).

Both strands of influence presume that a harmony of good can be established for a nation—one by the providential "hidden hand" effect of the individual pursuit of self-interest and autonomous moral reasoning, the other by the centralized propagation and enforcement of a solidarity that reinforces collective identity. Both became background beliefs that rejected theology as necessary in public discourse, although personal piety was encouraged and forms of civil religion were functionally cultivated. The purpose of this paper is to identify where these older theories proved inadequate and to show that an orthodox, catholic, reformed, and ecumenical set of theological insights—more than personal but independent of the state—is required for a public theology in our day. This public theology is needed to constrain the egoistic selfishness to which the liberal influence leads and the collectivist bureaucratization to which the statist tradition leads.

The debates between these older traditions have brought us a set of two-agent theories—the individual and the state—with contending views of how to combine them into a whole. Both purport to enhance the common well-being, with ongoing debates about the economic benefits or liabilities of alternative reliance on individual responsibility or on collective governmental action to generate or redistribute goods that are part of the common life. They have also brought considerable confusion as to what is truly "liberal" and what "conservative." Depending on the context, each affirms more liberty for each individual person to seek his or her own ends with the least political constraint. Or each affirms the governmental mobilization of resources, by coercive means as necessary, to liberate repressed and oppressed people so they can reap the benefits of the common good. As one wag put it, the liberal wants to liberate sex and use government to control money; the conservative wants to liberate money and use government to control sex. Both tend to see religion as a private preference and theology as its opinion.

The attempts to give theoretical coherence to views that are simultaneously individualist and statist have, over the centuries, prompted two major attempts to offer a more coherent vision. They parallel the more libertarian and the more liberationist themes already mentioned. One attempt is rooted in the classical philosophical-political presumption that each individual person (or thing or activity, including politics) has its own natural entelechy, as was variously argued by Plato and Aristotle. And, if these are properly discovered in thought and followed in practice, we will be led to the flourishing of the whole. That in turn will habituate each member into the paths of virtue. This view that has been argued in recent years by the disciples of neoconservative Leo Strauss and the postliberal Alasdair MacIntyre. The other attempt, doubting that natural moral goods can be discovered, seeks to construct a "social contract" as we find in the utilitarian legacy of J. S. Mill, in the romantic voluntarism of J.-J. Rousseau, and in the more recent neo-Enlightenment rationality of John Rawls.[3]

---

3. The British scholar of jurisprudence William Twining has attempted to set forth a wider view on this basis. See his *Globalization and Legal Theory* (Evanston, IL: Northwestern University Press, 2000). However, he seems quite unaware of the

It is doubtful that any of these models can offer an enduring view of the common good. The doubt derives from three concerns. One concern is philosophical: if the good is obvious to reason as natural law, why can't everyone discern the good? Or if the constructed contracts are rational and desirable, why doesn't everyone choose them?

A second concern is political: the unit of focus is no longer a classical polis or a modern nation. Both now involve an "us" that is too small to be genuinely common. While these political units remain as basic centers of power, law enforcement, and cultural identity, they are increasingly dependent on various spheres of civil society that have a sovereignty of their own beyond politics. The academic, economic, technological, and religious worlds, for example, have substantially escaped the constraints of any political order, and they shape politics as much as politics shapes them. Further, even each "sovereign" political unit now operates in a global context of relatively sovereign powers that resist attempts of any one unit to claim full sovereignty. Other nations, economic organizations, and popular opinion around the world (shaped by academic, media, and religious authorities) react negatively when any one political unit, even a superpower, seeks to execute its will without regard for the moral sentiment of the community of nations.

Even after the older European ideas of a "balance of power" have faded with the end of the Cold War, the United States, and other potential superpowers such as the European Union or China, have to operate in a much expanded context and must take account of each other.[4] Cooperating nation-states, even close allies, of course, may have temporary and even sharp disputes about policy. But standing alone, no single one or wider "block" is "common" enough or "good" enough to provide *the* model for what increasingly looks like a global future. Moreover, these "blocks" do not share either an interpretation of natural virtue or of a binding social compact that can define and enforce a common good. In short, neither the neoclassical nor the revised contractarian theories now seem able to provide a persuasive view that can integrate moral wills into the wider common purpose. Neither seems able to offer a vision for a comprehensive view of how to organize the many common goods when multicultural and transnational developments dominate our globe.

The third and most important reason for doubt is that neither the retrieval of classical teleological views nor the resuscitation of modern social contract theories is theological. Both views doubt that the knowledge of God is reliable and necessary to the understanding of good. They tend to see philosophy or science as universalistic and theology as inevitably particularistic and incapable of engaging in

---

critique of contractual-utilitarian views set forth, for instance, by the Nobel-Prize-winning economist Kenneth Arrow in *Collected Papers of Kenneth J. Arrow* (7 vols.; Cambridge, MA: Belknap, 1983–85). Arrow argues that a social equilibrium and rational definition of the common good cannot be attained on these bases.

4. The fact that some American policies seem imperialistic is likely a mark of moral hubris. They are likely to inhibit efforts to be effective advocates of the principles of justice that the U.S. episodically attempts to establish.

those forms of public discourse pertinent to the defining of the comprehending polity. Certainly it is the case that faiths and religions are particular, and some theology is little more than a rationalized megaphone for them. But it could be that other kinds of theology are more universal in that they can offer critical evaluations of all forms of particular faiths that do not reach toward God, who alone is, by definition, universal. That would include the faith of those nontheological thinkers who deny that there is anything more comprehensive than rational philosophical reasoning, or the faith of those who religiously believe that goodwill can, by itself, come to agreement about and actuate the common good.

It would, of course, be foolish to ignore the human capacities to reason, recognize virtues in others, make choices, and negotiate our interests by various agreements. And who can deny that many theologians have caused theology to curve in on itself, and to abjure any attempt to shape the moral architecture of civilizations, as it did in its most creative moments over the centuries? Still, it cannot be held that philosophy, politics, social studies, or economic calculations alone are either entirely benign or sufficient by themselves either to discern the good or to guide humanity to the best form of the common life. Philosophical and scientific discernments or contractual constructs and agreements may have seemed to offer convincing accounts of the structures and dynamics of the common life at certain stages of sociopolitical history. However, the *intellectus* of the one and the *voluntas* of the other were more often generated and guided by deeper repositories of religious conviction than they acknowledged. They degenerated into rationalism or the will-to-power when they failed to acknowledge their source and norm. To put the matter in overtly theological terms: God is what sustains the common life, and the human capacity to flourish in community and goodness erodes over time if God is excluded from consideration.

It would be more universalistic to argue that only God is ultimately good, that only God comprehends what is genuinely common in life, and thus that only God can guide the diverse powers and spheres of life to their proper ends. If that is so, then theology is the obvious first discipline to use in sorting the pertinent questions, precisely because it does not reduce God to something less than what is common and good. Thus, Thomas Aquinas used Augustinian theology to transform the teleology of the Greek polis, and Calvin used biblical motifs to transform contractual notions from Stoic jurisprudence in the Roman republic. Their work opened the door to deeper and wider understandings of dynamic, complex structures that could be faithful to the self-disclosure of God in Jesus Christ and simultaneously bring a modicum of order to the variety of commonalities and goods of civilization. They did this by pointing to God's purposes, which surpassed natural ends and human desires, and God's law, which surpassed the edicts of empires and the codes of nations.

In contemporary life such ideas have been developed further, although just below the radar of much theology, philosophy, and science. Still, they have issued in theologically based polities of a "hierarchical-subsidiarity" and a "federal-covenantal" kind. These are the two great theories that can give conceptual, ethical, and organizational coherence to the discussion of the common good. Both are pluralistic, although the former tends toward a vertically layered order and the latter towards a horizontal multiversity. Both recognize that there are many goods that have to be pursued to sustain life and meaning in history. Both have a profound place for the dignity of persons and importance of communities. And both are aware that they cannot resolve the tensions between the many goods entirely within history.[5] Both know that a "transcendental" frame of reference is required.[6]

However, the fact that a resolution of the conflict about what is common and what is good cannot be fully accomplished in history, as all serious theological views recognize, is not satisfying to those who want to overcome evil and immediately establish good by public policy. Thus, the twentieth century saw the rise and fall of highly impatient antitheological ideologies—neopagan and premodern on one side, or secular and modern on the other. These brought with them the bloodiest attempts to force resolution on the human condition that the world has ever seen. The reactions against these terrors have brought with them the repudiation of both the ontotheological traditions of antiquity and the willful constructions of modernity. They have produced both a resurgence of religions around the world, each claiming to have a comprehensive view, and a lively set of debates about religion as an inevitable and necessary factor in public discourse. Such happenings are puzzling to many neoclassical and modernist theorists and bizarre to postfoundationalist postmoderns, who see only fragmentation around them.

Yet, I believe that it is plausible to suggest that an alternative postmodernity is emerging, and that the most influential areas of the common life are creating an alternative postmodern global order today. This is manifest in many areas of education, technology, law, modern medicine, corporation-dominated economics, ecological movements, cross-cultural recognitions of excellence (as in Nobel Prizes), the media, and (most ambiguously) in the prospect of a widely resisted and morally suspect Pax Americana. All these were historically formed under the deep imprint of a theological legacy that has encouraged all parts of the society to obey universalistic moral laws. Thereby they are to develop their several vocations in ways that serve both the neighbor and divinely given yet pluralistic ends. Such newly cultivated spheres of the common life, generated out of this theologically shaped history, have brought us untold benefits even as they have challenged many cultures. At the same time, many of these spheres have tried to declare their autonomy from all theology. Nevertheless, they have the traces of these deep theological imprints embedded in their cultural forms and social practices. And current denials or ignorance of their own history means that they are often seen to

---

5. See the discussion of these matters in Nancy Rosenblum and Robert Post, *Civil Society and Government* (Princeton, NJ: Princeton University Press, 2002), esp. 223–64, the dialogue between John Coleman, SJ, and me over these matters. Cf. also the very important resource by James W. Skillen and R. M. McCarthy, eds., *Political Order and the Plural Structure of Society* (Atlanta: Scholars Press, 1991).

6. This sense of need for a transcendental frame of reference is why we, as a collection of theologians, are asked to address the issue at all.

be entirely without moral or spiritual inner guidance by their practitioners as well as their opponents.[7]

The loss of consciousness of such roots is made easy by the forms of natural theology that made God all too natural in one tradition and forms of confessional nationalism that made religion the legitimizing sanction for a given political regime in another. Hence, neither those who live and work in the globalizing spheres of life, those who administer them, those who teach others how to carry them on, nor those who enjoy their fruits—none of them understand what they are based on, how they work morally and spiritually, and why they have become so powerful. These spheres are displacing religious orientations, practices, and worldviews not rooted in the same traditions. In reaction, forms of religious militance that are arising around the world can be seen to be desperate attempts to reassert at least some kind of transcendent source and norm for meaning. They see the God-given structures of common grace by which virtue can almost be recognized and the conventional units of social solidarity that define their identity being swept aside. And, indeed, that is happening. The "powers and principalities, authorities and dominions" that Christians have held to be divinely ordained potentialities for the well-being of humanity and the honoring of God have repudiated their theological roots. In their fallen states, they are now transforming our lives, while their practitioners offer no theological or ethical rationale for what they are doing or why it should be done.[8] In contrast, both the hierarchical-subsidiarity model and the federal-covenantal model offer a theological orientation that can preserve, transform, and redeem the various spheres, practices, and worldviews that are, otherwise, being destroyed. These models perhaps even suggest the contours of a definition of the goods that could obtain in a hegemonic but highly diversified common world.

Today's militant neofundamentalist theocratic movements, however threatening, are fueled by the recognition of the emptiness of the purely naturalist or voluntarist views of the common good that are said to guide life in the most "advanced"

---

7. This is a central insight of major essays by Richard Osmer, John Witte, Allen Verhey, Ron Cole-Turner, Jürgen Moltmann, and Peter Paris in *God and Globalization*, vol. 2, *The Spirit and the Modern Authorities* (ed. Max Stackhouse with Don Browning; Harrisburg, PA: Trinity Press International, 2001). Yet all would surely bridle at the suggestion that a Pax Americana is a part of this development— a suggestion only being contemplated as one possible outcome of the recent conflict in Iraq and the fading of the United Nations as an international center for peacemaking or peacekeeping. If this is a likely eventuality, it is surely necessary for theologians and theological ethicists to engage the issues of what kind of civilization ought to be cultivated. It seems clear that the present national leadership does not have a clear or compelling theology of history or of governance to guide it.

8. Peter van der Veer recognized the problems more than a decade ago. See his *Religious Nationalism: Hindus and Muslims in India* (Berkeley: University of California Press, 1992). More recently, Mark Juergensmeyer has extended his earlier work on this topic also: *Terror in the Mind of God: The Global Rise of Religious Violence* (Berkeley: University of California Press, 2000). See also Robin Wright, *Sacred Rage* (New York: Simon & Schuster, 2001).

and "powerful" parts of the world. These movements are likely to fail, for they often want to adopt the benefits of these powers without accepting the metaphysical and moral assumptions on which the powers rest. Their own faiths are unable to accommodate to the residual theological core of these globalizing forces without changing those societies, the religions, and the personal convictions they want to preserve. The expected failure of these movements, however, is not likely to be because they are religious, as naturalists and humanists argue. Instead, they will likely fail because they do not recognize the primary discipline for the critical and self-critical examination of religious claims and ethical practices that determine the commonalities and goods they seek—theology. While only God can preserve the common life, theology offers the form of intellectual activity that also guides the will and provides the conscious critique of and the reconstructive ethic for social and political life. This position is no less true today than it ever was: We cannot define either what is common or what is good without God. Natural reason and voluntary agreement by themselves cannot get the common good right.

A Sociopolitical Hypothesis

A basic theological tenant is that all humanity is made in the image of God, and that we, by the common grace of creation, are enabled to participate in the formation and maintenance of the modules of ordered interaction that we call institutions. These modules are inevitably clustered into various spheres of life to preserve and enhance our common well-being. If so, we shall have to acknowledge that individuals and the various spheres of life pursue differing combinations of material, social, and moral goods. For as long as we can trace in history, these have been ordered into a pluralism of relatively stable cultures, ethnic groups, and religions. But what is distinctive about our contemporary condition is the recognition that these spheres can be multiplied. In fact, the idea that it is a good thing to form new institutions and constantly reform the various spheres of life is a primary mark of what sociologists call "differentiation"—a (if not the) distinctive feature of modern societies, in contrast to traditional ones. That differentiation has allowed various kinds of specialization of function and demanded the development of more highly differentiated personalities able to interact in more complex social settings.

Under conditions of globalization, such development is an increasing threat to traditional cultures, peoples, and religions. Now—except at one point, as we shall see—the decisive pluralism of modern life is not the clash of cultures, an awareness of ethnic difference, or even a pluralism of contending religions. Rather, it is a pluralism of social institutions, each pursuing its own end with no overarching vision of the common good. And this includes the sphere of politics, which for centuries has ordered the other institutions and spheres within a specific geographical territory.

Any realistic analysis of the various institutions of the common life also reveals that no one of these institutional spheres of life is capable of manifesting the common good unless it is formed into a community of commitment. Such a community would seek not only its own good but also federate with other institutional spheres to form a network of communities committed to a wider justice. It would allow for the freedom of other communities and spheres to cultivate their own good within an open vision of the whole. What accounts for this incapacity of each sphere, and what could overcome it? Certain strands of the Christian theological tradition have an account of these matters that may be decisive for the future. They hold that our fallen nature inclines us to pursue a competitive advantage over other persons and groups. A collective selfishness haunts every effort to cultivate the common good. But they also hold that, in spite of our sinfulness, what is "written on our hearts" is the residual knowledge that there are standards and purposes that stand over us all, even if they are not always clear to the natural capacities for reason. Still, they allow us to recognize that it is right and good to be called into covenanted communities of commitment, discipline, excellence, and responsibility. In federated dialogue and debate about these standards and purposes, we can recognize a "higher law" that is able to order our various pursuits of various goods in ways that our own efforts could not accomplish.

Further, it is one of the chief insights of the biblical tradition that a confederation of covenantal spheres and institutions—coupled with a recognition of the variety of ways these are formed among the multiple settings in life—enhances a "principled pluralism" for patterns of life that can generate a plethora of ends and goods.[9] Each within itself will have hierarchical and subsidiary elements. But even these will have to be subject to a more universal law than it can manifest or mediate and an acceptance of the fact that we are bound by God to purposes and people we do not chose.[10] Our wills are real but not sovereign. Covenantal possibilities are God-initiated and -sustained; they invite us to concrete embodiments of the laws, ends, and mercies that allow life to flourish in a community of communities. Insofar as they are "natural," they are in fact "creational," for they point to the Creator beyond what is natural, and what is natural is temporally created and subject to temporal transformation. Insofar as they are human agreements, they depend upon a "graced" consent to a partially common, but also distinctively particular, institutionalized community of commitment or sphere of such communities. The covenantal possibilities point to more ultimate goods that transcend what is possible in ordinary life, common goods that this tradition claims were inaugurated by Christ, who renewed the divine covenant for all humanity and pointed life toward a new future.

---

9. I am deeply indebted to the masterwork of Daniel Elazar, *The Covenant Tradition in Politics* (4 vols.; New Brunswick, NJ: Transaction, 1995–98).

10. When I state the matter in this way, I intend to notify any reader of my position. I think that the hierarchical-subsidiary model has validity and must be accepted as part of the whole orthodox, catholic, and ecumenical tradition. It is theologically best represented in classical Roman Catholic theology (with parallels to aspects of Confucian and Hindu theory, as I have argued elsewhere). Yet I think that model must finally be subordinated to a federal-covenantal model, best represented in Reformed theology (with parallels to features of ancient amphictyonic intertribal or feudal traditions and to modern associational theories of civil society, as I have also argued elsewhere).

The goods of these pluralistic, covenanted centers of principle, purpose, and practice do not easily converge and cannot be forced into any single model of the good in history without risking an increased centralization of coercive power. Yet previous hierarchical-imperial ages, more recent forms of bureaucratic statism, and current neoimperialist actions have shown the centralization of power to be the source of great social and ethical disaster. At the same time, each sphere, each institution within a sphere, and each person within each institution must acknowledge that all parts of the social system are tainted with the temptation to self-aggrandizement and rebellion against others. Thus, an ordered political government is required to secure the relative peace possible in history. But that political order is never competent enough to control the whole complex of activities that must be managed by individuals, associations, independent institutions, corporations, and federated spheres below and beyond the government itself. None of these modules of human commonality and potential good, including every political unit, last forever or can achieve the perfection of the good. Like persons, they become unstable, less focused, and less productive over time unless they are renewed by a spiritual power beyond themselves. Like cells in an organ, or parts in a machine, they die, break down, or come to an end. With spiritually renewed purposes, however, they can form new covenants or renew their older ones, generating new units, including new varieties of institutions and spheres. And our participation in these modules in quest of a just law to order their ever-changing interaction invites us to cultivate an ever richer array of personal and group potentiality. It points to a larger hope given by God for an expanded integrity and fulfillment beyond history, even if they are not able, together or individually, to bring the fullness of the common good within history.

This view, deeply associated with theories of a principled, pluralistic civil society and with concepts of a "free" society, does not presume that the goods of the various spheres of life all point in an obvious single direction any more than the contracted interests of persons do. Nor should they incline us to a solidarity of purpose in all areas of life. People have repeatedly failed to recognize the pluralism of spheres in society and attempted to establish a society dedicated to a single definition of the common good, sometimes religiously blessed, but usually based in naturalistic or voluntaristic orientations. Such strategy has been the chief source of the utopian and totalitarian efforts that have brought so much misery and death in recent centuries. These experiments have not only damaged hopes for a common good; they have also destroyed many of the common's goods, as rubble found in ecological ruins shows.[11]

We should surely take into account the fact that historic attempts to define the common good are most active in two processes. One is when a people's old traditions

---

11. See Charles Erasmus, *In Search of the Common Good: Utopian Experiments Past and Future* (Glencoe: Free Press, 1977). The older work by Norman Cohn remains highly relevant: *The Pursuit of the Millennium: Revolutionary Messianism in Medieval and Reformation Europe and Its Bearing on Modern Totalitarian Movements* (New York: Harper & Row, 1961).

and social order break down, usually because the influences of more complex civilizations are threatening their ways of life, and they cannot adjust to the new ones. The definitions of common good then are calls to retreat to the wondrous ways of the romanticized elders. The other is during the formation of a new collectivity, when new models are unclear. Historic examples include the transition from a hearth culture to the ancient polis, then from local city-states to the imperial city, from collapsed imperialism to a feudal society, and from that to the modern system of nation-states that we call the international community. Such transitions in the past were superseded by more encompassing and simultaneously diversified civilizations, usually brought about with considerable turmoil and suffering. Now, in turn, these historic models are being superseded by the prospects of a more encompassing global civil society, powered by modes of technological, communication, and economic organization, a global society with no political governing system. In such a context, every effort to identify and actualize the common good of some nation or class, some profession or independent sphere of human activity, without reference to the global state of affairs, will tend to render a romantic or a utopian program. And, if we try to organize the whole politically, we may well end up with but another arrogant imperial or theocratic system.[12]

Decisive in constructing an alternative is the reality of religion. Historically, the great world religions have supplied the metaphysical-moral visions that have woven the diversity of spheres present in complex cultures and the hopes of persons into comprehending visions of what is common and what is good for humanity. Yet the religions have recognized that the common good cannot be fully attained in this life. The great syntheses not only offered a portrait of the transcending reality; they also formed the inner moral architecture of the historic civilizations. These religions have, in other words, generated a profound and guiding sense of what the righteous order of things ought to be and what the good ends to be pursued should be. All are now being tested to see if they can cope with globalizing forces, with all the options brought to every part of the world by migration flows, media, travel, education, and missionary work. While it is clear that the religions and the cultures stamped by the great faiths have many things in common, they seldom have the same ultimate vision of the common good. Thus, we must find ways of engaging in the comparative evaluation of the world religions. That is where the issue of the common good in relationship to multiple definitions of what is common and what is good will find its knottiest problems. In short, this will require a public theology, one that must seek to operate in a much wider public than has been the case before. We will see that there are some areas of philosophically and theologically discerned ethics, especially deontological ones, where there are possibilities of overlapping consensus. There are other

---

12. In my attempt to draw attention to this issue in this essay, I draw freely from several previous efforts, especially here from *God and Globalization*, vol. 3, *Christ and the Dominions of Civilization* (ed. Max L. Stackhouse with Diane Obenchain; Harrisburg: Trinity Press International, 2002); and from my *Covenant and Commitments: Faith, Family, and Economic Life* (Louisville: Westminster John Knox, 1997).

areas, essentially ethological ones, which allow us to recognize comparative similarities and differences in the ways that complex societies are characteristically
organized, and to assess pragmatically those in need of expanded possibilities. And
there are still others, primarily teleological ones, that prompt us to point out differences that are not resolvable in any foreseeable period of history. Yet precisely
these differences will force us to make choices between our proximate ends because
they are variously shaped by visions of the ultimate end—eschatologies.

It is in interaction with other world faiths on the issue of eschatological
thought that the most difficult issues of the common good come to focus. This is
necessary because of how we live in a much expanded understanding of what is
common, and because the world faiths have distinctive views of what is ultimately
good and how that ultimate good is to be anticipated by or related to life in the
here and now. If the theologies of these world faiths are articulate, they will state
in one way or another the implications of the uncommon goods of their eschatology. This would be not only for persons, but also for the institutions and spheres
of society, which partially overlap with those of other traditions, and for the ways
their faith is inclined to interpret and apply their sense of the universal moral law,
which they share with other traditions.

Common and Uncommon Goods

One way of understanding the issues, perhaps the most pervasive way in contemporary thought, is represented by the recent work of Diane Obenchain. In a substantive article,[13] she accents the variety and multiformity that appear in historic
religious and cultural traditions. She views these traditions as secondary to the
common, ultimately universal, human effort to point to, identify, acknowledge, or
discover a relationship to the transcendent ultimate reality that each seeks to discern beyond what is empirical. The "more than meets the eye" is everywhere present to the sensitive soul. She is aware that this approach has come under periodic
attack for speaking of "religion-in-general," as if some form of spiritual Esperanto
exists.[14] But in a bold move, she challenges such critics to recognize how much the
Enlightenment view of transcendental reason depends on the Christian belief in
a transcendent God whose moral laws could be known, in principle, by all. This
matter is not always acknowledged, and it is sometimes obscured or denied by
religious authorities of traditions that have been challenged by the Enlightenment

---

13. Diane Obenchain, "The Study of Religion and the Coming Global
Generation," in *Christ and the Dominions of Civilization* (ed. Stackhouse and
Obenchain), 59–109.

14. A sharp rebuke to the emerging pluralist school of thought was recently set
forth by Cardinal Ratzinger, head of the Congregation for Doctrine of the Faith in
the Vatican. *Dominus Iesus*, a statement approved by the pope and issued on August
6, 2000, severely criticized the tendency to downplay distinctive Christian doctrines
and the exclusive particularity of Jesus Christ as taught by the Roman Catholic
Church (http://www.vatican.va/roman_curia/congregations/cfaith/documents/
rc_con_cfaith_doc_20000806_dominus-iesus_en.html).

to make a believable case for what they hold or stop setting it forth as universally valid. She demands a recognition that the Enlightenment, which expanded the quest for a more universal understanding of reality than many confessional theologies allowed, derived from nowhere else than those strands of Christian faith that gave rise to modern "Liberalism."

Her understanding of this relationship is compelling and has extensive implications for the understanding of the world religions. It helps account for the fact that we can recognize the integrity of another person's or another people's convictions, even if we find some of their beliefs strange and unbelievable for ourselves. It opens the way to mutual understanding, tolerance, and the acceptance of difference, in part because it recognizes that behind the difference is a human "faithing," a genuinely universal human phenomenon. Human "faithing" suggests a common knowledge that we are all related to a transcendent reality, which no one knows perfectly. Indeed, this view suggests a certain sadness with regard to those who claim that they have no such faith or no sense that there is or could be such a common, ultimate reality beyond the sensible world. It understands people who cannot grasp what all this "religious stuff" is about (in any tradition) as persons similar religiously to those who are tone deaf and thus cannot appreciate music, or color-blind and see all as gray, or frigid and can find no joy in sexuality. They see the world as flat in a moral and spiritual sense, as confined to a narrow range of human emotion and thought.

Thus, to put it another way, schools of thought that are not flat see both the profound humanity involved in, and ultimately the human-transcending ground of, highly pluralistic and diverse religious experience, even if they do not accent, or even approve of, particular theological systems or dogmatic, exclusive claims. On these grounds it would be quite possible to seek out and give priority to the general principles that seem to be universal in character, and to articulate why every great world tradition has a set of first principles much like those which Jews and Christians know as the Ten Commandments. Certain deontological principles of right and wrong—such as those also accented by philosophers of the Enlightenment: Locke's "self-evident truths" or Kant's "categorical imperatives"—are also honored by this kind of thought. Even more, this perspective leads to a sense of humility in the face of the "other," and to a willingness to dialogue with, learn from, and live in peace with those who believe differently and express their faith in distinctive rituals. Such a perspective implies a deep presumption of common human logic that, behind our differences, stands alongside faith. It also implies an eagerness to share what is held to be true, with the presumption that it can be and should be understood and tolerated even by those who do not share a particular faith.

In such approaches, we find a metaphysical, moral, reasonable, and finally theological view, systematically neglected or rejected in contemporary academia, that an unacknowledged foundation stands behind "secular" life and thought. This foundation entails a specific religious and ethical conviction that requires overt and systematic acknowledgment. Behind the interpretive attempt to recognize the formal validity of the truth-claims and the ethical sensibilities of the other religions is the profound presupposition that a basic, ultimate structure of meaning stands behind many differences. It can be experienced in pluralistic ways, is susceptible to reasonable discourse between culturally divided peoples, and can sustain dialogical efforts to find coherent, loving, and integrative ways of living together. All the various faiths may participate in, contribute to, and become fulfilled by the recognition of this reality.

But more, Obenchain holds that Christians rightly understand that this deep Logos is Christ, the one in whom Logos became incarnate and present to human experience. Christians can thus both contribute to the fuller understanding of its nature and seek to learn more about their own faith by studying the many manifestations of that Logos as it appears in other traditions.[15] It is not "religion" as a set of abstract doctrines that serves as a genus of which the various traditions are species. Instead, each of the great religious traditions is an expression of the Logos, to which all humans have access in principle. By that Logos it is possible for us all to understand one another. With the Logos all seek to relate in a variety of "religious" ways (including how they organize their societies). And the Logos becomes historically actual in Christ.

A quite different view of the religions arises, however, if we ask how, concretely, particular religions influence the various spheres of life in civil society, establish an ethos with legitimated common meanings, and thus potentially form or legitimate a civilization. These are vital questions in our global era. When we look at the religions with this question in mind, we see the reassertion of specific religions as political and cultural forces, with emphatic attempts to establish, or reestablish, societies based on particular religious traditions. Indeed, in parts of Africa, Latin America, northeast India, and the Pacific Islands, those rooted in traditional "primal" religions are attempting to gain their autonomy, after having been swept into artificially created nation-states by colonial governments. Moreover, resurgent Islam from the Middle East to Malaysia and Indonesia, Hindu nationalism in India, and Buddhist-sanctioned militance in Sri Lanka and Burma—all are evidence of a new particularism that seems also to accompany our era.

Thus, we turn to a second response to the religions, one that accents the differences between them. We usually do not appreciate the fact that certain strands of Christian theology shaped modernity, and now globalization, more fully than any of the other traditions. Several are critical of everything modern or Western and opposed to anything global. We face this unavoidable fact when modern, Western, differentiated patterns of life encounter other heritages that also have shaped civilizations and had their own impact on human history. Perhaps we can find points of convergence and contact at general transcendental and ethical levels.

---

15. It is this factor that allowed both the early Jesuit missionaries and the later Enlightenment philosophers to recognize profound similarities of Confucianism with their own predispositions to endorse "natural law" arguments and to develop concepts of "natural theology," even if it sometimes meant exaggerating convergences. See Lionel M. Jensen's remarkable, if controversial, *Manufacturing Confucianism: Chinese Traditions and Universal Civilization* (Durham, NC: Duke University Press, 1997).

But we also have to acknowledge that we have not found agreement on an enormous number of decisive social, political, and economic questions, and we are unlikely to find it soon.

Moreover, when we encounter other traditions concretely, it becomes clear that the institutional forms of life organized on the basis of differing faiths do not easily blend into a single pattern. If we are to interact with other societies, we shall have to see how primal religious myths, Confucian wisdom, Hindu devotion, Buddhist teachings, and Islamic revelations work out their implications in the various spheres of society. Indeed, we may find that some traditions are only awkwardly able to allow or to engage the patterns and dynamics of globalization. Several, indeed, are likely to contribute to the forces of resistance against globalization, running the risk of either being crushed or forced to modulate their own faith tradition if they chose to enter the discussion about our common future. A religion holding that "according to our sacred tradition, we are all one, and we all must share what we have equally" differs from a view holding that "all of the cosmos and all rightly ordered societies are stratified according to a divine plan."

Thus, when we turn from certain universalistic aspects of human "faithing" and deontological principles in ethics, we find that we must recognize partially overlapping diversity in the ethos of the cultures shaped by different religions. We can, for example, recognize that Jewish, Christian, Hindu, Buddhist, Confucian, and Islamic traditions all have a sense of the sacred duties of family life. Each tradition can recognize the realities of love and fidelity between husband and wife and parents and children in the other traditions. Yet each tradition structures the family differently. Indeed, contemporary social scientists and political theorists, including those who train diplomats and political leaders, are increasingly acknowledging that religions functionally have material correlations. They are modulating older models of understanding that focused more on material interests than on material implications of religious convictions.

In a very critical essay,[16] Scott Thomas shows that many specialists in these areas are beginning to recognize how much, directly or indirectly, religious claims, religious behaviors, and religious institutions continue to influence public affairs with shocking vigor. It is shocking at least to those who think of themselves as having surpassed that more "primitive" (or "medieval") stage of "mythical" speculation. Moreover, morally concerned Westerners and indigenous leaders of the "underdeveloped" regions of the world are seeking to extend the alleged benefits of modern, Western ways of organizing the spheres of life—democratic government, human rights, access to technology, efficient economic productivity, reliable medical care, and so on. In so seeking, they find that the capabilities of cultures to adopt and adapt these possibilities, or the inclinations to resist them as too

---

16. Scott Thomas, "The Global Resurgence of Religion and the Changing Character of International Politics," in *Christ and the Dominions of Civilization* (ed. Stackhouse and Obenchain), 110–38. He has developed these themes further in *The Global Resurgence of Religion and the Transformation of International Relations* (New York: Palgrave Macmillan, 2005).

socially "dehumanizing," depends on religious factors. Some foment an ethos that allows relatively easy adoption of these values; others foment resistance or are overwhelmed by the changes when they try to adapt to them.[17]

Thus, while we must recognize the commonality of all religions in certain respects, we must simultaneously recognize the different social implications that various religions and cultural traditions based on these religions have legitimated. At the level of, say, international diplomacy or development economics—not to mention missionary and relief work—it is quite clear that particularity and distinctiveness characterize each of the traditions. Each has its own social expectations and set of loyalties that tend to bend the society toward some polities and policies and away from others, and it becomes the responsibility of those who are engaged in work with people in these traditions to do so on their own terms. A kind of technology of religious adaptation becomes necessary. In fact, almost all of us who have seriously encountered other religions accept a pluralism of traditions functionally, without overtly judging the reality and influence of religious claims other than our own, even if we think them to be quite wrong. Failure to accept the functional validity and moral equivalence of incompatible religious orientations would be to risk perpetual conflict, resistance, and possible disaster.

The recognition of certain forms of universality at one level of religious and ethical reality and of other patterns of diversity and pluralism at another, however, still leaves open the question of any common good. One way of solving this issue is posed by Paul Knitter and his many allies. They not only display great sympathy for positions such as Obenchain's, they also recognize the concrete pluralism in social formation that is implied by the various traditions, as recognized by Scott Thomas. Knitter is one of the leaders of those who link the universalistic, Enlightenment-approving "logos" view of "pluralistic inclusivism" with a concrete sociopolitical postmodern recognition of "pluralistic diversity" of particular religions.[18] He does this by establishing a single teleological standard of the common good. On this ground, every religion, theology, worldview, or cultural practice is to be assessed. That standard is "liberation," a process that seeks to overcome poverty and suffering by bringing those who are marginalized, oppressed, or exploited to a condition of empowerment. There they, as persons and as social groups of which they are a part (class, race, caste, or sex), may find the freedom to be their own

---

17. See Lawrence Harrison and Samuel Huntington, *Culture Matters* (New York: Basic Books, 2001).

18. See Paul F. Knitter and John Hick, eds., *The Myth of Christian Uniqueness: Toward a Pluralistic Theology of Religions* (Maryknoll, NY: Orbis Books, 1987); as well as Paul Knitter's justly influential *No Other Name? A Critical Survey of Christian Attitudes toward the World Religions* (Maryknoll, NY: Orbis Books, 1985); idem, *One Earth, Many Religions: Multifaith Dialogue and Global Responsibility* (Maryknoll, NY: Orbis Books, 1995); and idem, *Jesus and Other Names: Christian Mission and Global Responsibility* (Maryknoll, NY: Orbis Books, 1996). Critiques of this view can be found in Gabriel Fackre, Ronald H. Nash, and John Sanders, *What about Those Who Have Never Heard?* (Downers Grove, IL: InterVarsity, 1995).

agents, their own subjects. This, indeed, is a standard of the common good shared today by many contemporary Christians, as well as by many secular activists, journalists and philosophers.

None of the world's religions want systematic injustice to be perpetrated, and all would approve of efforts to overcome human distress. But they disagree as to what is the source of the distress that needs to be overcome and what is able to overcome it. They all suspect that Knitter's account of the deepest nature of the distress and of what can provide remedy is a version of what modern, Western social-psychology has developed as a model of the ideal self in a perfect classless society. His diagnosis and prescription turns out to be less universal than he thinks. As one of his sharpest critics, Mark Heim, has argued, if we take Knitter's criterion (liberation as the defining norm for pluralistic inclusivism and diversity) as the only one, it would establish a single social view of salvation as a kind of political religion in itself. By this view all other religions and other claims about truth, justice, the human condition, law, and purpose in life would be evaluated. Here is a singular and thin view of the common good, one that has become a set of slogans in many contemporary religious circles. But this view of salvation implies that the fundamental sin from which humanity needs to be saved is a socially created one, amenable to a social solution. The view is dishonest insofar as it claims to allow pluralism, while it denies the pluralism it claims to affirm in that it dismisses any other orientation that does not agree that liberation and the maximization of freedom and equality is the end of all existence.[19]

In fact, several religious traditions are suspicious of the implications of this view. It not only manifests an unwarranted confidence in unfettered human freedom; it also makes equality the decisive regulative principle of justice. Further, it fails to recognize that those who are to be liberated are usually group-identified—a class, a race, or a gender. It also presumes that the liberation of a group guarantees the liberation of the individuals in it, as if the herd's identity has swallowed their personal identity. Moreover, the gaining of a desired autonomy is set as the ideal good; every autonomous lifestyle and way of life should be equally regarded. But the view presumes that these and only these political effects of a religion are its most important features.[20] Are these the ultimate purposes of a valid faith, and are these the first principles of life? This view does not seem to be at all respectful of the world religions. Does this not, in fact, fundamentally set them all aside unless they meet this one test?

---

19. S. Mark Heim, *Salvations: Truth and Difference in Religion* (Maryknoll, NY: Orbis Books, 1999), esp. ch. 2.

20. It is widely held that this view (pluralistic inclusivism and diversity of religions based on a liberationist perspective) was part of the target of the Vatican statement *Dominus Iesus* (2002). A quite different, but finally not incompatible critique of this view can be found in my *Christian Social Ethics in a Global Era* (Nashville: Abingdon, 1995), in dialogue with contributions from Peter Berger, Dennis McCann, and Douglas Meeks. This study attempted to clear the ground for further reflection on our situation.

The reason why the religions differ from this liberationist view and from each other is that they have different assessments of why life in this world is fraught with so much difficulty and distress, conflict and care, disease and death, terror and tragedy. The unity that religions have in "faithing," and by their faiths seeking to point to what is transcendent, brings an awareness that there are other standards, norms, and ideals that ought to govern life rather than the ones that often do govern it. And as has been argued, they may have common or at least quite similar knowledge of what ought to be universally binding with regard to moral laws: Humans ought to honor what is truly holy and respect just authority. They ought not murder, rape, torture, deceive, exploit, or bring wanton harm to other humans, to society at large, or to the biophysical universe that sustains life. Thus, the religions know that some things are wrong and that it is right to form character and social institutions that will avoid these wrongs. In these respects, there are "universal absolutes" about which religions, together, can remind wayward humanity. Yet, the religions differently explain why it is that humans are inclined to do these things and what it takes to overcome that inclination.

It is the key insight of Mark Heim, whose work is now under lively discussion, that religions and philosophies fundamentally differ as to what it is that we need to be "saved" from, and hence they promise different "salvations." He claims that each religion does actually recognize a fundamental problem as serious, and that each is authentic insofar as it does deliver on what it promises to do to relieve humanity from this problem. Let me restate his argument: If the underlying difficulty of human existence is that we break community with our ancestral way and its harmony with nature and thus lose our identity, we must recover and enter into the spirituality of the primal religions of our forebears. That is how we can find and actuate the common good of that tribal people of which we are a part. If the fundamental problem of the human condition is that we are too much attached to the things of the world, Buddhism can offer a way of becoming detached and overcome the common malaise of life. Or if we have not rightly obeyed the apodictic laws of God as delivered to humanity through the prophets, orthodox Judaism and Islam offer patterns of life that could well tell us how to find a more perfect obedience by righteous deeds and spiritual-intellectual submission. And so on through the other great traditions.

However, the most important insight that his argument advances is that we are forced into a new level of discussion between religions: What is the fundamental reality that inhibits the common good, and what has, does, can, or could overcome it?

The Most Common Uncommon Good

When Christians think about the good toward which all should aim, we think first of the messianic expectation present in the prophetic visions of the Hebrew Scriptures, and of the Christian conviction that the messianic age has begun in the life, death, and resurrection of Christ. In these, the kingdom of God was inaugurated, and it is already active within us and among us in a cosmic history that points to the New Jerusalem that is to come to us from the other side of the end of history. To hold such views is to deny the contemporary claim that there is no universal metanarrative that can be known by humans. In fact, the eyes of faith see, and hold that all discerning humans can recognize that each one of these motifs has special meaning for understanding the nature and character of the common good. The messianic expectation continues to be a theme that Christians share with Jews. Christians, of course, hold that the Messiah has come in Jesus Christ, yet the expectation is not completely fulfilled. Thus, when Christians speak about Christ coming again, they continue, as do the Jews, to be people of hope. As a Christian, one cannot turn to any particular moment in the past—creation, Sinai, even the incarnation or the resurrection—and say that all truth, knowledge, grace, and justice has been given. We always live in history with the utopia- and illusion-shattering recognition that all that we have that is good is but prologue, and that only in the ultimate future will we know final truth, and with it, true judgment and mercy.[21]

As H. Richard Niebuhr pointed out two generations ago, the motif of the kingdom of God, the dominating idea of Jesus' ministry as reported in the New Testament, has three fundamental dimensions.[22] By determining which one or which combination of these dimensions is being used at particular points, we could sort many biblical images of this idea and also every compelling philosophy of world history.

The first dimension is the sovereign reign of God over the public affairs of humanity. This bears the implication that there is a universal moral order that can be well enough known to write constitutions of relative justice for the ordering of the common life. With the renewal of the primal covenant in Jesus Christ, Christians have become more aware of this sovereignty of God. The wider world acknowledges that this was a turning point in universal history every time they refer to A.D. or C.E. The God who is creator of, lawgiver for, and providential sustainer of the world can be known more clearly when the Messiah is manifest.

The second dimension is the quite personal reign of Christ in the hearts of the believer. This carries with it a renewed capacity to find faith and hope, to love the neighbor, to engage in sacrificial acts for others, and to recognize that novelty is introduced as a factor in historical existence. We cannot find the meaning of life in the constancy of order, although order remains an inevitable and perennial reality at a profound level, in spite of disruption and distortion at the less ultimate

---

21. In his masterwork, Reinhold Niebuhr recognized this commonality between Jews and Christians and simultaneously identified the areas where differences remained. See his *The Nature and Destiny of Man*, vol. 2 (New York: Charles Scribner's Sons, 1943), esp. 6–34, sections "Where a Christ Is Not Expected" and "Where Christ Is Expected" in ch. 1. The differences are identified especially in ch. 2.

22. See H. Richard Niebuhr, *The Kingdom of God in America* (Chicago: Willett, Clark & Co., 1937; New York: Harper & Brothers, 1959). It is a mistake to see this only as an American view. Although he draws his key examples from the American theological tradition, he clearly holds that the three dimensions of the kingdom that he spells out are parts of the very structure of the idea.

level of existence. Without order, neither being or science would be possible. Nor can we find the meaning of life in the cycles of nature, although they do recur; nor can we find it in a singular logic of history that infinitely repeats the same dynamic interaction of factors. But we can find the meaning of life in the recognition that new realities can and have been introduced into time, and that one of them is paradigmatically of world-historical significance and is repeatedly capable of renewing the inner personal life of persons.

The third dimension is the expectation of the coming kingdom, a dynamic that breaks into time from beyond time and presses prophetically toward the overcoming of injustices and meaninglessness that beset our understanding of everything that dies and is temporal. The kingdom, already at work within and among us, points toward a New Jerusalem, a fulfilled and transformed city of the nations that is not yet and nevertheless invites us to live toward it. But we cannot attain this transformed city of and for the nations by even the best human act. This is the best good, the most uncommon good, and ultimately the only common good that can integrate all lesser goods. It is entirely a matter of God's doing.

Christians believe that the kingdom in its first two dimensions is made vibrantly present in the life, death, and resurrection of Christ, although we do not know with much precision what life in any other state would be. It is a hope-full assurance that decay, dust, and ashes is not the final chapter of human existence. Although these are indisputably real, and the end to which all come, they are not the telos of life. Moreover, the motif of the kingdom indicates that under God's rule, neither the church nor the many spheres of civilized life wherein the kingdom is active are empty of promise. However bleak the social situation looks at any given point in history, God allows these fragile reeds of social arrangement to bear the weight of promising possibilities in the midst of disconfirming evidence. Marriages may fail, but families continue. Governments fall, but new ones develop. Economic systems collapse, but alternatives emerge. Cultures are subjugated, but the artistry of their existence leaves indelible traces. Schools teach badly, but students learn. Hospitals do not cure, but compassion heals. Indeed, religions rise and fall, and many have died, but elements of those traditions are carried into renewed faith. Insofar as a constant reconstructive dynamic is directed toward discovering or recovering a God-oriented sense of principle and purpose, traces of the kingdom of God can be, more or less, discerned in the midst of the actual fragile structure of being and in the sinful and distorted events of history. Those able to discern these traces are called to be its agents in this life, in every sphere of existence.

Yet neither the personal trust in the resurrection promise, nor the discernments of the kingdom, even if acted upon with humility, courage and wisdom, can bring the ultimate good end. As one distinctive characteristic, Christianity does not hold that getting personal faith right or doing things right in the social contexts of this life can guarantee us of fulfillment of either our own best hopes or the most ultimate common good. It cannot even guarantee establishing the proximate common good of any given institution, spheres in history, or system of such spheres. A discontinuity, an eschatological break, even an apocalyptic gap stands between the very best we can imagine or do and the fulfillment of the divine purpose for all. Such things can only be grasped in symbolic terms; they are beyond the scope of ordinary personal or social programs and projections. In this regard, all the projects for personal or social betterment, captured in the concern for the common good, are put into another perspective.

Thus, we hold that the vision of the ultimate end—signaled in an anticipatory way by the resurrection and glimpsed in the gains that can be made in history as we discern and seek to actuate the kingdom of God in our common life—depends on something that is a radically uncommon good: a gift of grace that changes all. That is what allows us to live toward death without despair, and that is what empowers us to celebrate in society the modest gains possible as we seek to actuate a little more justice in our civil societies and a little more love in our hearts. It is also what demands that we do not overestimate our own heroism in dying well and do not hold that our societies, even the very best of them, can form the common good by good living. Should we face the prospect of death personally with confidence? Should we ask, "Death, where is thy sting?" Certainly, but we cannot do it without graced faith. Should we be active in seeking to restrain evil and establish that little more justice in the institutions of the civilizations of which we are a part? Certainly, but we dare not think that we can define the common good by teaching virtue or by political or military mobilization. We must recognize the temptation to self-celebration in our wanting to live beyond death or in making the limited range of our own soul or society the center of civilization.

The final good is deeper and more ultimate than any personal cultivation of virtue or any sociopolitical loyalty. Consider, for example, the words of the final chorus of the classic requiem mass as summarizing the elements of the ultimate good. After judgment and remorseful tears of repentance, we hear:

> May angels lead you to paradise.
> May the martyrs greet you at your coming
> and lead you to the holy city, Jerusalem.
> May the angelic choir receive you,
> and with Lazarus, once a beggar,
> may you find eternal peace.

This is a compressed version of the last few chapters of the book of Revelation. It has echoes of promise that this is also the fulfillment of the inbreaking of a promised future begun in the life, ministry, parables, death and resurrection of Jesus. The scene draws our attention to each particular person, for each one is of worth, although each will know defeat and death, with their inevitable loneliness. It points beyond the collapse of the hope that all that one wanted to be and do on earth is brought to the void. Still, persons are lovingly led by unseen powers to another kind of realm and welcomed into a communion of saints by those who have been persecuted for their faithfulness and righteousness. The lyric envisages another kind of companionship than envisaged in any national purpose or any progressive program.

Moreover, this paradise is not a return to Eden, and neither is it a recovery of some dreaming, primal innocence or an attained bliss of no-thing-ness. It is not the absorption of the personal soul into a cosmic oversoul, nor is it a rejoining of spirits with the departed ancestral elders. There is no sense of a tiny remnant of the select few who have proved their moral and spiritual merit. Indeed, there is no temple, no church, no politics except the Lamb who was slain and now on the throne. Rather, it is a gifted destiny that comes to us from another dimension as a complex civilization into which all the nations may bring their gifts. It is a city where engineered and artistically formed structures invite joyous exaltation in participatory cultural activity, where even the laws of nature are transformed so that trees bear fruit and healing leaves each month. There an exuberant spirit of holiness welcomes the least; even the most neglected beggar finds a just peace. It is the most uncommon, greatest good that has ever been imagined. To speak of it requires a theological imagination, one able to invite the global public to its portals.

The question, of course, can be asked as to what difference this eschatological vision makes to the question of how we organize the common life. The answer is, It makes all the difference in the world. The way we envision the ultimate and salvific possibilities for ourselves, humanity in general, and the biophysical universe impinges on our present and shapes our orientation to each sphere of life. The eschatological definition of redemption trumps and transforms every naturalist teleology or humanist contract or every hostile critique of culture. It thus reorders the decisive concept of what is common and what is good. We hold, with the classic tradition of Christianity, that the eschatological promise has already broken into the present and is both objectively as well as subjectively operating in the depths of history. Thus, we find that every believer is enabled to discern hints and glimmers of the fruits of the kingdom of God that is within and among us. Each is enabled to live toward the future with confidence in spite of the continued presence of sin and death. Each is enabled to accept a vocation to work in ways that point toward the new Jerusalem. Believers are graced to do all this with neither a utopian optimism nor a debilitating despair in reaction to sin and evil continuing to beguile the powers, principalities, authorities, and dominions that seek to lead humanity and history in entirely other directions.

In fact, faith allows us to seek to draw these powers too into covenantal relationships, so that they may serve the whole. It is the perennial function of government to establish just law and keep the peace. It best does this in a way that also beyond itself foments institutions able to preach and teach about truth, justice, and mercy. It is also the task of economic institutions to create wealth; those doing it best allow the support of families, educational, cultural, and charitable organizations without destroying the ecological order. The responsibilities of families, schools, hospitals, and especially religious organizations all differ. Nevertheless, they all pursue their own particular ends best if they too think beyond themselves and seek both to point toward the more ultimate ends of life and to acknowledge the alternative ends of other spheres of the common life.

Of course, all this theological sense of promise, with its inevitable discourse laden with symbol and poetic image, does not quite depend on "knowledge" in the

300 In Search of the Common Good

sense in which either the academic or the political community has confidence. To many people, the kinds of assurance that come from other sorts of evidence and insight seems much more secure; after all, to live toward an eschatological end is to live by hope, even by faith alone. That is, in part, because the evidence of what will ultimately happen in the future is not yet fully available, and a proper indeterminacy is required in our efforts to point toward the most promising possibilities. Intellectual, social, and political movements toward the common good—laden with elements of love, hope, and faith—have within them presumptions of what the good ends ought to be and yet are extremely difficult to prove by conventional means. Moreover, other religions, with which we now live, have other senses of what the chief problem is and what the ultimate end might be.

We may be able to argue, with good warrants, that the Christian tradition, when it has been faithful and dependent on this ultimate view, has helped to generate good aspects of technological orientations to life, economic development, democratic polity, and so on. We deem such aspects to be essential to the common good, and we notice when other traditions have functionally adopted them or want to adopt them.[23] But that is not a foregone argument, and some eschatological views are in fact strongly resistant to these developments. In any case, the "proof" that this vision and its fruits is or should be the vision of the common good for all is very difficult to offer. For that reason, other major aspects of moral discourse must be brought into play as we think about keeping an open prospect for such an ultimate vision to be discussed, to reveal new loci of operational promise in human affairs, or to be modified by new exposure to alternative perspectives.

Those other aspects of moral discourse are precisely a deontological understanding of moral law, embodied functionally today in international covenants of human rights. Such discourse includes an ethological analysis of dynamic social pluralism found in theories of sphere sovereignty and of subsidiarity as these bear on civil society. In brief, a serious discussion of the common good, from a theological-ethical point of view in our globalizing world, demands a recognition of the eschatological nature of the vision of the good for humanity. It demands universal standards of right and wrong and an operational pluralism to sustain dynamic openness to those possibilities. This is what theologically based perspectives have to offer to the world more than anything else.

---

23. See, for example, Lynn White Jr., *Medieval Technology and Social Change* (New York: Oxford University Press, 1962); R. J. Hooykaas, *Religion and the Rise of Modern Science* (Oxford: Clarendon, 1974); Eugene Klaaren, *The Religious Origins of Modern Science* (Grand Rapids: Eerdmans, 1977); John M. Staudenmeier, SJ, *Technology's Storytellers: Reweaving the Human Fabric* (Cambridge, MA: Society for the History of Technology and the MIT Press, 1985); David F. Noble, *The Religion of Technology* (New York: Knopf, 1998); and the discussions of these matters in *The Spirit and Modern Authorities* (Stackhouse and Browning). Parallel arguments can be found for economic development and political pluralism in, e.g., David Landis, *The Wealth and Poverty of Nations* (New York: W. W. Norton, 1999); and in my *Creeds, Society and Human Rights* (Grand Rapids: Eerdmans, 1985).

Killing for the Telephone Company

Why the Nation-State Is Not the Keeper of the Common Good

William T. Cavanaugh

The fact that Pope John Paul II and the American Catholic bishops spoke out so forcefully, clearly, and repeatedly against the preemptive war on Iraq launched in March 2003 has been a great embarrassment to some politically conservative American Catholics who were accustomed, they thought, to having the pope on their side. One of the primary ways of mitigating this embarrassment has been to cite the statement in the Catechism of the Catholic Church (2309) indicating that evaluation of just-war criteria "belongs to the prudential judgment of those who have responsibility for the common good." It is assumed that the state is responsible for promoting and protecting the common good; the Vatican's suggestions that legitimate action cannot be undertaken without the support of the United Nations are brushed aside. As a result, Weigel and Novak conclude that the opinions of the pope and bishops should be heard, but Catholics should defer to the authority of the president of the United States in deciding when a war is just and when it is not.[1]

In Christian social ethics the assumption is often made, with a minimum of examination, that the responsibility for promoting and protecting the common good falls to the state. In this paper I want to examine that assumption. All too often Christian social ethics begins from ahistorical and idealized assumptions about the state as protector and benefactor. They are ahistorical because they assume that the state has been with us since biblical times. The state, as Charles

---

1. George Weigel, "The Just War Case for the War," *America* 188, no. 11 (March 31, 2003): 7–10; and Michael Novak, "War to Topple Saddam Is a Moral Obligation," *The Times* (London), February 12, 2003.

Curran says, is "natural and necessary" and "based on creation."[2] It takes different forms—*polis* for Aristotle, *regimen principum* for Aquinas—but these different terms refer to the same essential reality; all historical forms of political community are conflated into the term "state."[3] These accounts are also idealized because they assume that society is prior to the state and broader than the state. Human society is represented as a pyramid: the family is at the base, other groups and associations are in the middle, and the state is at the top to coordinate and protect. The base has "ontological priority" to the state and calls forth the state to be at its service. Furthermore, "society is broader than the state and includes much more."[4] The state is just one limited part of society, but is established in nature with an important role to play: "The end or purpose of the state or government [is] the pursuit of the common good."[5]

What I find unhelpful about such accounts is the way that they float free from any empirical testing of their theses. Christian ethicists will commonly recognize that, in a sinful world, particular states always fall short of the ideal. Nevertheless, the ideal is presented not merely as a standard for Christian political practice but also as a statement of fact: the state in its essential form simply *is* that agency of society whose purpose it is to protect and promote the common good, even if particular states do not always live up to that responsibility. This conclusion is based on a series of assumptions of fact: that the state is natural and primordial, that society gives rise to the state and not vice versa, and that the state is one limited part of society. These assumptions of fact, however, are often made without any attempt to present historical evidence on their behalf.

This may be because such evidence is lacking. In this chapter I will examine the origins of the state and the state-society relationship according to those who study the historical record. I will argue that the above assumptions of fact are untenable in the face of the evidence. I will examine these three assumptions in order. First, unless one equivocates on the meaning of "state," the state is not natural, but a rather recent and artificial innovation in human political order. Second, the state gives rise to society, and not vice versa. Third, the state is not one limited part of society, but has in fact expanded and become fused with society. The primary burden of this essay is negative: in arguing these three points, I will attempt to present the case against seeing the state as the promoter and protector of the common good. Only in the conclusion will I make some brief comments on what this implies positively for Christian thinking and practice.

A preliminary comment is necessary: my analysis of the development and current condition of the state and nation-state is based on Western—that is, primarily Europe and the United States—models. The state and nation-state are

---

2. Charles E. Curran, *Catholic Social Teaching, 1891–Present: A Historical, Theological, and Ethical Analysis* (Washington: Georgetown University Press, 2002), 138–39.

3. Curran (ibid., 138) writes of the "state or political order" and the "state or the political community" as if they were simply interchangeable.

4. Ibid., 141–44.

5. Ibid., 144.

Western inventions. They have been exported to the rest of the world with varying degrees of success. In many Southern lands, the reality of the state and the sense of the nation are tenuous at best, and are mixed with other forms of political organization, such as tribal structures. Most of my examples are taken from the United States, though insofar as the nation-state has taken root elsewhere, similar dynamics can be seen in other contexts.

The State Is Not Natural, but Artificial

History of the Term

The word "state" is sometimes used loosely to refer to the political form through which a stable group of people is organized. Nomadic groups are usually the only kind of political community excluded from this definition, since it implies some form of geographical stability. The state is thus treated, as Engels says, as a necessary and ancient "product of society at a certain stage of development,"[6] and questions of, for example, "church and state" are perennial questions.[7] In more precise usage, however, "state" refers to a more limited development characteristic of modernity. The state emerged in Europe amid the late Renaissance and Reformation. As Bruce Porter puts it, "The state as we know it is a relatively new invention, originating in Europe between 1450 and 1650."[8] In this more precise sense the state is a political form based on the distinctly modern concept of sovereignty, which may be defined as "supreme authority within a territory."[9] As formulated by Bodin, Hobbes, and other lesser figures of the early modern period, the state claims *legitimate* authority—as opposed to mere coercion—a supreme authority that no lesser authorities within a recognized set of geographical borders may legitimately oppose. Sovereignty is a departure from earlier forms of governance in which people's political loyalties were based not necessarily on territoriality, but on feudal ties, kinship, religious, or tribal affiliation.[10] If a stranger committed a crime on someone else's land, it would be necessary to find out to whom he or she owed loyalty in order to know what law applied.

It is perfectly acceptable to use the term "state" in the looser sense, provided one is clear that it is not being used in the stricter sense. Confusion is produced when, as in the case of Curran (above), the two senses are intermingled. It should be made clear that, although political community may in some form be natural

---

6. Friedrich Engels, "The Origin of Family, Private Property, and State," in *The Marx-Engels Reader* (ed. Robert C. Tucker; 2d. ed.; New York: W. W. Norton, 1978), 752.

7. For example, Hugo Rahner, SJ, *Church and State in Early Christianity* (trans. Leo Donald Davis, SJ; San Francisco: Ignatius Press, 1992).

8. Bruce D. Porter, *War and the Rise of the State: The Military Foundations of Modern Politics* (New York: Free Press, 1994), 6.

9. Daniel Philpott, *Revolutions in Sovereignty* (Princeton, NJ: Princeton University Press, 2001), 16.

10. Ibid., 16–17.

and ancient, the sovereign state as we know it is not. One could claim that the modern state is just one more variation on the theme of the state, but that would be extremely misleading. In the first place, the term *status* began to appear in a political context only in the late fourteenth century, and until the sixteenth century it was used either to refer to the state of the ruler himself (*status principis* or *status regalis*) or to the current condition of the realm (*status regni*). The emphasis was on a personalized kind of rule embodied in the prince. Only in the sixteenth century does there arise the concept of an abstract "state" that is independent of both ruler and ruled. Machiavelli is a transitional figure in this regard, employing the term *stato* both to refer to the prince's powers and position, and to indicate an abstract apparatus above prince and people. By the mid-sixteenth century, the abstract usage had won out in French and English legal writing.[11]

In the second place, to treat the sovereign state as just one more variation on the ancient "state" is to misrepresent the radical nature of the modern state. As is often the case in the history of language, large etymological shifts followed profound changes in social organization. New vocabulary was needed to describe a radically new situation. To treat the modern state as simply a variation in the history of societies is to ignore the fact that there were no such things as societies in the sense of clearly bounded and unitary systems of interaction until the birth of the modern state. As Anthony Giddens says, traditional social systems are composed not of one society but many "societies." Hence, the modern unitary society that originated in Europe is highly exceptional.[12]

This brings us to the term "nation-state," which designates an even more recent development in the history of political organization. As the hyphen implies, the nation-state is the result of the fusion of the idea of the nation—a unitary system of shared cultural attributes—with the political apparatus of the state. Nations are most commonly united by some combination of shared ethnicity, language, or history, but nationality is not simply "natural" or "objective."

---

11. Quentin Skinner, *The Foundations of Modern Political Thought* (2 vols.; Cambridge: Cambridge University Press, 1978), 2:352–58.

12. Anthony Giddens, *The Nation-State and Violence* (Berkeley: University of California Press, 1987), 1–2, 52–53. Ernest Gellner discusses the transition from traditional social orders to unitary societies in terms of language: "In a traditional social order, the languages of the hunt, of harvesting, of various rituals, of the council room, of the kitchen or harem, all form autonomous systems: to conjoin statements drawn from these various disparate fields, to probe for inconsistencies between them, to try to unify them all, this would be a social solecism or worse, probably blasphemy or impiety, and the very endeavour would be unintelligible. By contrast, in our society it is assumed that all referential uses of language ultimately refer to one coherent world, and can be reduced to a unitary idiom"; Ernest Gellner, *Nations and Nationalism* (Ithaca, NY: Cornell University Press, 1983), 21. While Giddens is keen to emphasize the radical break that the modern state represents, he nevertheless uses the term "state" to include traditional class-divided social groups; for Giddens, the crucial transition is marked by the rise of the "absolutist state" and subsequently the "nation-state."

Ethnicity, language, and history are all themselves the result of contingent historical construction. The construction of a national sense is a matter of "common feeling and an organized claim."[13] Historically, this claim is first organized by the
state. It is only after the state and its claims to territorial sovereignty are established that nationalism arises to unify culturally what had been gathered inside
state borders. National claims tend to construct historical myths of origin stretch-
ing back into antiquity, but in the 1930s and 1940s Carlton Hayes and Hans
Kohn established the majority opinion that nationalism first appeared in the eighteenth century.[14] The nation-state first arose in the eighteenth century and
became prevalent only in the nineteenth century and following.[15]

Origins of the State

The above suggests something of the wide temporal gap between the modern
nation-state and the context in which language of the common good originated.
That caution registered, there is no question that the ground was prepared for the
modern state in the medieval period. In his work on medieval political structures,
Joseph Strayer locates the turning point toward greater administrative centralization somewhere around the beginning of the twelfth century. Although Strayer
acknowledges that once the state did not exist, he sees the embryonic "state" in
the increasing bureaucratization of civil authority in the twelfth century and
later.[16] Hendrik Spruyt says that Strayer overstates the early origins of the state,

---

13. "Nationalism," *The Blackwell Encyclopedia of Political Thought* (ed. David
Miller; Oxford: Blackwell, 1987), 354.

14. Carlton J. H. Hayes, *The Historical Evolution of Modern Nationalism* (New
York: R. R. Smith, 1931); and Hans Kohn, *The Idea of Nationalism: A Study in Its
Origins and Background* (New York: Macmillan, 1944). E. J. Hobsbawm refers to
Hayes and Kohn as the "founding fathers" of the study of nationalism and states that
their dating of nationalism has not been successfully challenged; *Nations and
Nationalism since 1780: Programme, Myth, Reality* (Cambridge: Cambridge
University Press, 1990), 9.

15. See, for example, Hendrik Spruyt, *The Sovereign State and Its Competitors*
(Princeton: Princeton University Press, 1994), 195 n. 2, where Spruyt distinguishes
between the state and the more recent phenomenon of the nation-state. Also
Benedict Anderson, *Imagined Communities: Reflections on the Origin and Spread of
Nationalism* (London: Verso, 1991); and "Nation-State," *The Dictionary of World
Politics* (ed. Graham Evans and Geoffrey Newnham; New York: Simon & Schuster),
1990), 258.

16. Joseph R. Strayer, *On the Medieval Origins of the Modern State* (Princeton,
NJ: Princeton University Press, 1970), 15–27. If Strayer is looser with the term
"state" than other historians, he is also looser with the term "sovereignty," seeing it
existing in fact but not in theory in the fourteenth century (9). What he means by
medieval "sovereignty," however, is simply the right of the king to be the court of
last resort in judging the law, whereas the early modern idea of sovereignty includes
making the law (102). Strayer also gives an early origin for nationalism, saying there
are "some signs of what might be called nationalism" in England, France, and Spain
in the seventeenth century (109).

but contends that, in the case of France if nowhere else, the basis of the state had been laid by the beginning of the fourteenth century.[17]

In his work *On the Medieval Origins of the Modern State*, Strayer narrates the gradual accretion of power to royal courts beginning in the twelfth century. The first permanent functionaries were estate managers hired to centralize, regularize, and keep account of the extraction of revenues from the lands and populations subject to the king.[18] Next to develop were royal courts of law. Courts of law were originally simply royal courts, that is, the "great men" who surrounded the king and made up his household. In the twelfth and thirteenth centuries, they were increasingly called upon to settle disputes, frequently by knights and lesser land-holders asking for protection against the wealthier nobles. The royal courts that developed were thus important to the king's struggle for power with the nobility. In general, the law became the principal tool of centralization and bureaucratization. By the fourteenth century, the governing apparatuses surrounding the king had "acquired their power largely by developing their judicial institutions and by protecting the property rights of the possessing classes."[19] By the fourteenth century, war had made royal courts increasingly reliant on taxation, which in turn required inviting representatives of the propertied classes to give their consent in occasional nonvoting assemblies. Such assemblies generally succeeded in shifting the tax burden more heavily onto the unrepresented classes.[20]

What is significant for our purposes is that Strayer's account leaves little room for the pursuit of the common good as an historical explanation for the rise of the state. According to Strayer, the development of regularized systems of revenue extraction and accounting, law courts, and assemblies were undertaken with reference to its advantages for particular parties—the royal household and the propertied classes—and without reference to anything like a common good. The common people came into the purview of the emerging bureaucracy almost exclusively as a resource for revenue extraction. At the same time, the very definition of what is common had begun a gradual transformation. The centralization of royal power involved a transfer of rights from local bodies that had previously been the primary referents of communal life. Legal right and the administration of justice were not created by royal power but were usurped from manorial lords, churches, and communities. If Strayer is accurate, this process took place to serve the particular interests of dominant groups, and not as the expansion of common space.

At this early stage, the ascendant civil bureaucracy did not yet refer to a unitary "common." In the absence of the sovereign state, there was no "society" to which a common good could be imputed. Europe was still a complex of multiple *societates* with a weak level of integration among them. The administrative reach of even the most bureaucratized royal courts was short and rarely touched the lives of the great majority of people. Significant elements of military power lay outside

---

17. Spruyt, *Sovereign State*, 79.
18. Strayer, *Medieval Origins*, 28–29, 69.
19. Ibid., 61.
20. Ibid., 58–68.

the control of the central apparatus. Political power was still a matter of the personal disposition of the ruler, and his or her rule was diffused into a jumble of overlapping jurisdictions and loyalties. Strayer characterizes the situation of kingly rule in the fourteenth century with this example:

> A king of France might send letters on the same day to the count of Flanders, who was definitely his vassal but a very independent and unruly one, to the count of Luxemburg, who was a prince of the Empire but who held a money-fief (a regular, annual pension) of the king of France, and to the king of Sicily, who was certainly ruler of a sovereign state but was also a prince of the French royal house. In such a situation one could hardly distinguish between internal and external affairs.[21]

This distinction between internal and external would eventually get sorted out, but only in the establishment of sovereign borders through the coercive aggrandizement of royal power. The state does not arise as the establishment of a uniform system of common good and justice on behalf of a society of people; rather, a society is brought into being by the centralization of royal power.

The agent of this change is war. Strayer says that the increased intensity of war in the fourteenth century and following was necessary to distinguish inside and outside, and he regards the process of state-building after 1300 as inevitable.[22] Charles Tilly, however, argues (against Strayer) that there was nothing natural or inevitable about the rise of the state. In 1300 there were still five possible outcomes open:

> (1) the form of national state which actually emerged; (2) a political federation or empire controlled, if only loosely, from a single center; (3) a theocratic federation—a commonwealth—held together by the structure of the Catholic Church; (4) an intensive trading network without large-scale, central political organization; (5) the persistence of the "feudal" structure which prevailed in the thirteenth century.[23]

Tilly also faults Strayer for too little emphasis on the coercive aspects of state-building.[24] Tilly's larger contention is that there was nothing natural or inevitable about the rise of the state; it triumphed in Europe because of its superior ability to extract resources from the local population.

Tilly and eight other scholars changed the focus of the study of the genesis of the state in 1975 with the publication of *The Formation of National States in*

---

21. Ibid., 83.
22. Ibid., 57–58.
23. Charles Tilly, "Reflections on the History of European State-Making" in *The Formation of National States in Western Europe* (ed. Charles Tilly; Princeton, NJ: Princeton University Press, 1975), 26.
24. Ibid., 43.

Western Europe. Previous approaches tended to posit the problem in terms of whether or not political managers successfully directed socioeconomic change—or "modernization"—toward desirable outcomes, including the survival of the political apparatus itself. As Tilly says, when the problem is thus framed, it reproduces the worldview of the high administrative official: the world is "out there" to be dealt with and transformed by means of government. For Tilly and associates, the question of which political forms would survive to become a sovereign, national state is best answered in terms of "whether the managers of the political units undertook activities which were expensive in goods and manpower, and built an apparatus which effectively drew the necessary resources from the local population and checked the population's efforts to resist that extraction of resources."[25] Building a state depended on the ability of state-making elites to make war, and the ability to make war in turn depended on the ability to extract resources from the population, which in turn depended on an effective state bureaucracy to secure those resources from a recalcitrant population. As Tilly puts it, "War made the state, and the state made war."[26]

Gabriel Ardant looks carefully at the empirical financial conditions of state- and nation-building and finds them intimately connected to the ability to make war. He shows how, in the period of European state-building, the greatest changes in fiscal burdens imposed on a population occurred because of war. At the same time, the most serious precipitant to violence, and the greatest spur to the growth of the state, was the attempt to collect taxes from an unwilling populace. Finally, the efforts at nation-building in the nineteenth century, including the efforts to broaden political participation, were due to the demands of war.[27]

The element of popular resistance contradicts the modernizing narrative that sees in the growth of the state the progressive increase of political rights. In the crucial period of state formation, the state either absorbed rights previously resident in other bodies (guilds, manors, provinces, estates) or eliminated them altogether, as in the enclosure of common lands.[28] Close analyses of the history of taxation,[29] policing,[30] and food supply[31] indicate that popular resistance to state-building was deep, broadly based, frequent, and violent. In England alone, the crown put down by force popular rebellions in 1489, 1497, 1536, 1547, 1549, and 1553, all responses to the centralizing efforts of the Tudors. Those asked to surrender men, crops, labor, money, and land to the emerging state did not do so without a fight.

---

25. Ibid., 40.

26. Ibid., 42.

27. Gabriel Ardant, "Financial Policy and Economic Infrastructure of Modern States and Nations," in *Formation* (ed. Tilly), 164–242. On war and nationalism, see also Hobsbawm, *Nations and Nationalism*, 83.

28. Tilly, "Reflections on State-Making," 37–38.

29. Rudolf Braun, "Taxation, Sociopolitical Structure, and State-Building: Great Britain and Brandenburg-Prussia," in *Formation* (ed. Tilly), 243–327.

30. David H. Bayley, "The Police and Political Development in Europe," in *Formation* (ed. Tilly), 328–79.

31. Charles Tilly, "Food Supply and Public Order in Modern Europe," in *Formation* (ed. Tilly), 380–455.

As Tilly says, "The state-makers only imposed their wills on the populace through centuries of ruthless effort."[32] It must be underscored, however, that state-making was not the motivating intention of state-making elites. The state was largely an unintended byproduct of these elites' pursuit of their own ends.[33]

In a 1985 article entitled "War Making and State Making as Organized Crime," Tilly suggests the analogy of the protection racket for the formation of the Western state. The claim that emerging states offered their citizens protection against violence ignores the fact that the state itself created the threat and then charged its citizens for its reduction. What separated state violence from other kinds of violence was the concept of legitimacy, but legitimacy was based on the ability of state-makers to approximate a monopoly on violence within a given geographical territory. In order to pursue that monopoly, it was necessary for elites to secure access to capital from the local population. This extraction was accomplished in turn either by the direct threat of violence or the guarantee of protection from other kinds of violence. The variations in the states produced are explicable in terms of variations in the difficulty of collecting taxes, the cost of military technology employed, the force available to competitors, and so on. In sum, as Tilly suggests, "A portrait of war makers and state makers as coercive and self-seeking entrepreneurs bears a far greater resemblance to the facts than do its chief alternatives: the idea of a social contract, the idea of an open market in which operators of armies and states offer services to willing customers, the idea of a society whose shared norms and expectations call forth a certain kind of government."[34]

This view of state-formation has gained wide acceptance. It builds on the early twentieth-century work of Otto Hintze[35] and is confirmed by the more recent work of Perry Anderson,[36] Hendrik Spruyt,[37] Anthony Giddens, Victor Burke,[38] and others. In his survey of state-making studies over the last three decades, Thomas Ertman is able to say, "It is now generally accepted that the territorial state triumphed over other possible political forms (empire, city-state, lordship) because of the superior fighting ability which it derived from access to both urban capital and coercive authority over peasant taxpayers and army recruits."[39] As for

---

32. Tilly, "Reflections on State Making," 22–24.

33. Charles Tilly, "Western State-Making and Theories of Political Transformation," in *Formation* (ed. Tilly), 633–38.

34. Charles Tilly, "War Making and State Making as Organized Crime," in *Bringing the State Back In* (ed. Peter B. Evans, Dietrich Rueschemeyer, and Theda Skocpol; Cambridge: Cambridge University Press, 1985), 169.

35. Otto Hintze, *The Historical Essays of Otto Hintze* (ed. Felix Gilbert; New York: Oxford University Press, 1975).

36. Perry Anderson, *Lineages of the Absolutist State* (London: New Left Books, 1974).

37. Spruyt, *Sovereign State*.

38. Victor Lee Burke, *The Clash of Civilizations: War-Making and State Formation in Europe* (Cambridge: Polity Press, 1997).

39. Thomas Ertman, *Birth of the Leviathan: Building States and Regimes in Medieval and Early Modern Europe* (Cambridge: Cambridge University Press, 1997), 4.

explaining variations within the dominant form of the sovereign state, Ertman says that "the work of Hintze, Tilly, Mann, Downing, and Anderson has already conclusively established that war and preparations for war tended to stimulate the creation of ever more sophisticated state institutions across the continent."[40] He insists that war was the "principal force" behind the expansion and rationalization of state apparatuses.[41]

In his recent book, Michael Howard sums up the evidence bluntly: "The entire apparatus of the state primarily came into being to enable princes to wage war."[42] The word "primarily" suggests that violence was not the only factor in the creation of the modern state. All of the authors mentioned acknowledge a variety of other interrelated factors, including the rise of capital markets, technological innovations, geographical position, the introduction of Roman law, and urbanization. It is perhaps best to say with Bruce Porter that war was the catalyst and *sine qua non* mobilizing the other factors in the formation of the state.[43] One need not romanticize the medieval period to conclude that, at least in its origins, the state is not appropriately categorized as the agency of society that has responsibility for the common good. Those who study the origins of the state would find such a categorization rather remote from the empirical evidence.

The State Is Not a Product of Society, but Creates Society

The conceptual leap that accompanies the advent of the state in the sixteenth century is the invention of sovereignty. The doctrine of sovereignty asserts the incontestable right of the central power to make and enforce law for people who fall within recognized territorial borders. Giddens contrasts borders with traditional frontiers, peripheral, poorly marked or guarded regions in which the power of the center is diffuse. In premodern Europe, authority was often marked by personal loyalties owed in complexly layered communal contexts. In the state, by contrast, borders mark out a unitary space in which the individual is subject directly to the center, which has the right to enforce its will through a monopoly on the means of legitimate violence within those borders.[44]

As an example of the complex premodern situation, Giddens cites the province of Sedan in the mid-seventeenth century.

> Sedan is often regarded as a distinct realm. But others have seen it as a
> boundary province of the larger state of France, in which the monarch

---

40. Ibid., 26. Ertman's project builds on this consensus in offering what he says is a better account of the factors that predict whether or not a state will have an absolutist or constitutional framework. Ertman contends that Hintze, Tilly, Downing, . and Mann do not adequately account for the "nonsimultaneity" of the process: not all states were affected by war-making at the same time; ibid., 15, 26–27.

41. Ibid., 4.

42. Michael Howard, *The Invention of Peace: Reflections on War and International Order* (New Haven: Yale University Press, 2000), 15.

43. Porter, *War*, 7, 24, 60–61.

44. Giddens, *Nation-State*, 49–51, 85–89.

was not able to sustain more than minimal authority. The hesitations of historians are not particularly surprising, reflecting in some part those current at the time. The dukes of Bouillon held direct lordship over the area, but owed some of their possessions to the bishops of Liege, who in turn were princes owing allegiance to the French crown. The ducal family relinquished Sedan in exchange for certain other areas in France. On occasion, this has been regarded by historical writers as the annexing of previously foreign territory, by others as the consolidation of royal power over French lands.[45]

What takes place in the modern era—not complete in some places until the late nineteenth century—is a reconfiguration of space that is much more profound than the creation of an expanded common space through the gathering up and coordination of formerly scattered elements into one. What happens is a shift from "complex space"—varied communal contexts with overlapping jurisdictions and levels of authority—to a "simple space" characterized by a duality of individual and state.[46] There is an enfeebling of local common spaces by the power of the center, and a simultaneous parochialization of the imagination of Christendom into that of the sovereign state. To say that the state "creates" society is not to deny that families, guilds, clans, and other social groups existed before the state. Rather, the state "creates" society by replacing the complex overlapping loyalties of medieval *societates* with one society, bounded by borders and ruled by one sovereign to whom allegiance is owed in a way that trumps all other allegiances.

The early modern theorists of sovereignty saw this dynamic clearly. As formulated first by Jean Bodin, sovereignty is the triumph of the one over the many, the creation of a unified simple space. As such, the sovereign must be "absolute" and alone, which means above all to be able to give law without being subject to law. The laws of the sovereign, "although they be grounded on good and lively reasons, depend nevertheless upon nothing but his mere and frank good will."[47] Because law is based on will, the sovereign cannot be subject to his own laws. The unity of the republic depends on the absolute singularity of the sovereign, who creates a simple space through his power.[48] Bodin thus unblinkingly asserts that sovereignty, and therefore the state, is created not by contract, custom, or natural right, but by sheer power. All other types of association are subject for their very existence on the recognition of the sovereign.

Hobbes, too, derives sovereignty from will, though he attempts to found legitimacy in the implied consent of the people. For Hobbes, the sovereign is the representative of the people, their own creation; it is from this that legitimacy derives

---

45. Ibid., 89.

46. I adopt the language of complex and simple space from John Milbank, "On Complex Space," in his book *The Word Made Strange: Theology, Language, Culture* (Oxford: Blackwell, 1997), 268–92.

47. Jean Bodin, *The Six Bookes of a Commonweale* (ed. Kenneth McRae; Cambridge: Harvard University Press, 1962), 92 (1.8), translation modified.

48. Ibid., 6.6.

and this that makes Hobbes the founder of liberalism, despite the absolutist form his government would take. The foundation of the state in Hobbes is not a common good but rather a shared evil: the fear of death. Each person is possessed of a "perpetual and restless desire of power after power, that ceaseth only in death."[49] Individuals in the state of nature do not occupy a common space, for each has a *jus in omnia*, a right over everything, which makes them enemies, locked in the war of all against all. The only way out of this condition is for each to surrender his or her will to the sovereign, who gathers up the many into one. Despite his derivation of legitimacy from representation, therefore, it is the state that first gathers people into society with one another.

This creation of a unitary space requires the absorption into the sovereign of the church and any other bodies that would threaten the unity of Leviathan. Sovereignty is absolute for Hobbes because the *jus in omnia* that each individual transfers to the sovereign is unlimited. If each individual is possessed of an inviolable will which is his or hers alone, then the only way such a will could be transferred or represented is by the encounter with another irresistible will. Yet for Hobbes, the individual is not oppressed but liberated by Leviathan. In his view, the state is not enacted to realize a common good or common telos, but rather to liberate the individual to pursue his or her own ends without fear of interference from other individuals. In the peculiar new space created by the state, the individual members do not depend on one another, but are connected only through the sovereign, like spokes to the hub of a wheel. Cardinal Bellarmine has written, as Hobbes reports, that "the members of every commonwealth, as of a natural body, depend one of another." Hobbes replies, "It is true, they cohere together; but they depend only on the sovereign, which is the soul of the commonwealth; which failing, the commonwealth is dissolved into a civil war, no one man so much as cohering to another, for want of a common dependence on a known sovereign; just as the members of a natural body dissolve into the earth, for want of a soul to hold them together."[50] Hobbes sees clearly that it is the state that enacts civil society, and not vice versa.

English liberalism would appear to fork into two paths, one of which dead-ends with Hobbes's absolutism and the other of which bears fruit in Locke and his followers among the framers of the U.S. Constitution. Locke, however, is dedicated to the same basic reconfiguration of space as is Hobbes. Commentators usually assume that Locke made an abrupt change of mind somewhere between his earlier absolutist writings, especially the *Two Tracts on Government* (1660–62), and his later, more liberal writings, notably the *Letter concerning Toleration* (1689) and *Two Treatises of Government* (1690). His thinking did certainly shift, but not regarding the fundamental importance of subordinating the church and other social groups to the state for the sake of public peace and order.[51] What Hobbes

---

49. Thomas Hobbes, *Leviathan* (New York: Collier Books, 1962), 80.
50. Ibid., 418.
51. Robert Kraynak points to the underlying continuity in Locke's development in his article "John Locke: From Absolutism to Toleration," *American Political Science Review* 74 (1980): 53–69.

accomplished by absorbing the church into the state, Locke accomplished by privatizing the church. Peace would never be attained if essentially undecidable matters such as the end of human life were left open to public debate. What is common is therefore redefined as follows: "The commonwealth seems to me to be a society of men constituted only for the procuring, preserving, and advancing their own civil interests. Civil interests I call life, liberty, health, and indolency of body; and the possession of outward things, such as money, lands, houses, furniture, and the like."[52] As A. J. Conyers comments, for Locke: "What is left to discuss in the public arena, therefore, is not the common good that creates society at the level of common affections and common goals, but merely the resolution of differing material interests."[53]

The political space imagined by Locke has two poles, the individual and the state. The state is enacted immediately from the need of the solitary individual to protect his person and possessions. The world belongs to all humankind in common, but it is quickly withdrawn from the common by human labor. Even the "wild Indian," who "knows no enclosure, and is still a tenant in common," establishes an exclusive individual right to whatever he appropriates from nature by his labor.[54] Here Locke breaks with tradition, for which property is social according to its use. As Aquinas says, "In this respect [of their use] man ought to possess external things, not as his own, but as common, so that, to wit, he is ready to communicate them to others in their need."[55] For Locke, by contrast, property is a strictly individual natural right, and the basis of the state. The purpose of the state is to establish and enforce laws that clearly separate what is mine from what is thine. Locke combines this emphasis on individual property rights, however, with a curious sort of utilitarian justification of the system of political economy as a whole. Locke says that no one may appropriate from nature more than he or she can use, because it would then spoil. With the invention of money, however, perishable goods may be translated into imperishable goods, allowing the legitimate accumulation of great wealth. The advent of an exchange economy also means, therefore, that the legitimate owner of any goods is not necessarily the one whose labor produced the wealth, provided that all exchanges leading to such ownership were free. The system as a whole is beneficial for each, however, for wealth is increased through labor and exchange, such that, Locke tells us, even the day laborer in England enjoys one hundred times the material conveniences of an American Indian.[56]

---

52. John Locke, *A Letter concerning Toleration* (Indianapolis: Bobbs-Merrill, 1955), 17.

53. A. J. Conyers, *The Long Truce* (Dallas: Spence Publishing, 2001), 130. See also C. B. Macpherson's classic *The Political Theory of Possessive Individualism: Hobbes to Locke* (Oxford: Oxford University Press, 1962), 194–262.

54. John Locke, *Two Treatises of Government* (New York: Dutton, 1978), 129 (2.5).

55. Thomas Aquinas, *Summa theologiae* II-II:66.2.

56. Locke, *Two Treatises*, 131–41. On this point, see Pierre Manent, *An Intellectual History of Liberalism* (trans. Rebecca Balinski; Princeton, NJ: Princeton University Press, 1994), 39–52. Manent argues that, as a result of Locke's justification of exchange as beneficial for all of society, there can be no concept of "social

The "society" that Locke's state enacts is coterminous with the market, to which individuals come to contract for certain goods, both material and political. Locke's simplification of political space into the oscillation between individual rights and state sovereignty—what Conyers calls Locke's "bipolar disorder"—relegates all other forms of common life—those based on biology, locality, common blood, common tasks, or common calling—to the status of the essentially private "voluntary society." What is common is common only by contract. Besides the Catholic Church, which Locke explicitly excepted from his principles of toleration, Locke's simple space could find no place for Native American tribes. Locke refers to the "inland vacant places of America,"[57] the Indians already having been theoretically eliminated by the stark simplicity of Locke's justification of sovereignty. "Thus, in the beginning, all the world was America," says Locke,[58] common but waiting to be appropriated to private use and exchange for the benefit of each and all. As Milner Ball's article in the present volume makes plain, the untranslatability of the Indians into American law and their consequent destruction is not simply the result of judicial malice but is inscribed in the very nature of state sovereignty. Simple space cannot accommodate the tribal structure. The formal equality of individuals before the law pits individual rights against the traditional tribal sense that the tribe, not the individual, is the bearer of rights.

From the sixteenth and seventeenth centuries, the classical theories of sovereignty that gave definition to the state do not yield much in the way of the common good. The foundational anthropology is strictly individual, such that the goal of the state is to secure the noninterference of individuals with each other's affairs. A new type of space is invented in which individuals relate to each other through the mechanism of contract, as guaranteed by the center. Public and private interest is seen to coincide, but the discourse thus shifts from good to will and right. The body politic does not pursue a common good, but seeks to liberate the individual to pursue his or her own ends. Contrary to Christian anthropology, the sovereign individual is presented here as the natural—not merely post-Fall—condition of humankind. In fact, however, sovereignty is not the mere gathering of the many into one, but the *creation* of sovereign individuals related through the sovereign state.

The nation-state presents itself as a way of reconciling the many into one, *e pluribus unum*, and thus serving the common good. However, this reconciliation only comes after the creation of a prior antagonism, the creation of a novel form of simple social space that oscillates between the individual and the state. Simple space is a dangerous fiction, however, because, as John Milbank puts it, "no action can be perfectly self-contained, but always impinges upon other people, so that spaces will always in some degree 'complexly' overlap, jurisdictions always in some

---

justice." Hayek is the true heir of Lockean liberalism. Justice is not subject to debate, but is "*always already realized* as long as property is guaranteed and protected"; Manent, *Intellectual History*, 46.

57. Ibid., 134.
58. Ibid., 140.

measure be competing, loyalties remain (perhaps benignly) divided."[59] If this is the case, then

> the issue of the common good most pointedly surfaces, not in the more abstract deliberations of governments, where, on the contrary, its reduction to utilitarian calculus or promotion of free choice will seem most seductively plausible, but rather in the ever re-encountered "boundary disputes" and occasions for collective action in the everyday lives of citizens. These disputes and occasions need somehow to be mediated, and where the reality of "community" fades, the attempt is made to more and more do so by the extension of merely formal regulation of human transactions (with its utilitarian and more predominantly liberal individualist presuppositions). More of life becomes economized and legalized, as legislation seeks—hopelessly—to catch up with every instance of "overlap," and institute more detailed rules of absolute ownership, whether by individuals, or legally incorporated groups: so much and no more *for you*; so far and no further *for you*.[60]

The result is not the common good, but an—ultimately tragic—attempt to ward off social conflict by keeping individuals from interfering with each other.

The State Is Not a Limited Part of Society, but Absorbs Society into Itself

Civil Society

At this point I would expect to encounter both agreement and disagreement from John Courtney Murray, still the dominant voice in U.S. Catholic social thinking about the state and common good. Murray agrees that the state is not the agency within a social order that has responsibility for the common good. The state concerns itself with the much more limited role of vigilance for public order. Murray would disagree in that his distinction of public order and common good follows his sharp distinction of state from civil society.[61] According to Murray, the state is the creation of civil society and is meant to serve it. The state possesses the coercive power necessary to maintain peace and order, but the real life of a social order takes place in civil society, the realm of freedom outside the direct purview of the state. Murray writes, "The pursuit of the common good devolves upon society as

---

59. Milbank, "On Complex Space," 281.

60. Ibid., 281–82.

61. Murray uses the term "society" to denote what today is most commonly referred to as "civil society," that realm of spontaneous social life beyond the direct reach of the state. To avoid confusion, I follow current usage; John Courtney Murray, "The Problem of Religious Freedom," in *Religious Liberty: Catholic Struggles with Pluralism* (ed. J. Leon Hooper, SJ; Louisville: Westminster John Knox, 1993), 144.

a whole, on all its members and on all its institutions. . . . Public order, whose care devolves upon the state, is a narrower concept." Public order includes important public goods, but not the common good as such.[62]

This distinction follows from Murray's understanding of the U.S. liberal constitutional framework. In liberalism the state does not pursue the good, but rather secures peace among varying conceptions of the good.[63] According to Murray, the American state does not, therefore, try to impose uniformity on the many, but limits itself through mechanisms of consent and checks and balances, so that the many may flourish. Here the many are not merely individuals but rather all those varying types of communal life Murray calls "conspiracies," meaning spaces where people "breathe together." He has in mind especially the churches and synagogues, but the principle applies to all those associations that intermediate between individual and state, all of which make for a strong civil society and the pursuit of the common good.[64] Sovereignty derives from the people and is not, as in Hobbes, alienated from them into a transcendent state. Sovereignty remains "immanent" to the people; power remains in the hands of the multitude through mechanisms of consent and checks and balances in government. In this view, liberalism is that constitutional regime that frees the intermediate associations of civil society by limiting the state. Unity exists strictly at the level of political conversation, and does not destroy the underlying pluralism of civil society.[65] The state, therefore, does not have direct responsibility for the common good, but nevertheless makes the pursuit of the common good possible.

This view of the state paints an attractively balanced picture, but unfortunately bears little relationship to empirical studies of how "intermediate associations" have fared under the state.[66] The rise of the state is the history of the atrophying of such associations. As Robert Nisbet makes plain, the state is not a limited agency arising out of—and created for the service of—local communities, families, and tribes. "If we look not to imaginary beginnings in the never-never land of ethnological reconstruction" but to the historical evidence, it becomes clear that "the rise and aggrandizement of political States took place in circumstances of

---

62. Ibid., 144–45. The three public goods included in public order are peace, public morality, and justice. The inclusion of public morality in this list indicates that Murray envisioned a more significant role for the state than more libertarian types of liberalism would allow.

63. John Courtney Murray, *We Hold These Truths: Catholic Reflections on the American Proposition* (Kansas City, MO: Sheed & Ward, 1960), 45–78.

64. Ibid., 5–24.

65. Ibid., 45.

66. Political scientist Michael Budde comments, "Murray's theory of the state, such as it is, can only be described as naïve, almost a direct transferal from civics texts to political description." Murray's conviction that the American people govern themselves through free consensus leads Budde to observe, "No testing of reality seems to have affected his assessment of American political institutions"; Michael Budde, *The Two Churches: Catholicism and Capitalism in the World-System* (Durham, NC: Duke University Press, 1992), 115.

powerful opposition to kinship and other traditional authorities."[67] The fundamental conflict of modernity, says Nisbet, is not between state and individual, but between state and social group.[68] The history of the state is the creation of an increasingly direct relationship between state and individual by the state's absorption of powers from the groups that comprise what has come to be called "civil society."[69] In other words, the state is not simply local government writ large. The state is *qualitatively* different; it is precisely that type of government that does *not* grow organically out of the self-government of social groups.

Prior to the rise of the state, central authority was weak and associations strong. Rights, honors, immunities, and responsibilities were attached to communities, not to individuals. The family, the village, the church, the guild, the university were held to precede the individual both in origin and in right. Associations did not depend upon royal authority for recognition. Such associations could, of course, be oppressive, and often were. The point here is not to romanticize the medieval period, but simply to show the relative strength of local association to central authority. Central authority, where it existed, was severely limited in its ability to override local custom and law. The most significant law was not positive law given by a legislator but the customs and rules that provided the inner order of associations.[70]

The state grew by absorbing the rights and responsibilities of this plurality of social groups. The state came to be seen as the sole source of law and as the guarantor of property and inheritance rights. The state took over many of the civil functions formerly belonging to the church, such as the system of ecclesiastical courts. The state claimed a monopoly on the means of coercion and facilitated the enclosure of common lands. The state claimed that the lesser association itself was, in effect, a creation of the state, a *persona ficta*. In many places Roman law, especially the Justinian Code, provided the legal vocabulary necessary to reenvision social relations as essentially contractual and subject to a sovereign lawmaker above the law.[71] In all places, war was the principal means by which the growth of the state advanced. Nisbet writes, "If there is any single origin of the institutional State, it is in the circumstances and relationships of war. The connection between kinship and family, between religion and Church, is no closer than that between war and the State in history."[72] War requires a direct disciplinary relationship between the individual and the state, and so has served as a powerful solvent of the loyalties of individuals to social groups other than the state.

The absorption of civil society by the state is manifested in at least three different ways in contemporary America. First is the exponential and continuous

---

67. Robert Nisbet, *The Quest for Community* (London: Oxford University Press, 1969), 100.

68. Ibid., 109.

69. Ibid., 104.

70. Ibid., 80–85, 110–12.

71. Ibid., 104, 112–13. See also Robert Nisbet, *Twilight of Authority* (New York: Oxford University Press, 1975), 166–71.

72. Nisbet, *Quest for Community*, 100–101.

growth of the state. Bruce Porter has documented this growth and concludes that war has been the primary impetus behind it. All but five cabinet departments and the majority of smaller federal agencies have come into being during wartime.[73] World War I produced a 1,000 percent increase in federal spending;[74] the increase in government in World War II was three times that of the New Deal, the majority of it in the nonmilitary sector.[75] After World War II the large bureaucratic state became a permanent feature of the landscape. Under the supposedly "anti-big government" Ronald Reagan, the federal government continued to grow, even in the nonmilitary sector.[76] Today, in response to the "war on terrorism," such growth is represented by the 170,000 employees of the new Office of Homeland Security, the second largest government institution behind only the Pentagon. Another recent example is the Pentagon's Total Information Awareness program, which will gather information on every American citizen from databases of credit card transactions, health records, ticket purchases, housing records, academic grades, and so on.[77]

Nisbet points out that the "absolutist" state of early modernity was in reality much less powerful than the contemporary nation-state, which has succeeded in establishing a direct relationship to every individual within its borders. Nisbet quotes Walter Lippmann to this effect:

> It does not matter whether the right to govern is hereditary or obtained with the consent of the governed. A State is absolute in the sense which I have in mind when it claims the right to a monopoly of all the force within the community, to make war, to make peace, to conscript life, to tax, to establish and dis-establish property, to define crime, to punish disobedience, to control education, to supervise the family, to regulate personal habits, and to censor opinions. The modern State claims all of these powers, and, in the matter of theory, there is no real difference in the size of the claim between communists, fascists, and democrats.[78]

---

73. Porter, *War*, 291–92. This figure includes the first five years after major wars. The total number of years that fall into this category add up to only one-fifth of the total of American history.

74. Ibid., 269.

75. Ibid., 278–80.

76. Ibid., 294–95.

77. According to congressional officials, Homeland Security is blessed with "unprecedented power for a federal agency to organize itself as it chooses, without congressional oversight." Homeland Security includes a new secret court before which the government is the only party allowed to appear. The Total Information Awareness project was headed by John Poindexter, convicted on six counts of masterminding the secret Iran-Contra connection under Reagan and lying to Congress about it; see Michael Ventura, "Weapons of Mass Deception," *Austin Chronicle*, November 29, 2002. In response to citizen concerns about privacy, the Pentagon has changed the name of the program to Terrorism Information Awareness, without changing the program itself; Michael J. Sniffen, "Anti-Terror Surveillance System Name Changed," *St. Paul Pioneer Press*, May 21, 2003, 4A.

78. Walter Lippmann, *A Preface to Morals*, quoted in Nisbet, *Quest for Community*, 102.

When Lippmann wrote those words in 1929, he could not have imagined the aston-ishing growth of state influence in the United States into the twenty-first century.

The second contemporary manifestation of the withering of civil society is the progressive enervation of intermediate associations. As Nisbet, Robert Bellah,[79] Robert Putnam,[80] and many others have documented, what exists is not Murray's free space of robust "conspiracies" but a society of individuals alienated from sub-stantive forms of common life. Intermediate associations such as the church, unions, and the family still exist, but they are expected to convey identities, virtues, and common ends in a context in which their relationships to production, mutual aid, education, and welfare have been absorbed into the state and the mar-ket.[81] Although potential solutions to the problem are hotly contested, the empiri-cal fact of the decline of intermediate associations is not. The Council on Civil Society, for example, which includes such diverse figures as Francis Fukuyama and Cornel West, William Galston and Mary Ann Glendon, is able to treat the dis-integration of "civil society" as a given.[82]

The third contemporary manifestation of the absorption of civil society is the symbiosis of the state and the corporation that signals the collapse of separation between politics and economics. Twenty-five years ago Charles Lindblom wrote in his landmark *Politics and Markets*, "The greatest distinction between one gov-ernment and another is in the degree to which market replaces government or government replaces market."[83] We live under the former type, according to Lindblom, in which corporate leaders not only buy influence over politicians, regu-lators, and public opinion, but the business executive him- or herself becomes a type of public official.[84] Lindblom could scarcely have imagined the extent to which the state now treats corporations as its clients. This is hardly surprising given the revolving door between government and industry. A brief glance at the current president's appointees illustrates this situation: The number two person at the Environmental Protection Agency was a lobbyist for the chemical giant Monsanto. The chief counsel to the IRS is a corporate tax attorney who won sev-eral high-profile cases defending corporate tax havens against IRS enforcement. The deputy secretary of the Interior Department was a lobbyist for the oil, gas, and coal industries. And on and on, ad nauseum.[85]

---

79. Robert Bellah, et al., *Habits of the Heart* (San Francisco: Harper & Row, 1985).

80. Robert Putnam, *Bowling Alone* (New York: Simon & Schuster, 2000).

81. Nisbet, *Quest for Community*, 54. Nisbet explicitly disavows any nostalgia for some bygone era. He believes that the existence of genuine community is empiri-cally verifiable, and that it has been eroded in the modern era. However, he does not think that all community is good in and of itself; communities can be corrupt and stifling. Nor does he want to return to past forms of community, but rather to ask what new forms of community are viable today; ibid., viii, 31, 106.

82. Council on Civil Society, *A Call to Civil Society* (Chicago: Institute for American Values, 1998).

83. Charles E. Lindblom, *Politics and Markets: The World's Political Economic Systems* (New York: Basic Books, 1977), ix.

84. Ibid., 170–233.

85. These are just a few of the examples cited in Molly Ivins, "Fox-and-Chicken-Coop Comparison Might Not Say It All," *South Bend Tribune*, August 26, 2001.

The point of these examples is that the state does not simply stand *over against* civil society as its oppressor. Indeed, the point of the transition from state to nation-state is the fusion of state and civil society. The nation-state fully realizes the claim merely articulated by the absolutist state to have direct access to governance of everyday life within a defined territory. As Giddens says, "The nation-state is a power container whose administrative purview corresponds exactly to its territorial delimitation."[86] For this reason, Giddens does not use the term "civil society" with reference to the nation-state; the nation-state is simply what sociologists mean when they say "society" in contemporary life. There is no "civil society" that stands outside the administrative and symbolic system ordered by the state.[87] With respect to origins, there is no unitary and organically preexisting civil society that gives rise to the state. Hegel was empirically correct in positing the state as the ground of civil society.[88] The state creates a unitary space that enacts a single system of social interaction or society. It is not simply that government has gotten big, and economic and social transactions of every kind must pass through the organs of the state. It is also that the state itself—as well as churches, schools, unions, and other associations—has been colonized by the logic of the market. Marx predicted that the state would wither away. What has in fact happened, as Michael Hardt says, is that civil society has withered, or more accurately been absorbed into the state.[89]

Nisbet thinks that the absorption of civil society in the United States is not systemic, but is due to the importation of the unitary idea of democracy from the Continent that, beginning in the late-nineteenth century, has choked out the native species of pluralist democracy.[90] Others, however, have more convincingly argued that there exists a deeper problem endemic to the modern notion of sovereignty. Popular sovereignty is supposed to solve miraculously the problem of the one and the many by subsuming the many of civil society into the one state as the

---

Another type of example of the fusion of state and civil society comes from the recent pro-war rallies organized by radio stations across the U.S. Most of the stations are owned by Clear Channel, whose chairman and vice-chairman have close business ties to President Bush. In 1998, the vice-chairman, Tom Hicks, purchased the Texas Rangers in a deal that made Mr. Bush $15 million on a $600,000 investment; Paul Krugman, "Channels of Influence," *New York Times*, March 25, 2003.

86. Giddens, *Nation-State*, 172.

87. Ibid., 21–22, 172.

88. G. W. F. Hegel, *The Philosophy of Right* (trans. T. M. Knox; Oxford: Clarendon Press, 1952), pars. 256–57.

89. Michael Hardt, "The Withering of Civil Society," *Social Text*, no. 45 (vol. 14, no. 4: Winter 1995): 27–44.

90. Nisbet, *Quest for Community*, 248–54. Although the basic contours of Nisbet's sociological and historical analysis of the weakening of associations are, in my opinion, entirely convincing, Nisbet's analysis of the rise of the state is incomplete and often idealist because of his neglect of economic factors. In other words, the dissolution of community is laid on the state as cause, without much analysis of the solvent effects of capitalism. Nisbet ended his career as an ideologue of neoconservatism at the American Enterprise Institute in the 1980s.

unitary representative of the multiplicity of wills. The problem, as Pierre Manent says, is this:

> If civil society is what is natural, and if the state is only its instrument, why is the state detached from society in such a definite way? Why does civil society not simply take it over again, bringing an end to this "alienation"? Conversely, if the body politic exists only through the Representative, then the Representative is more than a mere representative; he gives consistency to civil society and is the source of social existence. The distinction between civil society and the state, and their union through the idea of representation, sets off a natural oscillation between two extreme possibilities: the "withering away" of the state on the one hand, the absorption of civil society by the state on the other. It is a distinction that calls out for negation, a negation that can benefit only one of the two terms.[91]

In fact, civil society is not the natural source of the state, but both society and state are enacted artificially "from above." The spontaneous life of traditional social groups from below tends to be delegitimated because such groups tend not to be representative, that is, based in consensus. Interests from below will always need to be channeled through the state to achieve legitimacy, since only the state can gather the diversity of interests into a transcendent unity.[92] The state is the source of social life. In the absence of a common good or telos, the state can only expand its reach, precisely in order to keep the welter of individuals pursuing their own goods from interfering with each other. Where there is a unitary simple space, pluralism of ends will always be a threat. To solve this threat, the demand will always be to absorb the many into the one. In the absence of shared ends, devotion to the state itself as the end in itself becomes ever more urgent. The result is not true pluralism but an ever-increasing directness of relationship between the individual and the state as foundation of social interaction.

The fusion of state and civil society is, then, a consequence of the unitary space created by sovereignty, not an accidental feature of modernity. As the early twentieth-century English pluralists saw, a limited state can only be one that does not enact a single society. A limited state could only exist where social space was complexly refracted into a network of associations, where associations were not "intermediate associations," squeezed between state and individual, at all. In the view of John Neville Figgis, there is no single entity called "society." The state should be a *communitas communitatum*. "This is the true meaning of our word Commons; not the mass of common people, but the community of the

---

91. Manent, *Intellectual History*, 26–27.
92. Ibid., 50–52, 62–63. This is why, according to Manent, Lockean liberalism tends toward a monarchical executive power, despite Locke's explicit wishes that the legislative power be supreme.

communities."[93] For Figgis, common good is promoted only by communities of people united for a permanent end. Such communities have corporate personality that is independent of recognition from the state. They are publics in their own right. The pluralists thus rejected the reduction of such a diversity of publics to a single sovereign will. G. D. H. Cole regards the claim of a unitary sovereign to gather the diversity of wills into one as a ridiculous fiction. It is in fact the hijacking of legitimacy by a small fraction of the whole, and can only be made plausible by the subsumption of difference to state power. Representation should be, at most, the choice of personnel, and not the transfer of will to a sovereign power.[94] Whether or not Figgis's and Cole's positive recommendations for restructuring the state are possible is not my concern here. What is important is their recognition that unitary sovereignty or simple space is incompatible with a limited state. If this is correct, then the sovereign state can only be hostile to the common good as John Courtney Murray defined it, as the spontaneous life of the various "conspiracies" built around common ends.

The Nation-State

In the West, the state became the nation-state in the nineteenth century, when the vertical relationship of state and individual was opened to include a horizontal relationship among individuals, an increasingly cohesive mass relationship.[95] In the liberal nation-state, the flows of power are not simply from civil society to state, as in Murray, nor from state to civil society. The flows of power are multi-directional. In other words, when state becomes nation-state it represents the fusion of state and society. The state precedes the idea of the nation and creates it, promoting the imagination of a unitary space and a common history. But in contrast to the absolutist state, the nation-state does not merely enforce its will through coercion. In order fully to realize the doctrine of territorial sovereignty and extend governance to every individual within its borders, the participation of the many in a unitive project is essential. Nationalism becomes a popular movement founded on consent.

Since Kohn and Hayes, scholars of nationalism have emphasized that "nation," like society, is not a natural or "ontologically prior" reality, but one that is invented by the state. As E. J. Hobsbawm puts it, "Nations do not make states

93. John Neville Figgis, *Churches in the Modern State* (Bristol: Thoemmes, 1997), 80. For Figgis, the state exists only to provide some minimal regulation of interaction between such publics. The English pluralists should not be confused with American pluralists, such as Robert Dahl, who place great emphasis on intermediate associations but see such associations as conflicting competitors for influence over the state, which remains a neutral and unitary staging ground; see Paul Q. Hirst's Introduction in *The Pluralist Theory of the State: Selected Writings of G. D. H. Cole, J. N. Figgis, and H. J. Laski* (ed. Paul Q. Hirst; London: Routledge, 1993), 3–4.
94. G. D. H. Cole, "The Social Theory," in *Pluralist Theory* (ed. Hirst), 82–90.
95. Nisbet, *Quest for Community*, 101–2.

and nationalisms but the other way round."[96] Most scholars agree that nations are only possible once states have been invented, and that nations, even seemingly "ancient" ones, are the product of the last two centuries. Until the nineteenth century, states lacked the internal cohesion necessary to be nations. One way this can be illustrated is by looking at the use of language. As late as 1789, only 50 percent of the citizens of France spoke French, and only 12 to 13 percent did so "correctly." At the moment of the creation of Italy (1860), only 2.5 percent of the people used Italian for everyday purposes.[97] As Italian patriot Massimo d'Azeglio said, "We have made Italy; now we have to make Italians."[98]

Nationalist sentiments were promoted by elites in the nineteenth century by various means. The first was the increasing influence of the state over education, by means of which a common history and common myths of origin were told.[99] The second was the spread of standardized language by means of print media. Sicilians and Venetians might not have been able to understand each other's speech, but they were beginning to read mass-produced Italian media, which had a significant impact on the creation of Italy.[100] Finally, war had a profound influence on the rise of nationalism. The United States became a nation-state only after the crisis of the Civil War, and nationalism took a quantum leap in the massive mobilization of society for World War I.[101] The questions of language and war are often intertwined; a language is just a dialect with an army, as the saying goes.

In the field of nationalism studies, a minority of scholars, some of them identified as "ethnosymbolists," want to press the origins of nations farther back by studying the ethnic identities that are precursors of the modern nation. Liah Greenfeld, for example, dates the sense of "nation-ness" in England to the sixteenth century, though she claims it was the only nation in the world for the next two centuries.[102] Anthony D. Smith claims that the origins of nationalism can be

---

96. Hobsbawm, *Nations and Nationalism*, 10. This fact was recognized even by some of the great nationalist politicians. Colonel Pilsudski, "liberator" of Poland, said, "It is the state which makes the nation and not the nation the state"; quoted in ibid., 44–45. To say that nations are invented is not necessarily to say that they are simply therefore "false." Benedict Anderson criticizes Hobsbawm and Gellner for implying falsity. Anderson prefers to see nations in a more neutral way as being "imagined"; see B. Anderson, *Imagined Communities*, 6.

97. Hobsbawm, *Nations and Nationalism*, 60–61.

98. Ibid., 44.

99. See, for example, Patrick J. Geary, *The Myth of Nations* (Princeton, NJ: Princeton University Press, 2002). Geary shows how the "science" of European history was invented in the nineteenth century as a tool of nationalist ideology, especially in the case of Germany. Ancestors such as the "Visigoths" were invented to stretch the origins of the nation back to the dissolution of the Roman Empire, and this history was disseminated through state control of education.

100. Benedict Anderson, "Nationalism," in *The Oxford Companion to Politics of the World* (ed. Joel Krieger; New York: Oxford University Press, 1993), 617.

101. Porter, *War*, xvi, 12–14, 247.

102. Liah Greenfeld, *Nationalism: Five Roads to Modernity* (Cambridge, MA: Harvard University Press, 1992), 14.

traced back in some European countries to the fifteenth and sixteenth centuries. Ethnosymbolists argue that nations were invented not out of nothing but out of preformed ethnic experiences and consciousness. The difference between previous cultural formations and modern nations is one of degree, not of kind. Once formed, ethnic identities are remarkably stable over generations and centuries.[103]

The ethnosymbolists have been criticized for defining the nation so broadly that all kinds of cultural groupings qualify. Smith, for example, has been criticized for attributing fully developed group consciousness to premodern groups that had only vague ideas of what differentiated them from others. Smith also fails to give due weight to the lack of institutional basis for such groups, such that they did not and could not make claims to territory, autonomy, or independence. Most importantly,

> nationalism is not simply a claim of ethnic similarity, but a claim that certain similarities should count as the definition of political community. For this reason, nationalism needs rigid boundaries in a way that premodern ethnicity does not: "Nationalism demands internal homogeneity throughout the putative nation, rather than gradual continua of cultural variation or pockets of subcultural distinction." Most distinctively, nationalists generally assert that national identities are more important than other personal or group identities (such as gender, family, or ethnicity) and link individuals directly to the nation as a whole. In stark contrast to this, most ethnic identities flow from family membership, kinship or membership in other intermediate groups.[104]

Nationalism, in other words, demands the simple space that only state sovereignty can provide. As Geoff Eley and Ronald Suny argue, ethnic identities may be the raw materials with which the state works, but they are not simply precursors that develop in a linear fashion toward the nation. The nation represents a rupture in the history of social organization.[105]

The idea of the nation does not remain an elite idea, but becomes gradually more powerful among the lower classes in the nineteenth and twentieth centuries. Why were common people willing to sacrifice their lives for nations their grandparents had never heard of, as Benedict Anderson asks?[106] Ernest Gellner answers this question by drawing a direct link between the weakening of smaller types of association and the growth of the idea of the nation. The loosing of individuals from traditional forms of community created the possibility and need of a larger,

103. Anthony D. Smith, *The Ethnic Origins of Nations* (Oxford: Blackwell, 1986), 16.
104. Umut Özkirimli, *Theories of Nationalism: A Critical Introduction* (New York: St. Martin's Press, 2000), 185. The internal quote is from Craig Calhoun, "Nationalism and Ethnicity," *Annual Review of Sociology* 19 (1993): 229.
105. Geoff Eley and Ronald Suny, "Introduction," in *Becoming National: A Reader* (ed. G. Eley and R. Suny; New York: Oxford University Press, 1996), 11.
106. B. Anderson, "Nationalism," 615.

mass substitute for community. Loyalties are gradually transferred from more local types of community to the nation.[107] At the same time, there is a gradual opening of the sphere of participation to the masses of people of whom the state had previously taken only sporadic notice. The rise of rights language goes hand in hand with the rise of the nation-state, because political and civil rights name both the freeing of the individual from traditional types of community and the establishment of regular relations of power between the individual and the state. Marx was wrong to dismiss rights as a mere ruse to protect the gains of the bourgeois classes.[108] Individual rights do, nevertheless, greatly expand the scope of the state because political and civil rights establish binding relationships between the nation-state and those who look to it to vindicate their claims. The nation-state thus becomes something of a central, bureaucratic clearinghouse in which social claims are contested. The nation-state is fully realized when sacrifice on behalf of the nation is combined with claims made on the state on the basis of rights.[109]

Alasdair MacIntyre alludes to this dual aspect of the nation-state in the following memorable quote:

> The modern nation-state, in whatever guise, is a dangerous and unmanageable institution, presenting itself on the one hand as a bureaucratic supplier of goods and services, which is always about to, but never actually does, give its clients value for money, and on the other as a repository of sacred values, which from time to time invites one to lay down one's life on its behalf. . . . It is like being asked to die for the telephone company.[110]

MacIntyre thinks that the nation-state can and does promote certain goods of order, but he also contends that it is incapable of promoting the common good. Integral to the political common good is a distribution of goods that reflect a common mind arrived at by rational deliberation. Rationality in turn depends upon recognition of our fundamental dependence on one another. According to MacIntyre, the nation-state is an arena of bargaining among different group interests. In the absence of any generally agreed rational standard to adjudicate among such interests, decisions on the distribution of goods are made on the basis of power, which is most often directly related to access to capital. The sheer size of the nation-state precludes genuine rational deliberation; deliberation is carried

107. Gellner, *Nations and Nationalism*, 63–87.
108. Karl Marx, "On the Jewish Question," in *Karl Marx: Selected Writings* (ed. David McLellan; Oxford: Oxford University Press, 1977), 39–57, esp. 52–56. Marx was right, however, to describe the solvent effect of rights. Marx sees that the "rights of man" are not available to Jews unless they lose their ties to the Jewish community and consent to being treated as "self-sufficient monads"; ibid., 53.
109. Giddens, *Nation-State*, 205–6, 220–1; Tilly, "Reflections," 36–37.
110. Alasdair MacIntyre, "A Partial Response to my Critics," in *After MacIntyre: Critical Perspectives on the Work of Alasdair MacIntyre* (ed. John Horton and Susan Mendus; Notre Dame, IN: University of Notre Dame Press, 1994), 303.

on by a political elite of lawyers, lobbyists, and other professionals.[111] For the same reason, the unitive community that the idea of the nation offers is an illusion. The nation-state is not a genuine community, a functioning rational collectivity whose bonds make possible the "virtues of acknowledged dependence" necessary for the common good. As MacIntyre says, "The shared public goods of the modern nation-state are not the common goods of a genuine nation-wide community and, when the nation-state masquerades as the guardian of such a common good, the outcome is bound to be either ludicrous or disastrous or both."[112]

The influence of money over deliberation to which MacIntyre refers has never been a merely accidental feature of the nation-state. For one of the functions of the idea of the nation is to short-circuit the conflict of classes by subsuming both forces of production and domination into one. Instead of the overtly class-based rule of absolutist states, the nation-state invites all classes to participate in a unitary project. This requires the imagination of a common space in which internal differences are minimized and external differences maximized.[113] Class analysis is considered divisive and subversive to the national project. So, for example, in the public forum both sides of the NAFTA debate asked, "Will this treaty be good or bad for America?" Only a few marginal voices on the losing side were able to suggest that NAFTA would be good for some Americans and bad for others, specifically, good for capital and bad for labor. Claims for the interests of groups must be justified in terms of national interests, but the wealthier classes are far more effective at presenting their interests as being national interests.[114] This is why tax cuts for the rich in 2002 and 2003 could be passed off as an "economic stimulus package" meant to get laid-off workers back to the plant, and why dissent from this legislation could be criticized by the House majority leader as sowing divisiveness at a time of national crisis.[115]

---

111. Alasdair MacIntyre, *Dependent Rational Animals: Why Human Beings Need the Virtues* (Chicago: Open Court, 1999), 129–33, 141–42; also Alasdair MacIntyre, "Toleration and the Goods of Conflict," in *The Politics of Toleration in Modern Life* (ed. Susan Mendus; Durham, NC: Duke University Press, 1999), 139–44.

112. MacIntyre, *Dependent Rational Animals*, 132.

113. Tilly comments sharply on this process: "Hence the plausibility of doctrines of national self-determination to nineteenth-century Europeans—just so long as they were not dealing with their own ethnic/religious minorities"; "Reflections," 79.

114. See Giddens, *Nation-State*, 221. For those who need a reminder of the influence of money over governance in the United States, William Greider's *Who Will Tell the People: The Betrayal of American Democracy* (New York: Simon & Schuster, 1992) is breathtaking. In painstaking detail Greider chronicles exactly how corporations and wealthy individuals get what they want in Washington, and how common people are ignored and manipulated.

115. The fate of the Social Security trust fund is an especially egregious example of how this dynamic works. Over the last seventeen years, income taxes have been repeatedly cut, while the U.S. Treasury has "borrowed" $1.1 *trillion* from Social Security payroll taxes, 53 percent of which are paid by people who earn less than $20,000 a year. As economist Dean Baker says, "That's a huge transfer of wealth from low- and moderate-income people, who paid the payroll taxes, to people at the high end, who pay the bulk of individual and corporate taxes"; Miles Benson, "Politicians Must Cure $1.1 Trillion Headache," *St. Paul Pioneer Press*, August 6, 2001, 3A.

If the nation-state tends to elide actually existing internal differences, it tends simultaneously to accent external differences. National identity becomes one's primary loyalty, and that which separates one's nation from all others is highlighted. In terms of law, sovereignty assumes a condition of anarchy among states, and nationalism heightens general consciousness of this condition. What is "common" is reduced to what fits into national borders, and what is good can be purchased at the expense of what is good for other nation-states. The development of the nation-state in the nineteenth and twentieth centuries can be summed up as the completion of the contradictory process of alienation from local community and simultaneous parochialization of what is common to the borders of the nation-state. Neither movement facilitates the pursuit of a genuine common good.

Globalization

Understanding this apparently contradictory double movement is crucial to understanding the relationship of the nation-state to the process that has come to be called globalization. The accelerated worldwide economic and cultural universalization that has marked the move to post-Fordist types of production since the early 1970s is said to be trampling the borders of the nation-state and making sovereignty increasingly irrelevant. In some ways this is true, but it is important to see that the nation-state has been one of the primary promoters of this process. Globalization is, in part, the hyperextension of the triumph of the universal over the local, on which the nation-state is founded.

Capitalism and the state arose simultaneously as, respectively, the economic and political logic of the same movement. The state produced a centralized and regularized legal framework to make mechanisms of contract and private property right possible. The state sanctioned the enclosure of common lands to private use, thus "freeing" landless peasants to become wage laborers.[116] The state directly promoted international trade. The state universalized and guaranteed money, weights, and measures to facilitate exchanges. Taxation became centrally organized under the state, which effectively signified the decline of the land-owning aristocracy and the ascent of the bourgeoisie. Above all, the state contributed, as we have seen, to the creation of "possessive individualism," the invention of the universal human subject liberated from local ties and free to exchange his or her property and labor with any other individual.[117] The advent of the nation-state and popular sovereignty has only reinforced the close relationship between the nation-state and capitalism. Enormous outlays of "corporate welfare" are only one manifestation of this fundamental cooperation. More fundamentally, as we have seen, the nation-state serves to subsume class conflict and advance the interests of

---

116. Michael Perelman's excellent study *The Invention of Capitalism: Classical Political Economy and the Secret History of Primitive Accumulation* (Durham, NC: Duke University Press, 2000) shows how Smith, Ricardo, Steuart, and other classical economists abandoned their laissez-faire principles when it came to advocating government policies that forced peasants off their land and into factories.
117. Giddens, *Nation-State*, 148–60; Nisbet, *Quest for Community*, 104–5.

capital as national interests. As Michael Hardt and Antonio Negri write, even conflicts between individual capitalists and the nation-state work for the health of capitalism as a whole.[118]

The advance of globalization has indeed eroded the nation-state's sovereignty on several fronts. This may eventually open up interesting possibilities for the reimagination of more complex political spaces. For the moment, however, corporations are the primary beneficiaries. Capital is now more mobile than ever, and nation-states have little power to contain the flow of money and information across their borders. Corporations have become increasingly transnational, discarding loyalties to any particular locations or communities and moving to wherever cheap labor and unrestrictive environmental laws can be found. One might expect that the nation-state and globalization would be mortal enemies, but in fact that is not the case. Capital is free to move where it wants, but labor is not. The profitability of shutting down plants in Wisconsin and reopening them in northern Mexico depends on the national border—and border guards—that stands, in some cases, just a few hundred feet north of the maquiladoras. More striking is the fact that the nation-state regularly and quite deliberately advances its own apparent loss of sovereignty. The surrender of sovereignty over tariffs, trade regulations, and environmental laws in the creation of the World Trade Organization was promoted by the governing elites of nation-states, and nation-states remain the only bearers of legitimate violence to enforce such international agreements. The Commerce Department and USAID encourage and subsidize the movement of factories to overseas locations.[119] The 2002 "economic stimulus" package included $21 billion in incentives for U.S. corporations to use tax shelters in the Bahamas and other Caribbean countries. These examples are inexplicable if one assumes that the nation-state and globalization are simply opposed. What is happening is perhaps best described as the hyperextension of the state's subsumption of the local under the universal. Just as the state enacted a unitary national market, so now a global market is taking its place. Government has not disappeared but become decentralized and partially deterritorialized. The fusion of politics and economics has gone beyond national boundaries, and national governments are increasingly integrated into a transnational system of power distribution, of which transnational corporations and supranational organisms like the WTO are other significant components. Saskia Sassen criticizes those who "reduce what is happening to a function of the global-national duality: what one wins, the other loses. By contrast, I view deregulation not simply as a loss of control by the state but as a crucial mechanism for handling the juxtaposition of the interstate consensus to pursue globalization and the fact that national legal

---

118. Michael Hardt and Antonio Negri, *Empire* (Cambridge, MA: Harvard University Press, 2000), 304–5.

119. For example, "Losing Our Shirts," *The Independent* (Durham, NC), April 6, 1994, on grants, loans, and advertising by USAID to encourage textile corporations to relocate factories overseas.

systems remain as the major, or crucial, instantiation through which guarantees of contract and property rights are enforced."[120]

If this is the case, then looking to the nation-state to defend the common good against the often brutal consequences of globalization does not appear promising. This is so not merely because the nation-state is increasingly powerless to oppose globalization, but because the nation-state at a fundamental level is not opposed to globalization. Nation-states may be resources for ad hoc resistance to the process of globalization, but in the long run, the prospects for resistance are undermined by the lack of autonomy of the political in the governance of nation-states.

Conclusion

The nation-state is neither community writ large nor the protector of smaller communal spaces, but rather originates and grows over against truly common forms of life. This is not necessarily to say that the nation-state cannot and does not promote and protect some goods, or that any nation-state is entirely devoid of civic virtue, or that some forms of ad hoc cooperation with the government cannot be useful. It is to suggest that the nation-state is simply not in the common-good business. At its most benign, the nation-state is most realistically likened, as in MacIntyre's apt metaphor, to the telephone company, a large bureaucratic provider of goods and services that never quite provides value for money.

The problem, as MacIntyre notes, is that the nation-state presents itself as so much more, as the keeper of the common good and repository of sacred values that demands sacrifice on its behalf. The longing for true communion that Christians recognize at the heart of any truly common life is transferred onto the nation-state. Civic virtue and the goods of common life do not simply disappear; as Augustine saw, the earthly city flourishes by producing a distorted image of the heavenly city. The nation-state is a simulacrum of common life, where false order is parasitical on true order. In a bureaucratic order whose main function is to adjudicate struggles for power between various factions, a sense of unity is produced by the only means possible: sacrifice to false gods in war. The nation-state may be understood theologically as a kind of parody of the church, meant to save us from division.[121]

The urgent task of the church, then, is to demystify the nation-state and to treat it like the telephone company. At its best, the nation-state may provide goods and services that contribute to a certain limited order—mail delivery is a positive good. The state is not the keeper of the common good, however, and we need to adjust our expectations accordingly. The church must break its imagination out of

---

120. Saskia Sassen, *Losing Control? Sovereignty in an Age of Globalization* (New York: Columbia University Press, 1996), 25–26. See also Hardt and Negri, *Empire*, xi–xvi, 304–9.

121. I make this argument at length in my book *Theopolitical Imagination* (Edinburgh: T. & T. Clark, 2002).

captivity to the nation-state. The church must constitute itself as an alternative social space, and not simply rely on the nation-state to be its social presence. The church needs, at every opportunity, to "complexify" space, that is, to promote the creation of spaces in which alternative economies and authorities flourish.

The theological rationale for such a move is founded in the biblical account of how salvation history interrupts and transforms human space and time. The word the earliest church used to describe itself was *ekklēsia*. In the Septuagint, the term *ekklēsia* was used for the assembly of Israel for various public acts, such as covenant-making (Deut 4:10), dedication of the temple (1 Kgs 8:14), and dedication of the city (Neh 5:7).[122] In calling itself *ekklēsia*, the church was identifying itself as Israel, the assembly that bears the public presence of God in history. In Greek usage, *ekklēsia* named the assembly of those with citizen rights in a given polis. In calling itself *ekklēsia*, the church was identifying itself as fully public, refusing the available language for a private association (*koinon* or *collegium*). The church was not gathered like a *koinon* around particular interests, but was concerned with the interests of the whole city, because it was the witness of God's activity in history.[123] At the same time, the church was not simply another polis; instead, it was an anticipation of the heavenly city on earth, in a way that complexified the bipolar calculus of public and private.

The medieval synthesis, though fused with static social hierarchies, at least preserved the biblical sense that the church was not a private association that mediated between the putatively universal state and the sovereign individual. When modern Catholic social teaching has insisted on the need for complex space, therefore, it should not be dismissed solely as nostalgia for medieval hierarchy. Pope Leo XIII's *Rerum novarum* (1891) noted that the "ancient workmen's Guilds were destroyed in the last century, and no other organization took their place." As a result, working people have been left "isolated and defenseless."[124] The solution, according to Leo, is the proliferation of associations along the lines of the medieval guilds, in complete independence from the state, and under the auspices of the church.[125] Critics have noted the vagueness and nostalgia of Leo's cure, but his diagnosis is insightful: the source of injustice is the modern creation of simple space, the individual cut loose from community and left isolated. Pope Pius XI's *Quadragesimo anno* (1931) also put forward an elaborate scheme calling for a proliferation of labor, religious, and professional vocational groups and

---

122. Peter J. Leithart, *Against Christianity* (Moscow, ID: Canon, 2003), 30.

123. Dieter Georgi writes, "Paul chose [*ekklēsia*] to indicate that the assembly of those who followed Jesus, the assembly called together in a particular city in the name of the biblical God, was in competition with the local political assembly of the citizenry, the official *ekklēsia*. The world is meant to hear the claim that the congregation of Jesus, gathered in the name of the God of the Bible, is where the interests of the city in question truly find expression"; *Theocracy in Paul's Praxis and Theology* (Minneapolis: Fortress, 1991), 57.

124. Pope Leo XIII, *Rerum novarum*, par. 2.

125. Ibid., pars. 36–43.

"corporations" not under the direct supervision of the state. The principle of sub-sidiarity was meant as well to keep the state from reaching down and distorting the organic life of community below.[126]

Unfortunately, the contemporary church often ignores the possibility that the church itself could encourage the formation of alternative social bodies; it usually treats the state as the potential solution to any given social ill. An anecdote from political scientist Michael Budde captures this problem:

> Once upon a time, I was hired as a consultant for a public-policy arm of state-level Catholic bishops' conference. The bishops, according to the institution's staff people, wanted to engage in rededicated efforts to con-front the realities of poverty in their state.
>
> What the church bureaucracy had in mind was something on the order of a new lobbying initiative in the state legislature or perhaps an expert conference on poverty in the state.
>
> I told them that they should attempt to take every Catholic in their state on an intensive retreat, with follow-up programs upon their return. Nothing the Church could do would benefit poor people more, I argued, than to energize, inspire, and ignite the passion of larger numbers of the faithful. Without attempts to "convert the baptized," in William O'Malley's phrase, the stranglehold of self-interest, isolation, and reli-gious indifference would continue to throttle church attempts to deal seriously with poverty in a global capitalist order.
>
> My advice, to put it gently, was unappreciated. I was fired. They had an experts conference. As far as I can tell, poverty in their state remained indifferent to their efforts.[127]

In this case the bishops were unable to imagine that the common good could mean the church itself creating authentically common spaces among the haves and have-nots, rather than advising the state on technocratic solutions to poverty.

The problem is not limited to liberal Christians who rely on the welfare state; in a different way it also captivates conservatives. The example cited at the begin-ning of this chapter is a case in point. In regarding the nation-state as responsible for the common good, the church's voice in such crucial moral matters as war becomes muted, pushed to the margins. Just-war reasoning becomes a tool of statecraft, most commonly used by the state to justify war, rather than a moral dis-cipline for the church to grapple with questions of violence. The church itself becomes one more withering "intermediate association," whose moral reasoning and moral formation are increasingly colonized by the nation-state and the mar-ket. To resist, the church must at the very least reclaim its authority to judge if and

---

126. Pope Pius XI, *Quadragesimo anno*, pars. 31–40, 79. Also, see Dennis McCann's essay in this volume.

127. Michael Budde, *The (Magic) Kingdom of God: Christianity and Global Culture Industries* (Boulder, CO: Westview, 1997), 1.

when Christians can kill, and not abdicate that authority to the nation-state.[128] To do so would be to create an alternative authority and space that does not simply mediate between state and individual.

How is this appeal "common" and not particular and divisive? In the first place, if the analysis of this paper is correct, then the nation-state is simply not the universal community under whose umbrella the church stands as one particular association. Not only does the nation-state carve the world up into competing national interests, but also internally, it is destructive of forms of commonality that do not privilege the sovereignty of narrow individual self-interest. In the second place, as Robert Jenson argues in this volume, the church is not a merely particular association; instead, it participates in the life of the triune God, who is the only good that can be common to all. Especially through the Eucharist, Christians belong to a body that not only is international, constantly challenging the narrow particularity of national interests, but it also is eternal, the body of Christ, that anticipates the heavenly polity on earth. Salvation history is not a particular subset of human history, but simply is the story of God's rule—not yet completely legible—over all of history. God's activity is not, of course, confined to the church, and the boundaries between the church and the world are porous and fluid. Nevertheless, the church needs to take seriously its task of promoting spaces where participation in the common good of God's life can flourish.

---

128. I examine this issue, and Novak's and Weigel's arguments, in greater detail in my article "At Odds with the Pope: Legitimate Authority and Just Wars," *Commonweal* 130, no. 10 (May 23, 2003): 11–13.

The Triunity of Common Good

Robert W. Jenson

What Is a Common Good?

It is often unwise to begin a discussion by "defining terms"—here, "common" and "good." If one does so begin, any offered preliminary definition should be vague.[1] Perhaps we will be safe, both as to historically appropriate provenance and as to needed imprecision, if we draw from the passages of Augustine's *City of God*[2] in which he in turn draws from Cicero[3] citing Scipio. Thus we secure both the Christian and the pagan authorities of our civilization's thinking about public matters, and by casting so wide a net we also secure an appropriately open concept.

There can, according to Cicero-Scipio according to Augustine, be a *res publica*, a public rather than a private "thing," only when an identifiable group of persons live in some mutually ordered fashion. There can be such ordering, such rule of law, only where there is prior community in virtue. Finally in this chain, there can be such community only where there is antecedent joint *amor*, longing, for some one thing, which is just so a "good." A common good, let us say, is an object of a shared

---

1. Perhaps we need not be so absolute as some followers of Wittgenstein.

2. For my interpretation of this text, with the references, see Robert W. Jenson, *Systematic Theology* (2 vols.; New York: Oxford University Press, 1997–1999), 2:73–88.

3. At one point in our group's discussions, several members pointed out that the West's understanding of political life was initially determined by the legacy from Cicero, rather than by that of either Aristotle or Plato. Also, in my judgment, the influence—whether malign or benign—of "the Greeks" in this matter is often overestimated.

longing that by funding certain virtues draws a number of persons to live together in mutually understood and practiced ways, that is, within some rule of law.

There are communities of various sorts and associations of various sorts and doubtless commonalities of other types than the famous two just mentioned. Each will have, if only apophatically—a point to which I will return—some common good specific to it, and perhaps also a specific way in which that good is common to it.

Some goods around which a group might cohere can subsist as goods whether or not such a group appears. A particular prime steak is in the butcher's display case, whether or not a dinner party forms around it. And the pseudouniversal "prime steak" also obtains with or without the organization of meatpacking firms. If, however, the diners or a shift at the packing plant join in a way that would survive their turning vegetarian or losing their jobs, it seems that they are now united by a good that does not obtain without the group. Being the-friends-who-met-at-that-dinner-that-turned-everyone-off-red-meat or the-gang-that-meets-at-Hansen's-Bar are not goods that would be there whether or not the groups in question subsisted. Nor, I think, are they instantiations or species of something like "post-revolting-dinner-friendship" or "male-bonding."

Thus, in the case of some coherent groups, the ontological status of their unifying good is unproblematic, since these goods can subsist without the groups that may gather around them. But other unifying goods seem to inhabit a different ontological mode. Do justice, familial love, and the like subsist independently of families, polities, and the like? If we are to distinguish communities from other commonalities, perhaps we may say that communities are those commonalities whose relation to their gathering good can provoke this very question.

It is a fateful question. For the circumstance that the common good of a community is not separable from the community that seeks it, may tempt us to suppose it has no independent reality of *any* sort. It would seem finally to consign it to the category of daydreams[4] or indeed dreams of a less harmless sort[5]—I will return to this.

Closely related to the plurality of sorts of commonalities and goods is the—in my judgment—vital if perhaps penultimate distinction between interests and goods. My interests, or the interests of some group of which I am a part, are what they are. I may be mistaken about them, but then I am indeed simply mistaken. It is in my interest—I think—that the stock market not collapse. Nor do convictions about how a just society would organize the supply and flow of capital, or about what I really ought to be doing with my money, change that eventuality in the slightest. If to some group I bring only my interests and others do the same, an overlap of our interests—or perhaps rather an overlap of overlaps—may indeed bind us firmly together. Is this ever all that happens? I am not sure.

---

4. Unless Plato as usually interpreted was right.

5. Several members of our group have been especially concerned to draw attention to this possibility. See the essays by Milner Ball, Cheryl Kirk-Duggan, and Josiah Young in this volume.

It anyway does sometimes happen that discourse occurs[6] and transforms the overlap of interests into a moral space. Arguing—or even violently disputing—with others in a public space constituted initially by interests, I may be led to see that my interest in the matter at hand *ought* not decide for the community, and you may do the same. Just thereby we may come to be united not or not only by the overlap of our interests—which remain what they were—but by the good that is the norm of these judgments. It is also important to note that this good may often be known only in this apophatic way, as the otherwise undisclosed ground of a feeling[7] that I ought not in this case demand my interest[8]—whether I continue to do so or not. That is, this common good may be known only in repentance, or indeed only in guilt.

Here, only partly by the way, is the problem of merely representative government: my representative can very well carry my interests to a forum where I am not, but he or she cannot there repent for me, which means he or she cannot there pursue the *good* on my behalf.[9] A representative can and should pursue the good of the polity to which I belong, but cannot *as* my representative.

A further import of the distinction between common interest and common good is to mitigate the alarm that concern for the common good sometimes arouses.[10] At least some of the cases adduced as instances of concern for a common good crushing or marginalizing individuals or minority groups are instead instances of intransigent insistence on a common interest, which will often be in conflict with interests of groups otherwise within some common forum, a conflict the minority party will likely lose.[11]

Within the way I have used the language, it is a near-tautology to say that no group held together solely by overlap of interests would have a common good. It is another question whether there could in fact be such a group. What I would

---

6. This is, to be sure, disputed by those with no hope. In political-science circles, it appears that the term is now "deliberation." Self-described "positivists" say that deliberation never actually produces or can be known to produce a better result than no deliberation; others variously maintain that it does.

7. Feelings may perfectly well grasp reality; they are or can be an apophatic mode of perception.

8. Kant had, surely, a point: sometimes when I know I ought to do something, if I ask why I ought to, I violate the mandate by asking the question. As Louis Armstrong reputedly said when asked what jazz is, "If you gotta ask, you ain't got it."

9. Here is a point of convergence with concerns of several other members of the group, who are suspicious of large centralized political structures.

10. Alarm was occasionally expressed also in our group.

11. Nazi anti-Semitism, often adduced, was a sheer hatred, explicable only outside the terms of the present discussion. Insofar as it bothered with motivations, those presented were the convictions that Jews had somehow been prominent against those who had "plotted" against German military force in World War I and could not be relied upon in future, that intermarriage with an inferior human strain was weakening the Aryan gene pool, and so on. The goods to which the party was allegedly dedicated—economic equality, societal discipline, recovery of German honor, and so on—were as much desired by Jews as by other citizens.

like to think is that no commonality actually comes together or perdures without some mutual commitment that is moral in character, that every commonality is united by some good common for it. In language other than that generally used in this chapter, but that is regular parlance for other contributors to this book, I want to think that not even the most coldly calculated association is grounded in *sheer* "contract," that all human commonality is finally grounded in "covenant" of some, however rudimentary or feeble sort.

In this volume[12] a case is made that powerful modern commonalities, notably the modern nation-state, originated by destroying communities indeed gathered around common good, and that in accord with this origin, the nation-state remains ill-fitted to any binding force but interest. I find this argument persuasive.[13] I wonder, however, whether even a nation-state could endure absent *all* common longing or aspiration, all common *amor*. Thus also the architects of the American state, arguably the modern state most consistently designed as mere mechanism, knew that their creation would not work without "civic virtue" in the larger community. It may well be that nation-states' civic virtue is left over from previous political arrangements. But could this run out altogether without precipitating the collapse of the state? Or perhaps creating a commonality that was hell itself, which God would hardly allow short of the End?

From a different point of view, another chapter in this volume[14] notes that—while it need not have been so—history has in fact given us the nation-state as the chief now-available domain of a common good. It argues that therefore our nation-states must have some claim to our support. This contention also has weight: we should not, in my judgment, be quite so suspicious of national patriotism as are some members of our group.[15] National sovereignty is now, to be sure,

---

12. William Cavanaugh, "Killing for the Telephone Company."

13. Yet one should consider Oliver O'Donovan's analysis of the notion of "state," which if correct would considerably modify such judgments; *The Desire of the Nations* (Cambridge: Cambridge University Press, 1996), 231–42. At the last session of our group, Jean Porter reminded me of an obvious point, that O'Donovan should get credit at several places in this paper.

14. Jean Porter, "The Common Good in Thomas Aquinas."

15. I perhaps owe readers some brief account of my own view of the nation-state. First, the genealogy presented by William Cavanaugh in "Killing for the Telephone Company" must indeed give one pause. Second is a consideration important for the fathers of the United States: a nation-state will usually be simply too large for the transformative power of discourse—or "deliberation"—to be effective in its most general arena. This is why they designed the national state as a mechanism of checks and balances and why Jefferson relied so much on smaller and more participatory subpolities within the nation, which have been declining in all typical nation-states. After recognizing both of these negatives, one must consider the alternatives. I am for myself not at all sure that a general sovereignty compound of multinational business, NGOs—many of them captive to statist ideologies—and such instruments of international law as actually seem to be developing will improve on the system of nation-states. At present, another sort of internationalism is also reasserting itself: empire. An American imperium is clearly in place and expanding. Again, I am less alarmed by this, and by the necessarily accompanying use of American arms, also at this writing in Iraq, than are most colleagues in this project.

being reshaped and perhaps undermined by the congeries of developments usually called "globalization." To the extent that globalization prevails, we must hope[16] that international corporations, the many and various international assemblies, agencies and courts, and "nongovernmental organizations" do not carry on without some binding *amor* beyond the interests of their "stakeholders." Otherwise the international order they constitute may prove as oppressive as any national tyranny.

The Common Good as the Political Good

It is time explicitly to add "the" to "common good" and thus arrive at the place to which I have been steering all along: in dealing with communities of the sort we call polities. My definition of "common good" was, after all, drawn from Augustine's book about the two great polities of God and this world.[17] What indeed would "*the* common good" be? We may say: It would be a common good whose subsistence and attraction is a condition of sharing other common goods. Alternatively but connected to that description, we may begin an approach to the eschatological considerations later to be offered by suggesting: "The" common good is the one that will survive the Last Judgment, that will be the bond of the new Jerusalem. And it is, I suggest, the political good that has this role.

Another vague definition is now required. By a polity, I mean something plausibly analogous to a Greek polis—or probably to a romantic image of the polis—which is why we use the word we do. A polity is a relatively permanent community whose life together is shaped and guided by binding moral discourse functioning as such. A polity surrounds an open place, a forum, where this discourse can happen; the place can be as small as a monarch's bed-chamber or as encompassing as an assembly of all the people. In it such matters are debated, with a plausible view to execution of decisions reached, as: "What shall we teach our children?" or "Under what circumstances will we use force against other polities?" A *polity*, as the tradition and I use the word, need not be a "state." It includes but is not exhausted in such things as legislatures and executives. Thus, political discourse in my sense embraces the sort of discussion and debate that another essay in this volume[18] calls discourse about "matters of the commonwealth," if only such discussions somehow go to determine the community's decisions.

Participants are to be "free persons," that is, persons not so bound to the satisfaction of necessary interest as to be removed from the transformative force of discourse. Much of the human race has routinely been viewed as bound in this fashion or indeed compelled into such bondage. That is a fundamental problem of all concerned for the common good, often adduced in our group.

---

16. I am myself undecided in the debate between Max Stackhouse and some other members of our group, about which is greater, the threat or the promise of globalization.

17. Augustine's word is *cives*, but behind his Latin stands the Greek name for structures like Athens or Sparta, *polis*, from which comes "polity."

18. Robin Lovin, "Public Discourse and the Common Good."

Empirically, it is apparent that many tribes, empires, dictatorships, and so on are not obviously polities in this sense.[19] But, analogously to a previously posed question, is human life possible with *nothing* of the authentically political? I do not think so. For human life, according to Jewish or Christian faith, is intrinsically moral life, and moral life is intrinsically mutual life. I contend that without membership in some community shaped in some (perhaps slight) degree by mutual moral deliberation, we are incapable of specifically human fellowship. "The" common good is the political good.

But what is this good? In the Bible it appears as "righteousness,"[20] a life together in which each one takes his or her particular position—as rich or poor,[21] female or male, countryman or priest—as an opportunity of service to each one other. "Ordered love" might be a translation. It is apparent that this good is its own reward. The attempt to define the common good of the polity is necessarily circular: a polity is a community that has this sort of common good, and *the* common good is the sort a polity has.

The Eschatological Good

It is perhaps the inseparability of communal goods from the communities they gather, and the resulting circularity of definition, that is the deepest reason for our worries about the common good. For if this is all that is to be said about the ontological status of common goods, it can look as though the good that gathers a community is invented by the community. It can seem that a community's dedication to its good is merely an attempt to lift itself by its own bootstraps. If this is indeed the situation, then in a community the advent of critical self-awareness must reveal it and bring the community crashing down to the earth of maneuvering interests. A hermeneutics "of suspicion" may then say that all self-described communities are really deluded commonalities of interest, and that when we talk of the good of a community, we are each really using the notion as a tool of his or her own interest.

Can there be another interpretation than such nihilism? If the common goods of communities are indeed not separable from their communities, might

---

19. Politics, properly so-called, are now perilously thin in the United States. In the national legislature, actual debate about what should be done has almost ceased; one need only watch C-Span for a time to see this. And the civil society of churches, town meetings, clubs, and so on, which for much of the nation's history carried most of its actual moral debate, has been largely declared "private" or closed down altogether. As the Mexican-American War (1846–48) was looming, the town fathers of Gettysburg, Pennsylvania, called for a general discussion of the citizenry. They invited the town's leading intellectual, a theologian and a man noted for unpopular antiwar views, to open the meeting with an address. When I lived in Gettysburg during America's adventure in Vietnam, such an event was inconceivable.

20. This interpretation seems to me congruent with Patrick Miller's essay in this volume and with his interventions in the group's discussions.

21. This does not mean that being poor is a good thing. Precisely the service due from the rich is emulation of the Lord's "preferential option for the poor." And as our Lord said, the rich are unlikely to run out of the poor to help.

they nevertheless have some reality other than that of their communities? I suggest: A community's unifying desire for some good and then the good itself occur *within* an encompassing historical reality that is *as a whole* teleological.[22] The common goods of communities are indeed not just there, like steaks or even the class of steaks. Their reality is that of way stations within the pull of a goal of all reality, and they disappear from sight if we abstract from that final goal. Nevertheless, *as* such way stations they are as actual as any other features of reality. "Familial affection," for example, subsists as families' *location* within an encompassing teleology of human life. By Christian—and Jewish?—interpretation of reality, there are communities and their goods because there is God as the final cause of his creation, drawing and leading it toward the perfection it will have in him. If we find it better, therefore, we might say that the only common good is God. But then we would have to invent some other word for the political common good, insofar as the church is not the only polity.

At this point we must be very strict in holding our language specifically to a *creation*. What God *creates* is not a something, which then may or may not have a history. What God creates is a history, which has an end and goal, thus making it a whole, a something. The great metaphysical divide is between those who think that a dramatic story can truly be told of the whole of reality, and those who think not; Judaism and Christianity are the paradigm instances of the first position. Prior to the end of any story, its bits hold together in that each event refers *figurally* to its successors, by virtue of some anticipation, some *amor*, of the story's end. Plainly, in the case of the universe, or of human history as a whole, such a story will not be plausible unless someone other than us is telling it. The creation is a history in which each event is given figural reference and attraction to its successors, by the draw of God the Successor.

Theological use[23] of the notion of *amor*, longing, comes from the Platonism which is one root of our culture. To fit it for Christian theological use, a sort of directional change was required. In a *creation*, ontological longing is not primally the relation of what is below to what is above, as with an unbaptized Platonism, but is the relation of beginning to end. That is to say, the longing that moves the creation is the figural dynamic of *drama*. And that is further to say, it is given in the surprise *persons* are to each other.

No account is dramatic unless it posits freedom and possibility, even if only, as in some plays of Samuel Beckett and his epigones,[24] as what is thematically

---

22. They are, as in some passages of Aristotle, "movers" penultimate to the "unmoved mover."

23. The great passage is from the opening of Augustine's *Confessions* (1:1): "You have made us for yourself, and our hearts are restless till they find rest in you."

24. Though actual followers of Beckett are impossible, each nihilistic drama as an individual must be its own genus. The resemblance to Thomas Aquinas's ontology of angels is perhaps not accidental. The authors of "theater of the absurd" indeed put themselves in the place of God, finding nothing else to put there, and rightly first created angels. They were proved, however, not to be God when they could create no further.

excluded or (what may be the same thing) as all there is. And freedom enters with persons. When you intrude on my life as an other than me and different from me, I am opened to the possibility of being other than I am. In a creation, persons meet through time, and just so the temporal dynamic of a creation is free longing.

There is a sense, therefore, in which "common good" is a teleological notion, and a related but different sense in which it is an eschatological notion. Christians and Jews must think that the goods that centrally define communities appear in a creation that is *not* a "tale told by an idiot." Human commonalities, and centrally among them polities, are *for* something; they occur within a universal teleology. Those who think history meaningless indeed have reason for their nihilism: one cannot read purpose from history's text, nor does the teleology of created history appear as the *progress* in which modernity hoped. Christians trust the gospel with its promises of fulfillment beyond the possibilities of history as it now moves; they look for an *eschaton*. Just so, we can know creation's teleology as well. "Common good" is an eschatological notion, as appears in several essays in this volume,[25] and only thus a teleological notion.

The end of these reflections would seem to be such propositions as the following. A polity both *has* a common good and *is* its own common good. The difference in which this dialectic is possible is dramatic and located in a *perichoresis*, a mutual interplay and even interpenetration of persons. The next step is an observation: only the triune God fully satisfies these stipulations.

The Good as What God Is for God

The community that has and is its good, with a longing that is not finally other than itself, and by a distinction of source and goal that is again not finally other than itself, is the community that the Father and the Son are among themselves in the Spirit. In the Scriptures, the eschatological fulfillment of Augustine's "city" is "the kingdom of God." But throughout the theological tradition, this political characterization of the *eschaton* is paired by an at-first-thought quite different characterization: the fulfillment of human existence is "deification" or the "vision of God." This notion too is scriptural, since "eternal" life, "perfect" righteousness, "boundless" love, and the like—all biblical evocations of the *eschaton*—can in fact only be *God's* life, righteousness, love, and so forth. If we are to have *eternal* life, this can only happen if we will share *God's* life, since (by a fine scholastic rule) God is identical with his attributes.

But if both eschatologies are true, then somehow entry into the kingdom of God must be entry into the triune life of God, and vice versa. That is, entry into the kingdom of God must somehow be entry into a polity that God himself is in himself. And that can indeed be the case, for classic doctrine of the triune God displays precisely a perfect polity. The following hardly describes what most religion

---

25. It notably appears in Dennis McCann's effort to discern a structure in Catholic social teaching's references to the common good ("The Common Good in Catholic Social Teaching").

thinks of as God, but it is indeed the way the doctrine of Trinity identifies the strange specific God of the gospel and the church.[26]

In the triune God there is a plurality of *social personae*: Father, Son, and Spirit each genuinely has a different role. This is true both in God himself—the Father begets and is not begotten, the Son is begotten and does not beget, the Spirit frees and is not freed—and in God's works, in the doing of which "all action . . . begins with the Father and is actual through the Son and is perfected in the Holy Spirit."[27] The three are nevertheless not three gods, precisely in that their communal *virtue* or *righteousness* is perfect; for each subsists at all only as his entire investment in self-giving to the others.[28] This righteousness itself is not a silent perfection, but occurs as a *discourse*, for the second identity, in whom God knows what God is, is a *Word*. Moreover, *decision* occurs in this discourse, since God is who and what he is *freely*, in his own eternal decision to be who he is. The divine "nature" that each has with the others, so that they are God instead of something else, and which is thus identical with their righteousness, is the *common Good* of the three; for to be God is to be the Good, first of all for God. And finally, in consequence of all the above, the eternal triune life is a space of *moral action*: we recognize "source, movement, and goal" in God himself and not just as adaptation to his relation with us. God is not eternal because he lacks such poles but because with him "there is no conflict between them."[29]

It is then a very traditional theological move, to say that "the common good" must be an intrinsically *analogous* term, whose primary referent is God and which applies to creatures just in that they derive their being from him. I wish to make that move. But how does it *work* in the present case? What is the *present* link between the common good as the Good that God is for himself, and the common good of this world's polities?

The Church as the Gate of Heaven

I propose that the link is the church. The church, said Martin Luther with his customarily vehement appropriation of catholic tradition, is "the gate of heaven."[30] Yet the church is very much a created community of this world.

It is a dominating feature of an extensive ecumenical ecclesiology, developed in the ecumenical dialogues that have proliferated since 1965,[31] that the church's

---

26. To the following, with overabundant reference, Jenson, *Systematic Theology*, 1:90–236.

27. Gregory of Nyssa, "Ad Ablabius" ("Not Three Gods"), 125.

28. This point was made fully clear to me by the writings of Wolfhart Pannenberg.

29. Karl Barth, *Kirchliche Dogmatik*, vol. II/1 (Zollikon-Zürich: Evangelischer Verlag, 1948), 690.

30. E.g., *Luther's Works* (American ed.; St. Louis, MO: Concordia, 1955–86), 43:599, "Go to the place where the word is spoken and the sacraments are ministered, and there set up the title, 'The Gate of Heaven.'"

31. Whatever other fruit the dialogues have not born, they have produced a body of good theology, most of it ecclesiology.

life and institutions are shaped by the triunity of God's own life—so long, anyway, as the church does not altogether defect from its own being. The church's unity is constituted in worship of God the Father, its animating communal spirit is the Holy Spirit himself, and its place within God's action is that of (again stealing from Augustine) the *totus Christus*, the unitary reality that the risen Christ is with his own body (the church).

In this ecumenical ecclesiology, the oneness of the community of which these things can be true, is *koinōnia*, communion. Each local church is the church as a communion of persons; the one church is a communion of communions. And if there are intermediate levels—patriarchates, provinces, or perhaps even "confessions" in fellowship—these too are communions of communions. The concept of *koinōnia* became dominant in ecumenical ecclesiology precisely because of its simultaneous applicability to the unity of the three triune identities and to the unity of the church.

Each of the characters just noted has its concrete ecclesiological consequences. What follows is hardly more than a chance selection from among them.

The church worships God the Father. Thus its prayer and offering are conducted within a directing triune framework: in most contexts, the church prays *to* the Father, with the Son, in the power of the Spirit. And because prayer is the church's determining discourse, its life as a whole has this dynamic orientation. The church, directed to the Father, the single first source and goal of all things—in classic Trinitarian language, the *Monarchos*—is thus a sort of monarchy (see below).

The church's unity is constituted in worship of the one God, in jointly enacted desire for the one possible fully common good. Therefore, so long as the church does not utterly cease to be church by ceasing to worship the true God, its gravest defections and strifes cannot undo its unity in adoration, for God is indeed but one for all.

Here readers may object that Aristotle, whose political doctrines were controversial in our group's discussions, would too much approve of the church thus described. He distrusted democracy and taught that some one person or class must finally be responsible, and in our discussions, just this teaching was instanced against him:[32] whether one person or one class or one nation rules, others just so are ruled. Yet on the other hand, if a community dedicated to some one good is not to be a sort of machine, it would indeed seem that its good must be available personally and not just as an abstract ideal. Are we then left with a choice between a mechanistic state and one or another divine right or *Führerprinzip*? Some theorists of democracy are suspicious of the very notion of common good, just because it seems to confront us with these alternatives.

But whatever may be true of other communities, the church does not face this choice. For the church's monarch is present within the body not in naked sovereignty but by the Son and the Spirit. I move first to the Spirit.

---

32. In discussion, particularly Josiah Young found in Aristotle's influence a root of considerable evil in Western history; see his essay "Good Is Knowing When to Stop."

If a community has some common good, it must be animated by some common spirit. In remarkable agreement, both the Old Testament and the Greek thinkers use "spirit"[33] for personal freedom, the "wind," which both animates the one whose spirit it is and blows others about, liberating them from stasis in their present moment. Now *amor* is a mode of spirit. If then a community is united in a common *amor*, it must be animated by a common spirit; we do indeed speak of the spirit of all sorts of groups, from athletic teams to research projects. It is the particularity of the church that the spirit animating its unity is the very Spirit of God.[34]

Thus, the church's obedience to the Father, its *amor* insofar as the *Monarchos* is its object, is not slavish. For the church is drawn to the Father precisely by and in a freedom that is nothing less than the Father's own Freedom, who indeed is the same one God as the Father. The Freedom in which the Father is the universal monarch is therefore the very freedom in which the church obeys him. Moreover, the church is—short of its entire apostasy—the community whose inner freedom cannot be quenched and whose freedom from outward tyranny must always triumph, for its freedom is God.

Thus the church, as one in *amor*, lives within the life of the triune God. Are there then four in God, rather than three? No, because the church is in the Trinity— and the Trinity in the church—only as the church is in a certain way identical with the Son. It is immediately vital to specify that "in a certain way"; simple identification of the church with Christ has been a perennial and unhappy temptation.[35]

The church is "the body of Christ." In Paul's use of the phrase in 1 Corinthians, the predication initially[36] functions not as a metaphor but as an analogous predication: as I am my body, so is Christ the church. If you want to find me or even assault me, you look for a body that is I. If the world wants to find the risen Christ, if only to attack him, the world must look to the church. Yet as my body I am available also to myself; just so I am in this way different from my body. So it is as the church that the risen Christ is available to himself; he is—and indeed here in Ephesians and Colossians there is metaphor—the "head" of the body. Most significantly, as I can and must discipline my body, so the risen Christ can and too often must discipline the church. *Ecclesia semper reformanda*, it is said. "The church is always to be reformed," but not necessarily by us.

It is in this differentiated identity with Christ that the church indefectibly worships the Father and is animated by the Spirit. What must always be in our minds when thinking of the church as a community is the Eucharist, a public space where the one God gives himself to his community, where in consequence all sorts and conditions of humanity drink from one cup and eat of one loaf, and their parliament of prayer is a perfectly *participatory monarchy*.

---

33. *Ruaḥ* in Hebrew, or *pneuma* in Greek.
34. To say this, we do not, I think, have to settle the question on which the Western tradition has divided: Is the love that binds the church the Spirit himself, or a created gift of the Spirit?
35. Though a temptation to which perhaps no one has ever actually fallen.
36. See 1 Cor 10–11.

I do not think we should go further than this, in drawing lines from the triunity of God to the structure of the church.[37] The *koinōnia* that constitutes the church is not directly an image of the divine fellowship, as if God's relation to what is other than himself were a matter of reproducing himself at successive levels of remotion.[38] Instead, it is because the three mutually, each in their role, create *and* inhabit the church, that the life of the church has a structure corresponding to their unity and difference.

The degree to which the churches falsify this ecclesiology is only too well known. In this age the church is a struggling, tempted, and ambiguous participant in the divine polity. But the church is nothing less than that.

The Church as Mediator between God's Polity and Earthly Polities

The triune God is the only good that can be common to all. Thus this God is the final if usually unacknowledged object of the love that unites all other polities. The one tag of Augustine that everyone knows, that our hearts are made for God and find rest only in him, applies not only to persons but also to communities.[39] The church is the polity in this world that, sometimes despite strenuous efforts of its leaders and members, seeks this good explicitly, and as a public entity displays its seeking to the world. Christian theology must therefore summon the chutzpah to say: all earthly polities perdure—so long as they do perdure—by longing to be what the church in fact is.

We mislead ourselves if the model of our thinking is "the church and the larger community." The church *is* the larger community.[40] Or we can put it thus: What exists, as polities united by a common good, is the church and parodies of the church. Parodies can be good.

Two questions present themselves: How does the presence of the church mediate the analogy of other created polities to God? And does knowledge of this mediation enable any judgments about actual history and politics? A final section of this essay will be devoted to that second question.

The church's mediation of polity is in one aspect historical. All earthly polities perdure by longing to be what the church in fact is, the community whose common good is God, though they misidentify the object of their longing. Where the church is historically present to another polity, this longing is empirically presented with its true object. One need have no illusions about the state of the church or its public appearance to say that every such meeting is a decisive challenge to earthly polity, before which it may fall but by which it may also be enabled to perdure. For precisely those characters of the church that it cannot

---

37. In an early session of our group, I was warned against a perceived tendency to do so.

38. Yet this is the scheme of much religion and philosophy.

39. To the following, again compare O'Donovan, *The Desire of the Nations.*

40. I do not mean that the church in this world is the governing community, in James Skillen's sense in "'The Common Good' as *Political* Norm." Though again, why should that *not* sometimes be the best arrangement?

shed without ceasing altogether to exist—as noted above—are those which make the necessary object of political longing.

Thus we will know that China has recovered from its lapse into barbarism not when it fully joins the system of world trade or ceases to make international mischief, but when it welcomes the presence of the church—and particularly of the more plainly transnational Roman Catholic Church. The Roman Empire's uniquely able governing class promptly recognized the threat of the numerically and economically insignificant nascent church. And the many centuries during which the church was the acknowledged counterpart and judge of Western polities—for all that hindsight recognizes the faults of "the Constantinian settlement" so clearly—were a uniquely creative time in political understanding and practice.

To be sure, in the whole of history most polities have not had to deal with the church. If the church mediates between polity as it is founded in God and *all* earthly polities, its mediation must be metaphysical as well as historical. There is an eschatological radicalization of an Aristotelian principle[41] that seems to me appropriate to Christian theology. A condition of the creation's providing any eschatological perfection as a possibility is an anticipating actuality within the creation of that perfection. If there were within creation no actual polity gathered by the one fully common Good and enjoying the freedom of the Spirit, if there were no actual polity celebrating Eucharist, creation would not be such as to enable polities animated by longing for inalienable good and constituted in some—however pitiful or even sinister—sort of freedom and *koinōnia*. There could be no polities at all. The occurrence within creation of the church and of its meeting with some polities is a metaphysical condition of there being earthly polity.

Judging the Good in History

Readers will have noted a frequency of such weasel phrases as "perhaps" or "I am less alarmed than . . ." in the foregoing, whenever the discourse turned to judgments about history or policy. This is because—in the relation between the good that God is, the polity the church is, and other polities—such judgments are in my estimation underdetermined.

Every merely earthly polity, I have said, perdures by longing for what it cannot have except by abandoning its rebellion against the Creator; in which case it would no longer be a merely earthly polity. There is thus a profound contradiction at the heart of every such polity. We may follow Augustine's analysis of that contradiction. Every polity but the church is gathered by love for some partial good, which just because it is partial can be appropriated in self-love rather than in the joint love that makes the community. Thus, the common good of a merely earthly polity simultaneously binds the community together and solicits its members to turn against one another. Every polity but the church is exposed, by the very good that brings it together, to the political form of self-love, in Augustine's phrase, to the *libido dominandi*, "lust for domination."

---

41. Aristotle's principle that actuality is prior to possibility.

Theological judgments of political history must therefore always be dialectical— if not indeed downright slippery. To provide an example—and one that subliminally underlay some discussion in our group—let me again use the phrase "Constantinian settlement" to refer to a historical nexus more complex than the phrase suggests. Some contemporary theologians regard the relation between church and state established under Constantine and his successors as a primal fall of the church. But can we indeed say that the Constantinian settlement ought not to have happened? Should the bishops, when the rulers moved to co-opt them into a last effort to hold a disintegrating civilization together, have simply refused such a service? I think not, if we are to love our neighbor.[42] Undoubtedly, the church was thereby in some ways perverted. But just as undoubtedly, the centuries of Christendom[43] that followed uncovered unique possibilities of political freedom and human creativity.[44] The Constantinian settlement is now at an end. Is that a good or a bad thing? It is hard to say.

There have been many forms of polity. I have in effect suggested that the eschatological polity will be a participatory monarchy, a monarchy in which all members share the life and discourse of the monarch. It seems reasonable to think that earthly polities may be judged by their anticipation of this goal. If we do this, we will surely judge that the best earthly polity, all else being equal, would be what is sometimes called a participatory democracy, if provided by Providence with wise and humble moral leaders.

But all else is rarely equal, and that again widens the field of judgments. "Imperialism," for a drastic example, is a very bad word in most contemporary discourse; but it is not clear (again!) that empire may not sometimes be the best available solution to the problems of peace and justice, the best available opening to the eschatological city. Again, if one must have large nation-states, merely representative democracy (despite what I said against it) is no doubt better than no democracy at all. And while it undoubtedly seems arrogant to attempt—as the rhetoric goes—to "impose" liberal values on cultures whose history does not immediately support them, we surely should in each case inquire: What are their alternatives? One could continue at some length in this vein.

Given a historically actual spectrum of possible polities, some judgments can, I think, be more apodictic. No polity but the church has the one God for its

---

42. It does not alter the point when we recognize that the bishops undoubtedly had less Christian motives as well.

43. I speak of Christendom of a general European regime in which the polities of this world had to reckon with the presence of the church as the polity that would finally triumph.

44. An instance of these dialectics emerged in our group. James Skillen, while admitting that the generalizing and abstracting character of modern political structures *can* create a desert between the state and the individual, in which "mediating" structures wither, does not think this is inevitable. Jean Porter then observed that modernity's political structures are in part the products of Christianity's position within Western history. William Cavanaugh, on the other hand, argued that it has been war that has done the universalizing, to create structures inherently inhospitable to community. I think they are *all* right.

explicit gathering good, since a polity that did would *be* the church. But whatever good is common to a polity will shape its life, and some partial goods are better than others, by knowable norms. Thus, for example, there have been and doubtless will be theocratic polities; some have honored Moloch, and others the Buddha principle. Christians should disapprove polities gathered around baby-sacrifice or the like, and in love for their fellow humans oppose their power and even when possible their perdurance.[45] On the other hand, we may find it promising to search for shared moral standards with a Buddhist polity.[46] Some secularized polities have recently honored the Dialectic of History, which once seemed a nicely secularized deity but proved bloodthirsty. Over against state socialism, we may (as everyone does and I just covertly did) cite Churchill's maxim that democracy is the worst form of government except for all the others.

As for the norm of such judgments, the church need look no further than the Ten Commandments. If there is natural law, they republish it; if not, they are all we have or need.

---

45. Thus Spanish Franciscans debated whether the Aztec practice of human sacrifice made military removal of the Aztec regime a just war. The conquistadors did not, to be sure, wait for the outcome of the debate. But the justice or injustice of the conquest is not determined by the conquestors' motives, or even by other horrid things they did while changing the Aztec regime. We have to measure the intervention itself by just such considerations as were adduced among the Franciscans.

46. How should we characterize Islam? Much, including perhaps the general survival, suddenly depends on strict honesty in viewing the phenomena.

Contributors

Milner Ball is Caldwell Professor of Constitutional Law at the University of Georgia School of Law and a member of the Presbytery of Northeast Georgia.

William T. Cavanaugh is Associate Professor of Theology at the University of St. Thomas, St. Paul, Minnesota.

Victor Paul Furnish is University Distinguished Professor Emeritus of New Testament, Southern Methodist University.

Robert W. Jenson is Senior Scholar for Research at the Center of Theological Inquiry in Princeton, New Jersey.

Cheryl A. Kirk-Duggan is Professor of Theology and Women's Studies; Director of Women's Studies, Shaw University Divinity School, Raleigh, North Carolina; and ordained minister in the Christian Methodist Episcopal Church.

Jacqueline Lapsley is Associate Professor of Old Testament at Princeton Theological Seminary.

Robin W. Lovin is Cary Maguire University Professor of Ethics at Southern Methodist University.

Dennis P. McCann is Wallace M. Allston Professor of Bible and Religion at Agnes Scott College in Decatur, Georgia.

Patrick D. Miller is Charles T. Haley Professor of Old Testament Theology at Princeton Theological Seminary.

C. Eric Mount Jr. is Rodes Professor of Religion Emeritus at Centre College, Danville, Kentucky.

Jean Porter is John A. O'Brien Professor of Theology at the University of Notre Dame.

James W. Skillen is President of the Center for Public Justice and editor of the Center's *Public Justice Report* (quarterly) and *Capital Commentary* (biweekly).

Max Stackhouse is the Rimmer and Ruth de Vries Professor of Theology and Public Life at Princeton Theological Seminary.

Josiah U. Young III is Professor of Systematic Theology at Wesley Theological Seminary, Washington, DC.

Index

352

In Search of the Common Good

Baker, Dean, 326n115
Balentine, Samuel, 26n30
Ball, Milner, 51, 168–69. *See also*
Native Americans and the common
good in performance
Barth, Karl, 24n26, 238–39, 239n68
Beatitudes, 205–8, 209
Beckett, Samuel, 339–40, 339n24
Beeson, John, 228n1
Bellah, Robert N., 177, 186, 319
Bellarmine, Robert Cardinal, 312
Beloved (Morrison), 220–21
Bernardin, Joseph Cardinal, 145
Black Church, 223–24
Black Elk, 229–35, 239–40, 249–50
conversion and catechism of,
235–36
vision and gift of, 230–31,
233–34, 249–50
See also Native Americans and the
common good in performance
Black Elk Speaks (Neihardt), 229–35,
232–35, 239–40, 249–50
Black Reconstruction (DuBois), 222
The Bluest Eye (Morrison), 191,
201–5
Blumenfeld, Bruno, 65n25
Bodin, Jean, 303, 311
Bonaventure, 99–100
Bonhoeffer, Dietrich, 238
Boring, Eugene, 206
"Bowling Alone" (Putnam), 176–77
Bowman, Carl, 178n27
Buber, Martin, 171
Budde, Michael, 316n66, 331
Burke, Victor, 309
Bush, George W., 247
Butler, Elizur, 248

Cahill, Lisa, 175, 178, 179–80, 182
Calvin, John
and Aristotle, 268–69
biblical motifs and the common
good, 282
and common good as political
norm, 267–69, 267n21
God and Holy Spirit, 238, 238n56
and the Ten Commandments,
29, 40n58
Cassidy, John, 57n57
Catechism of the Catholic Church, 301
Catholic Bishops of Appalachia,
172–73
Catholic Bishops of the Columbia
River Watershed Region, 183

Catholic Social Teaching and modernization, 7, 92, 121–46
accommodation phase, 127–28,
137–41
and conservatism, 146
consolidation phase, 128–29
critical engagement phase, 127,
132–37
current phase, 141–45
defined, 121–22
development of, 124–29
and early definitions of common
good, 137–41
and eschatological common
good, 143, 145–46
and fascism, 136–37
Gaudium et spes, 123, 124,
127–28, 137–42, 141
and globalization, 144
historical responses to modernization, 124–45
and John Paul II, 121, 128–29,
141–45
and liberal Catholicism, 125, 126
and modernization's threats to
the church, 125–26
papal authority and the modern
papacy, 125–26, 142, 142n10
and "pro-life" stance, 144–45
and Protestant reformers, 124–25
and *Quadragesimo anno*, 122,
123, 132–37
and *Rerum novarum*, 123, 124,
127, 130–33
resistance phase, 126, 129–32
social justice and the common
good in, 134–36, 140
social order and the common
good in, 145–46
and the subsidiarity principle, 5,
146, 175, 175n16, 185
term "the common good" in
documents of, 123–24, 132–45
and Vatican II, 121, 127–28,
137–41
Cavanaugh, William, 254. *See also*
nation-states and the common good
Center for Theological Inquiry, 1
Centesimus annus (John Paul II), 123,
128–29, 142, 143–44
Cherokee Nation v. Georgia (1831),
241–42
Cherokee tribe, 241–42, 248
China, 271, 281
Cicero, 4, 62, 277, 333